DE LASCASES
ST JULIEN, MÉDOC
Btles 1972
CHATEAU BEYCHEVELLE
1er GRAND VIN

CRU D'ALESME
BECKER
MARGAUX

CHau MONTROSE

CHATEAU HAUT-BATAILLEY
PAUILLAC
MÉDOC

D0349070
ST ESTÈPHE
MÉDOC

CHAU LA LAGUNE
GRAND CRU CLASSÉ
HAUT-MÉDOC

REGUM MENSIS ARIS QUE DEORUM
CHATEAU d'ISSAN

CHATEAU BRANAIRE
DULUC DUCRU
ST JULIEN (MÉDOC)

MALESCOT ST EXUPERY
GRAND VIN
MARGAUX

CHAU LA LAGUNE
GRAND CRU CLASSÉ
HAUT-MÉDOC
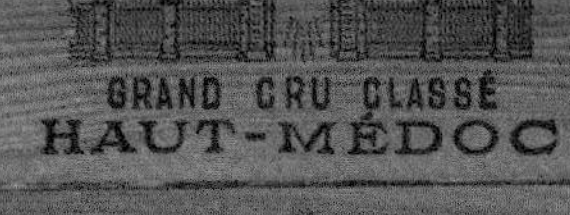

CRU D'ALESME
BECKER
MARGAUX
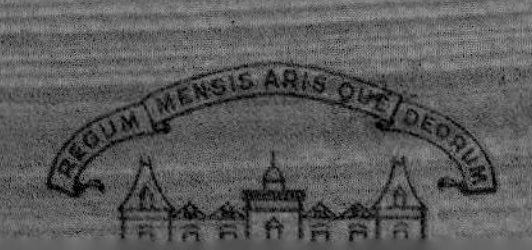
REGUM MENSIS ARIS QUE DEORUM

LÉOVILLE
POYFERRÉ

CHATEAU BRANAIRE
DULUC DUCRU
ST JULIEN (MÉDOC)

CHATEAU PRIEURÉ LICHINE
Margaux-Médoc

1er GRAND VIN
PICHON-LONGUEVILLE

Château
Mouton Rothschild

MIS EN BOUTEILLES AU CHATEAU
CHATEAU COUFRAN
ST SEURIN DE CADOURNE
(HAUT-MEDOC)

CHÂTEAU
CALON-SÉGUR

CHATEAU DE MARBUZET
SAINT-ESTEPHE

# The Great Wine Châteaux of Bordeaux

# THE GREAT WINE CHATEAUX OF BORDEAUX

*Text by* Hubrecht Duijker

*Consultants* Pierre and Bernard Ginestet *English consultant* Pamela Vandyke Price

Times Books

First published in Great Britain in 1975 by Times Books, the book publishing imprint of Times Newspapers Limited, New Printing House Square, London WC1X 8EZ
Produced by Spectrum International Publishing, Amsterdam


Art direction by Will van Sambeek Design Associates, Amsterdam
Printed in the Netherlands by Smeets Offset, Weert

ISBN 0 7230 0139 1



Photographs in this book by Peter van der Velde. Some additional photographs by Photographie Burdin, Hubrecht Duijker, Château Mouton-Rothschild and Boudewijn Neuteboom. The photograph by Cecil Beaton on page 119 (top, left) is reproduced by courtesy of Château Mouton-Rothschild. The photograph on page 184 (top) is reproduced by courtesy of Château Ausone.
Maps, plans and drawings by Otto van Eersel, Jan ten Hove, Jan Klatter, Will van Sambeek and Eddy Schoonheijt. The paintings on page 129 (top) are reproduced by courtesy of Château Lafite-Rothschild.

For Julie, with whom I have shared and hope to share more good bottles than with anyone else.

In the text I have quoted from some of these recommended books about wines – and particularly those of Bordeaux – and am grateful to those concerned.
J. M. Broadbent, *Wine Tasting*, London 1973
C. Cocks & E. Féret, *Bordeaux et Ses Vins*, Bordeaux 1970 (12th ed.)
Maurice Healy, *Stay Me with Flagons*, London 1940
Charles Higounet et al., *Le Vignoble de Château Latour*, Bordeaux 1974
Alexis Lichine, *Encyclopaedia of Wines and Spirits*, London 1967
Edmund Penning-Rowsell, *The Wines of Bordeaux*, London 1969, 1973
Cyril Ray, *Lafite*, London 1968
Cyril Ray, *Mouton-Rothschild*, London 1974
Philippe Roudié, *Le Vignoble Bordelais*, Toulouse 1973
Frank Schoonmaker, *Encyclopedia of Wine*, London 1967
Pamela Vandyke Price, *Eating & Drinking in France Today*, London 1972
Harry Waugh, *Bacchus on the Wing*, London 1966
Harry Waugh, *The Changing Face of Wine*, London 1968
Harry Waugh, *Pick of the Bunch*, London 1970
Harry Waugh, *Diary of a Winetaster*, London 1972
Harry Waugh, *Winetaster's Choice*, London 1973

# Contents

# Foreword

The great Blaise Pascal wrote: 'A multitude that is not arranged into unity is nothing but confusion.' This could be applied to modern mathematics. But I would like to quote these words in a very different sense from that intended by the author of the *Pensées*, one which I feel is appropriate for a foreword to this work on the wines of Bordeaux, which it is my pleasure to introduce.

The amateur lover of fine wines often feels some hesitation about the wines of Bordeaux. There are so many of them. Around the capital of Aquitaine, there is a multitude of names, vineyards and growths. This diversity can lead to ambiguities. It may make the beginner unsure, and can even mislead the connoisseur. On the other hand, it is interesting, even fascinating, to compare all these noble wines, to study their histories and to discover and select those among them with a special appeal. They represent an infinitely subtle gamut of colours, bouquets and flavours, renewed again each vintage, that need to be explored and experienced again and again.

I am particularly pleased to invite the reader to this marvellous tour of the vineyards of Bordeaux. Each of the regions discussed has a character all of its own, which is shown to advantage in this book. In the Médoc, the Graves, St Emilion and Pomerol are concentrated the most famous wine estates in the world. For a long time they have deserved to be described in a well-illustrated volume such as this, for which Mr Duijker has taken the initiative. To him are due the thanks and congratulations of all wine lovers for the quality and impartiality of his text. Among the many books published on wines in general and those of Bordeaux in particular, this stands out in a distinguished way. In 1824, William Frank published the first edition of his *Traité des Vins du Médoc.* Since then, millions of words have been printed on the subject. But apart from the fine albums edited at the turn of the century by A. Danflou and Ch. de Lorbac – now collectors' items – there has not been a single book on the great wines of Bordeaux that combines a sound text with fine illustrations.

Now here is this book. I keep admiring the beautiful photographs in this volume, and the detailed, precise text, which sometimes gives information never made public before. Many members of the wine trade will find some unexpected facts here, and all wine drinkers and wine enthusiasts will find what they want to know about Bordeaux wines . . . and in the process become very thirsty.

So, I raise my glass of wine and propose a toast to your health and to the success of this book.

*Bernard Ginestet*

# Introduction

Anyone who decides to write a book about the wines, the châteaux and the people of Bordeaux is plagued by Hamlet-like doubts about which wines to include and which to leave out. To describe them all is impossible, unless you restrict yourself to some very brief comments. After much deliberation it was decided to devote this book to Bordeaux red wine châteaux that are in the highest classification. You will therefore find the *grands crus classés* of the Médoc and Graves, and the *premiers grands crus classés* of St Emilion. So as not to disregard Pomerol (which as yet has no official classification) two great estates from this district have also been included. Each one of the châteaux discussed has been visited, quite a few of them on several occasions. Personal impressions are recorded in this book, based generally on the information, tasting-notes and so on which I have gathered over the years. Since wine is after all a highly subjective matter, I can only hope that the readers' experiences may correspond to some extent with mine.

I am greatly indebted to all those people who have helped me by generously giving me some of their precious time, knowledge and hospitality. I cannot, alas, mention them all by name, but most of them are mentioned elsewhere in this book. There are a few, however, to whom I am especially grateful: M. Thierry Manoncourt of Château Figeac and M. Jean-Bernard Delmas, Chairman of the Union des Crus Classés de Graves. My thanks are due also to Bruno Prats, Chairman of the Syndicat des Grands Crus Classés du Médoc. Without his invaluable help I do not think I would ever have been able to finish this book. Finally, I should like to mention my good friend Herman Mostermans, one of the most dedicated Bordeaux people I know.

*Hubrecht Duijker*

*Left:*
*In the winter, after the vintage, it is particularly easy to see how meticulously the vines are planted. The distance between the rows varies in each Bordeaux district. In the Médoc and the Graves it is usually 1·80 metres, elsewhere 2 to 2·20 metres.*

*Bottom left:*
*At Château Gruaud-Larose they have a collection of vines in spirits. Of the black grapes, the Malbec ripens first, followed by the Merlot and finally the Cabernets. With white grapes, the Sémillon ripens first. This difference can greatly influence the style of the vintage, because districts with a large percentage of Merlot (such as St Emilion) may sometimes have finished vintageing before picking has begun in the predominantly Cabernet district of the Médoc, just a little more vulnerable to changes in the autumn weather.*

*Below:*
*The first years of a great wine. The series of drawings illustrates certain highlights of the wine making.*
**A** *The black grapes come in. At traditional estates they have been collected in wooden douils (illustrated) which are loaded on a cart and then emptied into the de-stalking machine. A douil holds enough grapes to make a 225-litre cask of wine. The de-stalker ejects the stalks and pips, while the only slightly crushed grapes are pumped up into the fermentation vats. The skins are not removed because their pigments give the wine its colour.*
**B** *The first fermentation takes place in vats made of oak, cement or steel. The wooden vats are the least practical but wholly traditional. During the first fermentation the skins and other solid matter float on the surface and form a thick*

# Wine

It is not true that the right soil, the right climate and the right vines will suffice to produce a great wine. Of course all these are essential conditions, but after the grapes have been picked the grower certainly cannot consider that his work is done and that the wine will make itself.

On the contrary, wine making requires all a grower's experience, attention and skill, for its art consists of transferring the full quality of the grapes to the wine, which is easier said than done. A single error of judgement in the process can have disastrous effects on the wine, and there will not only be a direct financial result but perhaps also detract in the long term from the reputation of the estate; the consumer who has once been disappointed by a particular bottle will not rush to order the same wine a second time.

It is not only the meticulous care and skill of the proprietor and his staff that count, his whole attitude is of fundamental importance. In the last resort it depends on the choices and decisions which the proprietor is continually having to make about whether a great wine will be made or not. It is he who decides about the upkeep of the vineyard, the choice of equipment, the number of people employed, the procedure to be followed at every stage of wine making, the length of maturation, and so on. Usually, at any estate it is truly the owner – or his managers – who makes or mars the wine, because the natural factors at each property remain more or less constant. The ups and downs of the châteaux described in this book are largely due to the people behind the wine. A good proprietor must be prepared to devote his time, his money, and in fact his whole life, to making the wine as perfectly as he is able, which is why the most famous growers are idealists.

What has to be done to transform the right grapes, once they have been picked, into a red wine of breed? First, it is essential that the equipment and the place where the wine making is done are clean. The newly-born wine is extremely vulnerable and an easy prey for all kinds of bacteria. When harvest-time arrives and the grapes have been picked, they are first tipped into a de-stalking machine, the *égrappoir*. This machine ingeniously separates the stalks, to which the pips are attached, from the grapes themselves. During this process the grapes are slightly crushed but not pressed. They are then pumped or otherwise transferred to the fermentation vats, or *cuves*, where the first and most important fermentation takes place. This is the *fermentation alcoolique* or *fermentation tumultueuse* (alcoholic or turbulent fermentation). This is a highly complex process in which the sugars present in the fruit are converted by the action of wine yeasts into alcohol and carbon dioxide gas. This process takes 7 to 12 days and stops of

*layer, or* chapeau *(hat) which remains there for a determined period – nowadays not long. This is pressed after fermentation* (**C**) *and the result is sometimes added to the first pressing to give tannin.*

**D** *The young wine has been transferred to oak casks,* barriques, *where it will mature for at least 1½ years. Many* grands crus *use new casks for part of the wine each year, some use only new ones. This is good for the wine, but expensive; not only because of the cost of the casks but also because each new cask absorbs between 7 and 10 litres of wine. After the first fermentation the second, slower fermentation takes place. It is for this reason that the casks in the first-year cellar or* chai *have loose bungs, often of glass, which allow carbon dioxide to escape. In its first year the wine develops its character and later, having completed its basic development, matures up to bottling.*

**E** *Because 8% to 12% of the wine evaporates annually, the casks must be topped up at least twice a week during the first year, so as to limit the wine's contact with the atmosphere as much as possible. Too much air after a while may make it break up.*

**F** *The wine continues to throw off various deposits, which is why it is racked into a fresh cask every 3 to 4 months. This is usually done with a pump, which introduces air into the top of the cask to be emptied. The process is called racking or* soutirage. *It is repeated while the casks are in the second-year* chai, *where they are normally moved just before the next vintage.*

**G** *Two or three months before the wine is bottled (and sometimes earlier) fining takes place. This is a process whereby the wine is fined with the white of fresh eggs, anything between 3 and 8 eggs being used to a cask. The egg whites are beaten with a twig whisk in a wooden bowl, called the* bontemps, *and folded into the wine. The whites attract and hold any particles in suspension.*

**H** *After the wine has been racked for the last time, bottling follows, often with modern bottling machines, but sometimes by hand from the cask. For some months afterwards the wine suffers from bottle sickness and, as when it is being racked or fined, is not really fit to sample. Some bottle age is always good, but this depends on the wine and the vintage.*

SOME COMMON TERMS

*Appellation d'Origine Contrôlée, A.O.C., A.C.:* legally controlled designation of origin
*Barrique:* Bordeaux cask of about 225 litres
*Cave:* cellar
*Chai:* above ground wine store in Bordeaux, where in many regions cellars cannot be excavated because of the shallowness of the soil
*Chef de culture:* man responsible for the vineyard
*Cru:* growth
*Cru bourgeois:* growth below the classed growths but often of good quality
*Cru exceptionnel:* top growth between the bourgeois and classed growth
*Cuve:* fermentation vat
*Cuvier:* vathouse
*Fouloir-Egrappoir:* de-stalking and crushing machine
*Gérant:* general manager of a property
*Cru Classé:* wine included in one of the official classifications.
*Grand vin:* a term without official meaning, but signifying the finest wine from an estate
*Maître de chai:* cellar master, responsible for the work in the cellars
*Mise en bouteille:* bottling
*Mise en bouteille au château, mise du château:* the bottling has been carried out at the estate owning the vineyard
*Négociant:* shipper
*Propriétaire:* owner
*Récolte:* harvest, vintage
*Régisseur:* overall director or manager, to whom the *maître de chai* and *chef de culture* are responsible
*Tonneau:* about 900 litres. The archaic *tonne* is the measure of capacity of a ship, dating from the days of the Bordeaux wine fleet in the middle ages
*Viticulteur:* wine grower



its own accord once virtually all the sugar has been converted. It stands to reason that the higher the sugar content in the grape, the higher the alcohol content in the wine, and vice versa. In poor years a little sugar may be added to the must, otherwise the wine would remain too frail. This practice is legal, though very strictly controlled, and is known as chaptalisation. Red wine gets its colour from the skins, which are also left in the vat. For white wine, white grapes are pressed and only the juice or must, without the skins, is fermented.

During fermentation heat is given off, but the temperature must not rise too much. The general rule is that the fermenting mass should not exceed 30° C; 35°C tends to kill the yeasts. At many estates 27°C to 28°C is considered the ideal temperature. At châteaux with the traditional oak or with cement fermentation vats the wine may be put through a cooling unit to ensure that this temperature is not exceeded; this is one of the reasons why more and more properties are switching to water jacketed stainless steel vats, through which cold water can be directed, often by thermostatic control.

After the first fermentation a second, more gentle fermentation takes place, the *fermentation malolactique*. In many instances the wine has already been transferred to casks. This second fermentation is essential to red wine, which loses some of its hardness, its acids and its colour. Here too the grape aroma is transformed into the beginnings of a bouquet. Moreover, the wine becomes less vulnerable to sickness. The ideal temperature for the second fermentation is 18°C–20°C. The wine is then racked into fresh casks because lees or sediment has formed in those already used.

The next stage is the *assemblage*, or the mixing of the different casks. Most of the great châteaux process their grape species separately, and less successful casks will not be mixed. After this the wine is left to mature for a considerable time, at the greatest châteaux remaining in casks for at least 1½ years, though 2½ years is not unusual. During maturation the casks are regularly topped up, and now and again the wine is racked into a clean cask. Towards the end of the maturation period in wood the wine is fined with egg whites, racked a final time and bottled. All the leading estates now do the bottling themselves. Of course, the wine then continues to mature in the bottle.

The question is often raised of why it is in the Bordeaux area that wines are made with *le goût le plus fin du monde*, as the Duc de Richelieu put it two centuries ago. Apart from the human factor, what is so special about this particular part of the world? The answer must be that in Bordeaux there is a unique combination of natural elements. Everything natural for man to be

*Below:*
*Diagram showing the natural factors which influence the quality of wine.*
**A** *Complex soil with layers of gravel and sand, light and often rather poor, is the best soil for most vineyards.*
**B** *The older the vine, the longer its roots and the deeper they seek nourishment. This improves the quality of the wine and makes it more constant.*
**C** *In each wine region and district some vine species give better results than others. This depends, among other things, on the soil content and the climate.*
**D** *Sunshine is, of course, essential for vines as it develops the sugar in the grapes. But too much sun can shrivel them.*
**E** *A mild climate with sun, rain and wind is preferable. Too much rain increases the yield, but the quality is inferior: the grapes are too swollen with water.*
**F** *One short hailstorm can ruin a whole crop. Fortunately they usually occur in small areas, sometimes hitting one vineyard but sparing its next-door neighbour.*
**G** *Something any grower is afraid of: frost. In spring even light frosts may kill the young shoots, diminishing the production later on. Snow in itself is not so dangerous.*
**H** *The best vineyards are usually drained by a stream. Vines do not like having wet feet.*
**J** *A vineyard on a slope often has a better exposure to the sun.*
**K** *Pruning is necessary to ensure that the vital sap is not spread between too many grapes. The number of vines per hectare and the maximum yield entitled to the* appellation contrôlée *are strictly regulated. In this way the grower assists nature to achieve the best possible results.*

*Right:*
*What a well-kept Bordeaux vineyard should look like.*



able to make a great wine is here, and in such proportions that all these elements are in perfect harmony with each other. The climate is right, so is the soil. It is as though a great composer had been at work here and had written a perfect symphony where no instrument dominates, but in which each contributes to the whole.

### What nature does for the wine

It begins with the soil. If this does not satisfy certain requirements there is no hope of making a great wine. In general, a poor soil with a complex structure is needed to make a fine wine with many gradations in its bouquet and flavour, because it is from the soil that the vine draws its nourishment and the wine gets its character. This complex soil structure is found in many areas of the Gironde – especially in the Médoc and the Graves. Over the centuries rivers have carried many different kinds of pebbles down to the estuary of the Gironde, including types of gravel from the central Pyrenees, the Massif Central and the valleys of the Lot and the Aveyron. Sometimes these forms of gravel (*graves*) can be seen on the surface, but usually they are to be found in a broad layer in the subsoil. The drainage too must be exemplary, as nothing is more ruinous for vine roots than a wet subsoil. Many famous vineyards are situated on slopes or on plateaux drained by little streams or a river – with the added advantage of better exposure to the sun.

For quality in a wine the vine must grow in a mild climate, where extremes in

The vines not only draw their nourishment from the soil but also actually produce it. They do this through foliage. Two processes go on during the day: with the help of sunlight, carbon dioxide is assimilated, oxygen given off and sugar formed. At the same time, carbon dioxide is given off and the sugar combusted. The former process is called carbon dioxide assimilation, the latter breathing. Each day the build-up of sugar is greater than the amount combusted, and part of this reserve is passed to the grapes. So, in sunny years the grapes receive a lot of sugar, in less sunny years, less. It is the sugar which is later converted into alcohol during the first fermentation.

*Below:*
*The vine is a climbing plant which seeks support with its curling tendrils; in its wild state, the woody stem can become thick and many metres in length. For wine production, the vine is rigorously pruned. Many varieties of vine are cultivated, differing in the size and colour of the leaves and grapes and in the type of grape yielded.*
**A** *pruned* Vitis vinifera.
**B** *green shoot with ripe bunch of grapes.* **C** *flowering branch with leaves and tendrils.*
**D** *flower bud; the small, greenish flowers form close clusters.* **E** *flower in full bloom.*
**F** *wilting flower, in the centre the pistil.* **G** *pistil where the fruit will develop.* **H** *seed (the pips of the grape) which is embedded in the ripening fruit.*
**J** *cross section of the seed.*
**K** *longitudinal section of the seed.* **L** *section of the grape.*

*Right:*
*Splendid bunches of grapes immediately before being picked. For all the great red Bordeaux a blend of various grapes is used: Cabernet Sauvignon, Cabernet Franc and Merlot dominate, followed by Malbec and Petit Verdot. Creating one wine from the given species is no easy task. Each estate requires its own kind of make-up; in each vintage different varieties react severally.*

temperature are the exception rather than the rule. Or course, sunshine is needed for the vines and their fruit to develop, but rain is equally vital. The ideal climate is considered to be one which is not quite sub-tropical. Too much sun gives unwieldy, tough wines; too much rain gives weak, thin ones. Bordeaux has an admirable climate, with mild winters, sunny springs, dry summers and not too rainy autumns.

In the Bordeaux region only a few vine varieties may be used – those which produce the best results in this region and on this soil. They are planted in various proportions in the respective sections of the vineyard. The choice of vines and their percentages is therefore of importance. But once the choice has been made that is not the end of the matter, for regulations must be followed for the spacing and care of the vines, going on the principle that with wine quality and quantity are inversely proportional. There must not be too many vines to a hectare: the maximum in the Médoc is around 10,000. As mentioned before, a poor soil, perhaps of gravel or limestone (as in St Emilion), is best. Nor must vines produce too many grapes, because then their juice will be spread among too many bunches. Rigorous pruning, a highly skilled operation, is carried out several times a year, done in a different way in each district. Finally, the age of the vine is also important: only old vines have long roots which can extract everything the soil has to offer, though their yield is less. It is often said that 'the vine must suffer'; the more difficulty it experiences, the better the grape.

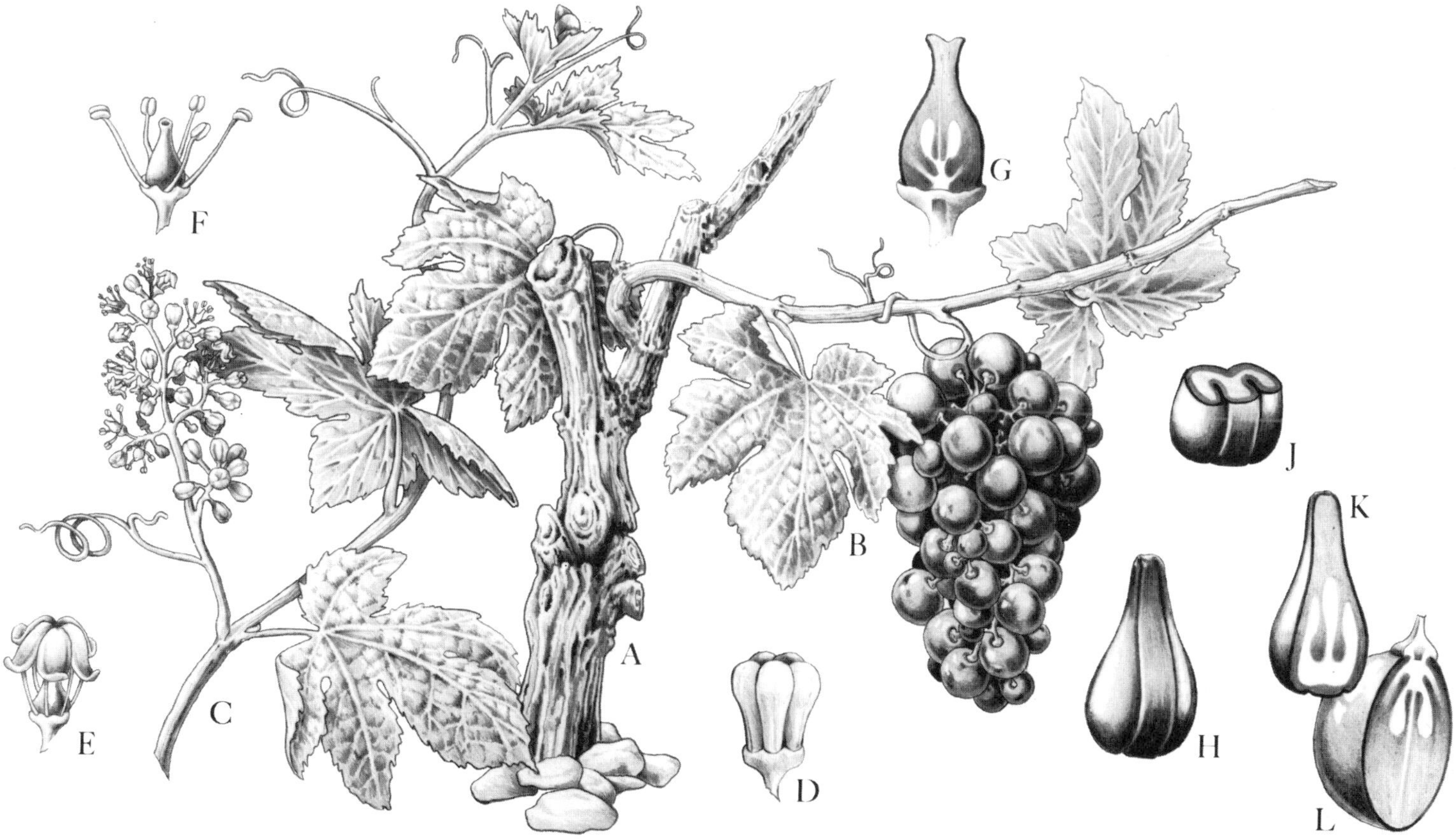

All wines should be stored lying down, so that the cork does not dry out and permit air to enter because of the shrinkage; this would cause oxidation

The ideal cellar temperature is 12°C, but constancy is most important. The less temperature varies, the better.

Before drinking any fine wine, stand it up for at least 24 hours where it is to be drunk. The deposit will subside and the room temperature gradually be acquired.

The moment to open the bottle has arrived. Cut the top edge of the capsule to below the rim of the neck – or remove the whole capsule if this is easier.

Wipe the top of the exposed cork and the bottle rim to avoid any dirt contacting the wine as it is poured.

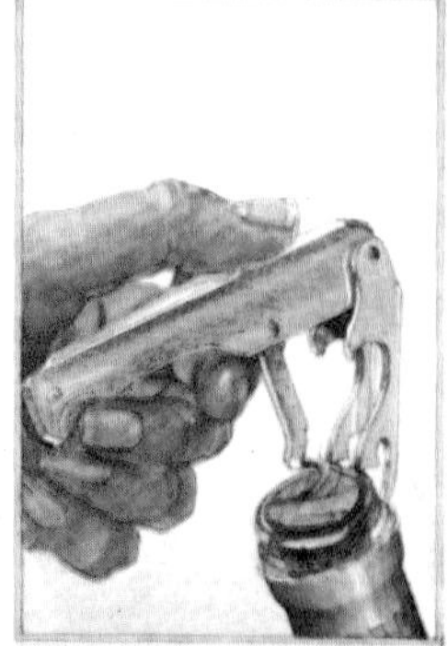

The best corkscrews have a smooth open screw, not a sharp or pointed end, which breaks the cork. Once the cork is drawn, wipe the inside of the bottle neck.

# Drinking and Enjoying Bordeaux Wine

Wine is something special. Unlike other alcoholic drinks, it is not a beverage which, left in the bottle, just sits there, waiting to be drunk. On the contrary, wine is alive, sensitive to air, light, temperature and vibration. What is more, the very greatest wines can develop in bottle, though this does not apply to all wines. It is no use storing branded table wines for years, because they may then taste more like vinegar than like wine. The finer red Bordeaux, however, are supremely suited to maturation in the bottle. In their youth they may be characterised by a hardness or astringency, but with years this gives way to a gentle, fascinating softness.

What is the best way to store wine? It is happiest in a kind of hibernation, lasting sometimes for years. The 'cellar' room in which the bottles rest must be cool (preferably around 12°C), dark and vibration-free. A real cellar is ideal. There should be adequate ventilation, but no draughts. It should ideally be damp rather than dry. Leave a bucket of water there to evaporate if it is too dry, for dryness will shrink corks, and bring on wine too fast. A disadvantage of damp is that the labels may deteriorate – so put paper over the bottles, and of course keep a note of what wines are where. Only a wine snob minds about the label, but you do need to know what the wine is.

Those who have no cellar need not despair. In most houses there is some suitable place where wine can be stored. The most important thing is a constant temperature. This can, if necessary, be higher or lower than the ideal level as long as there are no great fluctuations. Then there are the special insulated wine bins which have been on the market for some years. They are not cheap, but if you keep several hundred bottles at home they can save you worrying about the wines' possible deterioration.

The life of a wine naturally depends on its vintage, and on the way it is made. Today some clarets are ready for drinking much earlier than they would have been fifty years ago. In general, 8 to 12 years is possible for a fairly good year, 15 to 20 years for a fine one, and even longer for a great vintage of a great wine.

### How to serve Bordeaux

The rule about serving wine at 'room temperature' was made before the days of central heating, and many people now drink claret virtually tepid. This does little to show off the wine, which is probably at its best between 17°C and 19°C. (The average room temperature today is likely to be over

Left:
Cork is expensive, so a good cork is a sign that great care has been given to the wine. The finest clarets should have 'full long', or 2 inch corks, but most now use the $1\frac{7}{8}$ inch Bordeaux cork.
From left to right: a still unused (and therefore somewhat thicker) cork from Château Latour; one from Château La Lagune 1964; and for comparison corks of a Burgundy Chambertin Clos de Bèze 1969, an Alsace, an Italian Gattinara, a German Moselle and a Bollinger Champagne.

*A fine wine generally has some deposit and should be decanted. You need a spotlessly clean decanter and a candle. You may decant younger wines as well to bring them on slightly by aeration.*

*Pour the wine carefully into the decanter. The lit candle should be positioned below the neck of the bottle, so that you can immediately see any sediment as it rises. Pour slowly, and leave this deposit in the bottle.*

*Sniff the empty glass to check it for cupboard or detergent smells. Then pour out enough for a couple of mouthfuls.*

*First look at the wine, and enjoy its brilliant tones of red to tawny, according to its age.*

*Then, after having swirled the wine round in the glass, sniff the bouquet. The nose of a wine tells you a great deal about its personality.*

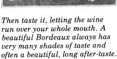

*Then taste it, letting the wine run over your whole mouth. A beautiful Bordeaux always has very many shades of taste and often a beautiful, long after-taste.*



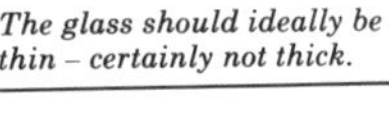

*The glass should ideally be thin – certainly not thick.*

*The glass should be plain – the colour of the wine should be seen clearly.*

*The bowl should also be plain. The wine needs no adornment by way of decoration.*

*The glass should not be too small. When two-thirds filled it should contain about five small mouthfuls. In wine regions it is usually only filled about a third.*

*To swirl the wine round and enjoy the bouquet, hold the glass by the stem or the foot.*

*The proportions of the glass should be harmonious and the base steady.*

*Opposite page, above:*
*Everything is prepared for the decanting of a magnificent claret.*

*Opposite page, centre:*
*A private wine cellar. There are many types of wine racks on sale, which may be made of metal, wood or plastic.*

*Right:*
*Anatomy of a good wine glass.*

20°C.) Of course, a higher temperature will not ruin the wine, but it will affect the way it tastes – many people would say distorting it in various ways. A warmer wine, for example, tends to have a rather exaggeratedly powerful bouquet and a slightly diminished taste. It goes without saying that wine should never be quickly warmed. It must be gradually brought from storage temperature to the ideal 17°C to 19°C. A wine which is insufficiently *chambré* can best be brought to the right temperature by clasping the glass, or even the bottle or decanter, in your hands.

Fill the glass only a half or two-thirds full, so that the wine can be freely swirled around. This best releases the bouquet.

As far as the wine itself is concerned, do not be afraid of deposit. It still happens that in restaurants the *sommelier* receives complaints that a wine has sediment in it. This is a sign of ignorance, for sediment is usually a sign of quality, for the wine lives on this. If it is filtered and recorked before sale, it will be merely a shadow of itself. Deposit is a completely natural thing which a wine throws to a greater or a lesser extent according to its vintage. Correct handling and decanting will prevent it from getting into the glass.

*Above:*
*In Bordeaux six bottle sizes are used. From left to right: the half bottle (37·5 cl), standard bottle (75 cl), magnum (300 cl), jéroboam (450 cl), and impériale (600 cl). 1 litre = 100 cl. The first three sizes are the most usual. The larger the bottle, the longer the development of the wine. The classic Bordeaux bottle is in fact used elsewhere as it is admirable for wines throwing a deposit, which can be held back in the shoulder. For comparison, a Burgundy bottle and a flûte d'Alsace.*

*Right:*
*A festive-looking table laid with glasses and decanters of the* Académie du Vin de Bordeaux. *This is a group of about 80 châteaux from the districts of Médoc, Graves, Sauternes, St Emilion and Pomerol. In addition, leading shippers are affiliated to it, plus people from the world of art, letters and science. The main objective is to ensure that the good Bordeaux wines are presented, served and tasted in the correct manner. The* Académie du Vin de Bordeaux *acts as a guarantor of the reputation of Bordeaux wine. One of its activities is the publication each year of a vintage table. The glassware was specially designed in Baccarat crystal and bears the Academy's coat of arms.*

# Gastronomy à la bordelaise

You may sometimes come across people in Bordeaux who say that they do not drink. They may consume 4 litres of wine a day, but this is not regarded as 'drinking', while one dram of whisky is. But you will never find anyone who says he does not eat. The Bordelais enjoy life and good food is a part of the good life. At twelve noon everything stops for the midday meal, and it often depends entirely on the company, the dishes and the wines as to when work begins again. You must allow at least two hours for a week-day lunch; Sunday, the gastronomic high spot of the week, may see the family at home or in a restaurant. The regional specialities are very popular: the true Bordelais never gets tired of his famous *entrecôte* grilled over the prunings of the vines – *grillé aux sarments.*

**Bordeaux specialities**

It is an impressive experience to witness Sunday lunch in some small, unostentatious eating house. This will always be packed. Often whole families will be gathered round a table, from grandfather down to the toddlers. A typical meal begins with *hors d'oeuvres*: smoked Bayonne ham, small shellfish, marinated mushrooms and beetroot, which might be followed by some Arcachon oysters. The main dish consists either of a gigantic steak, a leg of lamb, or roast chicken. Then come the cheeses – invariably including red-skinned Dutch cheese – and finally ice-cream or a *gâteau.* This five-course meal will be accompanied by about a bottle a head at least, followed by coffee and Cognac – and the bill even today may be reasonable. The *décor* in these little restaurants is always simple, and the same goes for the service, but the quality is excellent and everyone has a thoroughly good time talking, laughing, eating and drinking.

Bordeaux has more luxurious specialities, too, such as the *foie gras des Landes*, which is certainly not inferior to goose livers from the Périgord or Alsace. There are also *cèpes à la Bordelaise*, large, flat, rich mushrooms with a singular flavour, which are usually prepared with shallots and a pinch of garlic. The most curious speciality is lamprey, an estuary creature prepared rather like *coq au vin*, in a red wine sauce with diced bacon. The lamprey, a primitive eel-like creature with a mouth like a suction pad, is rich and satisfying to eat. And of course all these delicacies are accompanied by local wines.

**Which wines with what**

Despite what you may have heard, there are no laws in gastronomy that decree exactly which wines must be drunk with what food. Thank goodness, because by experimenting with combinations of wines and foods you can have fascinating adventures which will make good topics of conversation. Drink what you yourself enjoy and keep on experimenting. Of course there are a few general guidelines:

- Match the wine with the character of the dish (or vice versa), so choose a delicate Margaux with lamb and a fine Pauillac with game. Neither the wine nor the dish should dominate: good gastronomy is true democracy.
- Do not skimp the wine any more than you would the food.
- Serve simple wines before better ones, young before old, dry before sweet, white before red.

*Bon appétit!*

Pâté de foie gras *goes well with a light claret or a dry white Graves, but in Bordeaux it is sometimes served with a great Sauternes.*

*In and around Bordeaux, leg of lamb, especially that of Pauillac, is a favourite dish. One of the fine wines of the Medoc is ideal with it.*

Steak de veau *in a cream sauce requires a supple, delicate claret, perhaps a Margaux.*

*Below:*
*The pleasures of food and drink are greatly appreciated in Bordeaux – as they should be everywhere.*

Surprisingly enough, Dutch cheese is often found in Bordeaux, although more accurately it is a French version of Dutch cheese. This curious occurrence originated in the 18th century, when the Dutch had the largest mercantile fleet in the world. Holland had about 15,000 cargo vessels, England 3,000 and France 500. The Dutch transported the wines of Bordeaux throughout the world, using whatever was available as ballast to fill their ships when the vessels went to collect the wine. Dutch cheese was often used, which is why this type of mild cheese, which goes so well with all kinds of red Bordeaux, is still popular in the district.

In the Bassin d'Arcachon, 60 km from Bordeaux, there are vast oysterbeds, among the largest in Europe. In 1969 the production was 13,500 tons. Oysters have been found at Arcachon for a long time – they were known at the time of Rabelais – but they have only been cultivated on a large scale since 1856. Those cultivated today are both the classic oyster – *ostrea edulis* – and the so-called 'Portugaise' – *crassostrea angulata* – grown since a Portuguese ship carrying some went down there.

A special local delicacy is the small-grained Gironde caviar, from the Gironde estuary where the sturgeon is able to survive.

Apart from its famous red and white wines (dry, medium dry, sweet) Bordeaux also produces some pink or rosé wine and *mousseux* or sparkling wine. The *vins mousseux* are largely made in St Emilion and also in St André-de-Cubzac and Bourg. A well-known liqueur from this region is Vieille Cure, and so is Lillet, a type of vermouth. Fine de Bordeaux is a brandy which has been evolved by farmers who are currently having difficulty in selling their white wine, especially in the district of Blaye. They used to supply the Cognac producers of the Charente, but since the stricter application of the *appellation contrôlée* this is no longer permitted.

## Gastronomy à la bordelaise

*Fish is mostly accompanied by dry white wines such as Graves; sole in a red wine sauce is a dish that is better with a fairly light-bodied claret.*

*Raw ham with a little claret is always popular as a starter – sometimes accompanied by melon. In Bordeaux the* jambon de Bayonne *is a speciality.*

*The famous* entrecôte bordelaise *should be grilled over vine prunings. It is prepared with shallots, red wine and seasonings and is ideally accompanied by a good glass of claret.*

*Dutch cheese with its bland, simple taste shows off any claret to advantage.*

*Pheasant deserves a fairly full claret, such as a Pauillac or a St Emilion of a good vintage.*

*Grapes, peaches, pears and nectarines are perfect partners for a sweet dessert wine such as Sauternes, served well chilled.*

*Robust St Emilions or full-bodied Pomerols or Médocs go well with game.*

*Blue cheeses, such as Bleu d'Auvergne, need a fairly assertive wine to go with them. A very strong cheese can overpower a delicate red wine.*

*No French meal is complete without fresh, crisp bread.*

*Brie, often considered the 'king of cheeses', is excellent with a fine red Graves of Margaux, or one of the more subtle clarets.*

*Wine is adversely affected by vinegar, mustard and anything very strong or piquant, so be cautious with such seasonings if you have a good bottle.*

*Oysters are often served in the Gironde with a dry white Graves.*

*Left:*
*In Bordeaux it is often said: 'From a good vineyard you must be able to see the river.' This glimpse of the Gironde, with a ship just passing by, is seen from the Médoc. Across the river are the districts of Bourg and Blaye.*

*Opposite page, right:*
*The port of Bordeaux just as the early morning mist is lifting.*

*Opposite page, centre:*
*This old print demonstrates how little the port has changed over the years.*

*Opposite page, bottom:*
*The Fountain of the Three Graces by Visconti in the Place de la Bourse.*

*Opposite page, far right:*
*The* Maison du Vin. *The official bodies can be found here, and visitors can obtain detailed information about all aspects of the wine. One side of the building stands on the Allées de Tourny, once the site of a vineyard. Today you will find no vine roots under the ground, only a car park.*

# The Town and Region of Bordeaux

'Take Versailles, add Antwerp and you get Bordeaux', was how Victor Hugo once described the sixth largest city in France. Like all the other major French towns, Bordeaux also has its new districts with rather characterless blocks of flats, but there is still the lovely heart to which the great author was referring. Here you find fine examples of 18th century architecture, such as the Grand Théâtre with its impressive row of columns, the Allées de Tourny and the houses and buildings on many streets and avenues. Then there is the wide river Garonne with the quaysides, parts of them very old, from which local products (including, of course, wine) are shipped to all parts of the world.

### Shops, cafés and restaurants

Bordeaux is the centre of the former province of Guyenne or Aquitaine, and the capital of the *département* of the Gironde; it is a large town with about 550,000 inhabitants including those who live in the suburbs. The centre is worth hours of wandering and exploring. The busy shopping street, the rue Sainte-Cathérine, runs directly north-south and is 1145 metres long, enough to bring even the most enthusiastic shopper to his or her knees out of sheer exhaustion, if not bankruptcy. Then there is the elegant *Cours de l'intendance*. Facing the Grand Théâtre is the Café de Bordeaux, where everyone meets. Inside now it is garish with fluorescent lighting and plastic surfaces, but outside there are numerous tables on the wide pavement, which is a favourite meeting-place for visitors and locals.

Across the Allées de Tourny from here is the Maison du Vin, where the official bodies connected with wine are housed, and opposite this is the Vinothèque, a kind of supermarket where lovers of Bordeaux wines can wander round to their heart's content and where all the *grands crus* and many other wines can be bought (but unfortunately not at low prices). From here it is a short walk to Dubern, a famous restaurant recently restored to its former glory by master-chef Roland Flourens. There are many more places where the gourmet can find excellent food – these are often tiny bars which you can only discover with the help of a resident. Each of the Bordeaux wine establishments has its favourites, where guests are entertained.

### Artistic town

Is it a coincidence that in the capital of the world's finest wine-growing district so much attention is devoted to art? Probably not; love of the wines of Bordeaux and of the arts go hand in hand. Every year the May Festival is held in Bordeaux, attracting artists from all over the world who come to this wine town and play to music-loving audiences. Among the many foreign guests who have appeared are Artur Rubinstein, Yehudi Menuhin, Andres Segovia, Marian Anderson, the New York City Ballet, the London Festival Ballet and the great symphony orchestras of Philadelphia and Boston. Bordeaux also has its own philharmonic orchestra which gives regular performances in the town.

### Economic centre

There is, of course, also a commercial and industrial Bordeaux. The city has some thriving industries, including refineries, shipyards, metal-works, foodstuffs and chemical installations. It is a bustling, busy place where the traffic quite often gets as congested as it is in Paris. Just outside Bordeaux there is a huge exhibition centre which was opened in 1969; the largest building is 845 metres long and looks out over an artificial lake covering 160 hectares, near which two luxury hotels have been built. Education and science are represented by a university campus around which five villages have been built to accommodate the students.

### About 23 centuries old

Anyone seeing the Bordeaux of today would hardly imagine that about 300 years before Christ a Gallic chieftain, called Burdigal, decided to found a settlement on this site. It is this obscure Gaul whose name, in a somewhat corrupted form, is perpetuated in the name 'Bordeaux'.

Many tribes and peoples, including the Visigoths, the Moors and the Vikings, tried to occupy the town and surrounding districts, but none with as much success as the English. When Henry Plantagenet married Aquitaine's Duchess Eleanor in 1152, the whole of south-west France came under his sway. In 1154 he became King of England, and his French possessions continued to belong to the English crown until 1452, when the English were driven out of France. During that period the wine had become very popular in England, where it was known as claret. The quality was jealously guarded even then: anyone who stole grapes lost an ear, as did those who tampered with the wine or made bad casks.

### The district round Bordeaux

Not all the land round Bordeaux is taken up with vineyards: of the agricultural land a third is planted with vines. To the east there is a varied landscape of undulating hills and plateaux, intersected by the valleys of the Garonne, Gironde and Dordogne. Narrow roads lead to small villages, the occasional old town and many wine châteaux, which may resemble either farms or genuine castles, but are usually something in between. There is also extensive woodland, especially to the south-west of the city in the flat region of Les Landes. You can wander about here for hours without meeting a soul. Then there is the coast with its beaches, and the lakes of Carcans and Lacanau. Many Bordelais have little houses in the country somewhere here, where they spend weekends and part of the summer. If you are a lover of wine, of the peace and tranquillity of the countryside and of a town like Bordeaux, you should plan a holiday in this wine province.

### Wine organisations and institutions

Bordeaux is also the seat of many organisations, institutions, brotherhoods and other bodies connected in some way with wine-growing and wine-making. The most important and best-known is the

The Town and Region of Bordeaux

Institut National des Appellations d'Origine Contrôlée. This is based in Paris, but there is a regional committee in Bordeaux. It is a semi-official institution which controls the *appellation contrôlée* wines and the conditions under which they are produced. It is always ready to defend the interests of the wines and wine producers of France. The French government makes a point of consulting the I.N.A.O. on questions in this field.

The official Institut National de la Recherche Agronomique has several research stations in the Bordeaux region. Here agricultural experiments are carried out; not just on vines but on many other crops as well.

Much more specialised is the world-famous Station Oenologique of Bordeaux, which for almost a hundred years has played the major part in the continual improvements in vinification methods and hence in the quality of Bordeaux wines. Courses in œnology are given regularly.

Wine growers, merchants, wine brokers and other experts are united in the Conseil Interprofessionel du Vin de Bordeaux. Its objects are fairly general: studying and organising the market for Bordeaux wines, enforcing the existing rules (such as *appellation contrôlée*) and offering a meeting-place for all wine professionals.

Finally, I must obviously mention the select society of the Syndicat des Grands Crus Classés du Médoc, in which the majority of the great classed growths of 1855 are included.

Right:
*Vintageing in Macau. Despite the increased mechanisation to be found in many activities, grape-picking is still done by hand almost everywhere, although experiments with mechanical harvesters have been carried out, and with some success.*

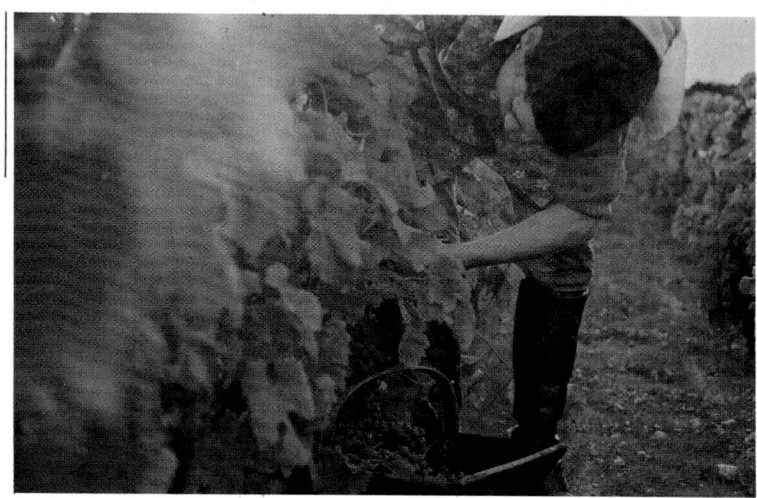

# Official Classifications and Vintage Charts

### The Médoc classification of 1855

Below is given the famous classification of 1855, comprising at this moment 5 first growths, 14 second, 14 third, 10 fourth and 18 fifth, a total of 61. It is remarkable that up to now only one alteration has been made to this list: in 1973 Château Mouton-Rothschild was promoted from the second to the first *grands crus*. Apart from this everything has remained the same as in 1855. This does not mean that everyone is content with the classification as it stands, for much can happen in 120 years: proprietors change, land is exchanged, some châteaux cease to exist – Desmirail, for example, has been swallowed up by Palmer. Also, in the existing classifications there are several châteaux which, if the categories related solely to quality, would now deserve a higher status, and conversely some should be demoted (or perhaps even be taken off the list). Besides, time has not stood still elsewhere; there are a number of wines being produced at non-classified châteaux which can show just as well as the *grands crus* at blind tastings.

The reason for the classification of 1855 still being used is probably that it is almost impossible to make a new one. The wisest course is therefore not to accept blindly the classification and the order of châteaux as indications of quality; the only viable criterion is the wine itself, not name or category. It is therefore a good idea, if possible, to begin the study of Bordeaux in the company of an experienced authority.

The price the wines might fetch was the major factor on which the classification of 1855 was based. It was reasoned that the best wines fetched the highest prices. It was the brokers of Bordeaux who drew up the classification and the Chamber of Commerce sanctioned it for the Paris Exhibition. In fact the brokers had been using a similar classification for years: the first dates from as far back as the beginning of the 18th century. Thus the official classification was more of a formal confirmation of an existing situation.

For the sake of completeness, it must be mentioned that in addition to the Médocs and Château Haut-Brion (the only Graves château to be included), 27 sweet white Sauternes were also classified. (The spelling of the names in the list is according to present usage.)

*Premiers crus*
Lafite-Rothschild, Pauillac
Margaux, Margaux
Latour, Pauillac
Mouton-Rothschild, Pauillac
Haut-Brion (Graves), Pessac

*Deuxièmes crus*
Rausan-Ségla, Margaux
Rauzan-Gassies, Margaux
Léoville-Las-Cases, St Julien
Léoville-Poyferré, St Julien
Léoville-Barton, St Julien
Durfort-Vivens, Margaux
Gruaud-Larose, St Julien
Lascombes, Margaux
Brane-Cantenac, Cantenac
Pichon-Longueville, Pauillac
Pichon-Lalande, Pauillac
Ducru-Beaucaillou, St Julien
Cos d'Estournel, St Estèphe
Montrose, St Estèphe

*Troisièmes crus*
Kirwan, Cantenac
d'Issan, Cantenac
Lagrange, St Julien
Langoa-Barton, St Julien
Giscours, Labarde
Malescot-St Exupéry, Margaux
Cantenac-Brown, Cantenac
Boyd-Cantenac, Margaux
Palmer, Cantenac
La Lagune, Ludon
Desmirail, Margaux
Calon-Ségur, St Estèphe
Ferrière, Margaux
Marquis d'Alesme-Becker, Margaux

*Quatrièmes crus*
St Pierre, St Julien
Talbot, St Julien
Branaire-Ducru, St Julien
Duhart-Milon-Rothschild, Pauillac
Pouget, Cantenac
La Tour Carnet, St Laurent
Lafon-Rochet, St Estèphe
Beychevelle, St Julien
Prieuré-Lichine, Cantenac
Marquis de Terme, Margaux

*Cinquièmes crus*
Pontet Canet, Pauillac
Batailley, Pauillac
Haut-Batailley, Pauillac
Grand-Puy-Lacoste, Pauillac
Grand-Puy-Ducasse, Pauillac
Lynch-Bages, Pauillac
Lynch-Moussas, Pauillac
Dauzac, Labarde
Mouton Baron Philippe, Pauillac
du Tertre, Arsac
Haut-Bages-Libéral, Pauillac
Pédesclaux, Pauillac
Belgrave, St Laurent
de Camensac, St Laurent
Cos Labory, St Estèphe
Clerc Milon, Pauillac
Croizet-Bages, Pauillac
Cantemerle, Macau

### Classification of Red and White Graves

It is strange that with the exception of Château Haut-Brion no red Graves was listed in the classification of 1855, for the vineyards of this district are the oldest in Bordeaux. Possibly they were going through a difficult period and they fetched less per *tonneau* than the better known growths of the Médoc; perhaps it was to a certain extent a question of discrimination. Be that as it may, the Graves châteaux have since made their own classification. After a great deal of preparation and an even longer wait this became operative by ministerial decree in 1959. Both red and white wines are classified, with the result that some châteaux get a place in both (in the Graves estates both red and white wines are frequently made). Wisely, however, no hierarchy has been established between the various châteaux. Haut-Brion is also included in this classification.

*Crus classés: Red*
Bouscaut, Cadaujac
Haut Bailly, Léognan
Domaine de Chevalier, Léognan
Carbonnieux, Léognan

Right:
View of the town of Pauillac under extreme weather conditions – just after a thunderstorm.

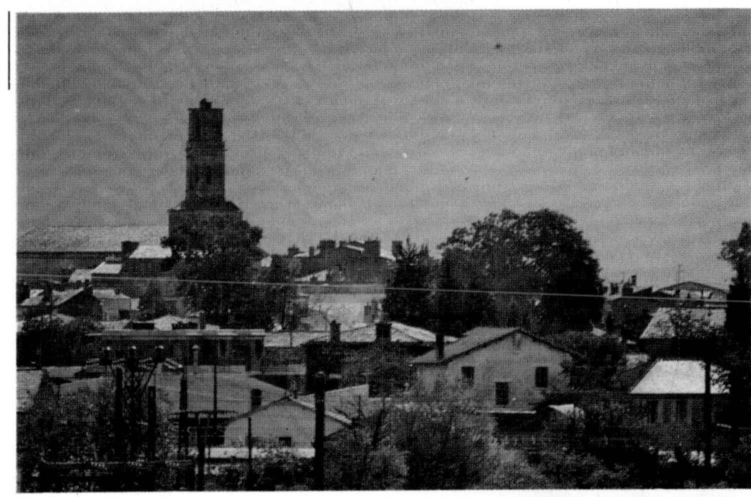



de Fieuzal, Léognan
Malartic-Lagravière, Léognan
Olivier, Léognan
La Tour Martillac, Martillac
Smith Haut Lafitte, Martillac
Haut-Brion, Pessac
Pape Clément, Pessac
La Mission Haut Brion, Talence
La Tour Haut Brion, Talence

*Crus classés: White*
Bouscaut, Cadaujac
Domaine de Chevalier, Léognan
Carbonnieux, Léognan
Malartic-Lagravière, Léognan
Olivier, Léognan
La Tour Martillac, Martillac
Laville-Haut-Brion, Talence
Couhins, Villenave-d'Ornon

**Classification of St Emilion and Pomerol**

St Emilion and Pomerol are not included in the classification of 1855. So, as in the Graves, St Emilion has made its own classification. Pomerol, however, has not yet done so: in this district there is no official classification (although there is an unofficial one headed by Château Pétrus). From the terminology used in St Emilion, it is clear that the classifications of the various districts cannot be compared. There is no legal definition of the use of the terms *grand cru, cru classé*, and so on. Each district interprets this in its own way, so that a St Emilion *grand cru classé* does not necessarily indicate a wine of the same quality as a classified growth of the Médoc or Graves.

What is the situation in St Emilion? Someone once wrote that this district has so many *grands crus* that you can compare it with a South American republic: there are almost as many generals as soldiers! Since 1969 St Emilion includes 83 *grands crus classés*, 12 of which are entitled to the designation *premier grand cru classé* (with Ausone and Cheval Blanc in class A and the rest in class B). Besides these there are the *grands crus* (not *classés*); this is not, however, a fixed classification but a fluctuating one. It is awarded each vintage, after the wines have been sampled. In 1971 juries sampled 244 wines, of which 234 eventually received the status of *grand cru*. So from the 1971 vintage there are no less than 317 *grands crus de St Emilion* in circulation in three different categories – a third of all the châteaux in the district! The classification is revised every 10 years, the next revision being due in 1979.

*Premiers grands crus classés A*
Ausone, St Emilion
Cheval Blanc, St Emilion

*Premiers grands crus classés B*
Beauséjour Duffau-Lagarrosse, St Emilion
Beauséjour, St Emilion
Belair, St Emilion
Canon, St Emilion
Figeac, St Emilion
La Gaffelière, St Emilion
Magdelaine, St Emilion
Pavie, St Emilion
Trottevieille, St Emilion
Clos Fourtet, St Emilion

*Grands crus classés*
L'Angélus, St Emilion
l'Arrosée, St Emilion
Baleau, St Emilion
Balestard-La Tonnelle, St Emilion
Bellevue, St Emilion
Bergat, St Emilion
Cadet-Bon, St Emilion
Cadet-Piola, St Emilion
Canon-La Gaffelière, St Emilion
Cap-de-Mourlin, St Emilion
Chapelle-Madeleine, St Emilion
Chauvin, St Emilion
Corbin, St Emilion
Corbin-Michotte, St Emilion
Coutet, St Emilion
Couvent-des-Jacobins, St Emilion
Croque-Michotte, St Emilion
Curé-Bon, St Emilion
Dassault, St Emilion
Faurie-de-Souchard, St Emilion
Fonplégade, St Emilion
Fonroque, St Emilion
Franc-Mayne, St Emilion
Grand-Barrail-Lamarzelle-Figeac, St Emilion
Grand-Corbin, St Emilion
Grand-Corbin-Despagne, St Emilion
Grand-Mayne, St Emilion
Grand-Pontet, St Emilion
Grandes-Murailles, St Emilion
Guadet-Saint-Julien, St Emilion
Haut-Corbin, St Emilion
Haut-Sarpe, St Emilion
Jean-Faure, St Emilion
La Carte, St Emilion
La Clotte, St Emilion
La Clusière, St Emilion
La Couspaude, St Emilion
La Dominique, St Emilion
Lamarzelle, St Emilion
Laniote, St Emilion
Larcis-Ducasse, St Emilion
Larmande, St Emilion
Laroze, St Emilion
La Serre, St Emilion
La Tour-du-Pin-Figeac (Bélivier), St Emilion
La Tour-du-Pin-Figeac (Moueix), St Emilion
La Tour-Figeac, St Emilion
Le Châtelet, St Emilion
Le Couvent, St Emilion
Le Prieuré, St Emilion
Matras, St Emilion
Mauvezin, St Emilion
Moulin-du-Cadet, St Emilion
Pavie-Decesse, St Emilion
Pavie-Macquin, St Emilion
Pavillon-Cadet, St Emilion
Petit-Faurie-de-Soutard, St Emilion
Ripeau, St Emilion
Saint-Georges-Côte-Pavie, St Emilion
Sansonnet, St Emilion
Soutard, St Emilion
Tertre-Daugay, St Emilion
Trimoulet, St Emilion
Trois-Moulins, St Emilion
Troplong-Mondot, St Emilion
Villemaurine, St Emilion
Yon-Figeac, St Emilion
Clos des Jacobins, St Emilion
Clos La Madeleine, St Emilion
Clos de l'Oratoire, St Emilion
Clos Saint-Martin, St Emilion

**Appellations contrôlées**

When buying Bordeaux wine it is wise to make sure that you check the *appellation*, for many famous châteaux have namesakes of lesser repute in other districts. For example, Château Cantemerle in Blaye is

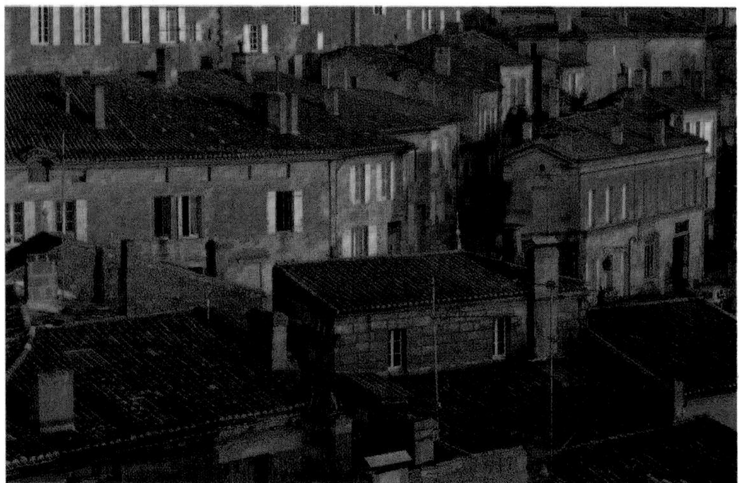

*Left:*
*The mediaeval town of St Emilion, which in itself is worth a visit. The fields around the town are almost exclusively planted with vines – hardly anything else is cultivated.*

*Left:*
*A view of the charming village of St Estèphe in the Médoc.*

List of the official *appellations d'origine côntrolées* currently in use in the Bordeaux region.

*Médoc*
St Estèphe (red)
Pauillac (red)
St Julien (red)
Moulis or Moulis-en-Médoc (red)
Listrac (red)
Margaux (red)
Haut-Médoc (red)
Médoc (red)
Wines that do not completely fulfil the requirements of their *appellation* may, in certain conditions, be declassified to lower *appellations*, such as Haut-Médoc, Médoc, Bordeaux supérieur and Bordeaux.

*Graves, Cérons, Sauternes and Barsac*
Cérons (white)
Barsac (white)
Sauternes (white)
Graves (red)
Graves (white)
Graves supérieures (white)
Wines that do not completely fulfil the requirements of their *appellation* may, in certain conditions, be declassified to lower *appellations*, such as Cérons to Graves supérieurs, Bordeaux supérieur and Bordeaux; Barsac to Sauternes, Bordeaux supérieur and Bordeaux; Sauternes to Bordeaux supérieur and Bordeaux; the others to Bordeaux.

*Right bank of the Garonne*
Ste Croix-du-Mont (white)
Loupiac (white)
Côtes de Bordeaux-St Macaire (white)
Cadillac (white)
Premières Côtes de Bordeaux (red)
Premières Côtes de Bordeaux (white)
Wines that do not completely fulfil the requirements of their



not at all the same as the Château Cantemerle in Macau. Similarly, Domaine de Beychevelle in St André-de-Cubzac, good though it may be, cannot be compared with Château Beychevelle in St Julien. There are ten estates with the name Beauséjour, nine of which begin with the prefix Vieux-Château, seven with Latour in their name and six with Lafite or Lafitte. So it is important to ascertain that you have the right name and the right *appellation.*

If a wine wishes to be granted the right to an *appellation d'origine contrôlée*, a legally controlled designation of the place of origin of the wine, then it must satisfy certain statutory requirements. The wine must come from a particular defined region, from certain prescribed vine varieties. These must be planted and cultivated in certain ways, and no more than a certain maximum number of hectolitres may be produced per hectare; also, the wine-making process is subject to regulations and the content of the wine must be regulated and attain a certain stipulated level of alcohol. The *appellation contrôlée* (always mentioned on the label) is therefore a guarantee of where the wine has been grown and made, and by implication an indication of quality, as being made according to certain rules. At the top of this page and the next you will find a complete list of the *appellations* to be found in the Bordeaux region.

### The vintages

A Bordeaux merchant once told me: 'The growers here are almost always pessimistic about the forthcoming vintage: they hope that it will make the prices of previous years rise. If you are to believe them, the first quarter of the harvest will not lead to anything, the second is destroyed by night frost, they lose the third in a hailstorm, they reject the fourth quarter due to rot, and they eventually harvest the fifth quarter . . .'

This is vintage talk. Months before the grapes are picked or are even ripe, forecasts are made, and there are more as the time of picking approaches. Once the wine has been made the public gets numerous reports, and for many these immediately represent the final judgement on that particular vintage. Unfortunately, however, little account is taken of the fact that it is difficult, if not impossible, to judge a wine in the first few months after it is made. Even the owners of the estates will not commit themselves at this stage.

Just how difficult it is to judge a wine's potential at an early stage may be seen by the fact that many years are initially over- or under-estimated. Examples are the many 'years of the century' (how many more will there be before the year 2000?) and 1966, which some experts at one time held to be inferior to 1967. Accurate assessments of the quality of a year are of course given sooner or later, but even then must be viewed with caution. For what is this evaluation of a vintage? It is really no more than an agreed general impression of the wine, with reservations and exceptions.

This applies particularly to Bordeaux, France's largest area for quality wines. About 33,000 growers in the Gironde produce between 3·5 and 5·7 million hectolitres of wine a year in an area covering 103,000 hectares; about 12 times that of Burgundy, 11 times that of Alsace and 7 times that of Champagne. The wine which is produced is then categorised among 29 different *appellations* for red and 19 for white. It is therefore impossible to put all these wines from all the growers under one single heading.

The brief descriptions of the vintages on the opposite page, compiled by experienced judges from each of the regions, must be read in this light. In every poor year, good wines are made, and in every good year poor wines are made. Wine farmer A, for example, may have got in his grapes just before the rain, whereas his neighbour B has not. Farmer C, on the other hand, decides to postpone picking in the hope that the rain will soon be over and the sun will shine again. Farmer D has hardly anything left to pick, because a hailstorm destroyed two-thirds of his crop a month ago. There are innumerable variants each year of growers with differing luck, more or less judgement. This is especially marked in an *année jalouse* such as like 1974. In such a year the quality of the wines differs widely, and many growers are jealous of neighbours who happen to have been fortunate; in vintages like these a great deal depends on the knowledge and expertise of merchants and shippers, for they have to pick out the wines early on in order to prevent their customers from making bad buys later.

The moral of this is that there are no years with nothing but good or bad wines: there are always exceptions, always borderline cases. Even in totally unsuccessful years it is possible to find some reasonably successful wines, although you do stand a better chance of making a right judgement in good years.

### Vintage Charts

*Médoc*

**1945** Remarkable vintage of very high quality
**1946** Light wines, now old
**1947** Great vintage now tending to decline
**1948** Very successful with full-bodied wines*
**1949** Rounded, popular wines, now ageing
**1950** Pleasant, sunny wines, now showing their age – a light year
**1951** An off year – few now in existence
**1952** Rather hard wines, slow evolution, potential great*
**1953** Wines of great charm and appeal – those that have lasted are still fine
**1954** An indifferent vintage
**1955** Powerful, sturdy wines, good but lacking grace*
**1956** The year of the disastrous frost; nearly all poor wines with high acidity
**1957** Low yield, wines remained hard for a long time, but are starting to soften
**1958** Below average
**1959** Big crop, great commercial success; excellent, now slightly lighter
**1960** Light year, pleasant wines
**1961** A great vintage; much charm, to keep for many years
**1962** Big crop, average vintage with charm and appeal – at peak
**1963** An off year
**1964** Fine autumn, then heavy rain at

*appellation* may, in certain conditions, be declassified to lower *appellations*, such as to Bordeaux supérieur and Bordeaux.

*Between Garonne and Dordogne*
Ste Foy-Bordeaux (red)
Ste Foy-Bordeaux (white)
Graves de Vayres (red)
Graves de Vayres (white)
Entre-Deux-Mers (white)
Entre-deux-Mers-Haut-Benauge (white)
Bordeaux Haut-Benauge (white)
Wines that do not completely fulfil the requirements of their *appellation* may, in certain conditions, be declassified to lower *appellations*, such as to Bordeaux.

*St Emilion and Pomerol*
St Emilion (red)
Sables-St Emilion (red)
Montagne-St. Emilion (red)
Lussac-St Emilion (red)
Parsac-St Emilion (red)
St Georges-St Emilion (red)
Puisseguin-St Emilion (red)
Pomerol (red)
Néac (red)
Lalande-de-Pomerol (red)
Wines that do not completely fulfil the requirements of their *appellation* may, in certain conditions, be declassified to lower *appellations*, such as Bordeaux supérieur and Bordeaux.

*Other wines of the right bank of the Dordogne*
Bordeaux-Côtes de Castillon (red)
Bordeaux-Côtes de Francs (red)
Côtes de Canon-Fronsac (red)
Côtes de Fronsac (red)
Bourg or Côtes de Bourg or Bourgeais (red)
Bourg or Côtes de Bourg or Bourgeais (white)
Premières Côtes de Blaye (red)
Premières Côtes de Blaye (white)
Côtes de Blaye (white)
Blaye or Blayais (red)
Blaye or Blayais (white)
Wines that do not completely fulfil the requirements of their *appellation* may, in certain conditions, be declassified to lower *appellations*, the first four to Bordeaux supérieur and Bordeaux; the red Bourg to Bordeaux; the Premières Côtes de Blaye to Blayais and Bordeaux; and the Côtes de Blaye to Blayais.



vintage time, hence varied quality; some robust, fruity wines
**1965** A year to discount – rained out
**1966** A fine summer making robust wines of character and depth, to keep
**1967** Bigger crop than 1966, wines of marked charm and elegance
**1968** An off year – little good wine made
**1969** Rather robust wines without much charm but plenty of fruit
**1970** Good quality and quantity; wines to lay down – a great vintage
**1971** Very charming wines, which may develop greatness; also to be laid down
**1972** A light year, many pleasant wines made
**1973** Quality varying; rather light, quick developers
**1974** Firmer than 1973 but an imponderable at present, so wait and see

*Red Graves*

**1945** A great vintage but a very small yield – still improving
**1946** A disastrous year
**1947** Charming and noble wines, which will not improve for much longer
**1948** Initially a hard vintage, now coming round*
**1949** Engaging but slightly superficial
**1950** A lot of wine made but essentially a light, agreeable vintage
**1951** Light, thin wines and a small vintage, certainly past its prime
**1952** Slow-maturing, balanced wines with much still to come*
**1953** A successful year from the start, well balanced, charming wines – the greater ones still delicious
**1954** Light, pleasant, short-lived
**1955** One of the best of the decade, fragrant, balanced, firm
**1956** Due to heavy frost, only a little wine and of poor quality
**1957** Another small vintage, rather hard wines
**1958** Rather thin, some drinkable wines, certainly over the top now
**1959** Very fine wines, harmonious, rich, compact; the biggest crop since 1953
**1960** Rather light but some very pleasant wines*
**1961** Fine, concentrated, big, slow to mature, keep for years yet
**1962** Well balanced, pleasant wines with much appeal, possibly now at their peak
**1963** Big yield but poor quality
**1964** Successful in this region, which vintaged early; fruity, compact wines, now developing well
**1965** Indifferent in general
**1966** Full, big wines with a fair amount of tannin; must be given time to mature
**1967** Harmonious, elegant and with considerable charm
**1968** A small vintage, quality negligible
**1969** Supple, pleasant, fragrant wines which become rounder as they mature
**1970** Abundant year with very good big wines to be laid down
**1971** Close in style to the 1970 vintage and sometimes even better; fine Graves
**1972** Mostly thin, frail wines, not very interesting, some pleasant to drink
**1973** Inconsistent vintage, some very pleasant wines but great variations
**1974** A rather inconsistent vintage, but more body, breed and potential than 1973

*St Emilion and Pomerol*

**1945** Warm year, very good
**1946** Poor wine, now too old
**1947** A great vintage, full-bodied, will not now get better
**1948** A variable vintage, now showing its age
**1949** A great vintage of assertive appeal
**1950** Average year, now old
**1951** Small, light vintage
**1952** Fairly good but of varying quality*
**1953** A very good vintage, but the wines are now declining
**1954** A poor year
**1955** Fairly inconsistent, but some good bottles
**1956** No production of any significance – frost
**1957** No production of any significance
**1958** No production of any significance
**1959** A reasonably successful vintage, though less so here than elsewhere
**1960** Fairly pleasing, light wines*
**1961** Great vintage with complete, big wines which can be left to mature for at least 20 years
**1962** Pleasant, lightish wines of definite charm
**1963** Minimal in every respect
**1964** Some very good wines made in this region
**1965** Poor year
**1966** Powerful, perhaps a little heavy, but certainly maturing well
**1967** Charming wines which are developing faster than 1966
**1968** Generally a poor vintage with a few drinkable wines
**1969** Seemed more promising than it has turned out, somewhat undistinguished
**1970** Very fine, big wines, for long-term maturation
**1971** Very good and pleasant wines which may also last a long while
**1972** A misleading vintage with much acidity; for drinking soon
**1973** An inconsistent vintage; reasonably fine, but care needed in selection
**1974** This vintage also shows large differences in quality but promises well

* *indicates that some wines of this vintage are past their prime*

*Left:*
*The long quay alongside the Garonne; much of the wine is shipped from here. Since 1973 more Bordeaux wine has been exported in bottles than in casks, and this trend is continuing.*

*Below:*
*Diagram of the production and export of Bordeaux wines with* appellation contrôlée *in several recent years.*

# The Trade

Foreign influence on the trade in Bordeaux wine has always been great. British and Dutch ships, more than French, carried the wines to the ends of the earth, and many foreigners set up in Bordeaux as wine merchants. Numbers of today's leading trading houses are of non-French origin. In his book, *Le Vignoble Bordelais*, Philippe Roudié says that Beyerman is the oldest house: it was established in the first half of the 18th century by a Dutchman. There followed Thomas Barton from Ireland (1725), William Johnston from England (1734) and Jean-Henry Schÿler from Germany (1739); to mention only a few famous names. The 19th century saw a flowering of the wine trade, with the result that more and more people began to go into the wine business: between 1855 and 1870 the town of Bordeaux included literally hundreds of large and small firms, some of them still in business. Guillaume Mestrezat came from Geneva and established himself in 1815, Léon Hanappier from Orléans (1826), Herman Cruse from Denmark (1819), Alfred de Luze from Germany (1820), Jean-Marie Calvet from Tain-l'Hermitage in France (1823), Eschenauer from Alsace (1831), the Frenchman Dourthe set up business in 1840. Later in the 19th century and at the beginning of the 20th century they were joined by Delor, Ginestet, Cordier, Sichel, Mähler and many others.

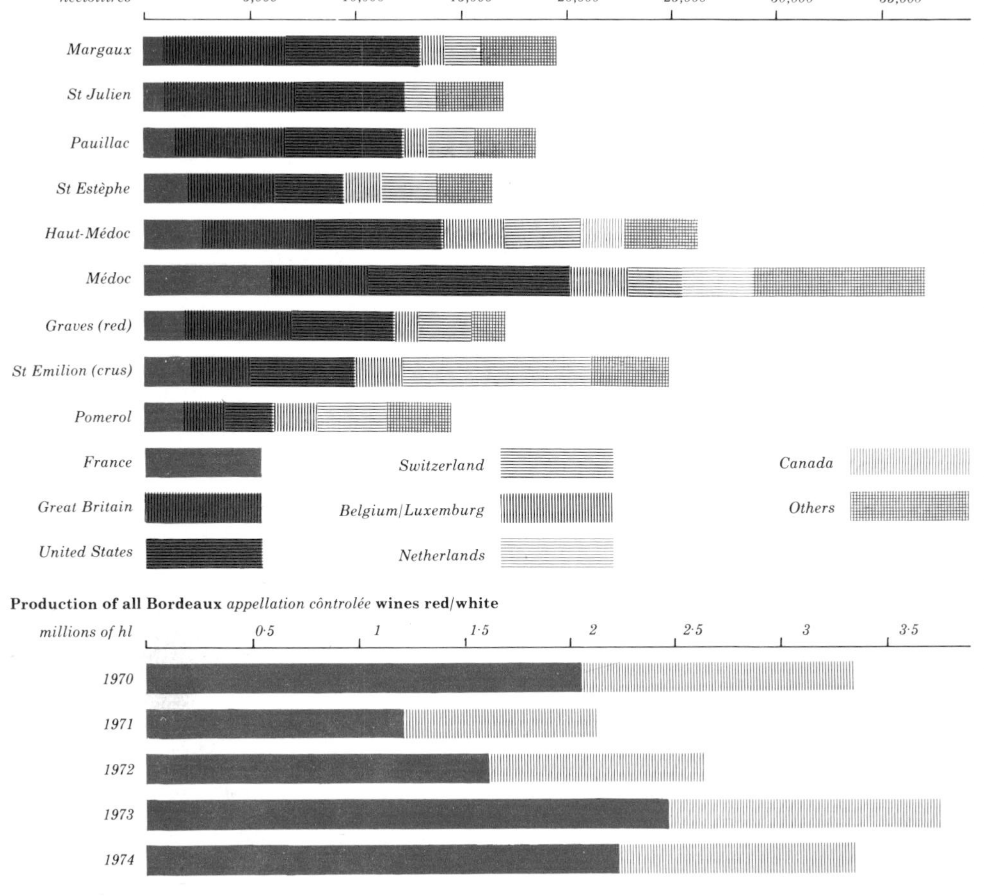


Production of all Bordeaux wines: 5·5 million hectolitres (1970), of which 48% red and 52% white.
Production of all French wines: 74 million hectolitres (1970), of which 75% red and 25% white.

### Contemporary changes in the trade

The wine trade created, established and made the international reputation of the wines of Bordeaux. Formerly, shippers bought the young wines in wood from the estates, took these into their cellars and matured them there. Such firms were called *négociants-éleveurs* – shippers and 'bringers-on of wines'. The intermediary between them and the growers was the *courtier*, or broker.

The present situation has changed considerably: the shippers can no longer afford to keep large stocks for long periods, and the leading estates now do the maturing and bottling of the wine themselves. The work of the broker is becoming less important now that there is more direct contact between the shipper and the grower or producer. Many of the Bordeaux shippers have exclusive rights to sell the entire crop of certain of the estates. This situation already existed where there were business relationships between certain estates and firms, but now many other estates also give a monopoly of their wines to a particular firm of their choice.

The role which the wine trade plays will therefore tend to develop in the future, stressing the role of the shipper or distributor. Firms in their position thus need not only a knowledge of wine but also an awareness of world markets and how to sell in them.

# The Châteaux

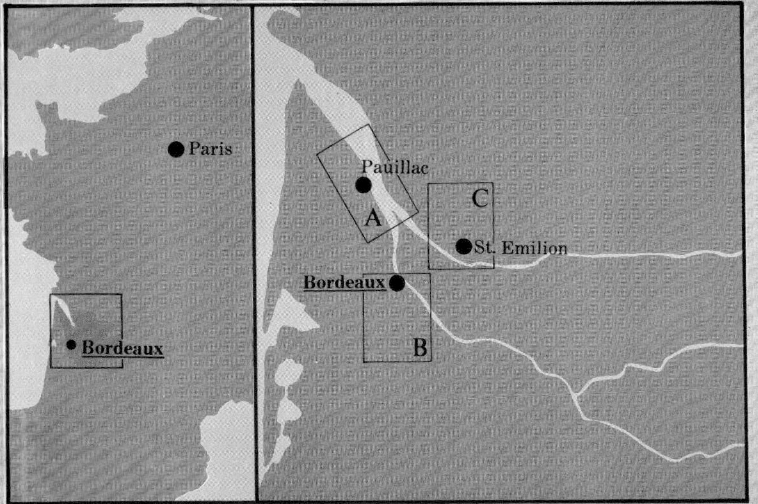


*Left:*
*The city of Bordeaux is situated 557 kilometres to the south-west of Paris. The city is in the heart of this famous wine-producing region, which is indicated in red on the key map. The three most important districts, each of them discussed in this book, are:*
**A** *the Médoc,* **B** *the Graves,*
**C** *St Emilion and Pomerol.*
*For a map of the Médoc see below; a map of the Graves will be found on page 143 and one of St Emilion and Pomerol on page 167.*

*Below:*
*The map gives a general impression of the Médoc, showing all the châteaux discussed in this section. The boundaries of the most important wine parishes are shown in dark yellow and their names are given, as well as the names of towns and villages, and next to each château symbol, the names of the individual châteaux. Please note that north is to the left of the page.*

# Map of the Médoc

The Médoc is a narrow strip of land to the north-west of Bordeaux. It is not a district renowned for natural beauty, but this is compensated for by the high quality of the wines. This is the most important wine area of the Gironde – and, for many, the most important in the world. In their youth the wines are fairly reserved and reticent, but over the years they acquire nobility and finesse. In the 7,200 hectares under vines it is the Cabernet Sauvignon grapes with their tough skins which dominate and give the wine its breeding. The Merlot gives the roundness and fragrance. There are about 1800 estates in the Médoc, almost all producing red wine. The district is divided into the Haut-Médoc (the southernmost part to just beyond St Seurin-de-Cadourne) and the Bas-Médoc, to the north. The great majority of the famous properties are situated in the Haut-Médoc, where six parishes have individual *appellations*. These are (in order of the amount of wine produced) St Estèphe, Pauillac, Margaux, St Julien, Listrac and Moulis.

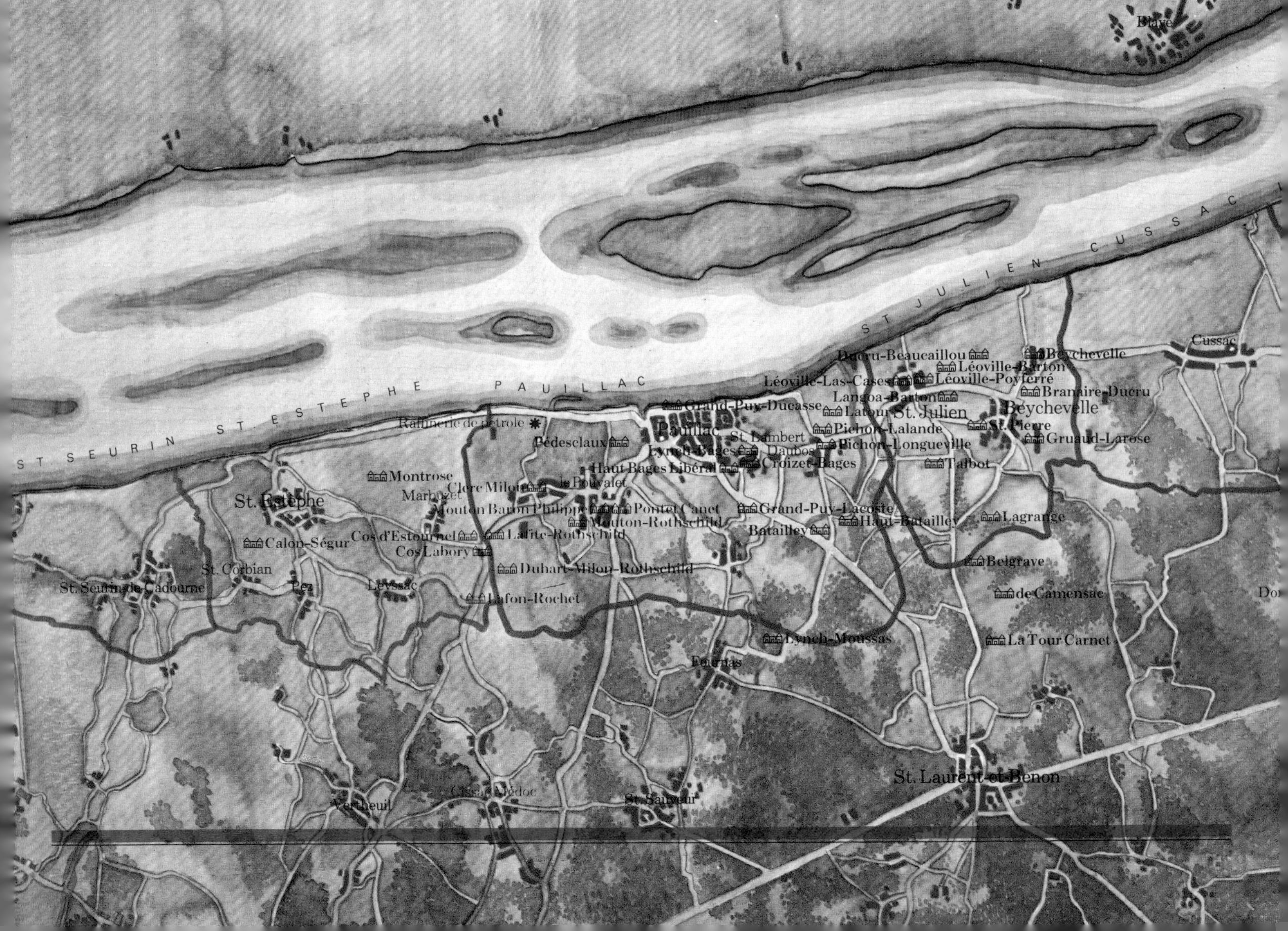

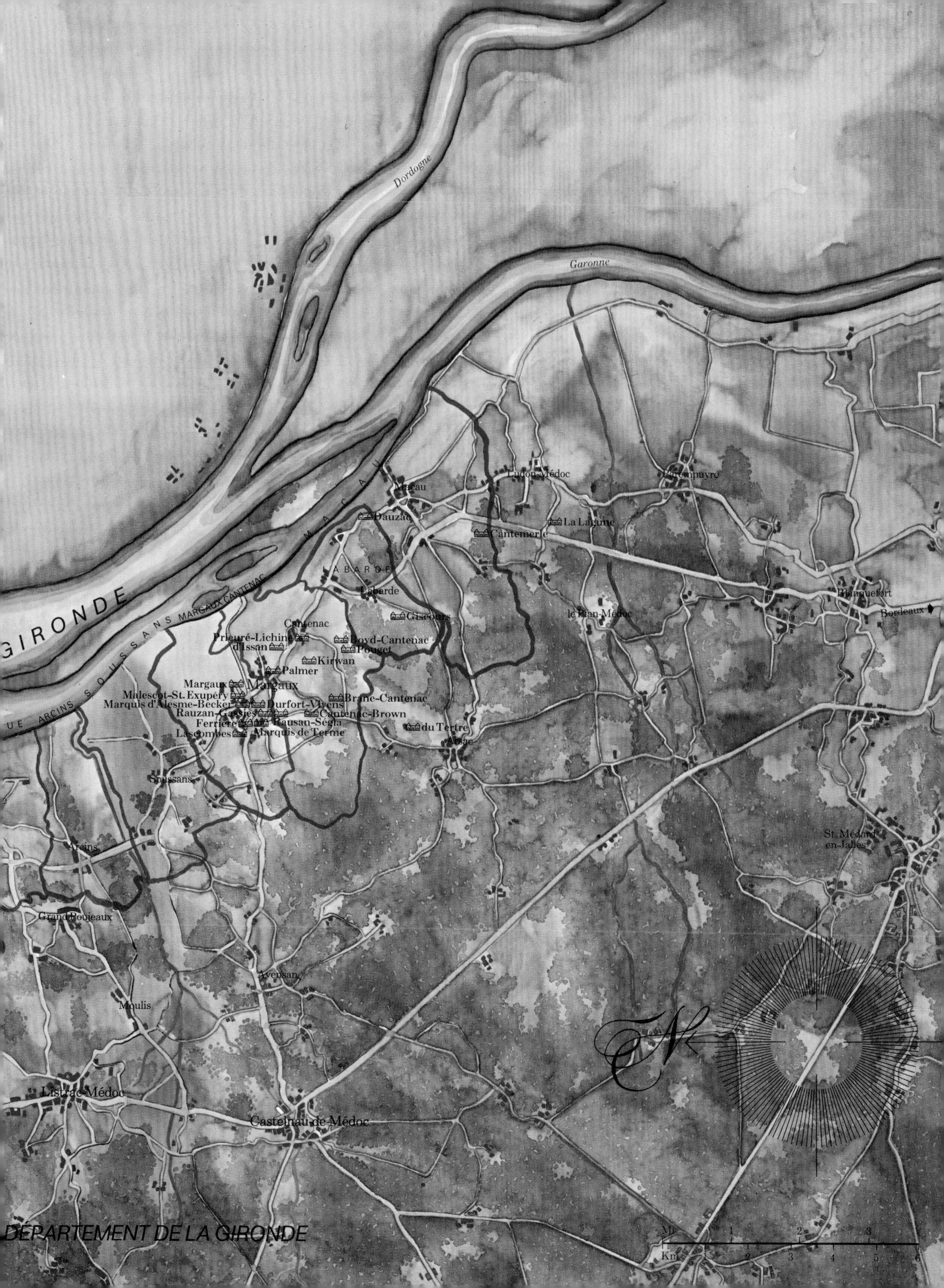
Dordogne
Garonne
GIRONDE
UE ARCINS SOUSSANS MARGAUX CANTENAC
MACAU
LABARDE
Macau
Dauzac
Ludon-Médoc
Parempuyre
La Lagune
Cantemerle
Labarde
Giscours
le Pian-Médoc
Blanquefort
Bordeaux
Cantenac
Prieuré-Lichine
d'Issan
Boyd-Cantenac
Pouget
Kirwan
Palmer
Margaux
Margaux
Malescot-St. Exupéry
Marquis d'Alesme-Becker
Durfort-Vivens
Brane-Cantenac
Rauzan-Gassies
Cantenac-Brown
Ferrière
Rausan-Ségla
Lascombes
Marquis de Terme
du Tertre
Arsac
Soussans
Arcins
Grand Poujeaux
Avensan
Moulis
Listrac-Médoc
Castelnau-de-Médoc
St. Médard-en-Jalles
N
DÉPARTEMENT DE LA GIRONDE
Mi 1 2 3
Km 1 2 3 4 5 6

La Lagune is the only Château which can be easily recognised from the air, because it has its name painted in giant letters on the *chai* roof. But there is no heliport yet in the Médoc.

La Lagune does not consist only of the 55 hectares of vineyard; the remaining grounds and the adjoining park extend over a further 45 hectares.

The Château is only occupied for a few months of the year by M. Chayoux's widow: she lives for much of the time at Ay, in Champagne.

*Right:*
*The label and the case stamp of La Lagune show the front of the Château. The offices and chais are situated on the left, round another courtyard.*

*Below:*
*A view of the Château's second-year cellar. With an average yield of 200 to 250* tonneaux, *there are at least 800 casks, each one of which must be moved from time to time – an exhausting operation! The Château uses only new, Bordeaux-type casks (recognisable by the oblique head staves). This is the traditional Bordeaux cask, but for today's often rough handling many châteaux have changed to the sturdier* barriques de transport.

GRAND CRU CLASSÉ
CHATEAU LA LAGUNE
HAUT·MÉDOC
APPELLATION HAUT-MÉDOC CONTROLÉE
1970
SOCIÉTÉ CIVILE AGRICOLE DU CHATEAU LA LAGUNE
PROPRIÉTAIRE A LUDON (GIRONDE) FRANCE
MIS EN BOUTEILLE AU CHATEAU
CHAU LA LAGUNE

3rd Grand Cru Classé

If someone were to forget what the major product of Château La Lagune is, the intricately wrought entrance gate would remind him immediately, for realistic corkscrews are worked into it. Other fine examples of wrought ironwork are to be found inside the property, such as the balustrade of the terrace and the lamp standards. Everything is spotless, not a speck of dirt is to be seen. Even the woodshed, which visitors normally do not see, is neat and tidy. But after all it is a woman who calls the tune at La Lagune. Her name is Madame J. Boyrie and she presides from a small office. This tiny, plucky woman has been *régisseuse* since 1964, the year in which her husband, who ran the estate, died. Mme Boyrie does an excellent job. Not only does she manage a permanent staff of about 47, she knows in detail exactly how to make an excellent wine, which usually pleases those who really know about Bordeaux – even competitors.

### A revived estate

This was not always the case. Although the estate – then Grand La Lagune – had in its day been famous, this century saw

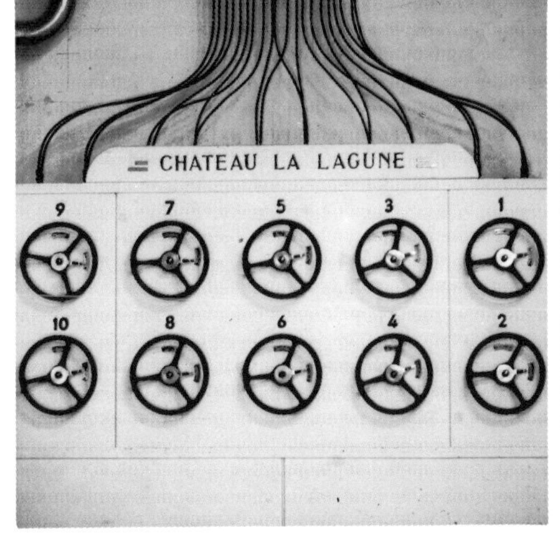


*Far left:*
*Château La Lagune has a shape characteristic of the Médoc, single-storied and called a* chartreuse. *It dates from 1730 and was designed by Victor Louis, who also designed Margaux and the Théatre de Bordeaux.*

*Left:*
*The impressive panel of the Téléflex equipment, with which the young wine can be sent from the fermentation vats to the various* chais *without coming into contact with the air.*

*Below:*
*Madame Boyrie, who is responsible for the work both in the vineyard and in the cellars.*



a period of decline. The production dropped to 15 *tonneaux* and the quality to below that expected from a classified wine. It was an idealist, Georges Brunet, who in 1958 bought the run-down estate, hoping to make fine wine there again. He began large-scale replanting and installed the very latest fermentation vats. In addition he devised a system of transporting the wine from vat to cask and racking from cask to cask entirely mechanically, which both facilitated the work and ensured that the wine came into contact with the air as little as possible. Unfortunately, however, it took too long for the enormous investment to pay, and in 1961 M. Brunet had to sell the estate. (It is interesting to note that he moved to Provence, where he now produces a good red wine, Château Vignelaure.)
The present proprietor of La Lagune is the Champagne house of Ayala, which has enabled the rehabilitation of the property to be continued, first through *régisseur* Boyrie and subsequently through Madame Boyrie, his widow.

### Sandy soil

La Lagune is the first classed growth to be seen as you travel up the Médoc from Bordeaux. The *appellation contrôlée* is Haut-Médoc. In places La Lagune adjoins the Cantemerle vineyard, yet the wines are entirely different. This is mainly due to the difference in soil where the vines of La Lagune grow; it is predominantly sandy, and in several places the water level is only one metre below the surface. It is also unusual in the southern Médoc for the vineyard of 55 hectares to be a single unit and not made up out of many small lots. The percentage of the Cabernet vines is fairly high: 50% Cabernet Sauvignon, 25% Cabernet Franc, 20% Merlot and 5% Petit Verdot. This undoubtedly helps to make the wines of La Lagune long-lasting. The production is 200 to 250 *tonneaux*.

### The scent of undergrowth

In the years immediately following the replanting of the vineyard, the wines were naturally less mature than they are now, and in fact the only bottle from this château which has slightly disappointed me was a 1960. 1962 was exceptional.
Since 1966 La Lagune has been producing profound wines which often need long maturing which is, however, richly rewarding. Whereas the 1966 vintage should not be drunk before the end of the seventies, the seven-year-old 1967 is already agreeably impressive. Besides a lovely pronounced bouquet, it has a rich, almost opulent flavour full of subtleties. A single sip can be enjoyed for minutes afterwards. In short, it is a very fine wine, in a year when it might have been rather light.
I also tasted a bottle of 1970, which everyone can safely leave to mature in their cellars until the mid-eighties: very dark in colour, a full, fruity flavour, rich, a wine which lingers in your mouth. Three other successful years are 1971, 1973 and perhaps 1974, which might even lie between those of 1970 and 1971. (The 1972 vintage suffered much from rain, with the result that the wine is already almost drinkable and must be consumed earlier than the others.)

What is the most distinctive feature of the wines of La Lagune? As with all great wines, this 'something' is very difficult to define. You could say that the wines of La Lagune are midway between those of the commune of Margaux and the red Graves, but that is of course not definite enough. La Lagune nearly always has a very deep colour; and its flavour is powerful and lingering; markedly so for a wine from the southern Médoc. Quite often it is fleshy – you can chew on it, so to speak – something which I would not say of its neighbours. Finally, the bouquet is highly individual. It makes me think of the scent of undergrowth in a wood still damp from rain. Others may be reminded of something completely different, but isn't that precisely why wine can provide the subject for fascinating discussions?
Anyone living in Britain, the United States, Belgium or Holland has a good chance of buying Château La Lagune, because these are the largest export markets.

APPELLATION HAUT-MÉDOC CONTROLÉE
1970
CHÂTEAU CANTEMERLE
GRAND CRU CLASSÉ DE MÉDOC
Héritiers Pierre J. DUBOS, Propriétaires
Macau-en-Médoc


*Below:*
*The label of Cantemerle, showing the impressive château façade, which is enlarged in the picture below.*

*Left and below:*
*The château, which has been extended several times. The oldest part can be recognised by the small round turret between the big tower on the left and the main building. Cantemerle was originally a simple, rectangular building with two wings standing at right-angles to each other. Later the two towers were added, and last of all the centre section, the main building.*

*Bottom:*
*Between the oak fermentation vats in the vathouse rails have been laid for a small railway truck which is used to transport heavy equipment. When this photograph was taken, the cart was filled with a large quantity of cases of the Château's wine – always of marked quality.*

# Chau Cantemerle

5th Grand Cru Classé

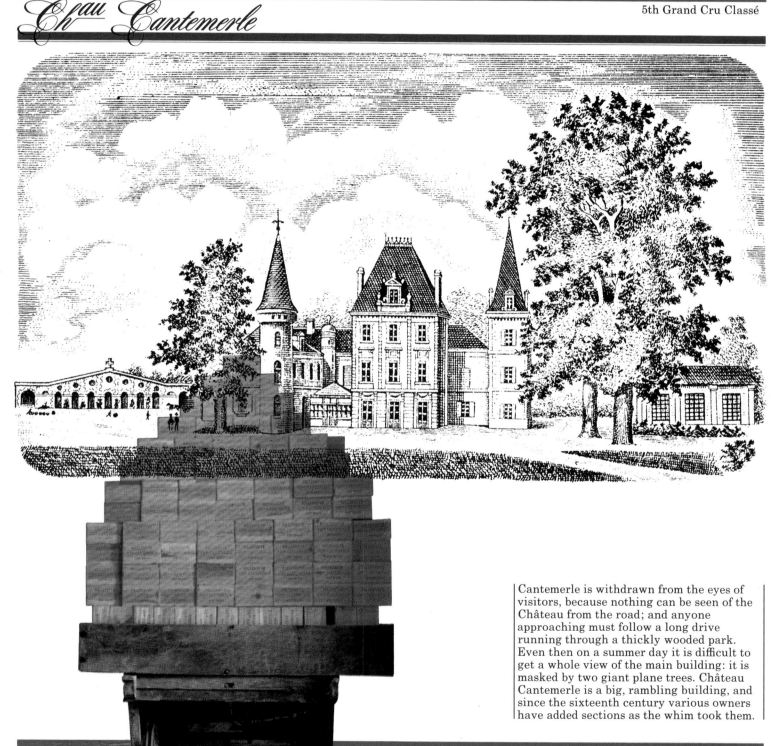

Cantemerle is withdrawn from the eyes of visitors, because nothing can be seen of the Château from the road; and anyone approaching must follow a long drive running through a thickly wooded park. Even then on a summer day it is difficult to get a whole view of the main building: it is masked by two giant plane trees. Château Cantemerle is a big, rambling building, and since the sixteenth century various owners have added sections as the whim took them.

*Left:*
*Another view of the Château, from the thickly wooded park, which has beautiful trees and a stream.*

*Bottom:*
*Michael Patarin is one of the cellar workers, working under M. Fraysse, who succeeded M. Laroza when the latter retired in 1967. Cellar master Fraysse is in turn responsible to the manager, Georges Constatin, whose father held the same position. In all there are 20 people permanently employed here.*

There is a charming story about the origin of the name Cantemerle. Centuries ago, during the time of recurrent warfare with the English, there was an enormous cannon on the estate, which for obscure reasons was called the *merle* (blackbird). One day an English unit came and camped on the estate, to the annoyance of the inhabitants. The soldiers plundered the cellars and soon became drunk and rowdy. The French stood by powerless, until one of them remembered the cannon. Very quietly the gun was moved out into the open, loaded and fired with a tremendous roar. The English were so startled that they took to their heels and fled. So the estate became Cantemerle – the blackbird that sang with effect.



### Last, but very far from least

None of this matters, for this is a property held in high esteem by all discriminating lovers of fine wine. A great many people have wondered about the fact that Château Cantemerle brings up the rear in the fifth and final section of the classed growths. But this merely shows how these divisions should not be taken as exact implications of quality – all classed growths are usually fine wines. It is certainly true that in good years Cantemerle, notwithstanding the rigid classification, deserves more than a last place, and this has actually been the situation for generations. In *Bordeaux et Ses Vins* of 1893, for example, the wine is listed as being ten per cent more expensive than the other fifth growths.

### A sleeping beauty of a wine

If you visit Cantemerle when things are quiet it is just as if time has stood still for everything there. You cannot see or hear the traffic going by on the road, the salons of the château are as they have been for generations and in the half-light of the *chais* a handful of workers methodically top up the oak casks as they have always done. The study of the manager, Bertrand Clauzel, is a dimly lit, dark brown room with gigantic leather armchairs and walls covered with paintings and old books. The Château has in its possession a document dating from 1573, which is a deed of sale exactly 4·56 metres long!

It comes as no surprise to discover that at this quiet estate the wine is made according to traditional methods. Almost everywhere in the Médoc you will see ingenious machines which remove the stalks from the grapes, but at Cantemerle it is still done by hand. The fermentation vats are of wood – the wine has no contact with metal. The ancient *chais* have black, cobwebbed ceilings. Here the wine is bottled, again by hand, the bottles being filled one by one from the cask.

What is notable is the general spaciousness. The *chais* and outbuildings are grouped around two large courtyards with a barrack-like appearance, and the presshouse has two separate entrances for the vintage to be brought in for, prior to the phylloxera disaster, Cantemerle produced almost double its present 80 *tonneaux*.

Today some 20 hectares supply the grapes for the wine of Cantemerle. They are planted with 40% Cabernet Sauvignon, 40% Merlot, 15% Cabernet Franc and 5% Petit Verdot. Although the whole estate totals no less than 328 hectares, there are no plans to extend the vineyeard. This is closely connected with the fact that Cantemerle is a family property: there is not enough capital to make large investments and extensions, if the wine's standard of quality is to be maintained.

### Ties with Holland

Two families have really made Château Cantemerle what it is today – those of Villeneuve and Dubos. It was Jean de Villeneuve, second president of the parliament of Bordeaux, who bought Cantemerle at the end of the sixteenth century, after which the estate remained in his family for nearly three hundred years. In 1892 the property passed into the hands Théophile J. Dubos and, later, into those of Pierre J. Dubos, a remarkable man who recorded every detail of vines and wines. In 1949 a group of Dutch wine-merchants celebrated his fiftieth anniversary at Cantemerle with a presentation blue Delft plate with his motto inscribed on it: 'Wine-making consists of a great many small worries.' M. Clauzel is the grandson of Pierre J. Dubos, who recently died.

It is no coincidence that it was Dutch wine-importers who paid this tribute, because Cantemerle has always had particularly close ties with Holland, for a long time far and away the largest buyer. Great Britain has now succeeded Holland as the largest buyer, and a good deal of wine is also shipped to the United States, Denmark and Switzerland. The wine, which is *appellation contrôlée* Haut-Médoc, invariably impresses even rival owners. For example, the 1966 vintage displayed the breeding and finesse of Cantemerle. The 1964 vintage, too – a difficult year in the Médoc – strongly appealed to me, though I found the 1967 vintage still rather reserved.

Cantemerle, the Bordelais say, never makes a bad wine. Not always obvious to the novice taster, its qualities develop slowly – the elegant, profound bouquet, subtly enticing flavour, length and beautiful after-taste, which combine to produce a classic claret possessing charm as well as nobility.

Arsac is by far the largest of the five communes which together make up the overall region of Margaux. Margaux itself covers 843 hectares, Labarde 475, Cantenac 1,417, Soussans 1,558, but Arsac is double this – 3,219 hectares. These figures of course refer to the total surface area and not to that of the vineyards.

The history of du Tertre goes back to the 12th century when it belonged to the *seigneurie* of Arsac. One of the later proprietors was the Ségur family, the same as in Calon-Ségur, which also belongs to Philippe Gasqueton's family. So the two estates have once again been united.

Twelve people are permanently employed at du Tertre and, apart from vintage time, there is always much to be done. In addition to the year-round routines of the vineyard, parts of du Tertre are in the process of being replanted.

*Right:*
*The bottles immediately after bottling, standing in the cases in which they will shortly be placed lying in batches of twelve. Close to the railway station in Margaux is one of the main suppliers of these wooden cases. As most of the châteaux now bottle their wines at the estate, such businesses are flourishing.*

*Below:*
*The Château seen some distance from the main entrance. The vineyard's raised situation is apparent, the gentle slope being of great importance for drainage.*

## Chau du Tertre

5th Grand Cru Classé

To reach Château du Tertre you have to follow a winding road for some kilometres into the hinterland of Margaux, in the direction of Arsac. Suddenly, on your left, you will see a hillock (*tertre* in French), completely covered with vines, rising up among some clumps of trees. This is the vineyard of Château du Tertre. The buildings are on top of the hill at the end of a bumpy drive. The château is ash-white in colour and looks very derelict – understandably, as nobody lives in it. The *chais*, on the other hand, are well cared for, as is the vineyard itself.

It used to be a different story. Château du Tertre is one of the many classed growths which had a difficult time during and after the second world war. Work was begun on restoring its reputation in 1962, when M. Philippe Capbern-Casqueton acquired the property. M. Casqueton is a totally committed wine-grower; his family has been connected with the wine trade in the Médoc since before the French Revolution. Another of his family's estates is the Château Calon-Ségur in St Estèphe, much further to the north, an estate which has a world name. When Château du Tertre changed hands M. Casqueton, together with his daughter, a fully qualified oenologist, started to restore the vineyard and buildings and to replace the fermentation vats and other equipment. He left the main building in the state in which he found it; he and his family already live very comfortably at Château Capbern-Casqueton, immediately behind the church of St Estèphe.

### Low yield

The vineyard of du Tertre covers over 45 hectares in a single unit. This is fairly unusual for an estate with the *appellation* Margaux; the vineyards of this commune

*Centre:*
*The bottling at du Tertre is fully automatic, though some other classed growths are still bottled individually by hand.*

*Below:*
*The functional, angular formation of the second-year chai contains the repetitive curves of hundreds of wooden casks.*

*Right:*
*Château du Tertre with its attractive little balcony, but alas, inside the building there are only ruins.*

are generally comprised of many small plots. Philippe Casqueton has planted a great deal of Cabernet Sauvignon: approximately two-thirds of the whole. The production is around 120 *tonneaux*.
Because it is always difficult to restore to its former place an estate that has declined, I asked M. Casqueton whether or not he gave special publicity to his wine. He replied: 'In fact all our publicity is based on the *déclaration de la récolte*. When we declare how much wine we are going to market as Château du Tertre, it turns out that we have produced 30% to 35% less wine per hectare than other châteaux – which can only mean that we are concentrating on the quality.'

### Built-in resistance to sea travel

The wine-making of du Tertre is traditional and the Cabernet Sauvignon plays a major rôle; this must be why its wines tend to retain a certain toughness for quite some time. I remember the 1967 vintage, which had a fine, delicate bouquet and a flavour which had a certain element of ripeness but also contained some hardness. As with everything about M. Casqueton, this has its reason: 'I noticed that wine which is shipped to the United States becomes a year older en route simply because of the continuous rocking movement of the ship. I have therefore tried to give my wines an extra, built-in resistance to this sea journey.' It will be understood from this that the United States is the most important buyer of Château du Tertre. Britain, Holland, France, Switzerland and Japan are also good customers.

Up to a point, the older the vines the better the wine a vineyard produces. I get the impression that the wines of du Tertre improve with each vintage. A striking example is the wine from the anything but superior year of 1972. M. Casqueton succeeded in making a pleasant wine with a good colour, bouquet and taste, and even charm. For a 1972 Margaux the wine also has quite a lot of body, which means it looks as if it may have a longer life than a great many other wines of that same year.

I found the 1971 vintage a good wine with a considerable amount of fruit on the nose and taste. Great refinement was not yet discernible, something which also applies to the much more powerful wine of 1970. This was very deep in colour, had a strong, fruity bouquet and a reticent, still hard taste. It is certainly not an unattractive idea to bide one's time in the company of the 1972 vintage from this up-and-coming Château until the 1971 vintage is ready, and then to sit back with the 1971 until the 1970 in its turn is ready for drinking – because this is the order in which the wines will mature.

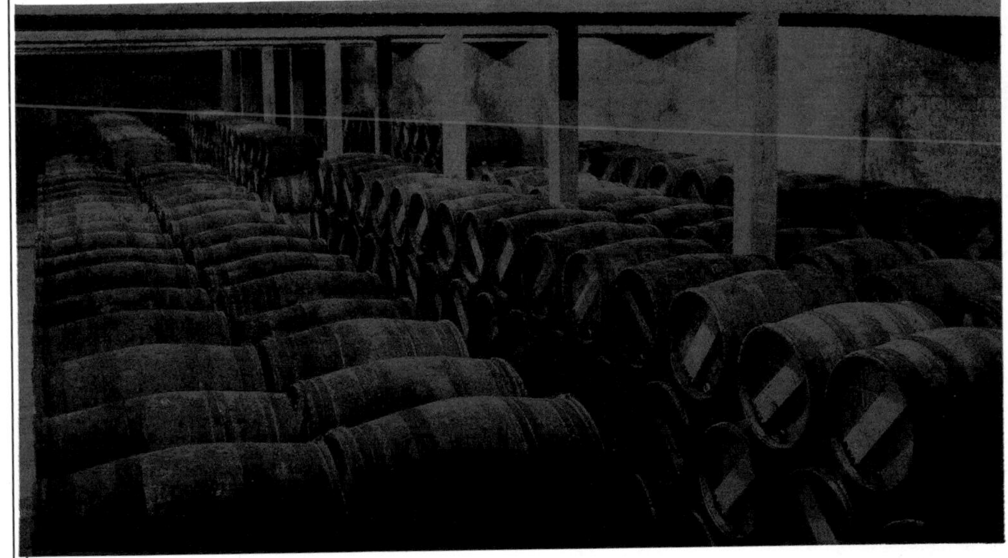

Château Dauzac
Margaux
APPELLATION MARGAUX CONTROLÉE
1970
Grand Cru Classé
HÉRITIERS EDOUARD F. MIAILHE
PROPRIÉTAIRES A LABARDE-MARGAUX (GIRONDE)
MIS EN BOUTEILLES AU CHATEAU


*Left:*
*Gables such as this give the house an elegant air.*

*Below:*
*One of the workrooms, with a solid mass of bottles and some of the robust women workers.*

*Bottom:*
*The bottles of Dauzac are 'dressed' one by one with loving care. The two women in the foreground do the labelling after the third one has fixed on the capsules.*

Powdery mildew is a type of fungus which can attack the grapes and wither them. The remedy is Bordeaux mixture, a mixture of copper sulphate, lime and water, with which the plants are sprayed. It is said that this remedy was discovered by chance at Dauzac. Nathaniel Johnston, the proprietor of this estate in the last century, noticed that children often picked the grapes from the vines growing by the wayside. To frighten them off he sprayed the plants with a harmless sulphur solution which turned the leaves a very unpleasant colour. Later it was these very vines that were not affected by mildew. Serious experiments were subsequently carried out at Château Ducru-Beaucaillou, another Johnston estate, and elsewhere.

# Château Dauzac

5th Grand Cru Classé

In the second half of the 17th century Ireland was no longer safe for the Catholics adhering to the cause of the deposed Stuarts, and many left the country. They were called the 'wild geese', because they scattered in all directions, although many had a preference for France. It is estimated that between 1645 and 1690 about 40,000 Irishmen found a permanent home on French soil, and Bordeaux, for centuries a well-known refuge, received its quota of Irishmen. The most famous of them is undoubtedly Count Jean-Baptiste Lynch, Mayor of Bordeaux from 1809 to 1815. The people of Bordeaux adored him, and when, in 1815, he was promoted by Louis XVIII to membership of the *Chambre des Pairs*, the inhabitants of Bordeaux presented a petition that they might be allowed to keep their mayor. The king acceded and decreed that Jean-Baptiste Lynch should remain honorary mayor for a further eleven months. During his term of office Lynch often lived at Château Dauzac, which had come into his family as a dowry in 1740. It was, however, not the only property belonging to this famous Irish family, which also owned La Macqueline, Pontac-Lynch, Lynch-Bages and Lynch-Moussas, to mention just a few. At present Dauzac belongs to the Miailhe family, and it is not surprising that the present owners once attempted to get the name of the Château changed to Dauzac-Lynch. This well intentioned plan, however, has not so far been successful.

### Whither Dauzac?

When the late Alain Miailhe bought Dauzac from an ice-cream manufacturer in 1966, much had to be done to get the wine back to something approaching the standard from which it had declined. At the start his efforts were reasonably successful. For example, 1966, the wine of the first Miailhe year, has a good colour, is particularly fragrant and not devoid of finesse. So the future of Dauzac looked bright. But unfortunately things changed after the death of Alain Miailhe, for the estate was inherited by three members of the family who find it difficult to get along with each other. This is often the problem with the great estates for, under French law, the *conseil de famille* requires complete agreement from all parties and, while negotiations go on, important decisions are shelved, perhaps being taken only after a great deal of time has been wasted.

### Fame in earlier days

All this, however, does not mean to say that the wine of Dauzac is now bad, merely that it could be better. In 1940 the Irishman Maurice Healy said in his famous book *Stay me with Flagons*: 'Dauzac is another wine that I think has been classed much too low. I have never drunk a bad bottle of Dauzac; and the 1920, 1924 and 1926

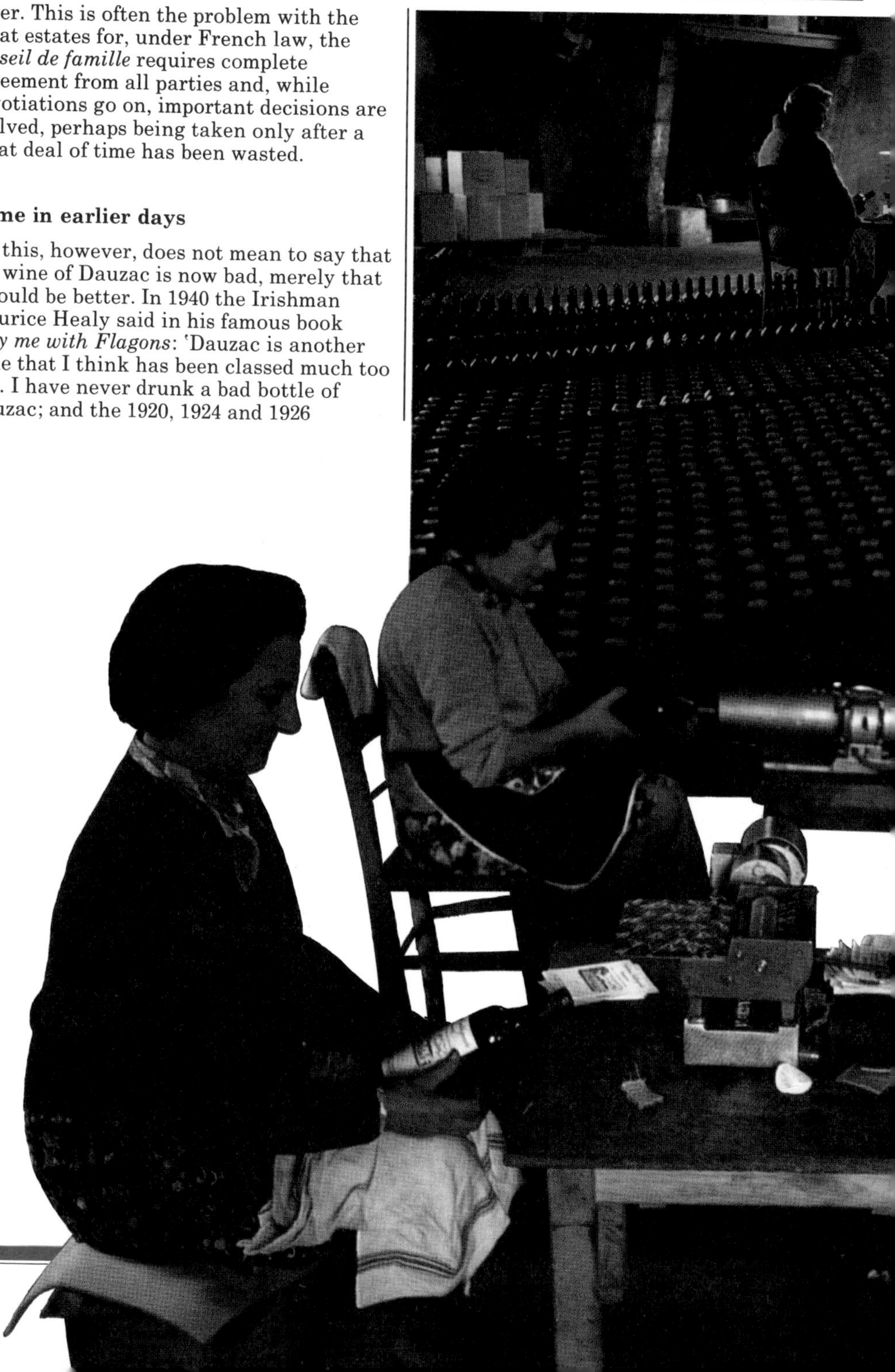

*Far left:*
*The château seen from the once-glorious park; no one lives there now.*

*Left:*
*One of the figures in the reception room.*

*Below:*
*A medal and a document recall the famous Jean-Baptiste Lynch, who was Mayor of Bordeaux from 1809 to 1815. Château Dauzac came into his family in 1740. In the narrow reception hall behind the* chai *there are more objects from the past for visitors to admire.*

Besides Dauzac the Miailhe family also has a majority holding in Pichon-Lalande and a small holding in Palmer. In the 18th century the Miailhes were wine-brokers; today they also have interests in Champagne.
The wine of Dauzac is mainly shipped to the U.S., Britain and Belgium.



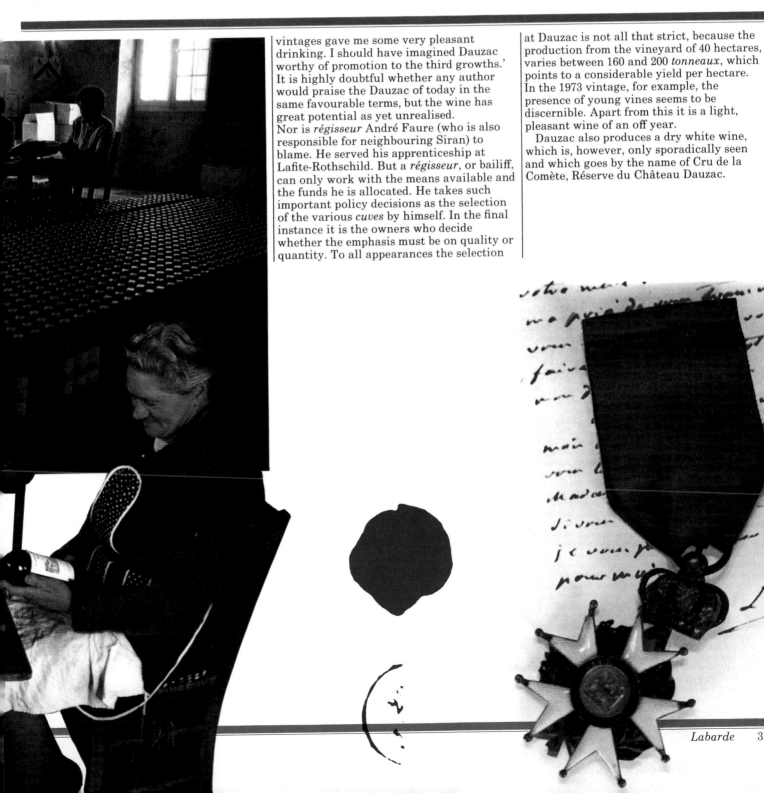

vintages gave me some very pleasant drinking. I should have imagined Dauzac worthy of promotion to the third growths.' It is highly doubtful whether any author would praise the Dauzac of today in the same favourable terms, but the wine has great potential as yet unrealised.
Nor is *régisseur* André Faure (who is also responsible for neighbouring Siran) to blame. He served his apprenticeship at Lafite-Rothschild. But a *régisseur*, or bailiff, can only work with the means available and the funds he is allocated. He takes such important policy decisions as the selection of the various *cuves* by himself. In the final instance it is the owners who decide whether the emphasis must be on quality or quantity. To all appearances the selection at Dauzac is not all that strict, because the production from the vineyard of 40 hectares, varies between 160 and 200 *tonneaux*, which points to a considerable yield per hectare. In the 1973 vintage, for example, the presence of young vines seems to be discernible. Apart from this it is a light, pleasant wine of an off year.

Dauzac also produces a dry white wine, which is, however, only sporadically seen and which goes by the name of Cru de la Comète, Réserve du Château Dauzac.

A few years ago a new bottle, the *'bordelaise Giscours'*, was put into use. It is heavier than most others. Because oxidation of the wine must be restricted to a minimum a 'full long' cork is used which goes deeply into the bottle. As a result the wine can be matured for periods longer than nowadays is usual without risk, but of course the glass is under slightly more pressure. The new bottles can be recognised by the Château name branded on them.

To my knowledge Giscours is the only *grand cru* with its own club tie. This has small, golden coats of arms of the estate on a purple ground.

At the Château stands the bed in which Empress Eugénie of France once slept on her way to the resort of Biarritz.

Chickens in their coops were traditionally kept in the vineyard; when released to range free they are insect pests.

A pleasant partnership of high fashion and fine wine was demonstrated at Giscours in October 1973, when Courrèges showed seventy models there.

Restaurant-proprietor Begout, of the restaurant Les Allées in Bordeaux, has created a recipe which is called 'La Truite au Vieux-Giscours'. The ingredients for four include a whole litre of Giscours – in the recipe, not in glasses.

*Bottom:*
*The Château stands impressively in a large park. The cellars extend under the main building; thanks to a series of underground storeys, the wine does not need to be pumped – gravity does the work.*

*Right:*
*Part of the cellar buildings. A large reception hall has been created in the vathouse. Among other things, visitors can examine an exhibit showing a cross-section of the soil on which the vineyard is situated.*

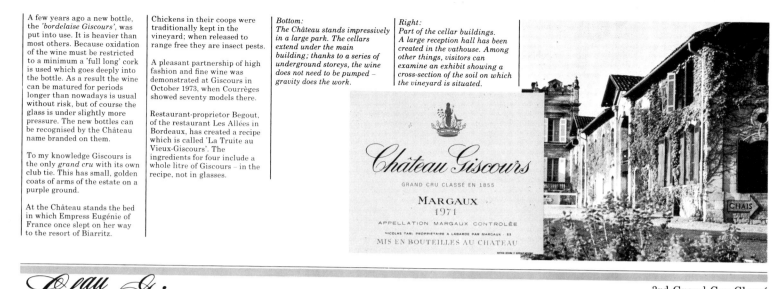

Château Giscours
GRAND CRU CLASSÉ EN 1855
MARGAUX
1971
APPELLATION MARGAUX CONTROLÉE
NICOLAS TARI, PROPRIÉTAIRE A LABARDE PAR MARGAUX · 33
MIS EN BOUTEILLES AU CHATEAU

## Ch^au Giscours

3rd Grand Cru Classé

Giscours is a lot more than just a château with a vineyard: it is a little world all of its own. The estate covers no less than 300 hectares, where in addition to viticulture various forms of agriculture and stock-breeding are carried on. Just behind the château there is also a magnificent, uncultivated wood, which the owners of Giscours preserve as a kind of monument to nature.

The vineyards cover 100 hectares, but that does not mean the whole of this area produces wine for Giscours; in fact only 72 hectares are in production, and of these yet another 7 hectares, with vines younger than five years, must be discounted, since these cannot be used for the *grand vin*, Château Giscours, *appellation contrôlée* Margaux.

However, the area under vines is still a considerable vineyard, and one which will grow in the future. Giscours is one of the very few châteaux with a vast expansion scheme at present being carried out. There are plans for an extra 28 hectares, which in due course will raise quite considerably the present average yield of 250 to 300 *tonneaux*.

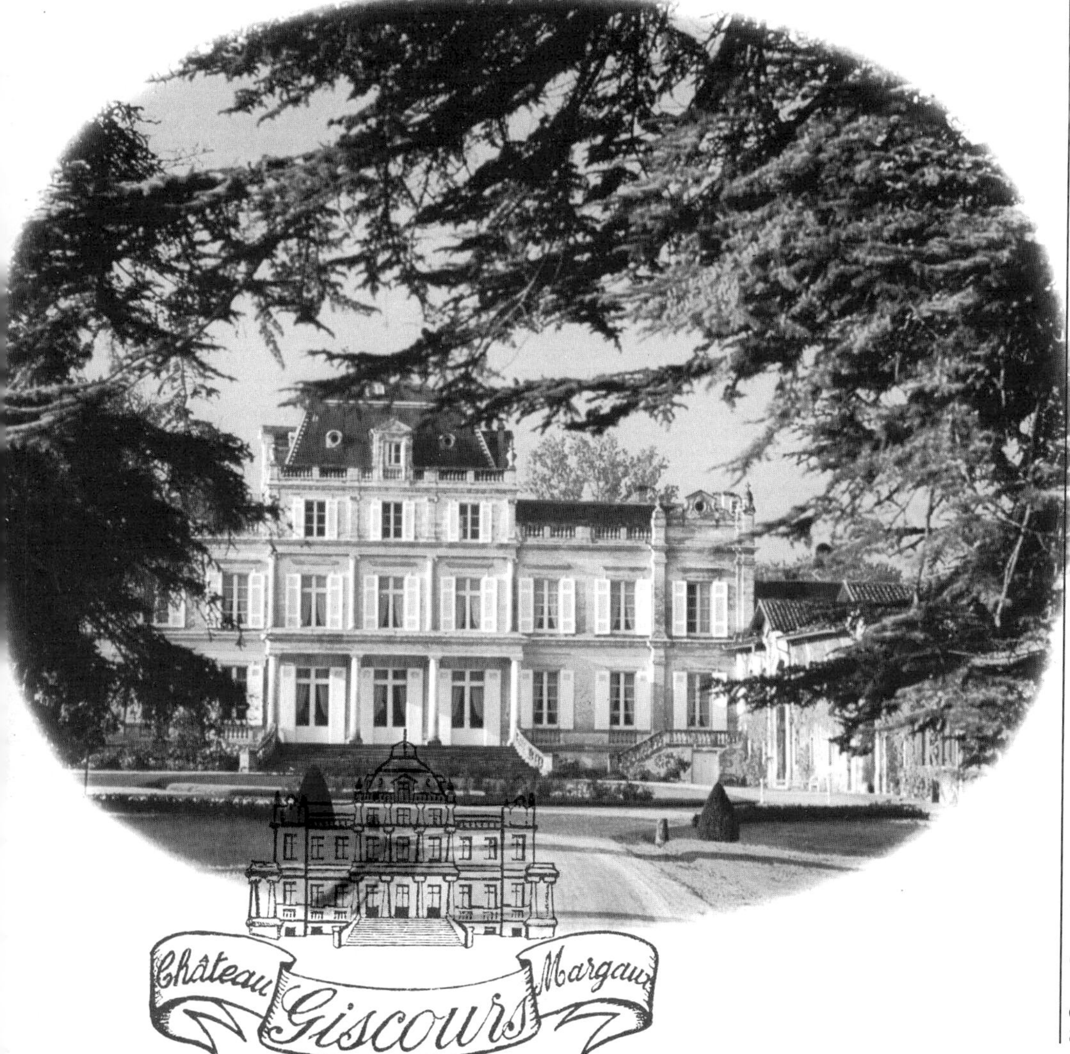


### Landscaping and making lakes

Although such an expansion scheme is in itself remarkable, something quite unique has been done here. For the sake of the vines alone a completely new lake has been excavated. I have seen it myself, and can testify that it is many times larger than the overgrown pond which is sometimes optimistically called a 'lake'. Ton after ton of earth has been dug out, creating a fairly deep basin for a real lake tens of metres wide.

The reason for this vast project is simply one of perfectionism. Those responsible for making wine at Giscours are determined to make a *grand vin*, and the new lake can make its modest contribution. What does this lake actually do? First of all it lowers the water-table, encouraging the roots of the vines to go deeper in search of food and drink, which will improve the quality of the wine. Second, this mass of water has a moderating influence at very low and very high temperatures, which can bring only benefit to the development of the grapes. And finally, trees and undergrowth which caused a certain immobility of the air when the barometer is high, thus increasing the chance of night frost in the spring, have been cleared. These reasons are justification enough for the existence of this unique lake. But how many *propriétaires* are prepared, or indeed able, to make such an investment on top of an already costly replanting programme?

### A highly dynamic estate

The active man behind this project is Pierre Tari, *président directeur général* of Château Giscours S.A. His family bought Giscours in 1947. The vineyard, at one time excellent, was then in a pitiful state: of the 80 hectares only seven were planted.

*Right:*
*Giscours, like many classed growths, has a laboratory of its own, where the wine can be studied, checked and controlled.*

*Centre:*
*The futuristic-looking machine with which the temperature can, if necessary, be slightly raised to ensure that nothing interferes with the satisfactory progress of the fermentation.*

*Bottom:*
*Cellar master Henri Castand, who has been working at Giscours for over ten years.*



Nicolas Tari, Pierre's father, became sole proprietor in 1952. He still lives at the château, but his son has been in charge of the day-to-day management since 1970. This probably came as a surprise even to Pierre himself, for as a young man he had very different plans. First of all he immersed himself in poetry and prose and then, obeying a centuries-old family tradition, he entered the army.

On his return from Algeria Pierre decided to become a wine-grower after all. His father and grandfather gave him his first lessons. After this he followed a university course in oenology. The Pierre Tari of today is a dedicated wine-grower who, in addition to his busy life as manager of his huge domain, still finds time for other important functions, including that of itinerant ambassador for the great wines of the Médoc. Each edition of his own periodical, *Giscours Réalités*, is proof enough of this, judging from the number of photographs of Pierre Tari making an appearance in one foreign country after another, where he does business and propagates the fine wines of his home country.

**Wine with a slow evolution**

The vineyard of Giscours consists of 75% Cabernets, 20% Merlot and 5% Petit Verdot. The yield per hectare is on the low side. A graph exists which shows that from 1964 up to and including 1973 an average of only 30·11 hectolitres was produced per hectare. Giscours is a wine which according to Pierre Tari distinguishes itself by virtue of its complex, elegant bouquet.

I should like to add something to this myself. For me Giscours is a wine which retains a trace of oak in its flavour for many years. As the years go by this diminishes, but it is still there, at least in the good wines made by the Taris. The Taris themselves claim that 1961 was the first year in which they made good wine, so there seems to be little point in tasting earlier vintages. I have thoroughly enjoyed the 1967 vintage on a number of different occasions, both at home and in restaurants. The 1969 vintage is perhaps slightly on the thin side for a Giscours, but it still has a fair amount of tannin. Even in such a light year you discover that Giscours is a wine with a long evolution. This applies particularly to the 1970 vintage, a classic, lingering wine which leaves on your tongue hints of good things yet to come. In 1971 and 1972 Giscours simply made good wine, but very little of it. In both years hail destroyed half the grape crop. In my notes I have given the 1973 vintage a slightly better rating than just 'good', and the same could well apply to the 1974 vintage. Or to put it another way: you can hardly go wrong with the recent years from this splendid estate.

*Left and below:*
*A panoramic bottlescape, and the large banners which are used on official occasions. Besides the* grand vin, *another wine is also made which is mainly the product of young vines. Large quantities of this wine are distributed among the employees: every man receives 56 litres of wine a month, for which he pays a symbolic amount, later refunded by means of a shrewd tax deduction. Anyone working at the Château thus drinks free!*

A pleasant tale is told that, after the siege of La Rochelle in 1628, Cardinal Richelieu, exhausted and ailing, convalesced with the Benedictines of Cantenac. He was offered the wine of Pouget and found it an admirable restorative. Back in Paris, he told Louis XIII of the excellent wine, which inevitably became fashionable. Even if Dumas omitted this episode from *The Three Musketeers*, it is a good story.

# Ch^au Boyd-Cantenac

3rd Grand Cru Classé

It is surprising that two châteaux with different names, different histories and different classifications should in fact be making the same wine. According to the proprietor, Pierre Guillemet, this is what is done. Guillemet's family have owned Pouget since 1910, and bought Boyd-Cantenac from the Ginestet family in 1932. Since then the grapes of the two vineyards, already adjacent, have been made into wine in the same vats, the same casks and the same *chais* by the same people.

The difference between the wines, as M. Guillemet frankly admitted, is purely psychological. Some people are of the opinion that the wines of Boyd-Cantenac are better, but that is probably due to the prestige of its higher classification. Boyd-Cantenac is also better known, both because there is more of it and because more is exported (to the United States, Britain, Belgium, Holland and Switzerland, among other countries).
The wine of Pouget goes exclusively to the house of Philippe Duboscq, which sells mainly to private French customers.
The size of the two vineyards thus becomes theoretical; it would be more accurate to talk of one vineyard of approximately 26 hectares with an average production of 100 *tonneaux*, of which two-thirds is sold as Boyd-Cantenac and one-third as Pouget.

## A wine that pleases

The wine-making itself is supervised by the famous Professor Emile Peynaud, *Directeur du Service des Recherches de la Station Agronomique et Oenologique de Bordeaux-Talence*. You will come across him several times in this book, because many château proprietors call upon the exceptional expertise of this learned man.
Professor Peynaud undoubtedly also advised which vine species should be planted in which proportions on certain plots to obtain optimum results. For a Margaux vineyard (both wines are sold under this name) the percentage of Cabernet Sauvignon is fairly high: 69%. This is made up with 7% Cabernet Franc, 19% Merlot and 5% Petit Verdot.

What always strikes me about the wines of Boyd-Cantenac is their roundness. Even at a very early age the wine appears to be without any sharp, hard edges and the greater its maturity the more marked this becomes. The bouquet – take, for example, the 1971 vintage – also gives a round

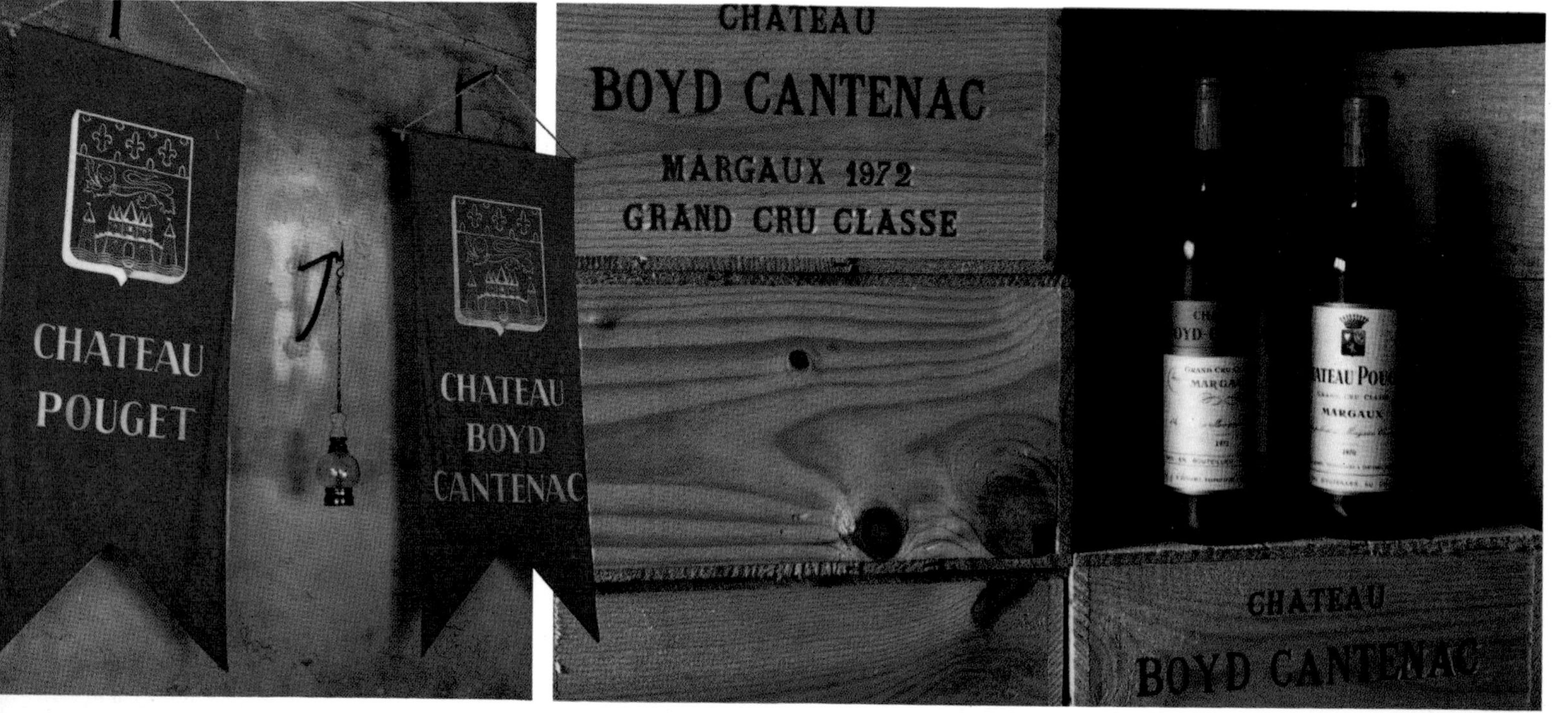

*Left:*
*M. Pierre Guillemet in his study. For many years he has been an antiquarian book collector, and he now has a valuable library.*

*Right:*
*Plan of the Château and its vineyards.* **A** *Château Pouget-Boyd-Cantenac,* **B** *vineyards belonging to the Château.*

*Below:*
*The bottles are still 'dressed' by hand. The cellars of Pouget are picturesque with their thick wooden beams, but they are on the small side, which is why in 1974 a new chai adjoining the old one was put into use.*

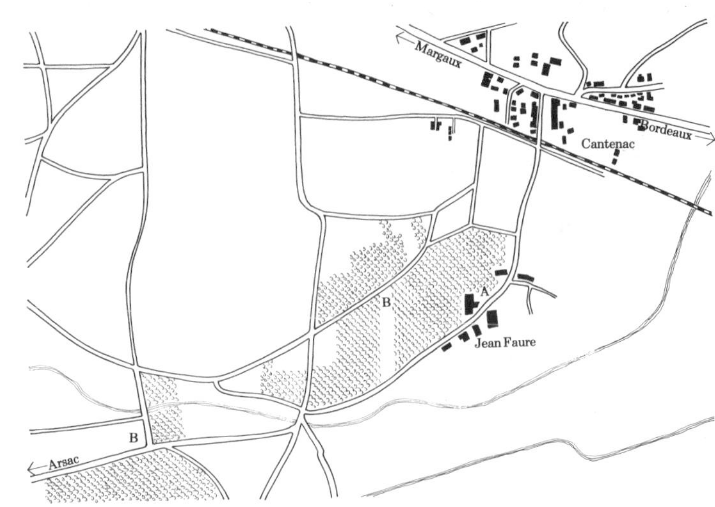


4th Grand Cru Classé

# Ch^au Pouget

impression, if one can say that of a smell.

### Recent vintages

The style of this sound wine is clearly Margaux, with the typical Margaux fruit. Some recent years which particularly fascinate me are 1970, 1971, and 1974.
As you might expect, the 1970 vintage is the sturdiest of the three, full of pent-up force and with a flavour that lingers a long time in your mouth. I give it a great future. The 1971 vintage is more supple; it is a wine which you would probably do better to drink with a quite mildly seasoned meat dish than with anything too piquant. Finally, the 1974 vintage is clearly better than the wines of 1972 and 1973. Its colour, fragrance and flavour promise to deserve the designation *très bon vin*.

### A little history

Although Boyd-Cantenac is the better known of the two wines, there is no such thing as a Château Boyd-Cantenac. The name is certainly to be found on signposts and walls, but the Château itself does not exist and has never existed. In 1852 the vineyard was separated from the neighbouring Cantenac-Brown, but this did not include a château. Mr Boyd, who at that time gave his name to the new estate, appears to have been of Irish origin. Pouget, on the other hand, does have a Château, where Pierre Guillemet lives. Originally the Château belonged to the Benedictines, who can be regarded as the founders of the vineyards of Cantenac, but it takes its name from the Pouget family, who managed the estate for more than 250 years, from 1650 to 1906.

### Taxation as an early classification

It is perhaps significant that shortly after the French Revolution, Pouget was rated slightly higher than in the classification of 1855. In 1795 a special tax was levied on all leading châteaux, and the better the wine sold the higher the levy. From an old document it can be seen that Widow Pouget was taxed 500 *livres* per *tonneau*, the same as d'Issan and 50 *livres* more than Brane-Cantenac, now a second growth. What was then called Boyd-Brown was taxed 550 *livres*, Kirwan 600, Palmer 600, Rauzan 700, Durfort 700 and Margaux 900: this was one of the earliest but not the first classification for the wines of the Médoc.

*Far left:*
*The small old parish church of Cantenac, and in the foreground a small section of the large cellars.*

*Left:*
*The branded château cork of Château Prieuré-Lichine.*

*Below:*
*A heavenly vintager in the beautifully kept park of the former Priory. This is only one of the many things worth seeing; in and around Prieuré-Lichine Alexis Lichine has art treasures which are attractively displayed.*

The production of Prieuré-Lichine has increased considerably over the centuries. In the first half of the 19th century it was 15 *tonneaux*; around 1893 it was 50; and now it is 130.

# Chau Prieuré-Lichine

4th Grand Cru Classé

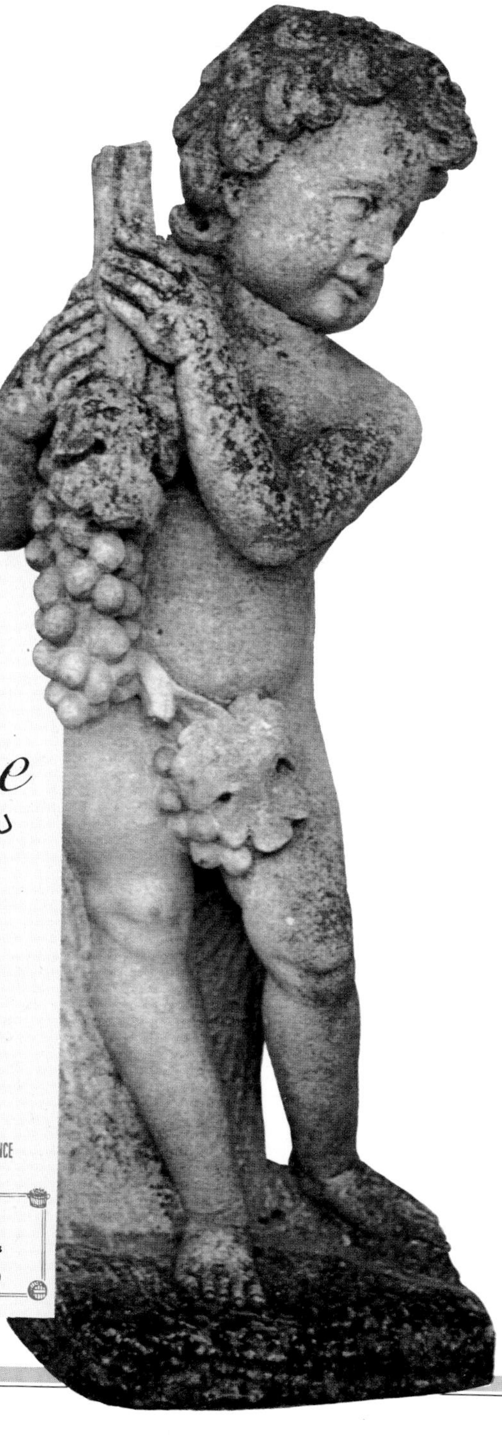

It is hard for a visitor to the Médoc to miss Château Prieuré-Lichine. Not only is it situated virtually on the *Route des Grands Crus* right in the middle of Cantenac, and a huge hoarding draws the attention of the passer-by to the Château, but also the proprietor, Alexis Lichine, has painted the shutters, doors and walls in turquoise, a rather frivolous colour for the Médoc, where mostly wine-red paint is used.
From other things as well it is clear that a great deal of attention has been paid to the appearance of the Château. On entering the forecourt through a small archway, you see a wall into which a unique collection of black metal firebacks has been set. And when you enter the new *chai*, which was completed in 1974, via the presshouse with its nine cement and three wooden fermentation vats, you will immediately notice that the casks there are varnished. This makes the *chai* look unusually clean: in the other châteaux they don't usually go to this trouble except for show, the result being deep purple stains on the light-coloured wood. In the first year the *barriques* are topped up three times a week and spillage is inevitable; the wine immediately seeps into the unvarnished wood. At Prieuré-Lichine, on the other hand, it can just be wiped off.
The Château is beautifully furnished and yet very much a home: in the Médoc the one does not necessarily mean the other. To the right and left of the front door are two large drawing-rooms, the one decorated in pastel shades, the other more sober.
A wealth of magnificent art treasures and a number of superb paintings in which wine plays a major rôle are displayed in them. Prieuré-Lichine also has a lovely dining room, which used to be the kitchen. The low ceiling is supported by massive brown beams and several dozen shiny copper pans provide fitting decoration. There are also several antique stoves, life-size and miniature.

Anciennes armoiries du Prieuré de Cantenac
Château
Prieuré-Lichine
GRAND CRU CLASSÉ
1970
MIS EN BOUTEILLE AU CHATEAU
MARGAUX
APPELLATION MARGAUX CONTROLÉE
Cette bouteille porte le Nº 02933
S. A. DE CHATEAU PRIEURÉ-LICHINE, PROPRIÉTAIRE A CANTENAC-MARGAUX (GIRONDE) FRANCE
SIEGE SOCIAL BORDEAUX (Gironde)
ALEXIS LICHINE & Cº
NEGOCIANTS A BORDEAUX GIRONDE FRANCE
SUCCURSALES Romaneche-Thorins (Saône & Loire) Chambéry (Savoie)

**Quality preferred to quantity**

The vineyard of Prieuré-Lichine was founded about three centuries ago by the

*Below:*
*The magnificent, ivy-clad Château façade, invisible from the road, because it is hidden by a fairly high wall. The two large drawing rooms are situated on either side of the entrance. The present Château dates from the beginning of the nineteenth century.*

In his *Encyclopaedia of Wines and Spirits*, Alexis Lichine writes about a piece of land he acquired called La Bourgade. This property belonged to the La Chapelle family from the 15th century to 1867. 'In 1667 Guy de la Chapelle presented wines from his vineyard to Louis XIV. They were placed in competition with Burgundies recommended by Fagon, the king's doctor. Nevertheless, the wines from La Bourgade remained among the favourites of Louis for many years.'

The *régisseur* of Prieuré-Lichine is M. Guilhem. He is in charge of a dozen men and has been at the Château since 1969

Cantenac and Margaux are communes with a large number of *grands crus* which belong to proprietors of non-French origin. Besides the American Prieuré-Lichine, there is Palmer (mainly Dutch and British), Rausan-Ségla (British), Lascombes (British), Kirwan (partly Danish) and Ferrière (leased by Englishmen).

Benedictine monks whose monastery was on the site of the present Château. It is therefore not surprising that the little church of Cantenac is adjacent to the Château. For a long time the estate was called La Prieuré, but in 1953 the *Syndicat des Grands Crus Classés du Médoc* approved the changing of the name to Château Prieuré-Lichine at the request of Alexis Lichine, who had bought the estate in the previous year with some American friends. As Lichine himself writes in his much-praised book, *Encyclopaedia of Wines and Spirits*, neither expense nor effort has been spared in improving the vineyard. For example, two metres of relatively poor ground were exchanged with adjoining châteaux for one metre of good; quantity thus being sacrificed for quality. In this costly manner Lichine succeeded in obtaining land from some châteaux with a higher classification, such as Durfort-Vivens, Brane-Cantenac, Palmer, Ferrière, Kirwan, Giscours, d'Issan and Boyd-Cantenac. In addition a great deal of attention was paid to the care of the vines, and wine-making methods were likewise improved. At present the vineyard covers approximately 30 hectares which are in production. A mixture of 50% Cabernet Sauvignon, 40% Merlot, 5% Cabernet Franc and 5% Petit Verdot yields an average of 130 *tonneaux* a year. It will come as no surprise to anyone that the U.S.A. is the largest buyer of Prieuré-Lichine, followed by the Caribbean Islands, Canada, Britain and Switzerland.

### A typical Margaux?

The wine is proof enough that all Alexis Lichine's hard work (he is regularly in residence at the Château) has not been in vain. The 1966 Prieuré-Lichine, for example, is a truly great wine, full of colour, fragrance, flavour, body and class. But don't think that it is heavy, because it is just the opposite. In it you can taste all the subtle delicacy of the wines of Margaux. It is since 1955, by the way, that Cantenac wines have been allowed to be sold under the *appellation* Margaux. The 1970 vintage is also a highly successful wine: supple, rich and yet robust enough to ensure a long, healthy future. The 1974 vintage is likewise full of promise. In my sampling notes I have only slight criticism for the 1967 vintage. The taste was to my mind a little on the tannic side at this comparatively early stage, this harshness lingering in the mouth. This unbalance was, however, amply compensated for by an extraordinarily good colour and a bouquet which can best be described as *très fin, très Margaux*.

Kirwan is situated right next to the railway and at least once in its history the train has been halted to stop especially so that visitors to the Château might descend. This was at the turn of the century when the Mayor of Bordeaux gave a great party at the Château.

*Below left:*
*This rather bewildered-looking stone lion has guarded the estate for generations.*

*Below:*
*The splendid garden of Kirwan. In the winter the most fragile plants are covered over or taken to the large greenhouse just to the side of the Château. Kirwan's interior is as charming as the outside of the house. Marc Schÿler's father bought a fine collection of paintings at an auction and these now adorn the hall and salons.*

CHATEAU KIRWAN
GRAND CRU CLASSE
MARGAUX
APPELLATION MARGAUX CONTROLEE
1966
Mis en bouteilles à Bordeaux par :
SCHRÖDER & SCHŸLER & Cie
ALCOHOL 11°5% BY VOL.
SOLE AGENTS
NEW-YORK, N. Y.
Dreyfus, Ashby & Co
PRODUCT OF FRANCE
TABLE WINE

# Chau Kirwan

3rd Grand Cru Classé

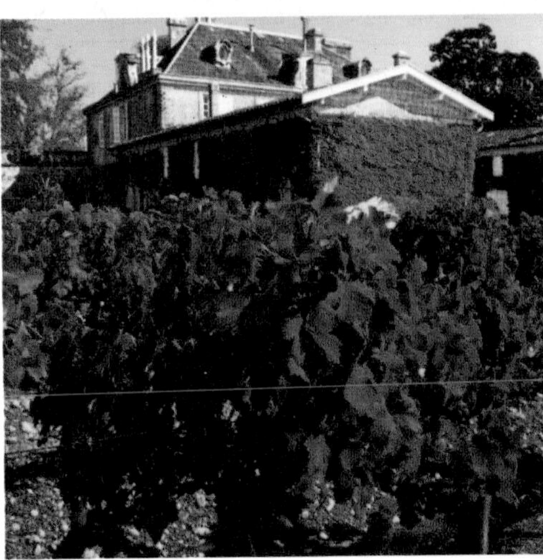

*Left:*
*The Château seen from the vineyard, which begins just behind the main building.*

*Centre:*
*The back entrance to Kirwan, with cellars and other storage facilities on both sides.*

*Bottom:*
*The vathouse. At Kirwan the traditional fine oak fermentation vats have gradually been replaced by new ones of cement.*
*Quality wines can be made in cement or stainless steel vats – and the upkeep is much simpler.*

The present proprietor of Château Kirwan is the Société Schröder & Schÿler et Cie, established in 1739. M. Marc Schÿler has retired as Danish Consul, the active work of the consulate now being done by his son, Jean-Henri.

Kirwan suffered greatly from the severe frost of 1956 when about 100,000 vines were destroyed; these have all been replanted.

Tennis is a popular sport in Cantenac Margaux. Bernard Ginestet and his wife often play with the Sichels (who live at d'Angludet) and there is also a well-tended grass tennis court at Kirwan.

# Château Kirwan

It is an amusing coincidence that one of the first artesian wells in the Médoc was dug in the grounds of Château Kirwan. It supplied no less than 300 litres of water a minute. As wine is not a liquid with which to slake the thirst, water is also essential. The history of Kirwan goes back to the time of the crusaders, the year 1147, when it was known as Château de Lassalle and belonged to Raymond de Lassalle. This nobleman left it to his heirs and they in turn to theirs, so the castle remained in the family until 1600. After that it changed hands several times until an Irishman, Mr Kirwan, married the daughter of the then owner, Sir John Collingwood, in 1776. Kirwan renamed the Château but was unfortunately unable to enjoy a long life there because his head rolled during the French Revolution. In the nineteenth century Kirwan was the property of M. Camille Godard, who – the annals relate – left the Château to the town of Bordeaux as he had no heirs. I get the impression, however, that M. Godard did have relations but for some reason or other begrudged them their inheritance, for in *Bordeaux et Ses Vins* of 1893 it states that the town of Bordeaux is the owner but that one Adolphe Godard has usufruct . . . Finally, in 1900, the Société Schröder & Schÿler (one of the oldest wine firms of Bordeaux) concluded an exclusive contract with the town of Bordeaux for the sale of the wine for ninety-nine years. Well before this contract expired, in 1926 to be exact, Kirwan became the property of the firm. Since then Schröder & Schÿler have been able to offer the wine of Kirwan in complete exclusivity.

## An elegant property

Curiously enough, Kirwan wine was sold for many years without the year being mentioned on the label. M. Marc Schÿler told me that Château Kirwan has only been sold with vintage labels since 1934.
M. Marc Schÿler lives with his family in the 18th-century Château from July to November. In 1973 the interior was completely renovated so that the growing number of foreign visitors could be properly received. The tapestries in the drawing room and the magnificent Charles X furniture made of lemonwood are in particular well worth seeing. One of the precious cabinets holds the key to the small family cellar, which is seldom shown to outsiders. This is where an ample amount of the estate's wine, dating back to 1943, is kept.

Immediately behind the Château is the vineyard, or at least a part of it, because the Kirwan vineyard is split up into a great many separate units. Approximately 30 hectares are productive and an extension project now in progress concerns a further 10 hectares. The Merlot (25%) and Petit Verdot (15%) are fairly well represented. Production averages 100 *tonneaux*.

## Flowers and bouquet

M. Marc Schÿler's wife has always done her best to fill the Château's splendid front garden in the summer with a glorious show of flowers. She has twice won prizes with her blooms. Is this perhaps why I find this Margaux so flowery, in both its nose and its flavour? Definitely not – but an interesting speculation! This was particularly marked in the 1973 vintage (an elegant wine of distinction, better than the 1972) and similarly in the 1959 Kirwan. Fifteen years after being harvested the latter wine had a velvety, reddish-brown colour, a superb, spring-like nose and a fine, elegant flavour: Kirwan at its best – a bouquet of flowers with no trace of excess.

Although M. Schÿler prefers his wine with game and even Roquefort cheese, I am inclined to serve Château Kirwan wines with simpler dishes, such as veal or roast pork, perhaps with a delicate sauce.

Due to the fact that for generations Schröder & Schÿler have exported almost exclusively to Germany, Scandinavia and a few East European countries, Kirwan is not very well known elsewhere. In recent years, however, the horizons have been extended somewhat, with the result that this delicate wine is now also available in the U.S.A., Britain, Belgium, Japan and elsewhere.

One of the best plots in the vineyard is called Champ de Bataille, the battlefield. However, although the Saracens fought here in AD 732, this piece of land takes its name from a less bloody episode. It is related how Maxime de Brane, whose interests were not restricted wholly to wine, once received from his wife a box on the ears so resounding that his hat flew off into the air. This anecdote is still chuckled over by the growers of Brane-Cantenac.

The watchword at Brane is tidiness; once a month a group of women go round actually dusting every individual cask.

The *chai* has its own watchdog – not a live one but an old vine which looks like a dog sitting down. This wooden guard has been mounted on top of a cask.

In 1838 Brane-Cantenac received its present name. In that year Baron de Brane wrote a letter to the journal *Le Producteur*, in which he stated that there had been so many changes on his estate, Gorse-Gui, in the past four years it was now right to speak of a completely new property, to which he had given his own name. 'For while the name of Gorse is highly regarded in Bordeaux and further afield, and rightly so,' wrote the Baron, 'so is the name of Brane.'

Brane-Cantenac came into the hands of the Lurton family when Lucien Lurton's grandfather bought it in 1925. Having travelled in North and South America, Lucien Lurton took over the running of the place in 1956. It was the worst possible one in which to start, because when the snow finally melted half the vines were found to have been ruined by frost. Not a drop of wine could be made at Brane that year.

For more than a quarter of a century the Château has had its own master cooper on the premises to make the majority of the new *barriques*. Each year new casks are used for about a third of Brane-Cantenac's harvest.

*Bottom:*
*The front of the château has not changed since it was depicted on this engraving.*

*Right:*
*Brane-Cantenac seen from the back garden. To the left of the steps is the large living room.*

*Right centre:*
*The label of the 1960 vintage, the wine which was originally not to be sold as Brane-Cantenac but which later proved very good indeed.*

*Far right:*
*Most of the work in the cellar is still done by hand, even the racking.*

*Bottom right:*
*The bottling of the wine in full swing.*

# Ch^au^ Brane-Cantenac

2nd Grand Cru Classé

The bouquet of Brane-Cantenac has always earned high praise. In earlier days, when the soft, westerly wind wafted the first scents of spring to the village of Cantenac the locals would say: '*Le Baron de Brane soutire ses vins*' (Baron de Brane is racking his wines). Today the wines of Brane-Cantenac still have a fine bouquet, although this only becomes evident when the wine is more mature and not when in cask, unless you are an experienced taster.

**1961, an outsider that came home**

Of all the vintages I have tasted the bouquet of 1961 was the best. It was outstanding. I drank this wine with a trio of international cheeses (Edam from Holland, Cheddar from England and Gruyère from France) at the end of a family luncheon at the château. It was in more than one respect a lively meal, because as well as the owner, Lucien Lurton, the party included his ten children. At this meal we also enjoyed the 1960 Brane-Cantenac, a worthy accompaniment to the grilled entrecôte. For a 1960 vintage the wine was unusually assertive and charming as well.

Lucien Lurton told me that initially no one, not even himself, thought anything of the 1960. They found it hard and mean and as a result the whole vintage was declassified to *appellation contrôlée* Bordeaux and was sold under Brane's second label, Château Notton. Fortunately, this declassification was not a serious disaster to the estate because the whole vintage totalled no more than 4,000 bottles. Ten years later, by accident, M. Lurton tasted the wine from this seemingly wholly unsatisfactory year, only to be surprised by a full, pleasant wine, which had nothing whatever in common with the meagre wine of a few years back. This is only one of the many surprises in the world of wine!

**The luck of the vintage**

Chance plays a part in winemaking. For example, in 1964 Lucien Lurton had arranged for a band of Spanish vintagers to come and vintage for him on a certain day. If fact they arrived about a week early, and evidently did not feel like going to another Château first. Lucien Lurton decided that he would set them to work picking at one. The vintage had hardly been made a day when it began to rain – for days on end, with the result that throughout almost all the Médoc the 1964 vintage was of variable quality. The exception was Brane-Cantenac, which produced a good wine with a sumptuous fragrance.

Can one taste something of the character of the maker in the wine? In the case of Brane-Cantenac this would seem to be true. Lucien Lurton is a friendly, quiet-spoken man, and his wine is soft, supple and harmonious: destined to be enjoyed by many. These qualities are clearly discernible even in the young wines, such as the 1970, in which the considerable amount of tannin was already balanced by an amiable, flowing taste, with some fruitiness also discernible. The 1970 vintage will undoubtedly develop into a great wine: the 1966 vintage is one already. The latter wine surpasses the 1967 vintage in every way, but even this vintage is a soft, supple, friendly wine which in no way belies its status of a second classed growth of Margaux – no mean appellation.

**Why Brane has its reputation**

One of the secrets of how Brane-Cantenac succeeds in making excellent wine is the strict selection. Only the very best is good

Château Brane-Cantenac

enough to be labelled as Brane; the rest, like the 1960 vintage, is sold as Château Notton. Lucien Lurton is not the only person responsible for making this important decision each year. He has called on the help of an authoritative outsider in the person of Professor Peynaud. Together they rejected all the vattings of 1960, 1963 and 1968. In 1965, 80% was found unsuitable and in 1974 about 35%. These few examples alone indicate how much you may have to lose commercially in order to make a great wine of consistent quality.

Another factor which is decisive for the quality of the wine is, of course, the situation of the vineyard. The vines are planted on the plateau of Cantenac, which is fringed by a circle of Cantenac estates. If you stand at the highest point, 23 metres above the Gironde, you will see not only Brane-Cantenac but Cantenac-Brown, Rausan-Ségla, Palmer, Prieuré-Lichine, Kirwan and Pouget as well. The vineyard of Brane-Cantenac covers 90 hectares, of which an average of 75 hectares are in production. The different vines are present in the following proportions: 60% Cabernet Sauvignon, 20% Merlot, 17% Cabernet Franc and 3% Petit Verdot. In normal years the production reaches 200 *tonneaux*. The wine is sold to some 40 different shippers and is therefore to be found in the catalogues of numerous wine-merchants in many countries all over the world.

The guests' bar at the Château has a fine collection of antique Cognac bottles. This is not surprising, as the house of de Luze also markets a Cognac of its own.

In the reception room at Cantenac-Brown a number of objects have been assembled which Messrs de Luze received on the occasion of their 150th jubilee. Several paintings also hang there, but unfortunately none by John-Lewis Brown, from whom the Château gets part of its name. The largest canvas is an exciting picture of hounds whose pads never seem to touch the ground at all!

Cantenac-Brown seems to have been called Brown-Cantenac at one time, but because of the confusion with Brane-Cantenac the name was wisely transposed.

*Below:*
*The rather English-looking château. Someone once worked out that it has as many as 370 openings: windows of all shapes and sizes, and doors. Only part of the château is occupied, by tenants who rent it from the owner. The main cellars are to the right of the main building.*

# Chau Cantenac-Brown

3rd Grand Cru Classé

Although the history of Cantenac-Brown goes back to the sixteenth century, the name itself is more recent. For centuries the château was simply called Château de Cantenac, until in 1826 John Lewis Brown bought the estate and shortly afterwards coupled his name to it.

Mr Brown, who was of British origin, was a Bordeaux shipper and a fair painter of horses. He bought the estate from the widow of François Coudac, an Amsterdam wine merchant, who had inherited it from Louis Massac, also of Amsterdam. Thanks to these two Dutchmen a great deal of goodwill was created in Holland, and for a long time this small nation was one of the largest buyers. Now, however, the United States, Britain, Belgium, Switzerland and Japan have also become interesting export markets for the wine, which, like other fine Cantenac growths, is now sold as *appellation côntrolée* Margaux, the name of the neighbouring commune.

One gets the impression that Mr Brown rather overdid it with his various acquisitions, because in 1843 he went bankrupt. The estate passed into the hands of M. Gromard, a banker. This man was perhaps more interested in money than in wine, for he badly neglected the vineyard.

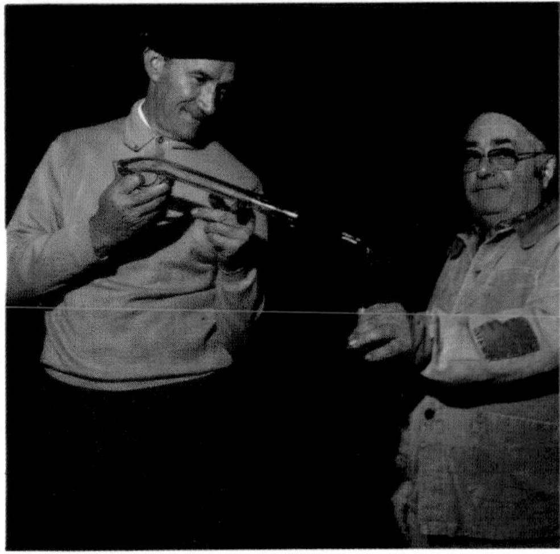

*Far left:*
*Two cellar veterans taste the young wine, which is drawn out of the cask with a pipette, or* velenche.

*Left:*
*A view of the new installation, which has been in use since 1968.*

*Below left:*
*In the background is the main cellar of Cantenac-Brown. Notice the beautifully painted pediment. The bottles shown in the foreground are empty, but there are about 100,000 full ones in the* chai.



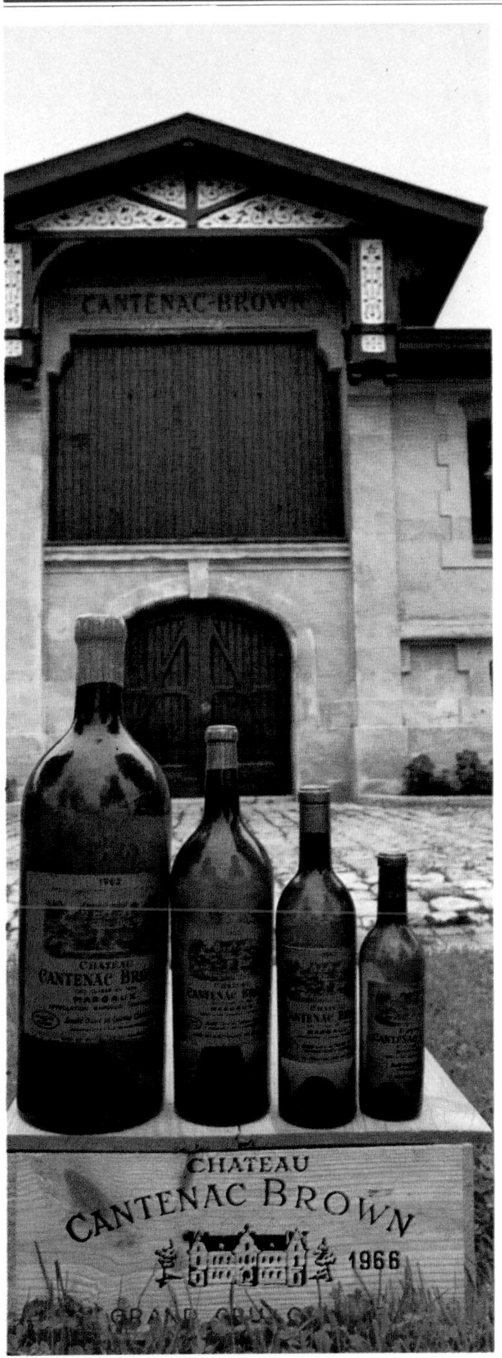


In 1860 he sold Cantenac-Brown to Armand Lalande, who already owned Château Léoville-Poyferré.

### British Victorianism in the Médoc

Lalande was an energetic and enterprising man. He immediately started work on replacing the vines, improving the *chais* and winemaking methods. His aim was to restore the Château to its former glory. He was also of the opinion that the existing château was not in keeping with the status of his wine, and he therefore ordered that a completely new house, in a more imposing style, should be built immediately behind it. It would seem that the architect (or was it the principal?) had a slightly bizarre taste, because the finished building is strongly reminiscent of a large British country house in mock-Tudor style. A silent homage, perhaps, to Mr Brown's forefathers – or an attempt to attract the English market? The building certainly looks like a Surrey export. The original château is still standing, a simple, angular house, connected to the new building by a storage area.

Monsieur Lalande's family remained owners of Cantenac-Brown until 1968, when it was taken over by the du Vivier family, which also ran the Bordeaux house A. de Luze & Fils. The latter was recently taken over by the British Bowater concern, but Cantenac-Brown has remained in the du Viviers' hands, with Bertrand du Vivier as manager; he also stayed on as *président directeur général* of de Luze. M. Bertrand du Vivier does not live in the château himself; part of the house is rented out. On the ground floor one of the drawing-rooms has been turned into a stylish reception room. Through a green painted bar with several fine paintings, you enter a pleasant salon completely furnished in 19th-century style.

### A 'vin de garde' – for keeping

Perhaps the penchant for the classical also plays a rôle in the making of this wine. My impression is that it is still made without many concessions being made to certain methods currently in widespread use. Every time I taste Cantenac-Brown I tend to think: 'That's how they must have made Bordeaux wines in the past'. In its youth the wine is very hard (in great contrast to its neighbour, Brane-Cantenac) and it takes many years for this ruggedness to be converted into a pleasing, powerful taste. The bouquet also needs a lot of time. For the first few years it is usually very reticent, and it is only after four or five years that it begins to open up. But once it has completely developed you enjoy a rich, elegant perfume which can possess a pervading quality – even in a fairly light year like 1962. Even as an experienced buyer of wines you should drink a mature Cantenac-Brown to be able to appreciate it fully, because tasting young wine is one amateurs seldom find pleasant, certainly not if the very young, ice-cold wine is drawn straight from the cask in the chilly *chai* with its dark earth floor. Cantenac-Brown is a classic wine for keeping. Be patient and serve a venerable old bottle one day as the highlight of a dinner on a special occasion – decanted of course.

### Trompe l'œil in the presshouse

Whoever enters the presshouses at Cantenac-Brown sees a row of shiny oak fermentation vats in perfect order. They are completely in keeping with the traditional image of this Château, but in this case appearances are deceptive. For behind the first presshouse is a second with metal vats, and it is here that the wine is made. Bertrand du Vivier has maintained the old ones to indicate the atmosphere of the cellars as they were in bygone days. There is nothing wrong with that, of course. There is also a lot of wood in the bottling area, where the occasional banquet or reception is held. The walls here consist of the actual packaging crates.

The vineyard of Cantenac-Brown was much larger before its separation from Boyd-Cantenac. Today the 30 hectares are planted with 70% of both the Cabernet species and 30% Merlot. The production averages around 130 *tonneaux*.

*Right:*
*The Château seen from the rear. The moat and the circular tower, which is just visible, are both, as may be imagined, really old.*

*Centre:*
*D'Issan is one of the most picturesque estates. The interior of the Château has been splendidly restored.*

*Bottom:*
*Manager Dulin has worked at d'Issan for more than 20 years and can identify himself completely with the fine wine he supervises through its beginnings.*

# Chau d'Issan

3rd Grand Cru Classé

The British have always liked the wine of Château d'Issan. In 1152 it was served at the wedding feast of Henry Plantagenet – later Henry II of England – and Eleanor of Aquitaine. The wine then, however, cannot be compared with the wine of today, as at that time there was no possibility of keeping it in closed bottles, and only the fairly light-coloured 'clairet' of the last vintage, served from the cask, was available.

On another occasion the English again

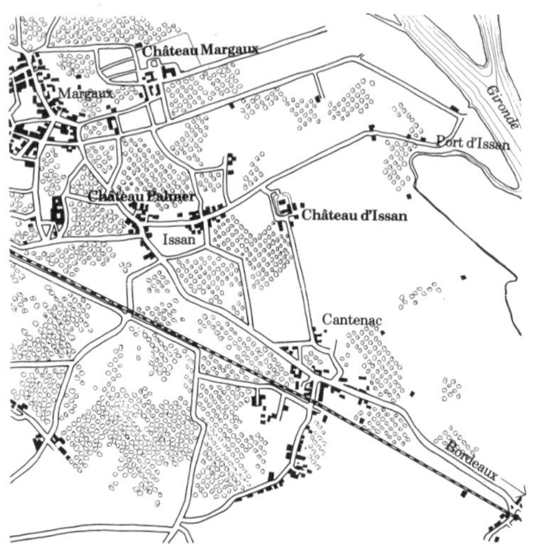


In May 1974 a German chamber orchestra gave a concert in the cellars for 500 people, an unusual instance of Franco-German co-operation in the worlds of wine and music.

The wine is still made in the traditional way, with the Château using large wooden vats.

In one of the *chais* at d'Issan the last royal crown of Bordeaux is on display. It is made of wrought iron and was once kept in the former palace, now the Town Hall.

The Château houses many art objects, including paintings, tableware and a magnificent fireplace dating from the Italian Renaissance.

*Right:*
*Many Margaux wines win prizes as well as world fame and popularity.*

*Right:*
*One of the large chais. Several years ago a large new cellar was built for the first-year wine. To the left of the picture you can see part of the former ramparts.*

*Centre bottom:*
*A workman fetches the hand pump which is to be used for racking, the process of transferring the wine into another cask. This is a procedure undertaken several times a year, so that the lees are left behind.*

Château d'Issan

CHATEAU d'ISSAN

showed a marked preference for d'Issan. After the Battle of Castillon in 1453, which put an end to two centuries of English supremacy in Guyenne, the English withdrew into the Médoc but they had their wits about them sufficiently to keep up rearguard skirmishes to gain time – and to ransack the cellars of d'Issan. Eventually the troops withdrew from Pauillac, taking with them enough wine to drown the sorrow of their defeat.

Britain is still an important market for this third classed growth, although Japan, the United States, Holland and Canada are also large export markets. The *appellation* is Margaux, as it is for other fine wines from the parish of Cantenac.

### Trees in the salons

As a mark of gratitude, the victorious king, Charles VII, gave the barony of d'Issan to the Comte de Foix, who was responsible for driving out the English. His family remained in possession until the beginning of the nineteenth century. During the early generations of the de Foix family the newly-acquired estate was not an attractive one because the English, in an aggressive farewell, had burnt the place down. It was not until the 17th century that the present beautiful château was built on the foundations of the old fort. Despite its squared-off shape its appearance is particularly graceful.

D'Issan was almost ruined a second time when the Germans arrived during the last war, and settled in there. It is thanks to the late Emmanuel Cruse that d'Issan has now been completely restored to its former glory. This cultivated man bought the estate in 1945 and spent virtually the rest of his life restoring both the vineyard and the house.

This involved a phenomenal amount of work. Photographs taken immediately after the war even show that trees were growing out of the windows! Emmanuel Cruse was also co-proprietor of Rausan-Ségla for a time, and when the latter was sold in 1956 many of the art treasures were transferred to d'Issan.

### A delicate bouquet of apples

Over the gate of d'Issan is inscribed *'Regum Mensis Arisque Deorum'* – 'For kings' tables and gods' altars'.
This claim is less immodest than it may seem, because the wine of d'Issan has certainly been the favourite drink of kings – even of the Emperor Franz Joseph of Austria. He preferred d'Issan to all other Bordeaux wines – and the court readily followed his example. Today one does not need to be a head of state to enjoy d'Issan, though drinking it copiously may encourage illusions of grandeur.

The wine of d'Issan has been in the background for some considerable time, but in the last decade it has come to the fore once again. Of the vintages I have drunk myself I found the 1967 a very striking wine, with a bouquet like the soft scent of apples, which was altogether very pleasant. The flavour was round and friendly, although still somewhat tannic. Characteristic of the wines of d'Issan is that they are fairly fleshy without, however, having the severity which one finds in certain other wines with the *appellation* Margaux.

The 1969 vintage was an attractive wine, a pleasant lightweight with a fine, delicate bouquet and still a slight trace of tannin. The 1970 vintage was more robust, though less overwhelming than other Médocs of that year. But d'Issan is definitely Margaux. The 1973 vintage had a good colour and was very fruity; it will develop into an elegant wine which should be ready to drink before 1980.

### Château-bottling at d'Issan now

The man behind the wine of d'Issan is M. Dulin, who came with M. Cruse and now works for his widow, who lives at the château in the summer. He is responsible for the vast cellars and the 33-hectare vineyard, of which an average of some 25 hectares is productive. The proportions are 66% Cabernet Sauvignon and 34% Merlot. The production is 80 to 100 *tonneaux* annually, and all the wine since the vintage of 1972 is château-bottled.

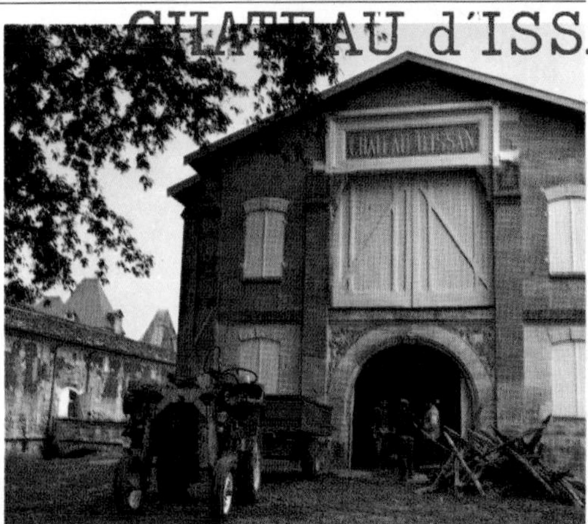

Palmer is one of the few châteaux where the grapes are de-stalked by *égrappage à main*. This is done by a skilled team who rub the grapes through a wooden griddle standing on a cart. Elsewhere, machines are generally used.

In the past not all the wine from Palmer was bottled at the Château. To distinguish other bottlings from the château bottlings the former had a white label with a line drawing, instead of a black label. The last time I saw this label was on the 1962, when Palmer made an outstanding wine – wherever bottled.

*Below:*
*The Château as it is depicted on the magnificent black label.*

*Bottom:*
*Glasses hang ready and waiting in the spacious reception hall. As elsewhere in the Médoc, visitors usually only taste the first and second year wines from the cask, sometimes a disappointment to people who are not used to them. Privileged and special visitors, as guests of the proprietors, may sample older vintages at luncheon or dinner. Any such guest should remember that 1945, 1959, 1961, the still much to young 1970 and 1971 are the outstanding vintages that now remain.*

# Chau Palmer

3rd Grand Cru Classé

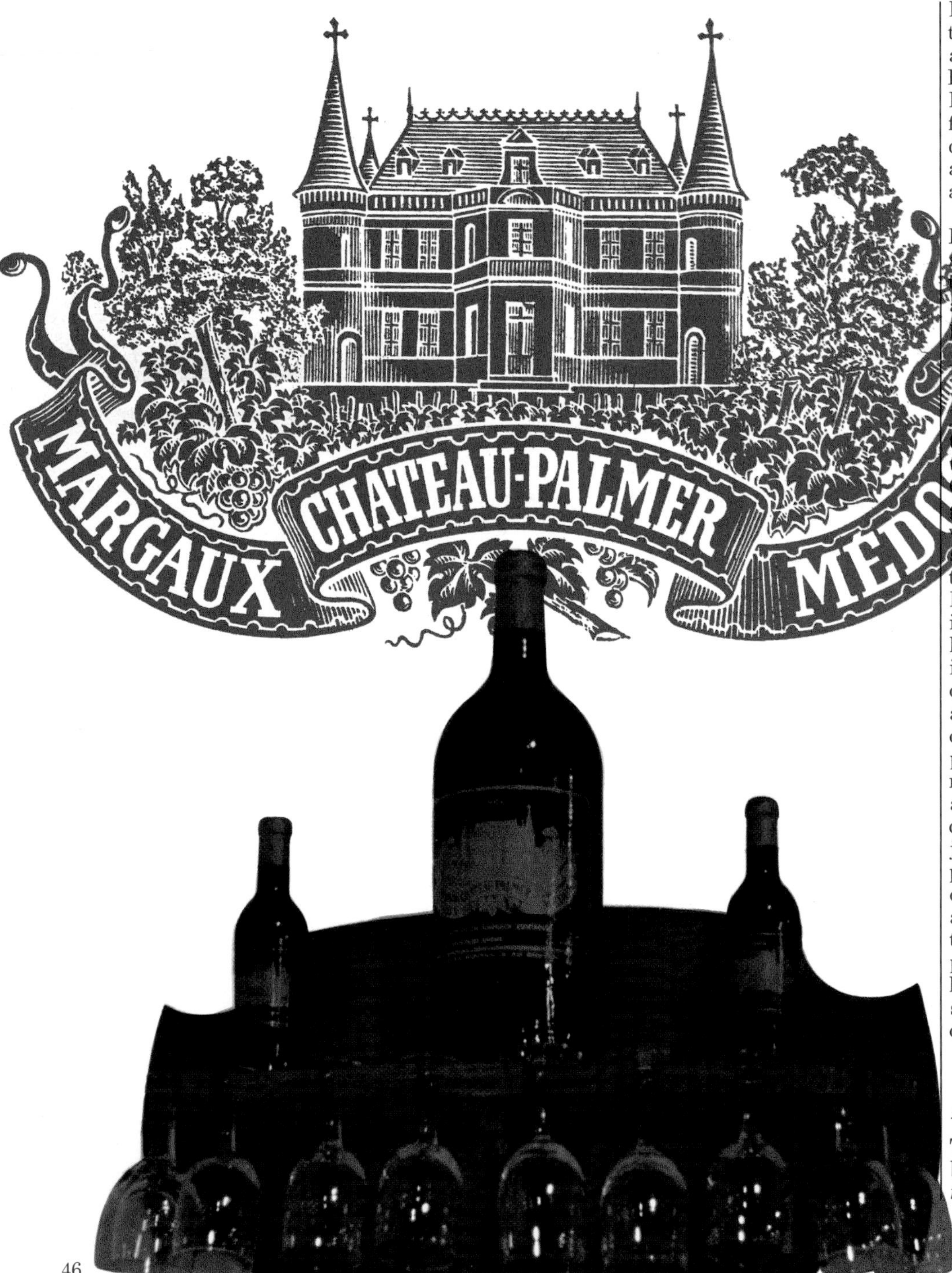


If you pass through Cantenac and drive in the direction of Margaux you will become aware of Château Palmer at some distance. Rising above the roofs of the village of Issan two spires can be seen, with three flagpoles carrying the flags of three different countries – Holland, Great Britain and France – all, incidentally, red, white and blue.

Château Palmer is the property of the Dutch family Mähler-Besse (59% of the shares), the British firm Sichel (31%) and the French family Miailhe (10%). The name and history of the Château make it particularly interesting.

The story begins with the British General Palmer who in the Napoleonic campaign was fighting with Wellington's army in the Peninsular War. As the French retreated, the British forces and their allies advanced through France and in 1814 occupied the Gironde. Palmer himself grew fond of the gentle countryside, and when Napoleon was finally defeated in 1815, he decided to settle in the Médoc, attracted to the life of the owner of a wine-producing estate.
He became increasingly interested and involved with his passion for wine-growing; he bought the Château de Gasq and immediately proceeded to add to it parcels of neighbouring vineyards. It became such an obsession that he ran deeply into debt in order to be able to continue to increase his property. He is supposed once to have come near to marrying a rich widow as a way of amassing more capital. But the lady in question learned of his mercenary motives just in time and the wedding did not take place. Nevertheless, General Palmer became one of the largest owners of his day, although after his death it was discovered that he was heavily in debt to a great many people, with the sad result that the estate he had so laboriously built up had to be sold piece by piece in order to pay off his creditors.

## A cherished property

The best section of the vineyard was bought by the Pereire family – rich, perhaps a little *nouveau riche*. You will still find their name

*Far left:*
*Yves Chardon who, together with his brother Claude and father Pierre, makes the wine at Palmer.*

*Left:*
*The grapes are brought in at Palmer in completely traditional style, as they might have been many years ago.*

*Bottom:*
*The château, seen from the front. If guests are being entertained to dinner the front is floodlit, the façade and towers gleaming white against the night sky.*



in Paris on a boulevard and a metro station. The Pereires turned out to be good owners, who invested large sums so as to give Palmer an increasing reputation. They may have regarded it as a status symbol, rather like keeping a racing stable. The exemplary attitude of the Pereires only became apparent after the economic crash in 1929, when first-class wines were not in demand; yet they continued to spend money on making a fine wine – unlike many other classed growths which had declined in quality through the 1914–18 war and during the years of depression that followed. Even the powerful Pereire bankers sustained losses, and one day the two brothers who ran Palmer had to inform the family that the coffers were empty. They asked that all shareholders should help by contributing a considerable sum of money. No one liked this idea: they enjoyed drinking the wine, but had no intention of paying extra for it. The two brothers then suggested that they should buy Palmer, but once again the family was adamant: they begrudged them the Château. So the brothers were forced to sell the estate on the open market at a time when money was extremely tight. The price was accordingly low: no more than a year's upkeep.

Henry Mähler-Besse's father saw his chance, and together with two wine brokers (brothers of the Miailhe family), the legendary Allan Sichel of the British firm and Bernand Ginestet (father of Pierre) it was decided to buy Palmer. Although the reputation of the growth had remained intact, the new owners had to pour money into the estate for years, especially as the second world war broke out shortly afterwards, and the house itself suffered severe damage from the Germans because it was used as a regional German military headquarters. Ginestet eventually sold his entire holding to Mähler-Besse alone.

*Left:*
*The first-year cellar. Notice the specially polished side bands on the casks; this is peculiar to Palmer. The statue in the background must be a substitute for the patron saint of wine, St Vincent, but is probably not the saint himself as there is no cross in his hands.*

*Below:*
*Using a small, circular wooden press, the lees are pressed. They were formed during the first, turbulent fermentation. The wine from this first pressing is often added in small quantities to the* grand vin *to give it a little more tannin.*

*Bottom:*
*One of the workers in the cellar, almost hidden behind his huge apron.*

Henri Mähler-Besse's father was simply Mr Mähler. When he married a Mlle Besse of a well-known Bordeaux family he coupled the name of Besse to that of the firm. People started calling him M. Mähler-Besse, and in the end his son Henri later had the name changed officially.

The harvest of 1934 was particularly plentiful, but because of the world financial crisis many châteaux had earlier reduced their orders for casks. But not Palmer: Henri Mähler-Besse can still remember that many owners came to him and offered him one full cask of their wine for two of his empty ones, they were so desperate for casks.

## An impeccable tradition

Nowadays, under the capable management of *régisseur* Pierre Chardon and his two sons Claude and Yves, some twenty men work in the cellars and vineyard. A total of 40 hectares are planted with 40% Cabernet Sauvignon, 10% Cabernet Franc, 40% Merlot and 10% Petit Verdot. Not so very long ago there was 60% Merlot, but as the vineyard was replanted some of the Merlot was gradually replaced by the Cabernet Sauvignon in order to make the wine slightly stronger. The production averages 120 *tonneaux* (*appellation* Margaux), which are mainly shipped to the United States, Britain, Holland and Belgium.

The wine is made in a wholly traditional fashion and stored in oak vats. According to the manager, Bertrand Bouteiller, the oak lends a little bit of tannin to the generally supple wine, especially since the fermentation vats are regularly renewed. In excellent years, like 1970, brand-new casks are used; in average years about half the casks are renewed.

Palmer is a wine that beginners can easily enjoy and which the experienced greatly respect. The late Allan Sichel was scrupulous about rejecting any vattings that did not attain the high standard he set for his beloved wine, and his son Peter, who was the first foreigner to become president of the Bordeaux Syndicate of Growers, has continued this tradition. The Sichels, with their associated family firms in Mainz, London and New York, have also continued the practice of encouraging students of the wine trade to come and make the vintage and to study wine seriously at Palmer. Many world-famous wine buyers, as well as numerous writers on wine, owe their start to their training here. Gradually the château is being refurbished, but the vineyard is always impeccable – it wins prizes for being well kept, just as Madame Chardon wins prizes for the gardens in front of it.

## Memorable vintages

The most memorable Palmer I have ever drunk is the 1961 vintage. The wine is still much too young, but it already has such a remarkable colour, perfume and flavour that I can hardly remember what we ate. After ten years the magnificent bouquet was still extremely fruity, and the flavour had a smooth, almost sweet style. Fate was to have it that not long after drinking this superb wine I met John Elliott, the well-known cellar master of the famous London restaurant, the Café Royal. He knew the wine well, and found it so great that he calls it 'the wine of the century'. As a result, the Café Royal has bought a generous amount. Another bottle which I look back on with pleasure is a 1959 Palmer, which I enjoyed at the Château itself during a dinner I had with M. Mähler-Besse. The wine had a dark colour, a rich, deep bouquet, which recalled memories of a mixture of ripe fruits, and a supple character full of velvety strength. It was still extremely vital and will certainly continue to mature for another 20 to 30 years. Another marvellous wine was the 1962, by some esteemed the greatest of this vintage: round, splendid, harmonious and with a taste lingering on in your mouth for minutes after you have swallowed. Other recent successful years are 1966, 1970 and 1971, immediately followed by 1967 and 1973. It is no wonder that Palmer, a great third growth, often commands prices only just below those of the first growths.

## Desmirail, the vanished vineyard

In some classifications Château Desmirail is still listed as a third growth. The estate, however, no longer exists. It was bought by Palmer in 1957 and added to the Palmer vineyard. Since then Desmirail has made an infrequent public appearance as Palmer's second wine, but it looks as if even this will not be done any more – the last time a small batch of Desmirail was seen was in 1965. This Château was at one time well known in Germany, because before the first world war it belonged to a Berlin banker, Herr Mendersohn. The buildings which were once Desmirail are still standing, and are now the private property of a Frenchman.

Margaux has its own glass, less severe and a little larger than that of the Académie du Vin de Bordeaux, engraved with the arms of the city.

Because Margaux is sold only through Maison Ginestet, there is less speculation in this wine than in other first growths, and the prices have remained more stable. The main markets are the United States, Britain, Japan, Holland and Belgium.

*Below left and right: This photograph of the 1974 vintage and the much older print on the right show how little things have changed at Margaux over the years.*

*Centre: Château Margaux, designed by Victor Louis, rightly always makes a deep impression on visitors.*

# Chau Margaux

1st Grand Cru Classé

Château Margaux is many things. More than any other classed growth, it makes a variety of impressions on the visitor, forming a picture which is as complete but also as complex as the wine itself. When you think of Margaux you at once think of art, architecture, hospitality, craftsmanship, history, gastronomy, indeed, a combination of all the things that embellish life. Perhaps this is why this Château has frequently served as a symbol for French civilisation? For example, after the last war when the first ship carrying flour arrived in a French port as part of the American Marshall Plan, the French wanted to give wine to the Americans in return for their bread, so the journey was made from Paris to Margaux to enjoy a banquet under the auspices of this Château. On the occasion of its 500th anniversary, the University of Bordeaux chose Château Margaux as the setting for a dinner with leading scientists from all over the world. In 1962 Chancellor Adenauer (*'Ich bin ein Bier-trinker'*) at his own request visited Château Margaux and said afterwards that he was delighted to have done so. 'Château Margaux', says Pierre Ginestet, 'represents the elite, perfection. It affords me great pleasure that my wine has always been so closely associated with cultural and intellectual life – with civilisation.'

### The quality of Margaux

Thinking of this, no one would suppose the wine of Château Margaux to be coarse, solid or inflexible, even if he has never drunk a drop. The wine is quite the

*Left:*
*The Château seen from the elegantly laid out park, which contains not only a large lake but an open-air theatre as well.*

*Below left:*
*Margaux is the only first growth whose classification is given in full on the label as* premier grand cru classé.

*Opposite page:*
*A glimpse of the vathouse. This is the domain of* maître de chai *Jean Grangerou, whose grandfather was also cellar master at Margaux.*

Before the grapes are de-stalked and crushed, they are dumped onto three sorting tables. Eight people at each table first sort out the rotten grapes, the unripe ones and the leaves. Only the juice from ripe, healthy grapes is used for the *grand vin* of Margaux, and even from these a selection is made.

Pierre Ginestet once met an American minister who confided to him: 'M. Ginestet, how glad I am to meet you! I have been drinking Château Margaux for years and I adore it. And do you know how I drink it? I take half a glass of Margaux from a good year, half a glass of strawberry juice and mix the two thoroughly. Delicious!'

The wine of Château Margaux is normally left to ripen for no less than 2½ years in the cask.

*Opposite page, centre:*
*The large first-year* chai*. Visitors' tasting samples consume 16 casks of wine every year.*

*Opposite page, far right:*
*Pierre Ginestet in the hall of his château.*

*Opposite page, below:*
*A collage of items which are on display in the reception room at Margaux. The late West German Chancellor, Adenauer, may be seen in the black and white photograph. He was just one among the many world-famous visitors to this outstandingly beautiful property.*

opposite: Margaux is the acme of delicacy; perhaps no other wine can be found or made which is more delicate. Whoever drinks Margaux is reminded of the scent of the most lovely flowers, of the subtle charm of fine porcelain, of intricate music for the harpsichord – in short, of many things which are exquisitely delicate and beautiful.

But do not imagine that the wine possesses only ephemeral and superficial qualities. Despite its superlative delicacy, Margaux is a wine which keeps well, needing time to reveal itself in all its beauty – however pleasant it may also taste in its youth. Taste, for example, the still dark 1970 vintage, only these few years after its birth: it has an elegant scent and taste. If you do not know Margaux, you might be inclined to classify it as a fine wine, pleasing to drink but without much potential. But the opposite is true! You may think that the wine has reached its peak, but in reality it will continue to mature and improve for years, especially if it is of a sunny year such as 1970, for Margaux seems to love the sun and the best Margaux wines are always produced in years with a high proportion of sunshine. This does not mean that the wine is disappointing in averagely good years, for it is said that it is then that this Château makes its most characteristic wines. In sunless years, however, Margaux has problems because the delicately constituted wine tends to become rather too light in body.

### Recent Margaux vintages

As with the other châteaux there is not much point in giving particulars of vintages which are now no longer available, or only at exorbitant prices, so I shall only comment on some recent vintages that I have been able to taste. The 1966 vintage has a magnificent, dark colour, followed by the distinctive, delicate, charming bouquet. The flavour is already typical Margaux, but will gain in richness as the years go by. The aftertaste is also remarkable. The 1966 Margaux may well excel the 1970 vintage.

The wine of 1967 is also striking for its outstandingly attractive nose, an almost sultry perfume full of concentrated floweriness. The constitution of the wine is a shade on the light side, the finish possibly slighter shorter than one has come to expect of this growth.

In 1964 – the year in which the rain came in the middle of the Médoc harvest – Château Margaux succeeded in making a good wine thanks to strict selection, because only grapes which had been picked before the rain started were used. This wine impressed me as extremely lively, and contained many surprising gradations of fragrance and flavour. Its colour was excellent.

1962 was also a superb Margaux year. The bouquet had a hint of violets, often associated with this parish; it was deep, distinguished, pure. The body seemed a little light, but was still in excellent harmony with the rest.

It goes without saying that the splendid year 1961 was a success, and the same applies to 1959. The 1959 vintage, at a dozen years of age, had a lovely tawny colour, a light bouquet and a soft, delicate, refined aftertaste: Margaux at its best, a symphony of colour, fragrance and flavour all in harmony. I drank this wine with a fresh Saint-Nectaire cheese from the French *département* of Puy-de-Dôme, and it was an ideal combination.

A wine which surprised me by its quality was the 1957 vintage. Seventeen years after having been harvested, it showed no sign of decline, and there was still a trace of tannin. Its nose was soft, ripe, almost sweet; its flavour lively and full of delicate shades.

### The Victor Louis chai

In the same way that you do not expect a churlish wine from Margaux, so you could not imagine it being produced in any simple farm shed. Such a wine must surely be born, reared and developed in surroundings to match its unique style. The château and the *chais* have classic proportions. The *chai* where the young

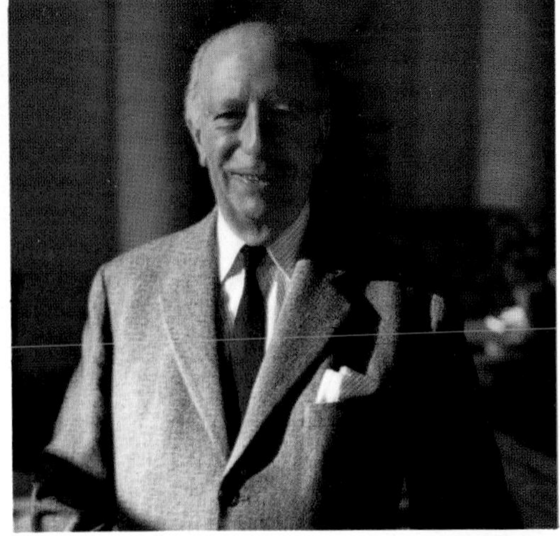

Château Margaux

wine spends the first years of its life in new oak casks is more like a wine cathedral than a wine store. It is 100 metres long, 23 metres wide, the high wooden ceiling supported by 18 white pillars, each with a diameter of 1·5 metres. Immediately adjoining this is the narrow private reserve of the owners, where there are 100,000 bottles, dating back to 1865.

Pierre Ginestet tells how this unique collection was saved from the ravages of the German occupying forces in the second world war: the wines, together with part of the Rothschild collection, were put at the end of the vathouse where there was still a reasonably large area not in use. The entrance was then concealed with such an enormous pile of empty cases that it discouraged even the most rapacious intruder from bothering to look and see whether there might perhaps be something behind them.

Visitors enter this same vathouse today from the private cellar through the inside of an empty wooden fermentation vat, an effective gimmick, which for a moment makes one feel almost as small as a freshly picked grape.

### The Margaux community

A whole court of craftsmen has been created at Margaux to work the vineyard and tend the wine. Carpenters, painters, bricklayers, mechanics, gardeners, tilers, smiths, electricians, cabinetmakers, plumbers and farmers live with their families in a complete village next door to the Château. This village is completely self-supporting, even to its own water and electricity supply. There is also a cooperage, which produces 600 new barrels per annum, all made by hand.

Because the estate has some further 150 hectares as well as the vineyard, it has a farm with cows who supply the necessary manure; among other things, a considerable acreage is also devoted to the cultivation of artichokes.

The vineyards cover about 75 hectares, of which about 70 are productive. Of the vines, 75% are Cabernet and 25% Merlot. The

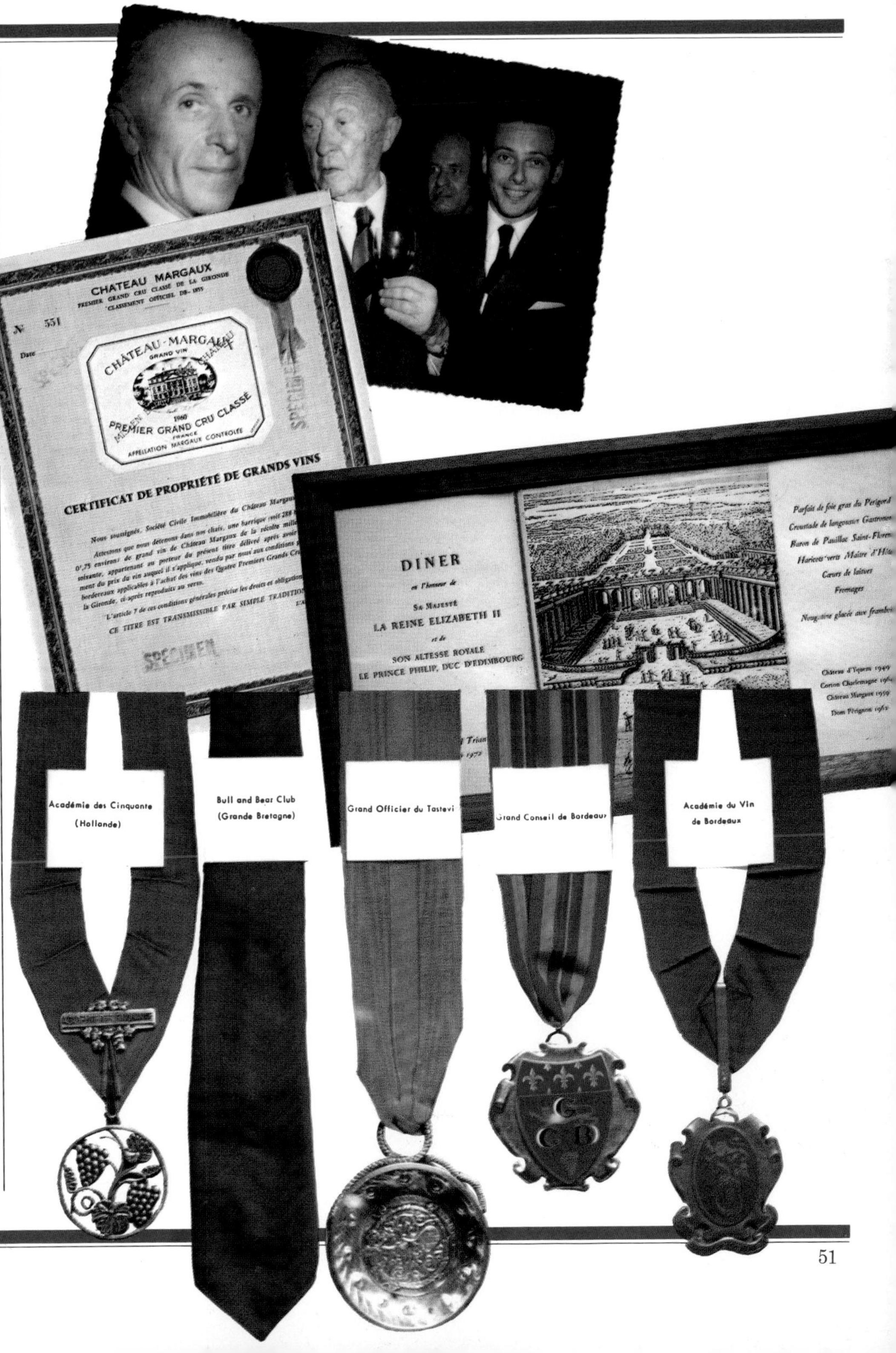

*Left:*
*The oldest of the 100,000 bottles stored in the private cellar is dated 1865.*

*Below:*
*Vintage time at Margaux. Of the 25 families virtually everyone who is fit and able to pick joins in, and even if the weather is uncertain, spirits are usually high.*

For a long time Château Margaux made a white wine, Pavillon Blanc. This has, however, been discontinued, because Pierre and Bernard Ginestet now feel that its quality is not sufficiently good to be coupled with that of Château Margaux. The white vines have therefore been uprooted, and another white wine has been launched: Pavillon Blanc de Ginestet. This has the *A.C.* Graves, and is not only thought to be better but is also cheaper than its predecessor. Whether Château Margaux will ever produce another white wine at the estate itself will depend entirely on the quality resulting from possible future replantings with better vine species.

When Chancellor Adenauer came to Margaux – and was presented, among other things, with a magnum of the year in which he was born – Pierre Ginestet was in Switzerland. Every other *propriétaire* would have hurried back to his Château to greet the high-ranking guest, but not Pierre Ginestet. With typical – and very French – calm, he said: 'I don't need to return. The Chancellor has come for the Château and the wine, not because of me.'

Château Margaux

production averages 160 *tonneaux*.

### Married to the estate

Everything is perfectly organised for the wine down to the last detail. The same is true as regards the proprietors of this estate, for they live in the superb mansion standing in the middle of a fine park at the end of a tree-lined drive. With its splendid flight of steps and its pillars it may remind visitors of the rich southern mansions in *Gone with the Wind*. The building, which dates from 1810, was designed by the architect Combes on the instruction of the proprietor at that time, Marquis Douat de la Colonilla.

Quite often similarly stately homes lack atmosphere inside, but Margaux is an exception. The château is lived in by M. and Mme Ginestet, and they have succeeded in making the drawing-rooms, with all their antiques, pleasantly home-like. Pierre Ginestet owns Château Margaux with his son Bernard; he feels it is important that the wine-grower should live on the land he cultivates. This can have its disadvantages, for it is not always easy for just two people to live in such a vast place, however beautiful and comfortable it may be (Bernard and his family live nearby at Durfort-Vivens). Moreover, it is expensive. 'An owner of a *grand cru* contracts a marriage with his vineyard,' says Pierre Ginestet, 'and that is just as in real life – for better, for worse. For a long time I have earned a lot of money with Château Margaux, and in the present economic climate I shall probably lose a lot. But I shall remain faithful to my land.'

*Right:*
*Château Durfort-Vivens as illustrated on the label – the bottle can be seen at the far right. The Vicomte de Vivens, one of the two men from whom Durfort-Vivens gets its name, knew a lot not only about wine but also about water: in 1840 he published a book about the River Garonne.*

*Bottom:*
*The chai is separated from the Château by a road. M. Lucien Lurton, the proprietor of Brane Cantenac and Durfort-Vivens, has collected a number of old objects associated with wine and the making of wine in the spacious entrance, including tools used in the making of casks and the old press, which in fact is not from Bordeaux. From 1975 the wine of Durfort-Vivens will be made in the Château's own cellars.*

# Chau Durfort-Vivens

2nd Grand Cru Classé

When Thomas Jefferson, the future president of the United States, visited Bordeaux in 1785, he immediately classed Durfort together with Rauzan and Léoville, as 'second quality' red wines after Lafite and Margaux, which he regarded as first-class wines. His judgement was proved sound, as in 1855 Durfort-Vivens was classed as a second growth.

The estate has not been in the hands of the Durfort and de Vivens families since 1866. After belonging to the Delor establishment and to Château Margaux, the vineyard and cellars were bought by Lucien Lurton from Brane-Cantenac in 1961. The château itself remained the property of the current owners, the Ginestets; it is now occupied by Bernard Ginestet and his family.

There is only a *chai* and a vineyard to see at Durfort, the latter covering 25 hectares (of which a good fifteen are productive). The vineyard is planted with 65% Cabernet Sauvignon, 20% Cabernet Franc and 15% Merlot. The production averages 40 *tonneaux*. I have drunk four vintages of Durfort-Vivens, and it is amazing how much it differs from Brane-Cantenac, which has the same classification and the same owner. All along the line Durfort has more hardness and less finesse. I have always found Durfort-Vivens a robust, almost wooden wine. Even a year such as 1967 seems rather severe. The 1964 Durfort is also fairly austere and is certainly neither supple nor very refined. The years 1970 and 1971 are very hard, as yet without any real promise of their developing into a delicate, fragrant Margaux wine in time to come.

It is, however, difficult and unfair to pass final judgement yet, since Lucien Lurton has not had the chance up to now of allowing a wine made by him to reach full maturity. It may well be some time before that day arrives, because the wines of Durfort-Vivens are traditionally slow to mature, partly because of the high percentage of the Cabernet grape. It will be interesting to see how this formerly fine wine will be made now it is in more responsible hands.

Below:
When the estate celebrated its 300th anniversary in 1961, a special label was issued.

Right:
Some of the 12 enamelled steel fermentation vats in the vathouse, which is situated to the right of the main entrance. Until 1969 wooden vats were used.

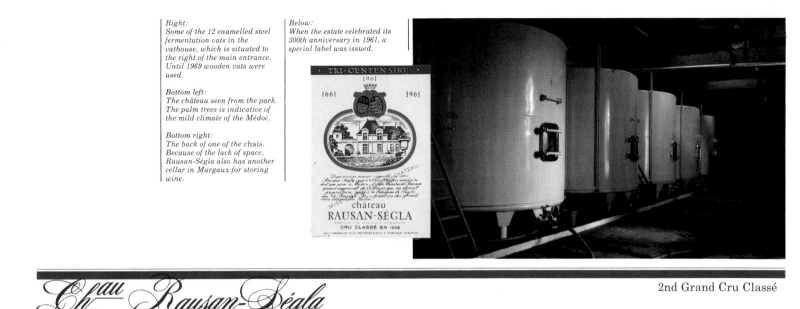

# Chau Rausan-Ségla

2nd Grand Cru Classé

Now that Mouton-Rothschild has been promoted to the first classed growths, Rausan-Ségla heads the second group. It is immediately followed by Rauzan-Gassies, which seems logical enough, since each of these estates occupies part of one and the same vineyard. Many of the well-known Médoc vineyards date from the 18th century, whereas Rausan goes back to 1661. The estate was then the property of Pierre des Mesures de Rausan, a wine merchant. During the French Revolution the vineyard was divided: about two-thirds went to the heirs of Baroness de Ségla and the rest to the politician Gassies. In 1866 Rausan-Ségla was bought by the father-in-law of Frédéric Cruse, whose family was to own the Château for ninety years.

The Cruses have done a lot both to the château and to the vineyard. They built a completely new main building and imported all kinds of furnishings from a château near Bordeaux which had been pulled down. Anyone visiting Rausan-Ségla and the gardens will come across strange stone tablets which are clearly older than the rest of the château. Many have proverbs written on them, some in Latin; there is probably no other estate where there is as much to read in stone as at Rausan. A touching and certainly authentic inscription is the one which states: 'Baroness Rausan-Ségla, 1761–1828, took delight in growing hydrangeas on this spot'. From 1956 the château belonged to M. de Meslon for four years; he in turn sold it to the British John Holt Group (which also owns the firm of Eschenauer). The château is not permanently occupied but has been refurbished so that wine trade guests can stay there.

## Chuck it into the Thames!

Great Britain has always been an important market for Rausan-Ségla. Centuries ago this was so, until suddenly the demand declined. This was not to M. Rausan's liking and he decided to do something about it. The problem was that the British no longer wanted to pay the price which M. Rausan considered his wine was worth. Letter-writing was of no avail, so one day the owner himself left on a ship laden with casks bound for London. But even this made no impression: the British would not buy. At this M. Rausan angrily shouted that he would never sell his wine at their preposterously low prices – he would rather throw it into the Thames. And he proceeded to do so. The first day a whole *tonneau* disappeared into the river, the second day another *tonneau* met the same fate. On the third day the merchants returned, offering a higher price.

Besides the British, the United States and Japan are now also large buyers of the 110 to 185 *tonneaux* which Rausan-Ségla produces each year.

## A vineyard of bits and pieces

Owners come and owners go, but a *régisseur*'s family often goes on from one generation to the next. Thus the grandfather of the present *régisseur*, Jean-Pierre Joyeux, began work at Rausan in 1897. His father took over in 1937, and Jean-Pierre in 1960. Before assuming this highly responsible post he already knew the château and its vineyards like the back of his hand. He was born at Rausan-Ségla and has worked there since 1944. He frankly admits that his task is a little simpler than his grandfather's, at least as far as working the vineyard is concerned, for in 1897 the 50 hectares of vineyard were broken up into no fewer than 215 different plots! By a process of exchange and other regrouping methods during this century the number has

Bottom left:
The château seen from the park. The palm trees is indicative of the mild climate of the Médoc.

Bottom right:
The back of one of the chais. Because of the lack of space, Rausan-Ségla also has another cellar in Margaux for storing wine.

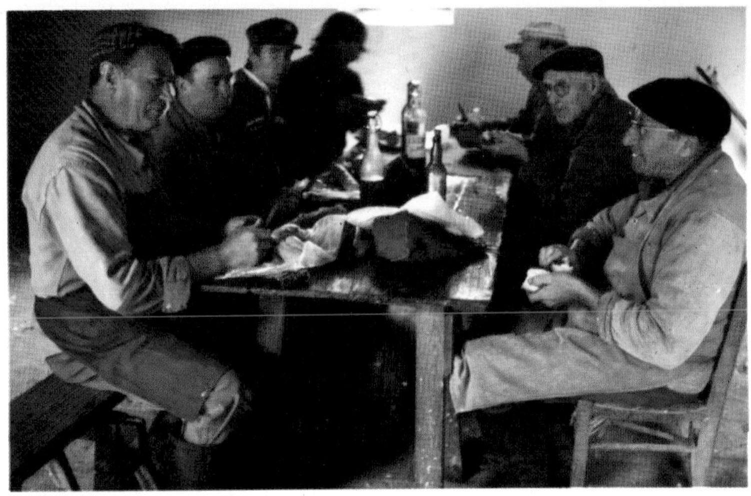

*Left:*
*A group of pickers enjoy a simple but sustaining meal (with plenty of liquid refreshment) during vintageing.*

*Bottom:*
*The entrance to the Château. The French and British flags are always flying, but if an important visitor arrives from another country his country's flag is hoisted as well.*

Anyone coming into the *chai* at Rausan-Ségla sees a huge vine high up on one of the walls. It was planted in 1820 and uprooted in 1928. It is extraordinarily large, with innumberable branches and long roots. It happens to be none of the well-known vine species cultivated today but one not used for some time – the Carmenère, which was not unlike the Merlot. A disadvantage of the Carmenère was that it usually only yielded well for five years and then almost completely stopped. This meant constant and costly replanting. The vine at Rausan is remarkable because it continued to grow for more than a century.

There are many things at Rausan-Ségla which have remained from when it was a Cruse estate. Opposite the reception hall hangs a poem by Frédéric Cruse; in a quiet spot at the end of the garden there is also a monument to Louis XI de Bourbon, Prince de Condé, who was born in 1530 and died in 1569 at Jarnac (not far from Cognac). This memorial has a reminder to the French nobility on it, which says: 'Let us not forget the noble cause for which he fell.' According to the manager, Jean-Pierre Joyeux, Louis de Bourbon was killed in one of the wars of religion, having been supported by many Bordeaux Protestants, among them the Cruse family.

now been reduced to six.

The vineyard covers 42 hectares and the following percentages of vines are planted: 50% Cabernet Sauvignon, 35% Merlot, 10% Cabernet Franc and 5% Petit Verdot. Like other Margaux estates, Rausan-Ségla gives preference to the Cabernet Sauvignon when replanting, so the percentage of this particular grape will increase.

### A smell of springtime

The most striking characteristic of Rausan-Ségla, I think, is its marvellous bouquet. Even in lesser years it is always well developed. I have been fortunate enough to drink a great many bottles of the 1960 vintage, a wine with a fine, springlike bouquet which reminds one of an orchard in full blossom. The better the year, the more pronounced is this superb nose. For example, there is the marvellous 1966 vintage, with its full and exquisite bouquet, rich in nuances, delicacy and depth. It makes you think of velvet, of soft fruit – and the longer you smell it, the more you discern.

The wine's taste is often slightly more assertive than its bouquet; although it was a pleasure to smell, the taste of the 1966 was really still rather hard. As regards the more recent years I recommend the 1970 and 1971 vintages. Nor will you find the wine of 1972 disappointing, though it needs a little time and is only a light year.
The 1973 vintage, however, is even lighter. In that year the Merlot was very important: *régisseur* Joyeux estimated that not 35% but 60% of all the 'must' (grape juice before fermentation) in 1973 came from the Merlot. The wine will be ready for drinking soon and will be pleasant, without pretensions.

When M. Rauzan, whose name is also spent with an 's', was still the proprietor, his wine was popular at the British Court in the last century. He was succeeded as proprietor of the estate by M. Vigueries, M. Rhone Péreire, M. Rigaud, the widow of M. Guiard, and the Puyo family, from whom Paul Quié eventually took over.

*Below:*
*Château Rauzan-Gassies seen from a section of the vineyard. It can be clearly seen that the Château adjoins Rausan-Ségla – the boundary is where the white painted wall ends and the ivy begins. Rauzan-Gassies looks out onto Château Palmer, and behind the photographer's back is the Château of Durfort-Vivens. The vineyard of Rauzan is split up into a dozen different lots to be found 'anywhere that Château Margaux is'. I was not able to check this statement, but it comes from someone who should know, the* chef de culture *Marc Espagnet. His colleague in the cellars is* maître de chai *Fernand Chauvin, who has already seen 15 years' service on this estate.*

# Chau Rauzan-Gassies

2nd Grand Cru Classé

You don't have to go far from Rausan-Ségla in order to reach Rauzan-Gassies – in fact the two Châteaux adjoin each other. At a particular point the brown outer wall of Rausan (with an 's') stops and the white wall of Rauzan (with a 'z') begins. This is of course due to the fact that the Châteaux used to be one property. When the property was divided, the château itself was allocated to Rausan-Ségla, so Rauzan-Gassies does not have a château of its own. There is a house, but you have to have a fertile imagination to regard this as more than a humble building.

One is naturally tempted to place the wines of Rausan-Ségla and Rauzan-Gassies on a par: after all, the wines come from different parts of the same vineyard. But this is a mistake you must never make; not only can slight differences in the angle at which the sun strikes the vineyards and in the composition of the soil cause considerable differences in the wine, but in addition a process of repartition has been going on in Margaux for generations, with the result that once-similar vineyards are gradually taking on another form. The last is something which has certainly happened in the case of the vineyards of Ségla and Gassies. Even then the list is not complete, because man also plays an important rôle. It is only thanks to his devotion, care and skill that a maximum result can be achieved alongside nature.

**An improving property**

To all appearances the human factor has been at fault this century at Rauzan. Most past critics have few good words to say for this second growth. I was therefore pleased to note that the son of Paul Quié (who bought the Château just after the second world war) is energetically subjecting the vathouse *chais* and in fact the whole wine-making procedure to a process of restoration. He is conscientious about the whole business and I imagine that the results of his costly efforts will be there for the tasting in a few years' time. It is never just one thing that makes a great wine; here more than elsewhere it is the sum of

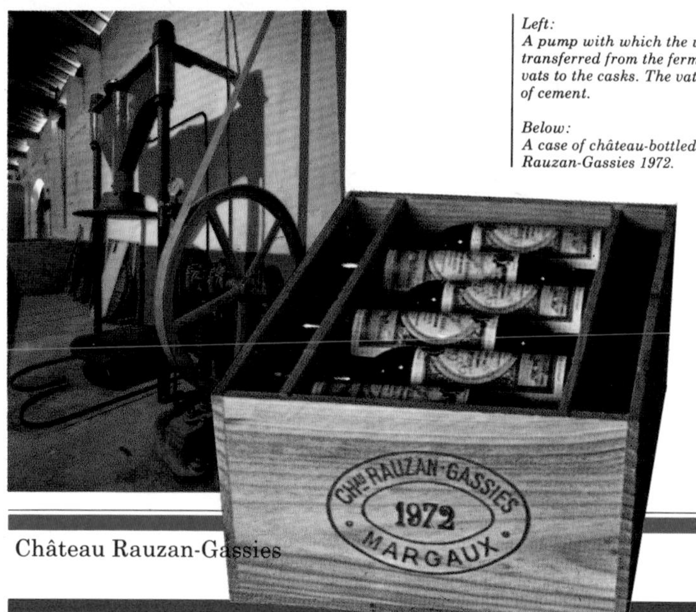


*Left:*
*A pump with which the wine is transferred from the fermentation vats to the casks. The vats are of cement.*

*Below:*
*A case of château-bottled Rauzan-Gassies 1972.*

There is a strange legend attached to the vineyard of Rauzan-Gassies. It seems that the vines of this estate have on several occasions miraculously escaped a disastrous hailstorm. This strange phenomenon is ascribed to mysterious little birds which are supposed to perch on the vines and fend off the hailstones with their wings. As with many good stories, however, eye witnesses are lacking.

The bottle racks for storage at Rauzan-Gassies, of thick metal wire, easy for stacking and for moving, are an innovation. The practical is gradually superseding the picturesque.

Rauzan-Gassies is a generally popular wine, notably in the United States, Britain, Belgium and Denmark.

## Château Rauzan-Gassies

the whole, which is more than the sum of the parts, that counts.

It happened that I was the first outsider to taste the 1974 vintage, even before members of the trade. Although the wine was a little tired from racking, it seemed promising. The colour was good, the taste full of fruit, the after-taste long. The 1973 vintage was a complete, rounded wine, lush and lingering.

### Ségla versus Gassies

The composition of the vineyard of Rauzan-Gassies is very similar to that of Ségla: about two-thirds Cabernet Sauvignon and Cabernet Franc, and the remainder Merlot, with a very little Petit Verdot. Some 21 hectares are in production, yielding an average of 90 *tonneaux*. Out of sheer curiosity I once put a bottle of Rauzan-Gassies next to a bottle of Rausan-Ségla of the same year, 1966, a year which not only produced a fine wine but a natural one, for the sugar-content of the grapes was so high that there was no need to resort to the practice of chaptalisation. This involves adding sugar to the 'must' in years when natural grape sugar is insufficient to produce a wine with the desired degree of alcohol. Both wines were château-bottled, each came direct from the storage cellars of its Château. These are my tasting notes: Colour – both good, the Rauzan-Gassies slightly darker. Bouquet – the Rausan-Ségla was the outright winner. The bouquet of the Gassies was hardly perceptible and what there was was less deep and less delicate; the two completely different. Flavour – to the surprise of those present the flavours were more similar than the bouquets. Here there was definitely a family relationship. The Rauzan-Gassies was lacking in charm, the taste almost uncongenial; it was still quite reserved. Finish (aftertaste) – both good, little difference. It would be a fascinating comparison to repeat in five or ten years' time with a later vintage from both properties!

*Right:*
*A lion rampant is shown on the label and on the nameplate.*

*Bottom:*
*The long low outbuildings Marquis de Terme are not used for storing wine but for tractors and agricultural tools. The actual* chais *are on the other side of Margaux. On the right of the picture you can see the fairly ornate château, which is not inhabited. The offices of the manager and his various staff are adjacent to it. There are 35 people permanently employed at Marquis de Terme. Immediately behind the offices is the vathouse with its big cement tanks, each with a capacity of 3,600 hectolitres.*

# Chau Marquis de Terme

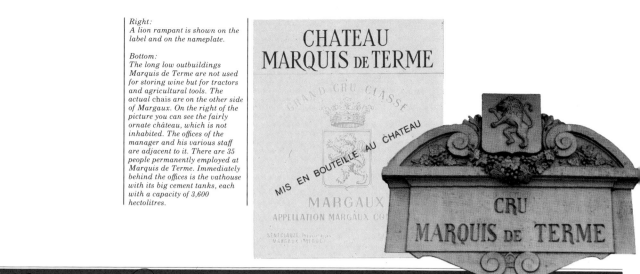

4th Grand Cru Classé

Although Château Marquis de Terme is only a stone's throw from the Rausans and Palmer, it is a little-known name in the international wine world. The reason for this is that the owners sell approximately 70% of their wine direct to private French buyers, so distressingly little is left for the rest of the world. What is exported goes mainly to Belgium, Holland and the United States. Nor, indeed, is the estate as yet organised for the reception of visitors, who can usually enter any property displaying a sign *'Visitez les chais'*.

Jean-Pierre Hugon is the rather laconic young *régisseur*, a position he has held since 1974. He works under the three brothers Sénéclauze, who own this fourth growth (the only one in Margaux), in a partnership. Their father, Pierre Sénéclauze, bought the estate in 1935 from one Armand Feuillerat. The person after whom the Château is named is *Seigneur* de Péguilhan, Marquis de Terme, who came into possession of the estate in 1762 through his marriage to the niece of M. Rauzan. We also find M. Frédéric Eschenauer among the list of owners.

### More than one wine made

For a long time the vineyard of Marquis de Terme was worked only with horses for the sake of tradition, but this is now a thing of the past, and here too the tractor has made its noisy appearance. The vineyard covers about 52 hectares and has an unusually high percentage of Petit Verdot (13%) and an unusually low percentage, for Margaux, of Merlot (9%). The rest is made up of Cabernets.
The château itself is a house with an overhanging, pointed roof. It is not inhabited. Adjoining the house are the modern offices, with the presshouse immediately behind them. The presshouse contains white-tiled cement tanks standing on red blocks. After fermentation the wine remains in oak casks for two to three years. The average 150 *tonneaux* are stored in a long, low *chai* well over a kilometre away on the other side of the village of Margaux.

*Right:*
*Vintage time in the Médoc. Bad weather may affect the quality of the vintage, but despite the pouring rain the pickers here are in good heart assisted perhaps by their daily wine ration.*

*Bottom left:*
*The lunch-break is over, the picking goes on.*

*Bottom right:*
*In a single swift movement the grapes are tipped out of the carrier's metal container.*

Not all the wine which lies here, incidentally, is sold as Marquis de Terme. A second label is used in lean years and inferior vattings: that of Domaine des Gondats. This is generally sold at half the price of its brother. In 1974 *administrateur* Pierre-Louis Sénéclauze quoted his French customers 22 francs per bottle for the 1970 Château Marquis de Terme and 11 francs for the 1970 Domaine des Gondats. In 1968 the wine was declassified to *appellation contrôlée* Haut-Médoc, and even lower to *appellation contrôlée* Bordeaux Supérieur.

**Could the wine be better?**

I can only comment on three fairly recent years of Marquis de Terme, because I have never come across a fully mature vintage. The wines tend to be high in tannin, which means that Marquis de Terme can without hesitation be counted among the potentially long-lasting wines. This was particularly marked in the 1971 and 1970 vintages. The 1971 wine was bottled in 1974 and to my mind will not be past its prime for twenty years. The colour is deep, still purplish, the bouquet reticent, the flavour less *fin* than that of the other great Margaux wines. The 1970 was even deeper in colour, and very much higher in its tannin content: it simply stuck to my teeth. There was a great deal of fruit in it, which is usually a good sign. The 1972 vintage has a good colour and traces of a fine bouquet. Once again there was a high proportion of tannin, although less than in the previous two wines. You should be able to start sampling the 1972 Marquis de Terme with pleasure somewhere around 1980.

All things considered I cannot include Marquis de Terme among the very best wines of Margaux, but then it is a wine which has yet to re-establish itself. That extra touch of finesse seems to be missing in the young wines – but who knows, perhaps this wine is a late developer, for whom life begins in later years!

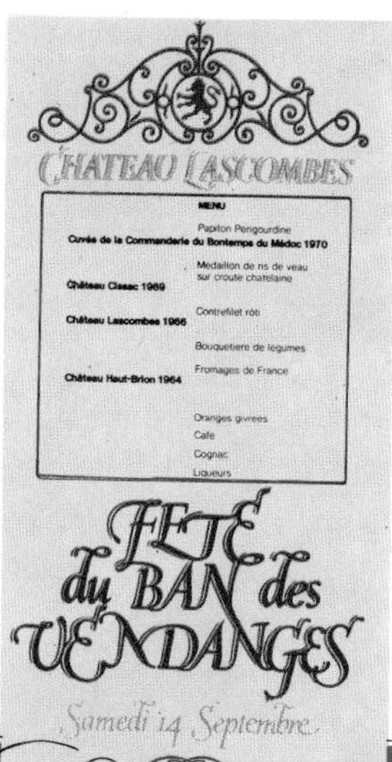

*Far left:*
*The menu for a banquet which was given in the new cellars of Lascombes on the occasion of the* Fête du Ban des Vendanges *in 1974. As many as 600 people attended. They ate at tables made from casks; gratifyingly, the 1966 Lascombes was the wine of the evening.*

*Left:*
*Lascombes is one of the estates which numbers its bottles. It is interesting to see whether a bottle was filled early or late.*

*Below left:*
*A panoramic drawing of Lascombes, updated with all its new cellars and other buildings. The château dates from 1904.*

Thanks to Lichine publicity the wine of Château Lascombes is shipped mainly to the United States, although other markets such as Britain and Holland are also regular customers.

The vineyard is not only very split up but very scattered as well. Plots are situated in three different communes – Margaux, Soussans and Cantenac – all three coming under the *appellation* Margaux, the A.O.C. under which the wine of Lascombes is therefore sold.

# Chau Lascombes

2nd Grand Cru Classé

Every great Médoc wine château has a long history and is proud of it. In many cases the château has been occupied and the vineyards tended by generation upon generation of the same family; in others, the estate has been sold frequently to many different people, some more interested than others in the fine wine they were supposed to make. Nearly always the names are remembered by the present owners, or at least recorded in old documents.

It was a certain Mademoiselle Hué who owned Château Lascombes at the time of the famous classification of 1855, according to the original document. The name of the Château was at this time spelled Lascombe (without a final 's'), and it was the fourth Margaux estate among the second growths, after Châteaux Rausan-Ségla, Rauzan-Gassies and Vivens-Durfort (*sic*).

Château Margaux was classed among the first growths, but it seems that at the time Lascombes was sometimes considered to be on a par with this famous estate. The agricultural journal *Le Producteur* of April 4, 1838, says: 'The estate of Lascombes is situated on precious soil, and it is planted with old vines of the best varieties. The quality of its wines has such a reputation that they can emulate those of Château Margaux.' We may feel that this flowery praise was somewhat exaggerated, but it does imply that the Lascombes wine was highly thought of at the time.

## Wine and art

The importance of Lascombes has certainly increased since the last century. The estate once formed part of Durfort, and when M. Loraique sold it in 1844 to M. L.-A. Hué for 90,000 francs, the vineyard was only 20 hectares. For some time after the sale the Château was called Petit-Lascombes; this was not intended to stress the smallness of the place, but M. Hué had made his son-in-law a present of the Château and his name happened to be Petit. Later it was bought by M. Chaix-d'Est-Ange, whose grandson Gustav took it over in 1867. In his time Gustav Chaix-d'Est-Ange was a

Lascombes gets more and more visitors every year, which they like. From March or April to August or September they average as many as 50 a day, contingents often arriving in busloads.

Because of the vast extension and maintenance work going on, the Château employs its own carpenter, painter and bricklayer.

*Right:*
*A small section of some of the stock of 1970 Lascombes still in the cellars – where demand will make inroads on this fine wine.*

*Centre:*
*The Château's striking main tower. At the bottom it is round and at the top angular! It is something of a landmark for anyone coming into Margaux from the north.*

*Bottom:*
*A voluptuous lady in the park who clearly thinks that a headdress of grapes is the only thing to wear.*

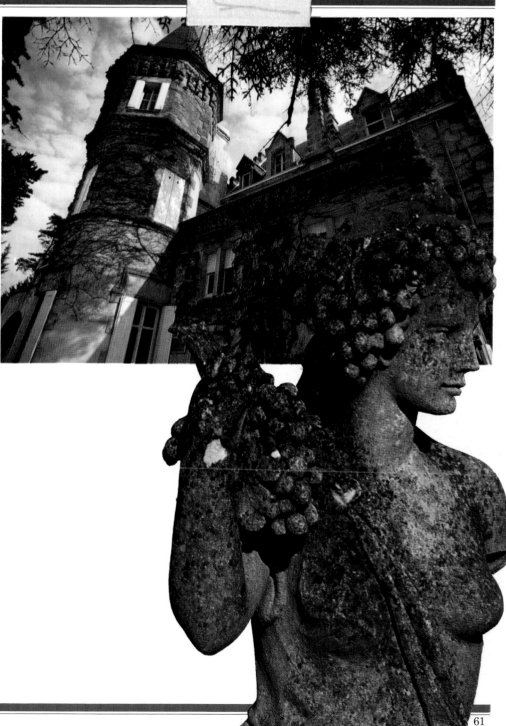

famous man for he was the lawyer who won the case of the Suez Canal for France against Egypt.

In the first half of the twentieth century Lascombes has had many owners; in 1952 the American, Alexis Lichine, and a few friends bought the estate and began to revitalise it. Typically, Lichine, already active in the world of wine in France, wished to restore Lascombes' glory. Careful attention was paid to the appearance of the château and the cellars, and it was Lichine's idea to organise an exhibition of contemporary art here every year with the theme *Vigne et Vin*. The standard of the exhibits was high, as can be seen from paintings now hanging in châteaux such as Prieuré-Lichine and Cantenac-Brown. However, in May 1971 Lichine sold Lascombes to Bass Charrington Vintners, one of the most important wine outlets of a vast U.K. brewery group. It is rumoured that the price was about two million dollars.

**Country house château**

The new owners have invested heavily in the estate, with the result that Lascombes is now one of the most impressive châteaux in the Médoc: curiously, the house itself, covered in creepers, has always had a somewhat English look. There is the influence of Victorian Gothic in the architecture – and certainly of England in the gardens.

In the autumn of 1973 the completely renovated *chais* were put into use. They are a delight to see: the outside is finished with white plaster, dark brown wood and red roofing tiles. Inside, indirect lighting reveals hundreds of casks in a spotlessly clean cellar which does not, however, lack atmosphere. Just as at Prieuré-Lichine, the ends of the *barriques* are varnished, which heightens the effect of cleanliness. There are even two large 'No smoking' signs in the big *chais*. These are not meant for the Château employees – they never smoke in the cellars anyway – but for the groups of visitors who might walk round with cigarettes alight. Those responsible

*Left:*
*A swimming pool has been built for executives and the guests who come to Lascombes. Half the cost could be paid for out of tax money, because the pool also serves as a reservoir to be used in case of fire.*

*Below:*
*In the hall of the château a cupola has been made as part of the restoration work.*

*Far below:*
*Cellar master Robert Dupuy, who usually conducts visitors round the* chais.

*Bottom:*
*A view of the brand-new vathouse. The tube complex in the foreground serves to cool the must during the first fermentation.*

The manager, Claude Gobinau, knows how to make excellent wine not only at Lascombes, but also on his own little estate in the parish of Moulis. This is a bourgeois growth which is called Cap de Haut. The production is around 15 *tonneaux* and it seems that the whole crop is sold to Holland.

At Lascombes up to 50% of new casks are used each year, the wine being left to mature in them for at least 18 months.

In the new *chai* at Lascombes stainless steel pipes have been laid in the floor, which carry the wine from one cask to another by means of compressed air. This is another innovation.

for making the wine at Lascombes wish to keep the air round the young wine pure.

The renovations have not been confined to the *chais*. The fermentation unit is also completely new, and consists of dark brown, tiled cement vats. There are also the pickers' quarters, bright and cheerful, with every modern convenience, showers and a modern kitchen. If you are thinking of becoming a grape-picker in the Médoc, you know where to go!

Last but not least, the château itself has also been drastically updated. There will soon be seven guest rooms with bathrooms, and several elegant reception rooms. There is even a swimming pool – one of the few in the Médoc – to refresh staff and guests in the hot summers of the Gironde.

## A mighty patchwork vineyard

Since 1971 the vineyard of Lascombes has been considerably extended: a total of nearly 25 hectares has been added to the existing 80 hectares. The only problem is that the acreage under cultivation is more split up than anywhere else in the Bordeaux region, so much so that a French official congratulated *régisseur* Claude Gobinau on what is proably a new world record: a vineyard made up of more than a thousand plots! This would be enough to make an ordinary man nervous, but not M. Gobinau. Not only does he succeed in joining a few more lots together each year, but the disunity has an advantage: the risk of hail, night frost and other hazards is reduced by being spread over a wide area. The vineyard consists of 45% Cabernet Sauvignon, 32% Merlot, 11% Cabernet Franc, 10% Petit Verdot and 2% Malbec. Although the last few years have seen a great deal of new plantings, a high average age of the vines is aimed at: half are 20 years old and more. The production of Château Lascombes is around 250 *tonneaux*, but will probably increase to nearly 300 in the coming years. This includes approximately 20 *tonneaux* of rosé which this estate makes. A small section of the vineyard is situated on flat ground down by the river which is unsuitable for the production of the *grand vin*; Chevalier de Lascombes is the name of this fresh, dry, fruity wine. It is sold in a slender, clear bottle under the *appellation contrôlée* Bordeaux Supérieur, and is named after the nobleman who once gave his name to, or got his name from, the Château.

## Lascombes in recent vintages

Judging by the 1967 vintage one would assume that Lascombes produced fairly light wines. This has a nice nose, a pleasing taste and a delicate constitution. But what a difference between it and the 1970! The latter is almost exceptionally firm for a Margaux wine, with a superb deep colour, a slightly reticent but highly promising bouquet, a fruity taste, adequate tannin and a long after-taste. The excellence of this wine is proved by the fact that at a huge banquet in Bordeaux it was awarded the gold medal by the wine merchants and agents of the region. It is obviously a wine which should be kept for at least ten years. The 1971 vintage is less assertive and will mature earlier. It has a good colour, a fine bouquet and a taste in which the breeding of a great wine is unmistakeable, though there is still plenty of tannin. The harvest of 1971 was below average. This was the first year, incidentally, to be put in the new Lascombes bottle, where the name of the Château is worked into the glass.

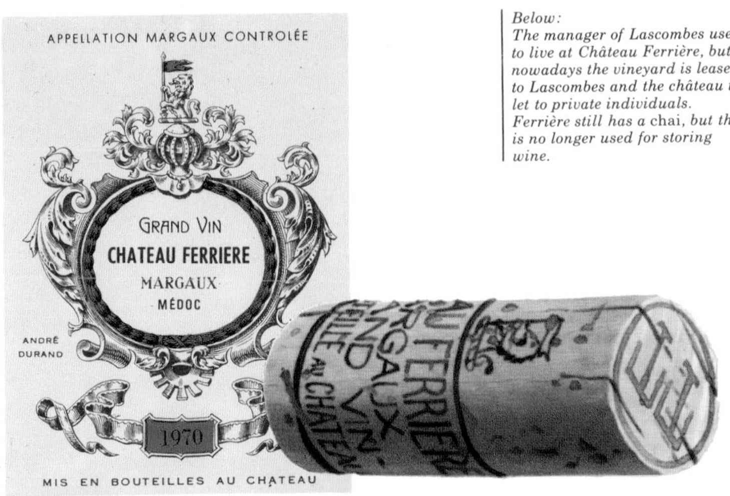

APPELLATION MARGAUX CONTROLÉE
GRAND VIN
CHATEAU FERRIERE
MARGAUX
MÉDOC
ANDRÉ
DURAND
1970
MIS EN BOUTEILLES AU CHATEAU


*Below:*
*The manager of Lascombes used to live at Château Ferrière, but nowadays the vineyard is leased to Lascombes and the château is let to private individuals. Ferrière still has a chai, but this is no longer used for storing wine.*

Ferrière derives its name from Gabriel Ferrière who was the royal Master of the Hunt in the 18th century. In 1777 he left the estate to his cousin, also called Gabriel Ferrière. His brother was later appointed Mayor of Bordeaux in 1795. In 1914 the estate finally passed out of the hands of the Ferrière family and was bought by Armand Feuillerat; at that time he also owned the neighbouring Marquis de Terme. M. Feuillerat gave Ferrière to his daughter, Madame André Durand-Feuillerat, as a dowry, and it still belongs to the Durand family. M. André Durand lives in Bordeaux.

To drink a bottle of Ferrière in the immediate vicinity of Bordeaux go to the hotel restaurant La Réserve at Pessac. This luxurious establishment is affiliated to the *Relais de Campagne* and it has Ferrière on the wine-list. The proprietor and chef is Roland Flourens, a gifted man who has also recently revived the formerly renowned Bordeaux restaurant, Dubern.

## Chau Ferrière

3rd Grand Cru Classé

Ferrière is in a number of respects exceptional. The wine, for example, can only be drunk in France, because the whole vintage is bought up by the exclusive group of country restaurants, the *Relais de Campagne*. This is possible because the production is the smallest of all the classed growths, no more than an average of 15 *tonneaux*, or 17,000 bottles. Another striking difference is that the Ferrière vineyard is leased to Château Lascombes, two minutes' walk away. Under the management of Lascombes' former proprietor, Alexis Lichine, Ferrière's vineyard was completely replanted between 1958 and 1964, with the result that both quantity and quality have, relatively speaking, greatly improved. Although Ferrière itself has a *chai*, the wine is made at Lascombes. In the cellars there I saw a separate row of casks containing the wine of this tiny property. The bottling is also done at Lascombes, where the entire estate and especially the *chai* have been splendidly modernised in recent years.

Another point where Ferrière differs from the other *crus* in Margaux is the location of the vineyard. A large part of it lies in the centre of the small town of Margaux, surrounded by a stone wall. In all, the vineyard covers an area of 5 hectares, which have a right to the name Ferrière and the *appellation* Margaux, and one hectare where rosé is produced to make Chevalier de Lascombes.

I have only tasted one Ferrière wine, the 1970 vintage. Naturally enough one automatically compares it with Lascombes, since both wines are today made by the skills of the same people, in the same cellars. Well, Château Lascombes is a second *grand cru* and Château Ferrière a third – and you can, I think, taste the difference. Compared with the Lascombes, Ferrière is slightly more rustic. The wine clearly has less fruit but more colour and more tannin. It may take more time to mature than the Lascombes of the same excellent year. It is a wine which undoubtedly has a good future ahead of it – and it is only to be hoped that the *Relais de Campagne* and their guests will be wise enough to allow this solid Margaux the time it needs.

*Left:*
*The labels of Malescot St Exupéry are numbered and state the exact number of magnums, bottles and half bottles produced. In 1971 there were 33,500.*

*Below:*
*The visitors' book of both Malescot St Exupéry and Marquis d'Alesme Becker, where visitors may sign their names. The books of many château would tempt autograph collectors.*

*Below:*
*The present Château dates from 1885 and was built in Louis XVI style on to the existing house. This was a friendly little building without pretensions. A picture of the original Château is to be found in the* Album de la Mère *of 1868, which Fernand de St Exupéry left to his heirs. The oldest cellar of the Château was built in 1861. Here is a small private reserve with several very old bottles, the oldest dating from 1878. The chais are gradually being renovated. The interior is being done up and the wooden fermentation vats have been replaced by ones of steel and cement.*

# Chau Malescot-St-Exupéry

3rd Grand Cru Classé

Château Malescot Saint-Exupéry is situated on the main street of Margaux. Two people are responsible for the double-barrelled name: Simon Malescot, attorney general to the king, and Count Jean-Baptiste de Saint-Exupéry. The former became the proprietor in 1697, the latter in 1827. The notable airman and author, Antoine de Saint-Exupéry, has also made this name well known.

Today the owners of Malescot are the hard working, wine growing Zuger family. Grandfather Zuger and after him father Paul Zuger had been in charge at Malescot, until Paul Zuger took over the estate in 1955 from the British firm of Seager Evans. Now his sons, Jean-Claude and Roger, are in charge of production, wine-making and also sales. Roger lives with his family at Malescot, while Jean-Claude and his father live at Château Marquis d'Alesme-Becker, which also belongs to the Zugers.

After the last world war Château Malescot was little more than a skeleton, but the Zugers have succeeded in turning it into a comfortable home once again.

## Wine for people with patience

The wine of Malescot comes from a vineyard of 23 hectares planted with 60% Cabernet, 30% Merlot and 10% Petit Verdot. The production averages 80 *tonneaux*, which is mainly shipped to Britain, the U.S.A., Switzerland, West Germany, Holland, Belgium and Japan.

A highly distinctive characteristic of this wine is its austerity which, for a Margaux, is fairly unusual. It is only after a long time that the delicate Margaux bouquet is released and the flavour becomes a little more friendly. Paul Zuger says: 'Yes, perhaps I make wines which require a great deal of patience on the part of the consumer!'

A very successful year was 1964, immediately followed by 1966. 1967 was a little lighter, but consequently is now pleasant to drink; obviously there can be more enjoyment from a developed but mature, light wine than from a reticent, inaccessible one. Typical of Malescot is the fact that the 1967 vintage shows no signs of fatigue even at the time of writing. On the contrary, the wine has a great deal of strength and is still a long way off its prime. To relieve the wine of some of its hardness Paul Zuger decants it some time before serving: in the case of the 1966 and younger vintages as much as three to four hours beforehand, because it is the young wines which need a lot of air in order to allow their bouquet and flavour to come to life.

The vineyard of Marquis d'Alesme Becker covers 15 hectares, of which 11 hectares are generally producing. The vineyard is planted with 50% Cabernet Sauvignon and Cabernet Franc, 40% Merlot and 10% Petit Verdot. The production averages 45 *tonneaux*.

The major foreign markets for Marquis d'Alesme are the United States, Great Britain, Switzerland, Belgium and West Germany. A small amount of the joint second label of this Château and of Château Malescot St Exupéry, Domaine du Balardin, is also sold to West Germany.

*Right and below:*
*Château Marquis d'Alesme Becker, still just as it looked in 1859. The father of Paul Zuger bought it in 1938, when he was already manager of Malescot St Exupéry. The large garden of Marquis d'Alesme adjoins the estate of Château Margaux.*

*Far right:*
*The Château gets its name from a marquis who contributed a great deal to the development of wine-growing in the Médoc. This property has been registered since 1616; justification, in 1966, for Zuger to give the label an overprint: '350th Jubilee'.*

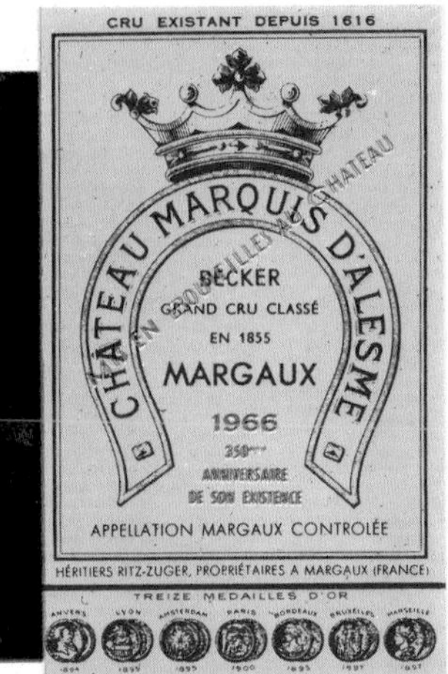


# Chau Marquis d'Alesme-Becker

3rd Grand Cru Classé

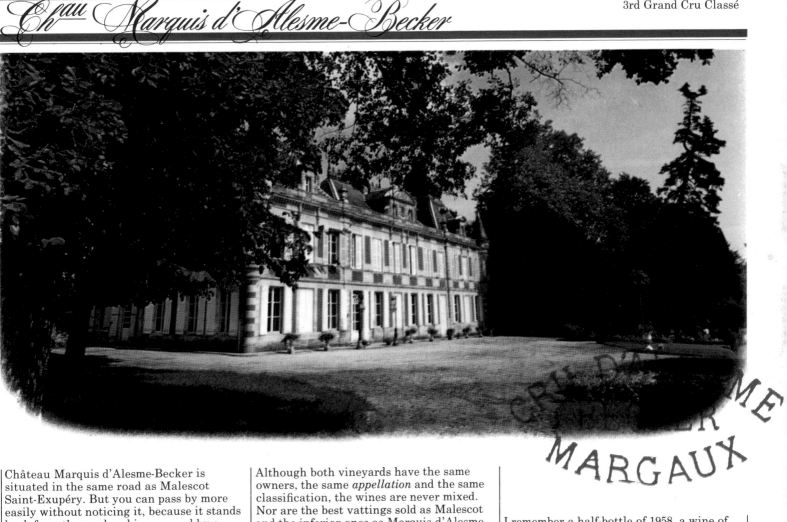

Château Marquis d'Alesme-Becker is situated in the same road as Malescot Saint-Exupéry. But you can pass by more easily without noticing it, because it stands back from the road and is screened by a park, which starts as a narrow strip between two houses and becomes increasingly wide as it gets further away from the road. The same applies to the château: at first sight it seems an optical illusion, because you are looking at it sideways on. In actual fact Marquis d'Alesme is a fairly ornate building, 12 windows wide, which fully deserves the title of château. From the charmingly furnished living rooms you look out onto the *chais*, where the wine will now be made and bottled. Before 1975 the wine was made at Château Malescot Saint-Exupéry, which belongs to the same Zuger family.

Although both vineyards have the same owners, the same *appellation* and the same classification, the wines are never mixed. Nor are the best vattings sold as Malescot and the inferior ones as Marquis d'Alesme. The wines are kept strictly apart, with one exception: the label of the second wine of the estates, Domaine de Balardin is a blend of the two, but this is only, of course, a blend of the lesser qualities.

There is a certain family likeness between Marquis d'Alesme-Becker and the wine of Malescot, but that is all. Generally speaking Marquis d'Alesme is less delicate and slightly less complex than Malescot. And whereas the latter is certainly not markedly delicate, Marquis d'Alesme can almost be classed as an indestructible wine. However long you leave it, it never seems to deteriorate.

I remember a half-bottle of 1958, a wine of an off year and moreover from a small bottle where it would have matured faster. It had a light brown colour, a respectable bouquet and – surprisingly enough – still some definite flavour. In other words, it was a typical Marquis d'Alesme.

Many wine-lovers buy a dozen bottles of good wine on the birth of a son or daughter, which is given to him or her as a 21st birthday present. Marquis d'Alesme-Becker lends itself perfectly to such a gesture, because even the off years have a very long life; at 21 years of age the wine will probably be feeling just like the happy boy or girl drinking it on coming of age.

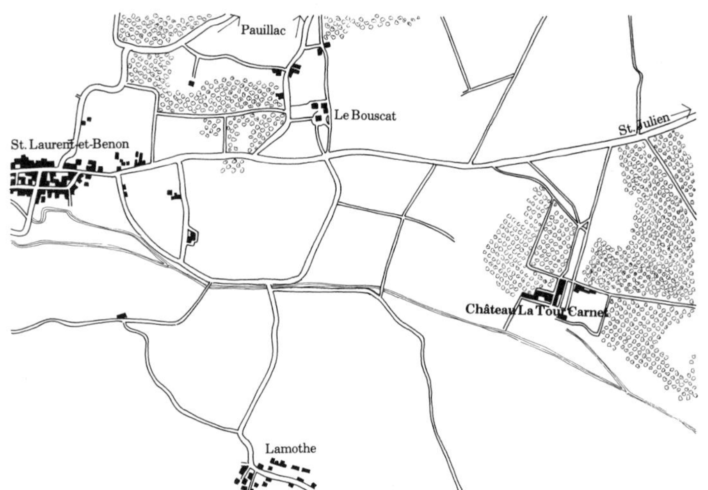


*Below:*
*Château La Tour Carnet is a genuine castle with a splendid tower, which forms part of the name. Most Médoc châteaux look nothing like the warlike, mediaeval bastion which one associates with the word castle, but this one is an exception. La Tour Carnet is encircled by a moat with two swans, which were specially fetched from England by Pierre Ginestet as being the most superior breed of swan. Other foreign dwellers on the estate are the 40 Dutch cows which supply the manure.*

When La Tour Carnet was for sale in 1962, it was even rumoured that the Queen of the Netherlands might buy it; but there are as yet no monarchs in the Médoc.

In 1965 M. Lipschitz tried to launch a non-vintage La Tour Carnet. To his great disappointment this failed. 'Why', he asks, 'can't the Bordeaux wine of poor years be treated like non-vintage champagne, which is a blend of several years?' But the claim of claret is in its vintage.

In the reception room is an attractive wine bar, which is made completely out of cases. This used to be the kitchen: in an adjacent room the large oven for baking bread can be seen.

Discoveries are constantly being made at many châteaux. At La Tour Carnet there is a secret passage – perhaps for a quick getaway – that comes out at Lesparre, far to the north.

# Chau La Tour Carnet

4th Grand Cru Classé

I first made the acquaintance of the wine of La Tour Carnet, one of the classed growths of St Laurent, entitled to the *appellation* Haut-Médoc, in one of those small but good restaurants in Bordeaux, which only the local merchants seem to know about. To accompany an excellent *entrecôte bordelais* I drank the then six-year-old 1966 La Tour Carnet, a wine which appeared a lot easier on the palate and far friendlier than most of the wines of the same year. In addition to an agreeable bouquet the wine had a ripe, soft flavour: very pleasant, but at the same time unusually advanced for a solid year like 1966. It was only much later, when I asked the present proprietor, Louis Lipschitz, about it, that I learnt the reason. He told me that he had bought the property in a very dilapidated state in 1962. The château

Right:
*The long drive leading up to the Château.*

Below:
*The archway under the broad tower used to be closed off by a drawbridge. Now there is only a fine wrought-iron gate which is usually open. On the right in the tower is M. Lipschitz's office.*

was a ruin, the vineyard virtually non-existent. Consequently, in the first two years (1963 and 1964) no more than 20 *tonneaux* were harvested as against 120 in 1974. However, the fact that the ground had lain fallow for years proved a great advantage for the young vines, which accumulated strength and made it possible to produce a successful wine like that of 1966 only four years after the first replantings. Naturally enough it was only a light wine, but thanks to the quiet force of the soil it had received sufficient body to be fully worthy of the distinction of its classification.

**From water to wine**

It almost goes without saying that the wines of La Tour Carnet will only gain in importance as the years go by. Proof of this is the 1970 vintage, which regales the eye with a deep, clear colour, the tongue with a fleshy yet charming taste and the nose with a glorious bouquet which makes you think of violets. This bouquet is highly characteristic of La Tour Carnet. As the vivacious Madame Lipschitz told me: 'The nose of our wine always reminds me of an exquisite scent. I am sometimes tempted to rub a small amount of wine between my hands and inhale the bouquet – just as you do with perfume.'

What is striking is that the Lipschitzes knew nothing about wine when they bought La Tour Carnet. That is to say, Louis knew how to open a bottle, but it went no further than that. Before buying La Tour Carnet he ran a shipping company. Wasn't that rather a big change? 'No, not really. I have switched from water to wine, and both of them are liquids, aren't they? You must make sure you have a good staff, good vines, good tools – and goodwill, because it calls for an extraordinary amount of hard work. What we have already done would normally take a generation.'

There is no doubt that a great deal of money and labour has been invested. The vineyard now covers 45 hectares (80% Cabernet, 15% Merlot and 5% Verdot), all the *chais* and fermentation vats have been renewed, and the Château itself has been completely restored. In addition there is the annual investment in brand-new casks, in which the new-born wine is put to mature two years.

**Château of treasures**

It is a pity that the people who drink La Tour Carnet (they live mainly in the United States, Belgium, Holland, Switzerland and Denmark) can not see the Château in real life but have to be content with the picture on the label. For La Tour Carnet is one of the few genuine castles of the Médoc. It dates from the 13th century, when it was known as Château de Saint Laurent. It takes its present name from the Seigneur de Carnet, who took up residence there in 1427. He was one of the many lords in the area who some 20 years later fell out of favour with the French king because he took the side of the English. Good wine was already being made there, too: in 1407, wine from this estate already sold for nearly twice as much as red Graves.

Anyone visiting the Château now takes a walk, as it were, down the centuries. This begins at the magnificent, 18th-century railings, painted blue, after which you pass the 17th-century workers' quarters. Then you see the moat and the 13th-century tower. After that you go into the main building; here the ground floor also dates from the 13th century, the upper floors the 17th century. Downstairs is the reception room where visitors can sample the wine, while upstairs there are a number of salons and an impressive hall, where neither expense nor effort has been spared in decoration and furnishings. You will find, for example, a magnificent, centuries-old safe, once proof of the skill and craftsmanship of a master locksmith. Louis Lipschitz never fails to demonstrate to visitors how this hand-made showpiece can only be opened via all manner of secret panels. And what lies inside? As you might guess: a bottle, a magnum and a double magnum of Château La Tour Carnet, the real treasures of this exquisite Château.

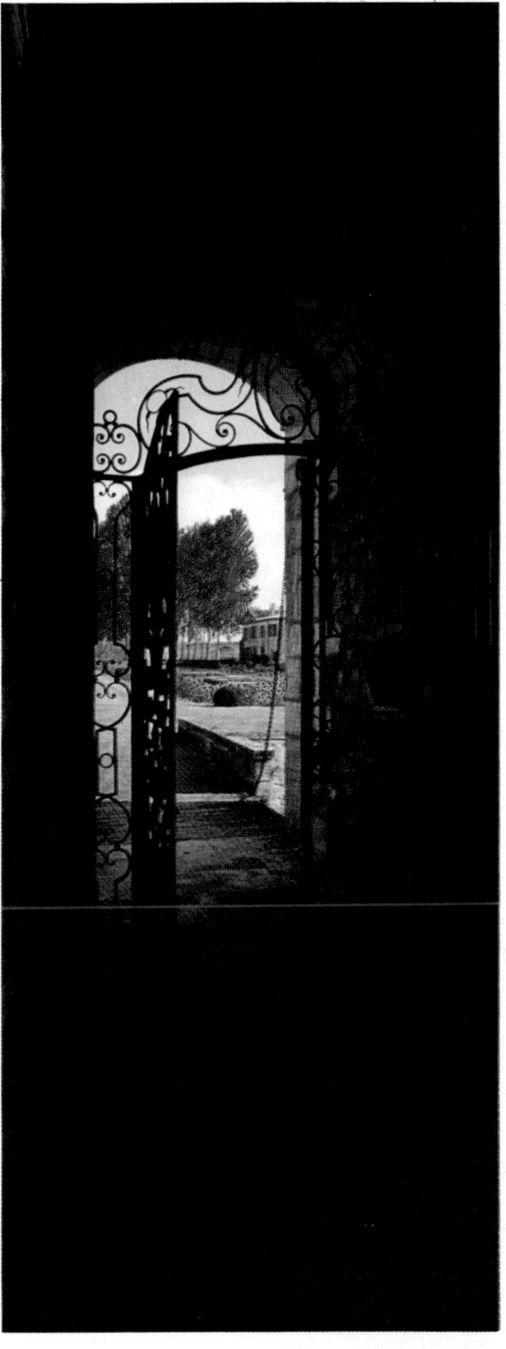

*Left:*
*A great deal of attention is devoted to the presentation of the bottles. Not only is the label very well designed, but for several markets another small label is often added on the back; this gives some more information about the Château and the work being done there.*

*Left centre:*
*Rear view of the château, which is not occupied; it is only used for offices, including the administration of Château Larose-Trintaudon, which also belongs to M. Forner.*

*Below left:*
*Long rows of wooden hoppers lie ready for the vintage to begin; on horse-drawn carts they will be taken to the vineyard and filled with grapes.*

5th Grand Cru Classé

# Ch de Camensac

Château de Camensac, *appellation contrôlée* Haut-Médoc, is by no means one of the best-known names in the classification of 1855. This is a pity, for the estate has since 1966 been producing excellent wines, which are perhaps the best of St Laurent. This is the work of two men: M. E. H. Forner (who together with two other people bought de Camensac in 1965) and the famous Professor Emile Peynaud, *docteur-ingénieur oenologue* (who gave his expert advice). At the outset they found themselves confronted with an estate which was completely impoverished. For many years the vineyard, the wine-making equipment and the Château had been entirely neglected. Looking back on the wines of that period M. Forner remembers: 'When we bought the Château we were forced to buy the whole 1964 harvest along with it. In the Médoc this was a reasonable year, but the wine of de Camensac turned out to be totally undrinkable. We tried to select the best casks and this wine was even bottled. They are still in our cellar. Ten, fifteen years after harvesting they are still unpalatable, and will remain so – in spite of being a classed growth.

Not discouraged by this Monsieur Forner, together with Professor Peynaud, set to work. They developed a seven-year plan for restoring the wine to its former status. It was lucky that the new owner had sufficient means at his disposal (he had been a contractor), because the Professor was exacting about what had to be done.

### Enormous investments justified

First of all the vineyard had to be completely restored. Only 15 of the present 56 hectares proved to be productive; the rest had to be replanted. The vines are 60% Cabernet Sauvignon, 20% Cabernet Franc and 20% Merlot – according to Professor Peynaud the ideal vine combination for this soil. Every piece of equipment had to be replaced, fermentation vats, bottling plant and so on. A third requirement was an extremely strict selection: only the very best vattings were to be used, which was bound to limit production seriously for the first few years. The last requirement is the most costly, because the investment involved recurs each year: Professor Peynaud insists on the use of brand-new oak casks for each vintage – a luxury which even many second growths cannot afford. But the result was reward enough. In a letter to M. Forner, dated 21 March 1969, Professor Peynaud wrote that at a blind tasting session the 1967 vintage had been classed on a level with the second growths. Similarly, in May 1970 the Professor was able to report that the 1969 de Camensac had finished second at a professional tasting of 14 different *grands crus*.

### St Julien and Pauillac together?

My personal view, after tasting the wines of de Camensac, is that they are the perfect

The elegance and bouquet of de Camensac are appreciated by the couture house of Courrèges and by Maison Coty, the perfume firm. Louis de Funès, a popular French comedian, is another customer.

M. Forner sells mainly through exclusive agencies in export markets such as Britain, the USA, Belgium, Switzerland, Holland and Denmark. It is therefore often difficult to find his wine in France, even in Bordeaux itself.

Emile Forner is a perfectionist. In each case of wine sold to French customers he includes a letter, stating how the wine should be served: not too warm and preferably decanted an hour or two in advance. Tactfully, he writes that his advice is not holy writ – but he hopes that his suggestions will show off the wine to best advantage. Even the French need guidance!

*Right:*
*The cement fermentation vats where the grape juice turns into wine, and the men who watch through the process the gradual development of the liquid.*

*Below:*
*All the wine of Château de Camensac is bottled on the estate. Here the necessary preparations are made to close the bottles with sound, strong corks. The stock of corks, with the name of the Château, the year and the* appellation *burnt into them, must keep pace with the supply of wine.*

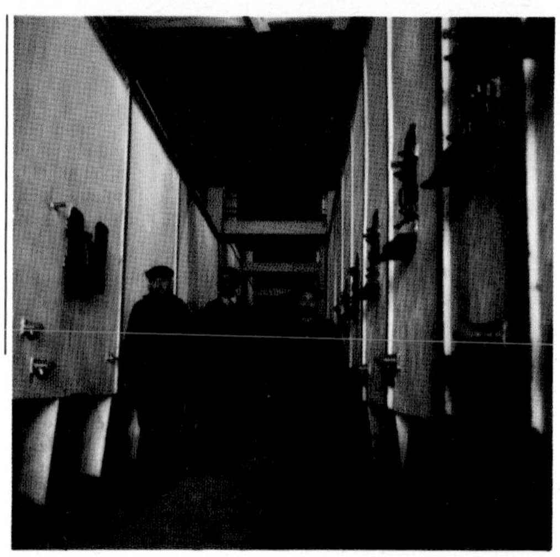



synthesis between those of St Julien and Pauillac. They are accommodating and have at the same time a great deal of body – even in lean years like 1968. At the beginning of 1975 I tasted a 1968 Château de Camensac and was extremely surprised by the deep colour, the full bouquet, the generous flavour and the still clearly discernible vitality: purely and simply a perfect example of a fine wine in a very difficult year. Two truly great wines are without a doubt those of 1966, 1970 and maybe 1974. I tasted the last from the cask. The first two had a deep, dark colour, the scent and flavour of fully ripe fruit and a marvellous completeness. The 1966 vintage was not unpleasant to drink, but will certainly continue to mature for a further 10 years. I hardly dare to guess at the possible life of the 1970, and the 1974 might well turn out to be nearly as good. It is reassuring to know that the production of de Camensac has already reached 200 to 250 *tonneaux*. Moreover, the vineyard can still be extended by some nine hectares.

### Future plans

Before other renovations are begun the Château and the park are being restored. The building dates from the last century and only served to accommodate the office, but guests are made welcome here now. From the front of the house there is a view over part of the vineyard, and from the steps at the back, over a large fir standing in solitary splendour, an undulating carpet of vines and a charming little park, which was still under construction when I visited the estate.

Everything that is being done at Château de Camensac speaks of expertise and the owners' unshakeable belief: 'We are a great growth and we shall be worthy of our calling!'

*Right and below:*
*The Château, seen from different angles. The building is assumed to date from somewhere around 1834. It is occupied by M. Edmond Gugès, but he has nothing directly to do with the making of the wine. Edmond Gugès is, however, a brother of André Gugès, whose sons Georges-Claude and Christian are in charge of the day-to-day running of the property. The château has a lot of old furniture, especially in the dining room, the reception hall and the salon, with its lovely stained-glass windows. Unfortunately, visitors are not normally allowed to visit the château; and they have to be satisfied with seeing the chais – interesting to wine lovers, but with less artistic appeal.*

## Chau Belgrave

5th Grand Cru Classé

My first experience of the wine of Belgrave was definitely not the most enjoyable. During a visit to the Médoc I happened to see a bottle of Château Belgrave, *appellation contrôlée* Haut-Médoc, standing between some ordinary table wines in a grocer's shop in Margaux. It had no year on it and cost 14 francs – not much for a classed growth, so I immediately bought it. This proved to be a mistake; the wine was very disappointing indeed. There was nothing in it reminiscent of a fine wine and I thought I detected something jarring in the flavour, giving it an unpleasant balance and taste.

When I later visited the Château I naturally asked about this. My questions were answered by Georges-Claude Gugès, the technical manager. In 1968 it was decided not to market any Belgrave, because the quality was too poor. The whole vintage of 70,000 litres was therefore sold to a merchant in Bordeaux for not more than 0·75 francs per litre, obviously with the intention of its being sold without bearing the estate name. To the amazement of the owners, however, countless bottles of Belgrave with no vintage appeared in many grocers' shops, at the high price of 14 francs! This in itself was bad enough, but the end of the wretched affair was by no means in sight, because the supply from the merchant turned out to be inexhaustible. Years and years later his customers were still receiving a full quota, and moreover Georges-Claude Gugès learnt that the wine merchant had even had extra labels printed. However, the world of wine is complicated and it does happen that a wine is sold in good faith as being one particular kind and then appears as something else: all the more reason for being careful about the sources of supply from whom you buy.

### A disappointing visit

I wish that my visit to Belgrave could have washed away the taste of the grocer's wine for good, but unfortunately that was not to be. I was disappointed with the reception room – there are limits to picturesque shabbiness – and it is impossible to resist commenting that attention to detail must be important with any product as sensitive

The latest edition of *Bordeaux et Ses Vins* lists three Châteaux Belles Graves, three Châteaux Bellegrave, one Château des Belles Graves and one Château Belgrave! Only the last was classified in 1855, so always note both the spelling of the name and the parish where the château is situated.

The man who gave Belgrave a great reputation was M. Bruno-Deves. After him the property was owned by M. Jules Canaferina, who was awarded in 1939 a diploma for his well-kept vineyard. He was the man who built the cellars which are still in use today.

Belgrave is one of the few châteaux that you can reach by train, for it is quite near the miniature railway station of St Laurent-St Julien, where once in a while a slow local train arrives.

In the reception room of Belgrave there is a sign with a comforting message: *'Pour éloigner l'heure du trepas, buvez Médoc à tout repas.'* This means: 'To postpone the hour of death, drink Médoc at every meal.'

*Right and below: Vintage time at Belgrave. The girl picks the grapes, putting them in a basket which she then empties into the metal container the carrier has strapped to his back. He in turn transports the weight of grapes to the main receiving holder, into which he tips his load with an adroit twist of his shoulders. The vineyard of Belgrave is not divided up but is in one piece. The average age of the vines is fairly old, half being 25 years old or more, a quarter 8 to 10 years and another quarter 4 to 6 years of age.*

## Château Belgrave

as fine wine. I was shocked by the presshouse and the *chais*. Everything looked filthy and positively dirt-grimed. The equipment seemed to be extremely out of date and very poorly maintained. There were even holes in the roof of the bottling hall. It is perhaps unwise for an outsider to comment, but the appearance was totally uncared-for. Why did everything seem so neglected? The Gugès family bought the property in 1956, and in my opinion they are jeopardising the reputation of this fifth growth, perhaps hoping to save money – but at the cost of quality.

The whole estate totals 80 hectares, of which slightly more than half are productive. The total yield is about 160 *tonneaux*, of which some is sold under the second label, Royale Darousse. The vine species are 45% Cabernet, 45% Merlot and 10% Petit Verdot. As I had expected, the wine was disappointing. As far as the 1970 vintage is concerned you would probably say there was little chance of spoiling it, but at Belgrave it cannot be considered successful. The bouquet was flat, without much fruit or finesse, the flavour was thin and without refinement, the overall impression being a rather meagre wine. Nor was the 1969 vintage a wine which was attractive; the wine was not exactly bad, but it could not be called good either. A velvety colour was followed by a reasonable nose, then a thin, rather hard taste without charm and nuance. Honesty forces me to add that I tasted these wines under the most thankless conditions, plus of course the psychological effect of the impressions left on me by the *chais*. At the correct temperature, with the right sort of food and in convivial company, these wines may perhaps show better.

An indication that I was unlucky is that at the Concours Général Agricole in Paris Belgrave was awarded a silver medal for its 1966 vintage and a bronze for its 1967 vintage. Apart from private French customers, the Château sells its wine to the United States, Great Britain, West Germany, Belgium and Holland.

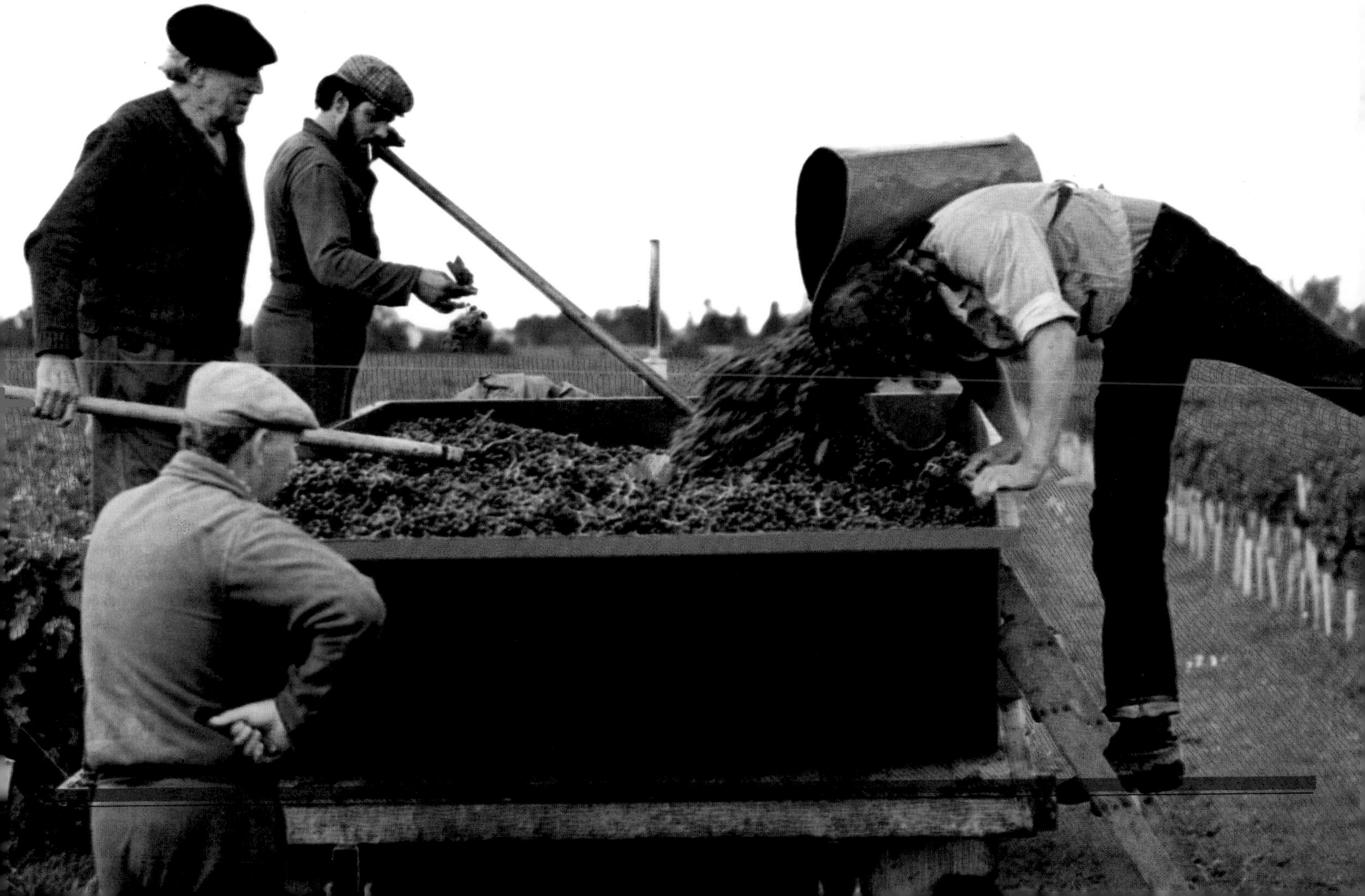

*Below:*
*Some of the interesting items connected with wine in the reception room at Ducru-Beaucaillou.*

*Bottom:*
*Château Ducru-Beaucaillou is imposing. Under the sweeping flight of steps are cellars, unusual in the Médoc, where the water is close to the surface of the ground. The Victorian towers make the Ducru label easy to pick out.*

*Right:*
*The Victorian hall inside the château. On the walls are several paintings from the Breughelian school.*

*Far right:*
*The wine museum, with a considerable number of old bottles, many of them dating from the 19th century. The cellar where the bottles are laid is at the lowest level of the château; it is very dark, as stores of wine should not be exposed to light.*

# Ch^au Ducru-Beaucaillou

2nd Grand Cru Classé

The first sight of Château Ducru-Beaucaillou makes you think that if a great wine isn't made here, then where else could it be? It is a majestic, square building flanked by two massive Victorian towers. In all its imposing glory it crowns the top of a hill rising above the Gironde. On the first floor are the charming rooms where the proprietor, Jean-Eugène Borie, and his wife Monique live. Below are the vast cellars where the harvests of two years lie maturing in predominantly new *barriques*.

**One of my favourites**

There in the half-light, on a fresh winter's day, I tasted several wines in the company of Monsieur Borie and the cellar master, André Prévôt, only to find my opinion confirmed that Ducru-Beaucaillou is one of my favourite Médocs. What attracts me in particular is its unmistakeable charm. Year in, year out this estate produces perfectly balanced wines, which smile back at you from your glass even while still young. Of course, when young they contain considerable tannin, but this is hardly a disturbing element, since it is the harsh tannins that give the wine the longevity to develop the fine, complex bouquet, smooth texture and mellow taste and aftertaste which make this wine extraordinary in outstanding vintages. At the beginning of 1975 I tasted the 1970 Ducru-Beaucaillou, a wine with a dark, almost black colour, a taste like baskets full of fruit, and a reticent but very charming smell. It is one of those wines which you should perhaps drink around 1985, but it proved a far from pungent experience for the palate. It is a wine which I can recommend to anyone with money, patience and a good wine merchant.

The same applies to the wines of 1971 and 1973, which are less exceptional but still of a very high class. I also drank a 1961 at Beaucaillou (with *entrecôte bordelais* and some cheeses. This was likewise a superb wine which has a long way to go yet before it is fully mature. The reason why the 1961

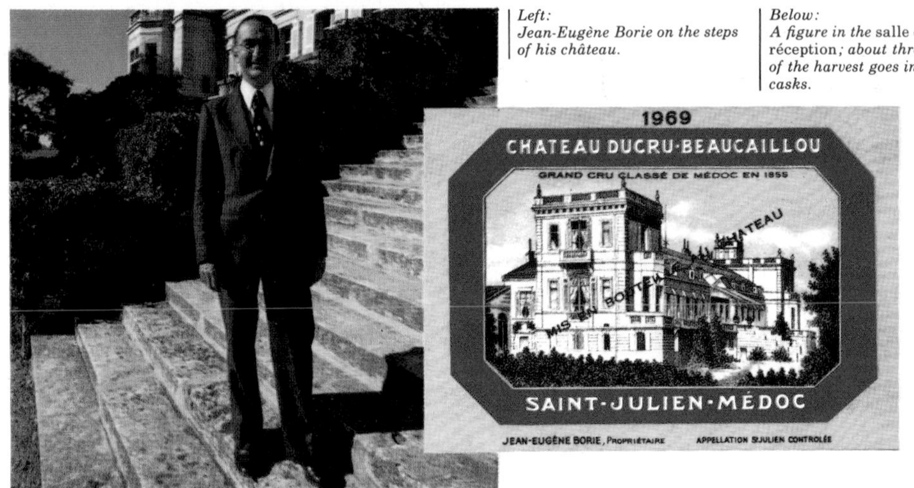


*Left:*
*Jean-Eugène Borie on the steps of his château.*

*Below:*
*A figure in the* salle de réception*; about three-quarters of the harvest goes into new casks.*

When I tasted the 1970 wine with the 70-year old *maître de chai* André Prévôt, he said: 'How beautiful this wine is – do you think I will live to drink it in its prime?'

Many *grand cru* châteaux have sets of plates bearing a picture of the château on them. These are made from old models by the firm of Haviland in Limoges. M. Borie is also on the board of this firm really as a hobby, although his son-in-law is an important executive at Haviland, which he vigorously promotes.

Château Ducru-Beaucaillou

at many châteaux was more successful than the (then) 'year of the century' 1959 is, according to Jean-Eugène Borie, largely due to the fact that wine-makers were better equipped in 1961 to deal with such an exceptional harvest. Should it interest you to know at what temperature this superior St Julien shows to full advantage, it is 18 degrees centigrade. Typical of the perfectionist streak in M. Borie is that while I was there he quickly checked the temperature of all the wines with a pocket thermometer.

### Early fame

In 1800, M. and Mme Ducru became proprietors of the vineyard of the *beaux cailloux*, or beautiful pebbles. The siliceous soil in many parts of the Médoc usually produces very good wines, and the wine of Ducru-Beaucaillou is no exception. Mme Ducru's father was in fact so fond of it that when he was chairman of the Bordeaux Chamber of Commerce he had the traditional glass of water replaced by a glass of Ducru-Beaucaillou. Unfortunately the story doesn't go on to tell us whether subsequent meetings took place under an increasingly inspired leadership, but who can doubt it!

It was on 3 March 1866 that Ducru-Beaucaillou changed hands for the fabulous sum of one million francs. The purchaser was the well-to-do wife of Nathaniel Johnston, Jr, a member of a famous Bordeaux merchant family. The Johnstons made the wine even better than it already was, winning numerous medals and other marks of honour. It was they who had the angular towers built, perhaps to make the grandeur of the building a fitting complement to that of its wine. Finally, in 1942, Ducru-Beaucaillou came into the hands of the Borie family. There was little left then to justify its former fame, for recent proprietors had neglected the quality of the wine over the years. Today's wines are proof of the successful revival. Château Ducru-Beaucaillou is now worthy of its place among the second classed growths. The Ducru-Beaucaillou vineyards cover some 43 hectares planted with 65% Cabernet Sauvignon, 25% Merlot and a 10% mix of Cabernet Franc and Petit Verdot. The annual production varies between 120 and 190 *tonneaux*, which find their way in the main to the United States, Britain, France, Belgium and Switzerland.

Beychevelle is not regularly inhabited, but the three proprietors of the Achille Fould family (Aymar, Etienne and Marie-Geneviève) have apartments which they sometimes use for short stays. Aymar Achille Fould is a famous man in France: he has been Secretary of State both for Defence and for Transport. His father Gaston held the post of Minister of Agriculture.

# Ch^au^ Beychevelle

4th Grand Cru Classé

*Opposite page, top:*
*The magnificent* cour d'honneur *of Beychevelle with its impressive cedar. In the summer hundreds of passers-by stop to photograph this graceful château.*

*Opposite page, bottom:*
*Bird's eye view of Beychevelle. In addition to the terraces the château has four separate courtyards. The cellars are on the far left.*

*Below left:*
*A glimpse of the second-year* chai, *noticeably cooler than the higher first-year* chai.

*Below centre:*
*Part of the vast reserves kept at the Château.*

*Right:*
*The little sphinx looks out longingly from the balustrade behind the Château at the waters of the Gironde. This is one of the most pleasant views of the river.*

Château Beychevelle

For Jean-Louis de Nogaret de Lavalette, Duc d'Epernon, 1587 was a memorable year, for in that year he acquired three things: the title of *Admiral de France*, a dynamic young wife called Marguerite, and as dowry the Château du Médoc. Very soon the estate was nicknamed Beychevelle, because all the ships passing on the river received instructions *baissez les voiles* (lower sails), as a mark of honour to the Admiral. The name Beychevelle remained, the owner did not. The Château passed through many hands before, in 1757, Marquis Brassier reconstructed the buildings on a grand scale. He replaced warlike battlements with peaceful balustrades and had a whole new château built in the style of Louis XV. This was done with the taste of the period, and it is one of the finer pieces of architecture in the Bordeaux region.

In 1875 the estate was sold to Armand Heine. His daughter married Charles Achille-Fould and their descendants – three in number – are the present owners. If they stand on the splendid rear steps, they can enjoy a view of an ornamental, Versailles-like garden and far away in the distance, at the end of a long stretch of lawn, the Gironde. The Château's name is responsible for the ship which appears on Beychevelle labels to this day.

**Appealing wines**

The vineyard has 48 productive hectares which are planted with 68% Cabernet Sauvignon, 28% Merlot and 4% Cabernet Franc. The yield is 200 to 250 *tonneaux*, which are largely bought by Britain, the United States, France, Belgium and Switzerland. (There is also a second wine, Clos de l'Admiral, which is still good for some 50 *tonneaux*, depending on the year of course.)

A decidedly great year is 1966; the 1970 and 1971 vintages also deserve the same designation. I find in them everything a wine should have or acquire: a beautiful, seductive colour, an elegant and yet rich bouquet, a generous, supple, distinguished flavour and a telling aftertaste.

In light years Beychevelle also makes pleasant drinking. The 1968 wine was charming, fragrant, with a feathery-light taste – lovely when you feel like drinking a good bottle of red Bordeaux. The 1964 vintage was a very successful wine, whose bouquet verged on the sultry with strong reminiscences of fruit.

**Differences in temperature**

The man immediately responsible for Beychevelle is *régisseur* Maurice Ruelle, assisted by *maître de chais* Robert Raymond, who dominates the vast (and yet really too small) *chais*. An unusual thing is that the wine changes temperature three times during its sojourn in the cellars. After fermentation is finished the wine passes to the casks in the first-year *chais*, where the temperature is slightly lower. In its second year it goes underground, rare in the Médoc. When bottling takes place the wine goes back to the wooden fermentation vats, which are only separated from the outside by a wooden roof.

M. Raymond maintains that the changes in temperature are very good for the young wine – and judging from the end product you can only believe him!

*Bottom left:*
*Bottles of Branaire-Ducru ready for packing and shipment. The major markets for the wine are Great Britain, the United States, Belgium and Japan. Apart from standard bottles, Branaire-Ducru is also available in half bottles, magnums, double magnums, jeroboams and impériales.*

*Bottom right:*
*Important aspects when judging a wine are its colour and limpidity, which is why dim cellars usually have extra candles around. Here* maître de chai *Marcel Renom samples a wine. M. Renom has worked at Branaire-Ducru since 1963 and is one of the 25 persons who are permanently employed at the Château. The overall management – apart of course from M. Tapie himself – is in the hands of manager Joseph Berrouet.*

The vineyard of Branaire-Ducru has many old vines: at least half are 25 years or more.

The wine families of the Médoc are often related. For example, the sister of Jean-Michel Tapie is married to M. Tari, the proprietor of Château Giscours.

As a mark of honour to the previous proprietors, the label not only bears the names of Duluc and Ducru, but also in the corners you will find the coronets of the noble families who succeeded M. Ducru: Marquis Carbonier de Marsar, Vicomte du Périer de Larsan, and Comte et Comtesse J. de la Tour.

# Chau Branaire-Ducru

4th Grand Cru Classé

I have always had a special, personal affection for Branaire-Ducru, because the 1959 vintage from this Château was one of the first really great wines I ever drank. No doubt the wine was then still much too young, but I vividly remember how a whole new world suddenly opened up before me: I had never dreamed how good wine could be. That one bottle told me more about wine than everything I had seen, heard or read till then. From that experience my wife joined me – we progressed to many other delights. In that moment the point of no return had been reached for our savings, our library and how we spend our holidays.

Now, some ten years later, I still find Branaire very attractive. It is above all a wine with character, with a taste and a bouquet all its own. Sometimes I discover a hint of violets, then of geraniums, then of almonds, and now and again of roses. The proprietor, M. Jean-Michel Tapie, rightly said: 'I have heard so many flowers mentioned when people describe our wine.' What is also typical is that Branaire-Ducru always makes a fairly solid impression, but never an aggressive one: in that it is typical of a fine St Julien.

I was impressed by the 1973 vintage, which I sampled from the cask. You could already taste something of the latent, delicate bouquet and the strong personality, but the most striking thing of all was the enormously long aftertaste, something that might not have been expected in this particular vintage when quantity rather than quality was the prevailing trait. The 1972 was lighter and the bouquet of

*Right:*
*The wine of Branaire-Ducru is not bottled until about 30 months after harvesting. The chai is partly underground, and has an aluminium ceiling which keeps the temperature constant. Note the cushions of black mould on the walls. Practically all the wine matures in new barriques, the oak used mostly coming from Central Europe; M. Tapie thinks it is better than French oak, because it tends to contain more tannin.*

*Below:*
*The orangery, now used for receiving large parties of visitors. Here a hundred people can lunch or dine comfortably; the ground is covered with neatly raked gravel. To the right of the orangery is a modern kitchen where the meals are prepared.*

*Bottom:*
*Front view of the old Château, which dates from 1794. Once through the front door you are in a spacious hall with rooms leading off it. The white stone staircase leading upward is a fine piece of design, dating from the same period as the construction of the château. The interior has been kept sober in style, unlike other châteaux where the decor is often exuberant and finishings elaborate.*

flowers was also present at an early age. The 1970 vintage is a truly great wine with a magnificent nose and a profound flavour, noble and masculine, but certainly not without charm.

### Non-vintage château bottling

Whoever visits Branaire-Ducru on a sunny day must make a point of wandering into the park, because there you will find a charming summerhouse on a hillock, which offers a view over the vineyards of St Julien. The vineyard of Branaire covers 45 hectares and is planted with 70% Cabernet, 25% Merlot and 5% Petit Verdot. The production averages 130 *tonneaux*. The château itself stands directly opposite Beychevelle and dates from 1794. It is sometimes occupied by the Tapie family, particularly during the school holidays; the children go to school in Bordeaux and so the parents live in town most of the year. This does not mean that Jean-Michel is not personally interested in his wine. Far from it: his profession, his Château and his parish are sources of great inspiration to him.
He regards the commune of St Julien-Beychevelle with personal affection. The area is small, the quality high; the number of estates is limited, but these are very well maintained.

Another of M. Tapie's pet notions is his view about undated wines. Most of the châteaux which experimented with non-vintage wines in the 1960s have since given up, but this does not apply to Branaire-Ducru. Jean-Michel Tapie thinks it pointless to have to sell a wine from a lean year either declassified, or under the estate name with the date. Whichever way you look at it, it remains an off vintage. He holds that it is better to improve such poor years by adding some wine from a greater year (obviously from the same Château). Then the customer gets a better non-vintage wine and the Château does not lose its profit. It is therefore a rule at Branaire-Ducru that a reserve of all good vintages is laid up to improve the indifferent years. The difficulty is that most consumers want to drink vintage wines, which limits considerably the market for a non-vintage at a high price. Most of the other châteaux have given up the practice, but for the time being M. Tapie is continuing to make non-vintage château wine.

### What's in the name?

Every now and again it is rumoured that Branaire-Ducru would like to shorten its name simply to Château Branaire. The parenthesised addition Duluc-Ducru would then be dropped. M. Tapie assures me, however, that he has no intention of altering the Château's original name. Both the former owners, M. Louis du Luc, oenologist, and M. G. Ducru, did so much to improve the growth in the nineteenth century that their names should continue to receive honourable mention on the wine's label. It is probably also thanks to the efforts of these two gentlemen that Branaire was given the status of a fourth growth during the last century – and Branaire is still justifying its reputation today.

M. Gruaud was a disciplinarian. To keep his staff hard at work he would keep a lookout over the property from the château tower. Woe betide anyone lazing in the vineyard or raising a bottle to his mouth! After each harvest M. Gruaud indicated by means of flags what type of wine had been made: the German flag meant a supple wine, the British flag an assertive wine, the Dutch flag something in between. This was a clever idea, although national tastes are no longer so sharply differentiated.

There is a song called *Le Roi des Vins*, which was sung for Gruaud-Larose-Sarget at the celebration for the *Exposition de Bordeaux* in 1907.

*Below left:*
*Front view of the Château. At the height of summer the only sound may be the hiss of the sprinklers watering the beautiful garden. In 1974 the park was awarded a diploma of honour by the* Société d'Horticulture de la Gironde.

*Below right:*
*In the vast entrance to the* chais *a number of medals are displayed. The wine of Gruaud-Larose has won awards for many years.*

*Below:*
*Stylish brands on the cases depict the Château.*

*Right:*
*The label of Gruaud-Larose, which is sold exclusively through the well-known shippers, Cordier.*

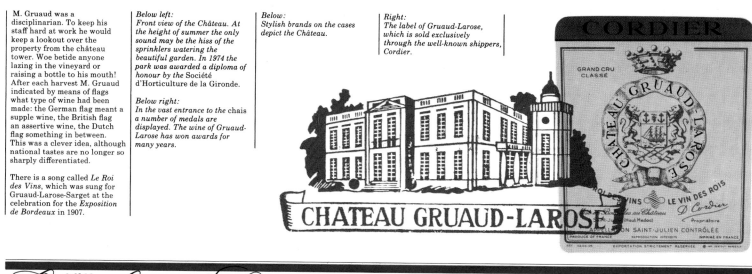

# Chau Gruaud-Larose

2nd Grand Cru Classé

Gruaud-Larose is certainly not the easiest of names for a Château which is largely sold in non-French-speaking countries. But it evolved because in 1757 M. Gruaud grouped a number of small vineyards together to form one large one, under his name Gruaud. Eventually a descendant of the first owner took over the property. His name was Larose, and he immediately linked this to the estate, hence Gruaud-Larose. In the nineteenth century the estate was split into two parts, both of which once again bore the name of their respective *propriétaires*. So for a long time there were two Châteaux Gruaud-Larose: one called Gruaud-Larose-Sarget, the other Gruaud-Larose-Faure. Finally the divided vineyard was joined together again by M. Désiré Cordier in 1936, and since then the reputation of this estate has steadily improved. M. Désiré Cordier did not add his name to the property, but a diminutive portrait of him used to be affixed to the Cordier bottle. This was intended more as a distinguishing mark for all the great wines from the house of Cordier than as a personal glorification, and from that time on the 'man with the moustache' appeared on the bottles of Talbot, Meyney and other châteaux, at least up until 1970.

## Selection of grapes

Georges Pauli, the technical manager of all the Cordier estates, is still young. He was not averse to reintroducing methods which were traditional at the beginning of this century. What is primarily involved is certain last-minute care of the vineyard prior to the vintage. What happens at Gruaud-Larose and Talbot is that three weeks before picking starts, workers go through the vineyard removing the leaves which cover the grapes. Now, in the last – often crucial – weeks the sun can strike the grapes directly.

Another unusual event takes place in July, at least in those years when the production threatens to become too vast. At this early stage quantity is already sacrificed to quality at Gruaud-Larose and Talbot by a selective cutting. Some grapes are cut off. These are not collected as they would be during harvesting, but simply fall to the ground and rot away. The remaining grapes grow and ripen more easily when this is done. So in this vineyard nature is to some extent forced to make a good wine in an indifferent year.

The size of the vineyard is proof enough that these practices are no mere sinecure: that of Gruaud-Larose alone covers 78 hectares, planted with 70% Cabernet

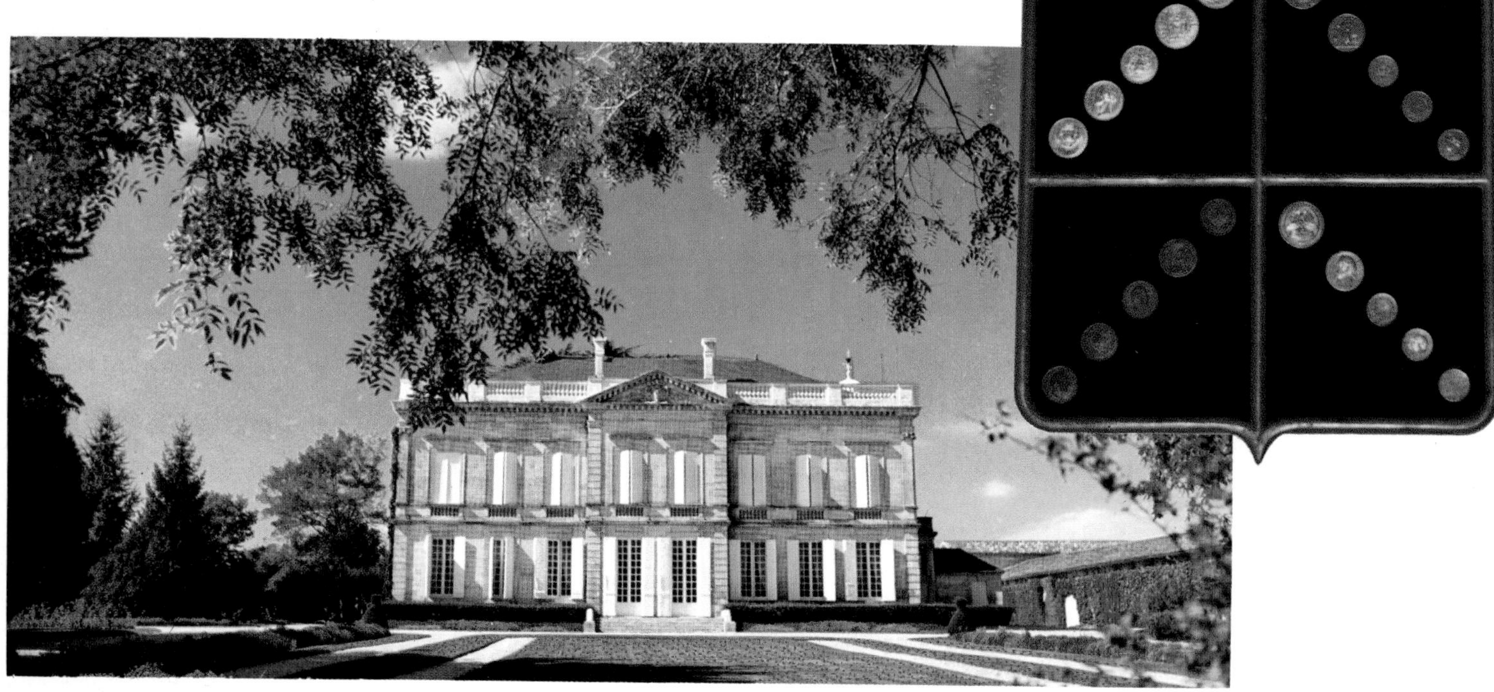

The guest room of Gruaud-Larose offers the comforts of both an old-fashioned four-poster bed and a modern air-conditioning unit.

The year 1965 was definitely not an auspicious one for Gruaud-Larose; not only was the harvest very disappointing, but one of the *chais* burnt down, with the result that half the 1964 harvest was lost as well.

In 1971 a 100-year old bottle of Gruaud-Larose-Sarget was bought by M. Zino Davidoff for 10,000 francs at an auction in the George V hotel in Paris.

At the Château two old hands are in charge of the vineyard and the cellars. They are *chef de culture* Raoul Gourdon, and *maître de chai* Lucien Moreau. M.

*Right:*
*View of part of the cellars and the vineyard from the Château tower. 780,000 bottles are stored in the cellar; the older ones are re-corked every 35 years.*

*Far right:*
*In the Château's own laboratory the evolution of the wine is carefully studied.*

*Below:*
*The spacious drawing-room, which is furnished in the style of Louis XVI and decorated in sugar-candy colours. The round sofa resembles a huge cream cake.*

*Bottom:*
*View of the elegant dining room, used for formal and official entertaining.*

Sauvignon, 20% Merlot, 5% Cabernet Franc and 5% Petit Verdot.

**King of wines, wine of kings**

It was M. Larose in the last century who gave the wine of Gruaud-Larose its great reputation. He publicised his wine to the French smart set, and launched an effective slogan which was a good piece of public relations: *'Le roi des vins, le vin des rois'*. Château Gruaud-Larose still uses this motto, which certainly is not particularly modest, on the label. To my mind it is misleading and perhaps out of step with Gruaud-Larose today, for it gives the impression that Gruaud-Larose is a powerful, masculine wine, when in fact it is one of the more amiable wines from the commune of St Julien. The oldest Gruaud-Larose I have tasted is the 1953 vintage, the youngest that of 1973 – and both of these have a graciousness and elegance which you would ascribe rather to a queen than to a king. Of course they possess strength, depth and fruit. But through this you taste their refinement. Someone once said that this wine made him think of the music of Vivaldi, and that I can well understand. But because the percentage of Cabernet Sauvignon is high and the young wine remains for at least two years in new oak *barriques*, this exquisite wine requires time to mature slowly.

I found the 1967 vintage, for example, very good indeed. Seven years after its birth the wine was as lively as ever and was still improving. The colour was lovely, the bouquet beautiful, full of diversity, the flavour was very pleasant, the aftertaste excellent. A great future undoubtedly awaits the 1970 vintage, and the 1971 vintage is another to be reckoned with. The latter was full of colour and fruit and might well be among the most successful Médocs of that year. The harvest of 1972 produced a less complete wine, but 1973 has a fine colour, flowery bouquet and a pleasant taste. It is a reassuring thought that Gruaud-Larose produces no less than 400 *tonneaux* per annum: a wine like this can satisfy a large public.

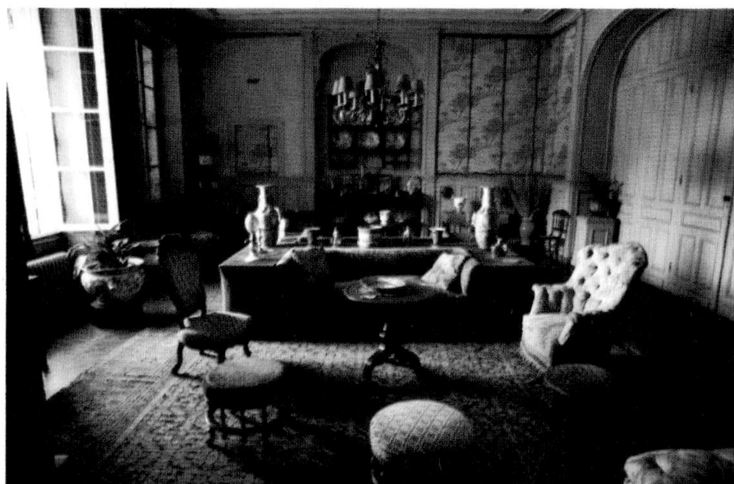

*Left:*
*One of the many drawing-rooms. Immediately next to it is a huge room with one of the largest billiard tables I have ever seen though quite in scale with the vastness of this château. But the cloth is torn – which is rather symbolic of the state in which Lagrange finds itself at present.*

*Below:*
*The impressive château. The tower was added later, in about 1820. At the back of the building hangs an old but still very loud bell, on which the date 1671 is clearly visible. The seigneur de Pauillac et de Lagrange was the proprietor at that time.*

# Chau Lagrange

3rd Grand Cru Classé

Lagrange is perhaps the only estate in the Médoc which has ever belonged to two different ministers: in 1790 Comte de Cabarrus, who governed Spain for Napoleon I, and from 1842 Comte Duchâtel, who was minister under Napoleon III.
In fact, the property does have an allure which seems worthy of high-ranking statesmen. It is situated nearly on the boundary between the communes of St Julien and St Laurent, in the middle of a park with centuries-old, towering trees, among which you suddenly feel very small and insignificant.

The estate comprises 162 hectares. It has been even larger in the past: there is a map dating from 1843 with a total of no less than 282 hectares. After the Château had been the property of M. Louis Mouicy between 1875 and 1919, it passed into the hands of the Société des Grands Crus de France. This society sold it again in 1925 to the Spaniard Manuel Cendoya (from the Basque Provinces), whose family still runs Lagrange.

M. Ignacio Cendoya is the manager. He lives in a comfortable little white cottage near the Château itself, which is only occasionally inhabited by members of the

*Right and below:*
*One of the entrances to the large chais. Lagrange is one of the few châteaux with more than enough space, and there are big courtyards, cellars, workrooms, all much larger than is really necessary. The grounds are sizeable, too. Formerly it must have been a monastery or hospice, as can be seen from the names of some of the plots, like La Chapelle and L'Hôpital. The vineyard is in one piece surrounding the château.*
*The French Larousse does not mention many châteaux, but in all the editions which have appeared so far Lagrange is mentioned alongside more famous names such as Lafite and Haut-Brion. No explanation is given.*

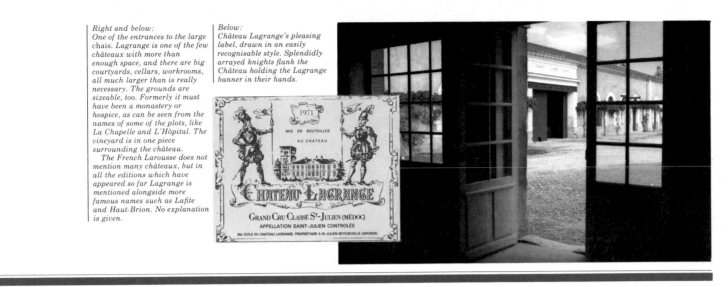

*Below:*
*Château Lagrange's pleasing label, drawn in an easily recognisable style. Splendidly arrayed knights flank the Château holding the Lagrange banner in their hands.*

family, mainly in the summer. For a very long time Lagrange had to manage with an excessive number of drawing rooms but without a single decent bathroom; however, this situation was recently rectified. It is a great pity that the oldest part of the Château was burned down in 1950.

### Unusual spaciousness

Because Lagrange used to make more wine than it does now there is certainly not a shortage of space, a problem with which some classed growths have been faced since switching to château bottling. Everything at Lagrange is spacious. You could play a game of football between the two largest *chais*, and there is any amount of other storage space which is only partly in use. Even the vineyard is a long way off its maximum capacity. At present approximately 50 hectares are under vines (with about 60% Cabernet grapes, 40% Merlot and a little Petit Verdot), but if needed – and it is feasible – another 30 hectares are available.

Few classed growths find themselves with such favourable circumstances. It would seem to me, however, that extension plans should be the least of Lagrange's worries. For before anyone starts thinking about stepping up the quantity (now around 150 *tonneaux*) something radical must be done about the quality, because I think something amiss has developed here.

### Wines that disappoint me – why?

In *Bordeaux et Ses Vins* proud mention is made of the fact that Lagrange has a number of sub-labels under which less successful batches, which are not good enough to bear the Lagrange name, are sold. Some of these names, such as Latour-Rauzan and Château St Julien, can be seen in one of the large *chais*. These secondary labels are no longer used and the wine is sold anonymously. But this does little to alter the fact that I have recently found Lagrange disappointing, especially considering its status as a third classed growth. I even found the 1970 Lagrange, which should normally speaking have been a good wine, unpleasant and without much bouquet, fruit or promise. The colour, too, was on the light side for that excellent year, the taste was somewhat thin, and moreover I found it a bit too dry on the palate.

I tasted the 1973 vintage from the cask, and once again I was disappointed, even though it is never ideal to taste what was anyway an 'off' vintage in this way.

I suppose that these wines will be drinkable in a few years' time, but they lack the aura of nobility which many other classed growths of the same years so obviously possess already. Or am I wrong?

Should the selection process at Lagrange be more rigorous? Should the vinification and the maturation of the young wines be done differently? I don't know. But one thing is probable – the family business (which may lack the capital for big investments) might benefit greatly from sound, expert advice from an outsider, because one thing is beyond dispute: if the soil is good, it must be possible to make a truly fine wine. You only have to look at the successful comebacks of so many other great classed growths.

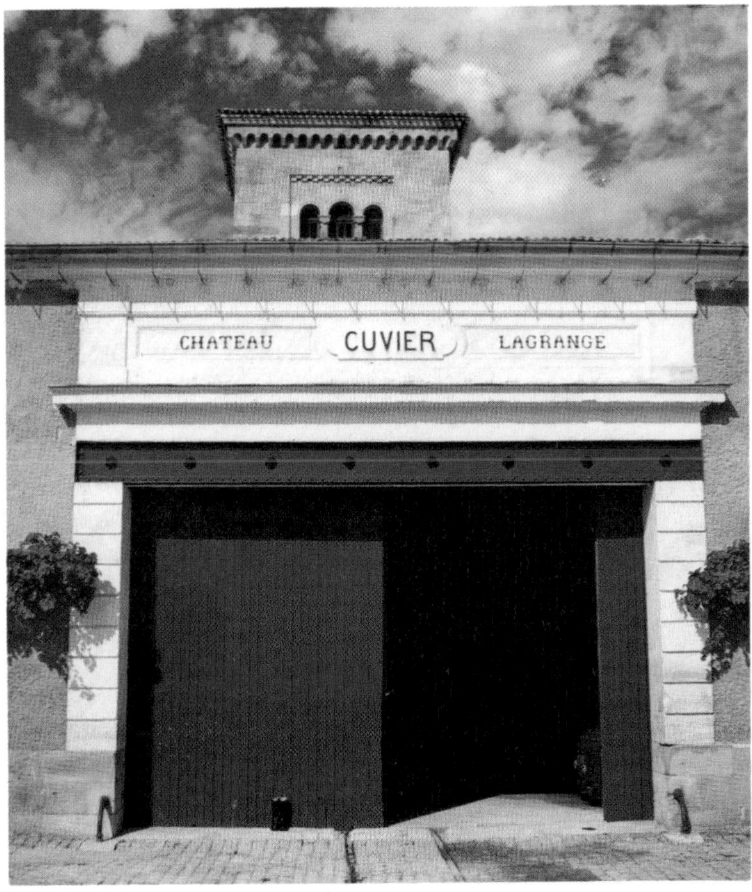

*Below:*
*Although the records of Château St Pierre go back to the middle of the 17th century, when it was called Serançan, the present Château is of a much more recent date, being built in 1875. Throughout the year, the flower-beds that surround it are full of colour. The small presshouse, with its steeply sloping roof, stands at right-angles to the house. The vineyard comes right up to the château, and in addition St Pierre owns many small plots scattered throughout St Julien. The largest is about 7 hectares.*

# Chau St. Pierre

4th Grand Cru Classé

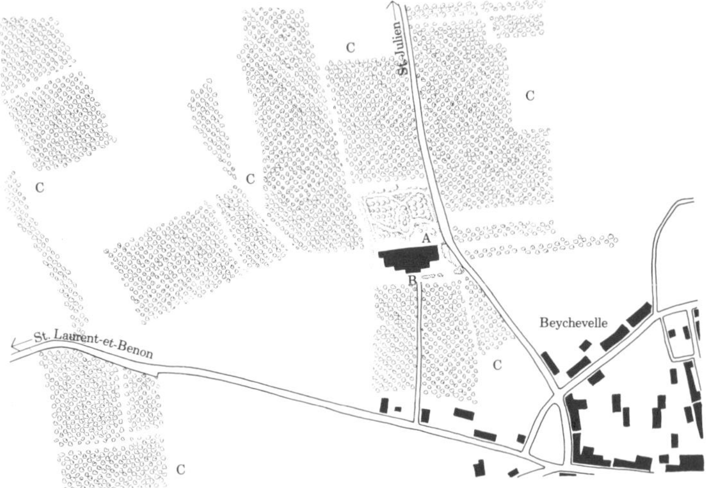


*Left:*
*Plan of Château Saint-Pierre and part of its vineyard. The big chai is in the village of Beychevelle, which lies just to the south of the château.*
**A** *the château,* **B** *the presshouse,* **C** *vineyards belonging to the estate.*

*Below:*
*Noble vines on the unique soil of the Médoc. Fine wine is made as the result of suitable grapes on the right soil, plus a favourable climate – and conscientious human care.*

Because the proprietors are of Belgian nationality, many vintagers come all the way from Belgium and also from Holland to Château St Pierre every year.

A reminder of the pre-motorcar era is to be seen at the entrance to the vathouse. Here two sculptured white horses' heads have been set into the wall, to which in earlier days real horses' reins could be tied.

There is currently a miniature extension project in progress at St Pierre, where a patch of land of only 0·8 hectares is being brought under cultivation again.

Manager Paul Sillon, who was schooled in his work by his father and had worked at St Pierre for over 20 years, died suddenly during the vintage of 1974. His place has been taken by the young Robert Moutinard, who has a small staff of 5 under him.

The small vats at St Pierre are nowadays made of cement, wood being dispensed with for practical reasons.

At St Pierre the wine is only bottled in two bottle sizes: normal bottles and magnum bottles – no halves.

# Château Saint Pierre

Although Château Saint Pierre heads the list of fourth growths in the classification of 1855, you might not suppose it was a great wine if you only looked at the house. This is just a homely building of essentially simple style. Like many Médoc châteaux, St Pierre is a property which might well be a delightful house in summer, but could be quite dreary during the wet and cold periods often characteristic of the Médoc winter. Yet the wine *is* something special.

## A vathouse of charm

The vineyard only extends to 17·5 hectares, and these are very broken up. The production averages 70 *tonneaux*; it used to be much more, but apparently a considerable part of the vineyard was sold to Château Gloria. Once the grapes – 63% Cabernet, 30% Merlot and 7% Petit Verdot – have been picked, they are collected in a small-scale but charming vathouse, with ornamental metal pillars. After fermentation the wines are transferred to wooden casks, which in turn are transported to a *chai* on the other side of St Julien, near Gruaud-Larose. There they remain for two years, after which they are sold to the United States, Britain and Belgium.

## Soft fruit

I have sampled a total of four recent vintages of Château Saint Pierre, 1967 being the oldest. The wine had a deep colour, a powerful, definite smell reminiscent of overripe fruit, and a reasonably firm flavour, which in my opinion was just a little too flat and short, although it was still very attractive.

The 1970 vintage was clearly better. This was a very dark wine, which clung to the glass and which also superbly exhibited Saint Pierre's most distinctive characteristic – the wine is quite obviously markedly fruity. The climate of the vintage, and the individual style of the winemaker, both contribute to the amount of fruitiness of a Bordeaux wine. Saint Pierre may evoke the luscious fruitiness of pears, peaches and similar fruits. In the 1973 vintage, too, this soft style was already evident, and also in the almost sultry bouquet. I found this wine distinctly better and fruitier than the 1972 vintage, which certainly had an excellent colour, but which missed some depth. The 1972 vintage will develop into a pleasant wine, suitable for drinking in the fairly near future.

For the young vines and lean years there is also a second label, Château St Louis du Bosq. The vintages of 1965 and 1968 were marketed under this label.

## Another property divided and reunited

Saint Pierre takes its name from Baron de Saint Pierre, who bought the estate in 1767 from the Cheverry family. The story goes that the good Baron was firmly convinced that his patronage would ensure him the right of entry to Paradise, since his nectar was what 'the Eternal Father delighted in as dessert'. After the Baron's death – unfortunately it is not known whether he reached his destination – the vineyard was divided. Part of it went to Colonel Bontemps-Dubarry, and part to Mme O. de Luetkens, his daughter, who sold her property to M. Léon Sevaistre at the end of the last century. As a result, there were two Châteaux St Pierre in existence for some time, St Pierre-Bontemps and St Pierre-Sevaistre, and you find these two names in old classifications or on old bottles. The two parts were reunited in the present century, as happened at Gruaud-Larose. This took place in 1922, thanks to the Antwerp family van den Bussche; Belgians still own Saint Pierre. Since the death of the brothers Pierre and Charles van den Bussche the estate has belonged to the family and to M. Castelein, a man in his mid-fifties who is also a relative.

*Left:*
*The grapes are hoisted up.*

*Bottom:*
*Château Langoa-Barton seen from the road to St Julien.*

In his cellar Ronald Barton has a fine collection of some 30 carafes, which ingeniously rest inverted and at an angle, on wooden slats. In this way they can drain completely and will collect no dust.

To his great surprise, during the last war M. Barton discovered a white wine in Beirut called Château Léoville-Barton, imported from Greece. The ensuing legal skirmishes cost a great deal of money and time, for he had to prove that he was proprietor of the French Château of that name. Eventually, however, he won the case, and in 1941 the rascally importer was heavily fined.

# Chau Langoa-Barton

3rd Grand Cru Classé

In a dip in the road between the village of Beychevelle and that of St Julien lies Château Langoa-Barton. Motorists are warned not to exceed the 60 kph limit; as the estate lies on both sides of the road pedestrians and vehicles regularly have to cross it, so the warning is a sensible one.

This is not the only reason why it is advisable to drive slowly, for the traveller can thus catch a glimpse of Langoa. The Château was built in 1759, and is still as graceful now as in its youth. It is a low, oblong structure with short towers at both ends. The building is raised above ground on a cellar set partly in the earth.

Langoa-Barton is occupied by proprietor Ronald Barton, whose great-great-grandfather, Hugh, bought it in 1821. The wine of Léoville-Barton is made in the *chais* of Langoa, for Hugh Barton made the first payment on this estate in 1822. Léoville Barton, like Léoville-Las-Cases and Léoville-Poyferré, was originally part of the whole Léoville estate. The other two châteaux had *chais* and houses left after Léoville was divided, whereas Léoville-Barton had none.

### Two wines under one roof

Because they have the same home and proprietor, Léoville-Barton and Langoa-Barton tend to be mentioned in the same breath. This does not mean, however, that the two wines are mixed. 'On the contrary', Ronald Barton told me over a glass of 1955 Champagne Roederer, 'the two wines are kept rigorously apart.' This is for a very good reason – they come from different soils and each has a distinct and different personality.

The vineyard of Langoa is mainly situated to the south of the Château in Beychevelle, that of Léoville to the north near the cemetery of St Julien. Of the two, Léoville gives the greater yield, approximately 100 *tonneaux* as against about 50 *tonneaux* for Langoa. The wine of Léoville-Barton also scores higher from a qualitative point of view. Although there is a distinct family resemblance with Langoa, Léoville-Barton is just that infinitesimal degree the finer of the two.

This is not always the case. Ronald Barton remembers a blind tasting session of six great growths of St Julien. The 1967 Léoville scored higher than the Langoa, but of the 1966 vintages, Langoa finished second and Léoville sixth! Mr Barton discovered just how enlightening blind tastings can be on another occasion, at a buffet lunch where the proprietors and the wines of the three Léovilles were all present. The wines were served and everyone recorded his impressions. To everyone's surprise none of the owners picked out his own wine!

*Right:*
*Until 1960 the striking label on the right was used for Léoville-Barton. Perhaps it does not have a classic style like the other great growths, but it is certainly distinctive. Ronald Barton was made to change it because of commercial pressures, and in 1961 a new label was issued. He found this one so awful that another design was made in 1962, which has proved a successful compromise and is still used.*

*Far right:*
*The traditional vintagers' soup being prepared. There is much rivalry about who makes the best in the Médre.*

*Bottom left and right:*
*Two other scenes typical of the hustle of vintage time. Léoville-Poyferré is run by Roger Delon, who succeeded his father in 1951.*

# Ch^au Léoville-Barton

2nd Grand Cru Classé

### A series of quality wines

Ronald Barton considers himself a traditional wine-maker. His wines are still made in traditional oak fermentation vats, and are then allowed to mature for two years, partly in new casks. Usually Barton wines benefit from a fair number of years' maturation before they are in their prime. A contributory fact is the fairly high percentage of both the Cabernet species (75%, with 20% Merlot and Malbec and 5% Petit Verdot).

Perhaps this is the reason why I know more old than young vintages from both châteaux, especially those of the 1950s. Of the two, Léoville-Barton is the better: the estate produces excellent wines in good vintages and good wines in moderate years. Examples of successful wines in light years are the 1950 and 1954 vintages.

The summer of 1950 was very wet, and to crown it all Ronald Barton lost half his crop in a twenty-minute hailstorm. But despite these misfortunes, the 1950 Léoville was a success. When I drank this wine it was nearly a quarter of a century old. The colour already had a fairly brownish-red tint, but was still surprisingly dark. The nose gave off a sweetish, soft, ripe perfume, and the taste turned out to be a mixture of various impressions: you tasted the wine's age but there was still some youthful vigour. I found it a sturdy wine, which was probably hard in its youth.

The Léoville from the off year of 1954 gave me much pleasure. It was quite an elegant wine, with a ripe and at the same time rich bouquet. The flavour lacked neither life nor strength. Truly a very lovely Bordeaux, with but one slight blemish: a rather short after-taste.

In the previous year, 1953, the weather gods had been well-disposed towards Bordeaux, which could be tasted in the wine of Léoville-Barton. A limpid colour, a delicate bouquet, an elegant, supple taste and lingering after-taste were in perfect harmony, exemplifying Léoville-Barton at at its best.

Even better was the 1959, which many consider the best wine of St Julien. It is not until you taste such superb wines that you realise how little tasting notes like 'ripe, thrilling bouquet, fine, velvety flavour, whole harmonious' may mean to those people who have never drunk such wines.

Recent good years from both châteaux are 1966, 1967, 1970 and 1971. From an historical point of view the 1971 Langoa-Barton should be interesting, because the wine was made exactly 150 years after Hugh Barton acquired the Château.

In one of the Château drawing-rooms hangs a portrait of Talbot. Sir John Looks very warlike, dressed in a suit of armour and with a sword in his hand. He has a proud moustache, wears a plumed helmet, a jerkin worked with *fleur-de-lis* and an ermine mantle. All this finery must have been very hot to wear.

Jacques Cordier is interested in vintage cars. In a garage near the Château he has several fine examples, including a Rolls Royce and, of course, a Talbot. Of the latter, there are apparently only 2 or 3 models left in Paris.

Because of the size of the estate and the extra attention paid to the vineyard, vintageing at Talbot it always hectic and hard. Normally some 120 pickers are needed; they receive board and lodging during the period of the harvest.

The coffer from which Sir John Talbot paid his soldiers is still in the Château's possession.

*Right:*
*Plan of Château Talbot, beautifully situated among its own vines in the heart of St Julien, a few kilometres from the village.* **A** *the château,* **B** *cellars,* **C** *the vathouse,* **D** *water tower,* **E** *reception room,* **F** *vineyards.*

*Bottom left:*
*The silhouette of Château Talbot, nowadays occupied by the proprietor, Jacques Cordier, and his wife.*

*Bottom right:*
*A bottle of Talbot 1968 – not such a good year, not bearing with the miniature of M. Désiré Cordier, Jacques Cordier's grandfather. The device is special to this particular Cordier wine.*

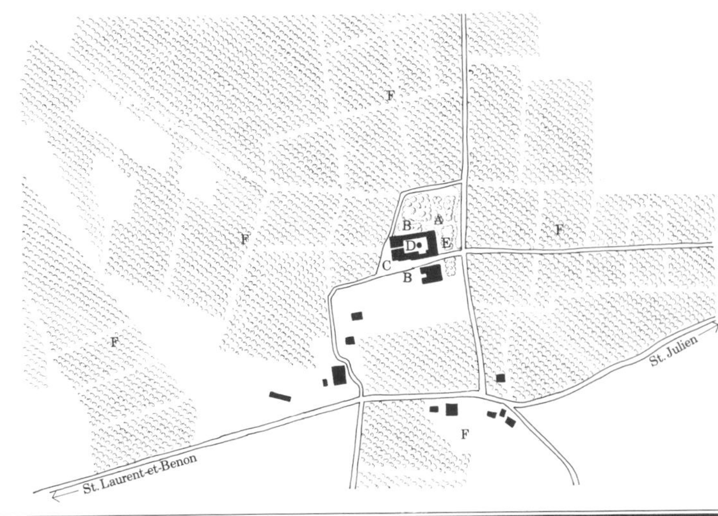

# Ch^au Talbot

4th Grand Cru Classé

This property is named after Sir John Talbot, Earl of Shrewsbury and Marshal of the English Army, although he probably only had his headquarters there before he left for Castillon in 1453, where he was defeated at the decisive battle which put an end to English ownership of Aquitaine.

### The Talbot treasure legend

Talbot has, however, left behind him the legend that before he left for battle, he buried some treasure at Château Talbot in one of the many underground passages, which even stretch as far as Cos d'Estournel and further north. Bordeaux became French again after Castillon, though the English still drank its wines. The treasure – if it ever existed – still lies hidden in the ground at the Château, and every now and again some optimist digs deep holes in the hope of finding a wealth of medieval relics.

Even if the marshal's treasure never existed, Talbot still has a treasure which is worth a fortune in the form of its magnificent vineyard totalling 83 hectares. This surrounds the château and is ideally situated, facing south-west. Just like Gruaud-Larose, this estate is tended as if it were an ornamental garden. The grapes are scrupulously watched and guarded against disease and it is often possible to pick them a week later than at other St Julien châteaux. Artificial fertilisers are never used; a herd of 80 cows is kept to produce manure for both Talbot and Gruaud-Larose. They graze on a part of the estate's remaining 77 hectares.

### Swimming pools of wine

The château is occupied by the owner, Jacques Cordier, and it must give him immense satisfaction to survey the meticulously kept *chais*, where the wine is made, stored and bottled. I was very much impressed by the presshouse, spotlessly clean, holding 25 white steel fermentation

Talbot is one of the few estates with its own water-tower, which is situated immediately behind the main building. So far they have never used it for wine – unlike more prolific regions.

For two centuries the estate was the property of Marquis d'Aux and his descendants, and the name of the Château used to be Talbot d'Aux.

The Château has a very large own reserve of some 100,000 bottles, the oldest wine dating from 1917.

The 30-odd persons permanently employed at Talbot are responsible to the manager, Jean-Marie Bouing.

In the reception hall there is a bronze figure which Georges Cordier received in 1937 as a mark of honour for *'la belle tenue de son exploitation viticole et agricole.'* This was a great compliment, especially in the difficult period of the 1930s. Even during the crisis the estate was immaculately kept.

*Right:*
*The large drawing-room with its magnificent beamed ceiling and a collection of antique Bordeaux porcelain displayed on the walls.*

*Bottom left:*
*One of the vast* chais, *where in abundant years about 1600 casks can be stored.*

*Bottom right:*
*Cellar master Michel Potier in his spotlessly clean vathouse. The fermentation vats date from 1968, but still look new – see how the lamps are reflected in the varnish.*

vats, each with a capacity of 16,000 litres. The bottoms of these vats are covered by sea-blue tiles, which reminded me of several huge, private swimming pools, except that these are filled with wine and not water. The production at Talbot is very large – 350 to 400 *tonneaux* – so there is a shortage of space in abundant years, when part of the vintage is stored not in Bordeaux *barriques* but in huge wooden casks with a capacity of 4,000 litres. (At Gruaud-Larose they do the same when necessary.) Generally, however, all the wine is stored in the usual casks for the regular period between 26 and 30 months. About a third of the casks are renewed each year.

### A bouquet of infinite fascination

When I was tasting the 1970 vintage in the company of the *maitre de chais*, Michel Potier, even he gave an exclamation of surprise as he sniffed the wine, so very formidable was its bouquet. Nor did it disappoint on the palate: it was a complete, well-balanced, fine wine. In 1980 it will definitely be a beauty. The nose of the 1966 vintage will also long remain in my memory. This was overwhelmingly beautiful. Did I smell undergrowth? Did I smell leather? Did I smell fruit? It was a magnificent gradation of various different impressions, with a lot of flavour and a good aftertaste. The 1967 vintage was a generous wine with an attractive, exuberant bouquet and a robust flavour. In all the wines the Cabernet Sauvignon was very obvious, which is logical, since 70% of the vineyard is planted with this vine, plus 25% Merlot, 3% Cabernet Franc and 2% Petit Verdot. Another successful year is 1964, which has produced a robust wine at Talbot with – once again – a superb nose. As regards the off years, the 1958 and 1968 were pleasing, light wines. I drank both of them in 1972. The 1958 vintage, by then 14 years old, was slightly past its prime, but certainly not unpleasant. The 1968 vintage was already the attractive brown of roof tiles – *tuilé*, the French say – it still had a fairly fruity flavour and an in every way respectable after-flavour.

In conclusion I invariably find that Château Talbot produces excellent wines, which makes the notion of fourth growth relating to quality quite unsound.

### The white wine of Talbot

Besides its red wine this estate also produces a white wine, which is called Caillou Blanc du Château Talbot. There is only a very limited production, because no more than two hectares are planted with white grapes (80% Sauvignon and 20% Sémillon). The quality of the wine is pleasant, but not spectacular: fruity, freshly-rounded, pleasant. There are dozens of other agreeable white Bordeaux wines, but because this is a curiosity and it bears the label of Talbot you naturally pay a lot more for it.

*Left and below: The grapes arrive at the presshouse of Léoville-Poyferré and are processed as quickly as possible. On the right of the left-hand picture is the wooden cart which catches the stalks and pips ejected by the égrappoir. The presshouse here is separate from the chais, the latter being on the other side of the main street of St Julien. The château shown on the label is probably a stylised impression of the parent château, which now belongs to Léoville-Las-Cases.*

# Chau Léoville-Poyferré

2nd Grand Cru Classé

Château
Léoville Poyferré
appellation St Julien contrôlée
1970
MIS EN BOUTEILLE AU CHATEAU

Like Léoville-Barton and Léoville-Las-Cases, Léoville-Poyferré is a part of the once mighty property belonging to the Marquis de Léoville. This great estate was confiscated during the French Revolution and auctioned. The sale resulted in its being divided into three parts: half went to Marquis de Las Cases and the remainder was divided up between Messrs Barton and Poyferré. In about the middle of the 19th century Château Léoville-Poyferré changed owners again. The person who took the estate over from Baron Poyferré de Céres was Armand Lalande, who is also involved with Cantenac-Brown. The present owners

*Far left:*
*Robert Lopez has already been maître de chai at Léoville-Poyferré for 20 years, and is one of the Château's 27 permanent employees.*

*Left:*
*The grapes are shovelled into the égrappoir by what is still the old method. At many properties nowadays grapes are tipped directly into a hopper with a huge spiral which automatically feeds them to the de-stalker.*



are united in the Société Civile des Domaines de St Julien. The Cuvelier family has a major say in this partnership, and M. Roger Delon is the administrator.

Whereas Léoville-Barton is actually housed at Langoa-Barton, Poyferré and Las-Cases stand side by side in the village of St Julien. The boundary between the two is not always easy to see. My first visit to Poyferré took a rather curious turn as a direct result of this. I had arranged a meeting with M. Delon, but did not know exactly where I was to meet him. As I came into St Julien I saw a large iron gate with a sign 'Léoville-Poyferré' at an entrance to a forecourt. I immediately concluded from this that I had arrived at the right place and made my way to the office. I gave my name and informed a friendly young woman that I had an appointment with M. Delon. She looked very surprised, because neither she nor M. Delon knew about my visit; but she went to ask whether M. Delon was free. After a quarter of an hour the message came back: he could not see me. Since I did not intend giving up without so much as a murmur, a polite but confused discussion ensued, and I suddenly realised why: I was not at Léoville-Poyferré at all, but at Léoville-Las-Cases!

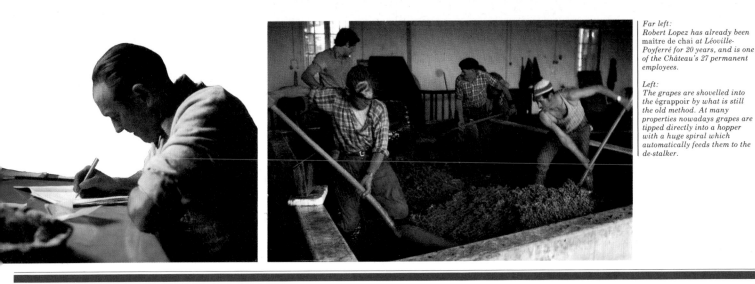

The sign on the gate is therefore misleading, but on the other side of the very same gate hangs a sign indicating Léoville-Las-Cases. So, depending on which direction you come from, you see either Poyferré or Las-Cases first. This has been done to indicate that the boundary between these two estates runs right through the middle – sometimes, I believe, even through the buildings. Why the mistake did not become apparent earlier was because both Poyferré and Las-Cases are run by a M. Delon – brothers. Luckily, however, Roger Delon was waiting for me on the opposite side of the street, where the *chais* of Château Léoville-Poyferré are situated.

## Due for a great revival?

The vineyard of Léoville-Poyferré extends to almost 45 hectares, and is planted with 50% Cabernet Sauvignon and Cabernet Franc, and 50% Merlot. The production fluctuates between 200 and 250 *tonneaux* (1974, for example, reached the 250 mark). Not all the wine is always labelled Poyferré: in 1963, 1965 and 1968 the whole harvest was marketed under the second label, Château Moulin Riche, for which Messrs. Cuvelier have the exclusivity.

You have only to consult any book on wine to discover that the 1929 Léoville-Poyferré is praised as being perhaps the best wine of that phenomenal year. This, of course, says nothing about present-day quality. I have the impression that Léoville-Poyferré declined somewhat, not only during the war but also in the post-war period. In themselves the wines of Poyferré are good, but the finishing touch seems to be missing – that touch of finesse in bouquet and taste which constitutes the difference between a successful and a fine wine. Sometimes Poyferré has a hint of bitterness, sometimes the bouquet is a little disappointing, or the taste is somewhat ungracious. These are minor details, but they become revelatory when this wine is compared with others that are just that much better.

The standard of the Poyferré wines is therefore still subject to criticism, but the future may be different. I found the 1966 vintage, for example, successful; the colour was deep, the flavour both firm and supple, the bouquet healthy. The wine might perhaps have had a little more finesse, but this may come with time. A bottle of 1966 Poyferré must at any rate be decanted well in advance. In the 1970 vintage as well I came across the suppleness typical of St Julien, in addition to great firmness. The nose was still reticent and, just as with the 1966, I felt a wish for more elegance. The 1973 contained a surprising amount of fruit – usually a good sign – and had a good colour, although not a very deep one. The wine was, I thought, better than the 1972 vintage. There was some tannin together with the amiability which always seems to be present in this good but as yet not quite outstanding St Julien wine.

*Right:*
*One of the wings of the original château, which is no longer lived in because, as with many Bordeaux châteaux, the estate belongs to vast numbers of the family who could certainly not share it between them. So it stands empty, but cellar master Jean Crété has his office in the left wing, together with the staff rooms and the headquarters of manager Paul Delon.*

*Centre:*
*Léoville-Las-Cases makes a very traditional claret – as this vintage scene indicates.*

*Bottom:*
*Las-Cases still uses horses in the vineyard, and of course they supply valuable manure for the vines.*

*Below:*
*The label indicates by its Grand Vin de Léoville that the three Léoville estates were once one.*

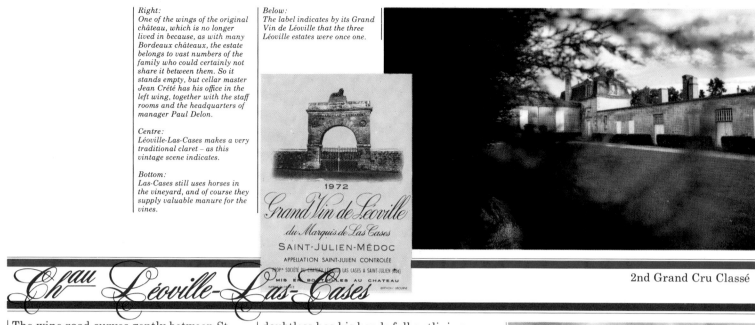

# Chau Léoville-Las-Cases

2nd Grand Cru Classé

The wine road curves gently between St Julien and Pauillac, and at this point is one of the most striking landmarks in the Médoc, the entrance gate to Château Léoville-Las-Cases. The arched gateway forms the entrance to *l'enclos*, the largest part of the Las-Cases vineyard, which is completely enclosed by a wall. Through the archway there is a fine view of the vines and the river, and of neighbouring Château Latour. There is, however, no sign of the Château of Las-Cases, for this is in St Julien itself, partially surrounded by another section of the vineyard. The grey building with its white shutters is uninhabited, and a short while ago part of the unused rear park was converted into vineyard. The only person who might regret this is the manager, Jean Crété, because his house lost part of its garden.

### Tradition maintained in the vathouse

Extending from one of the château wings is the vathouse. This is traditionally equipped with large oak fermentation vats. Their size is calculated according to the quantity of grapes that can be harvested in one day. When the fermentation is finished the wine is transferred to the large *chai* on the other side of the road for 18 to 20 months. This *chai* was built in 1912 and also serves as a reception room for guests. The visitors admire the long rows of *barriques* (about a third are new each year), and can also try out the old machines which were once used for filling and 'dressing' the bottles. Although they are old-fashioned now they are still in working order.

### A family concern

The family business, which the proprietors have been running for more than 260 years, is equally efficient. The members of the present Société du Château Léoville-Las-Cases are all descendants of the Marquis de Léoville, who bought the estate in 1712. The only problem is that such a family is constantly expanding, and eventually there may be dozens of different proprietors. Director Paul Delon, a very busy man, doubtless has his hands full outlining policies to all the owners and bearing responsibility for the day-to-day management of the estate.

### A world reputation

Château Léoville-Las-Cases totals 60 hectares of productive vineyard. The yield is considerable, averaging around 280 *tonneaux*. This is probably one of the reasons why the wines of Léoville-Las-Cases are widely known: in France, Britain, the U.S.A., Scandinavia, Belgium, Holland, Switzerland – all those countries where the great Médoc wines are in constant demand. It is not, however, only the large production that is responsible for the fame of Las-Cases, but also quality. Its wines are frequently among the best of the Médoc; this has been so at least since 1959, although before that date the Château passed through a difficult period.

### Aristocratic wines

Clive Coates, in *Wine Magazine*, sums up perfectly the present position of Las-Cases when he writes: 'Since 1959 Las-Cases has consistently produced wines which would be rated among the leading three or four Médocs after the first growths. Together with Palmer and Cos d'Estournel, the Las-Cases wines of the last decade have provided a nap selection for those of us who cannot afford to lay down Lafite, Pétrus, and Latour. Here again there was large-scale planting of young vines after the war, and this, coupled with a change in the vinification methods, has been splendidly successful.'

It is, I think, their aristocratic quality that is the most marked trait of Las-Cases. The wines are distinguished and, when young, are often somewhat reserved. The reason for this can partly be traced back to the traditional methods of production and the high percentage – 70% – of Cabernet Sauvignon, with 15% Cabernet Franc and 15% Merlot.

The 1959 was a sturdy, well-made wine with a perfect nose, to my mind slightly less

*Bottom right:*
*The impressive gateway leading to the 40-hectare enclosure of Léoville-Las-Cases. The wines are sometimes understandably guessed to be Pauillacs, because Las-Cases is on the parish border and its wines share the Pauillac nobility. The château, built at the turn of the 17th and 18th centuries, also has a lion above the door.*

The Marquis de Las Cases, descendant of the owner, was a historian who accompanied Napoleon into exile on Elba to write the great man's biography.

The large *chai* at the Château can be recognised by the tricolour of France which always flies at the top of the flagpole. If important visitors arrive the flag of their country is hoisted as well.

The grapes are transported in wooden tubs, which in the special wine vocabulary of the Médoc are called *douils*. This is a very old measure, the grapes from each douil yielding about 225 litres of wine, a whole cask, after pressing.

The second label of Léoville-Las-Cases is Clos du Marquis. This bears the *appellation contrôlée* St Julien. The wine is all château-bottled. Normally 10% to 20% of the total crop is sold under this name and label.

The 60-hectare vineyard covers less than half the estate, which extends to no less than 135 hectares. Nearly 40 workers are permanently employed here.



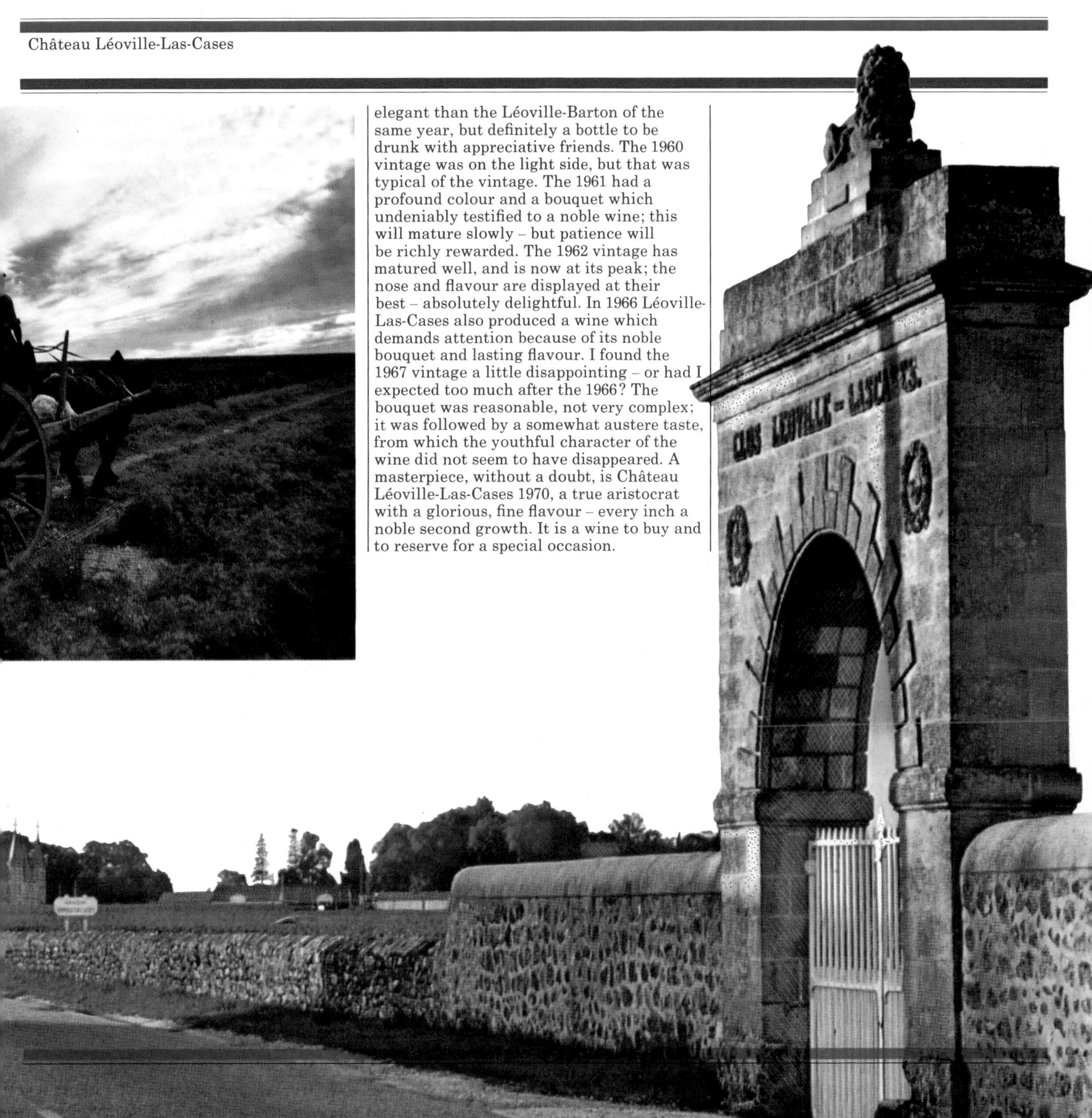

elegant than the Léoville-Barton of the same year, but definitely a bottle to be drunk with appreciative friends. The 1960 vintage was on the light side, but that was typical of the vintage. The 1961 had a profound colour and a bouquet which undeniably testified to a noble wine; this will mature slowly – but patience will be richly rewarded. The 1962 vintage has matured well, and is now at its peak; the nose and flavour are displayed at their best – absolutely delightful. In 1966 Léoville-Las-Cases also produced a wine which demands attention because of its noble bouquet and lasting flavour. I found the 1967 vintage a little disappointing – or had I expected too much after the 1966? The bouquet was reasonable, not very complex; it was followed by a somewhat austere taste, from which the youthful character of the wine did not seem to have disappeared. A masterpiece, without a doubt, is Château Léoville-Las-Cases 1970, a true aristocrat with a glorious, fine flavour – every inch a noble second growth. It is a wine to buy and to reserve for a special occasion.

A voluminous book has recently been published about a wine château, and deals exclusively with Latour. Its title is *La Seigneurie et le Vignoble de Château Latour* and it contains almost 700 large-format pages, bound up into two volumes. A group of people worked on this under the direction of Professor Charles Higounet of the University of Bordeaux, one of them being the brilliant Professor of Geology, Henri Enjalbert. The book is based on the comprehensive Château records; generations of cellar masters have kept a record of everything that has happened. The compilation of this work, which is written in French, took 10 years. The publisher is the Fédération Historique du Sud-Ouest, Cours Pasteur, Bordeaux.

# Chau Latour

1st Grand Cru Classé

'Château Latour bases its activities on the fact that today's tradition was yesterday's progress, and today's progress is tomorrow's tradition.' With these words director Jean-Paul Gardère outlines the philosophy behind the radical technical evolution which Latour has undergone since 1963. In that year the estate came under new management, as 51% of the shares were bought up by the Pearson Group of London, headed by Viscount Cowdray; Harveys of Bristol (a member company of Allied Breweries) had acquired a further 25%. The rest remained in the hands of a few Frenchmen, some of whom are descendants of the Alexandre de Ségur who acquired Latour in the 18th century. The price paid by the British was around the three million dollar mark; on top of this an estimated $750,000 (the equivalent of 4,300,000 francs) were invested in new buildings, *chais*, the fermentation unit and the vineyard.

### Bungalows for the workers

The largest item of 2,000,000 francs was not for the *chais* or vineyard, but for houses for the employees. At Lord Cowdray's suggestion work was started in 1964 on renovating the existing workers' houses and building new ones. These bungalows have every modern convenience including garages, television aerials, cellars and gardens. There will eventually be twenty-five of them in all. With the drift from the land, even in the Médoc reliable workers must be well housed.

In fact in all sections of the extensive renovation programme stress has been laid on the human element. Activities which are only done by hand because of tradition can in fact be a waste of time, as machines can often do the same work more quickly and efficiently – or so say the new owners. Consequently the work in the vineyard has largely been mechanised, and the *égrappage à la main* abolished. This work, the de-stalking and initial crushing of the grapes, required a team of 12 men; now one machine does the same job more quickly.

### All done by vat

The stage following de-stalking and crushing the grapes is fermentation. Here again radical changes have been made. In 1963 the old oak vats were deteriorating; one was already beginning to crack. They had to be replaced – but in what form? Stainless steel was chosen, first because this material is not only extremely resistant to wine but is also very easy to clean; second, because its intrinsic strength

For the Château's exceptionally successful second wine, Les Forts de Latour, the property of Gratadour, in the village of St Lambert, was bought in 1968; since then, two separate apartments have been built there, as well as a storage room for the bottles. It has now officially been decided to call the building Château Les Forts de Latour.

The managers of Latour cannot say precisely which countries constitute the largest markets for their wine, because once the wine leaves the estate they lose track of it. They presume, however, that their major clients are Britain, the United States, Belgium, Switzerland and West Germany.

*Below:*
*The 19th-century tower of Latour with the château on the right. It is said that this tower was made with stones from the fort built at this vantage point. A few years ago the tower was completely restored and redecorated. The château is only occupied intermittently by guests such as Lord Cowdray, chairman of the board of directors, Mr David L. Pollock, the managing director, and director, Mr Harry Waugh, who lectures and writes on wine in both the United States and Britain. Latour now vies for smartness with Mouton.*

*Opposite page, left:*
*Wrapping the bottles in tissue paper is a task still performed by hand.*

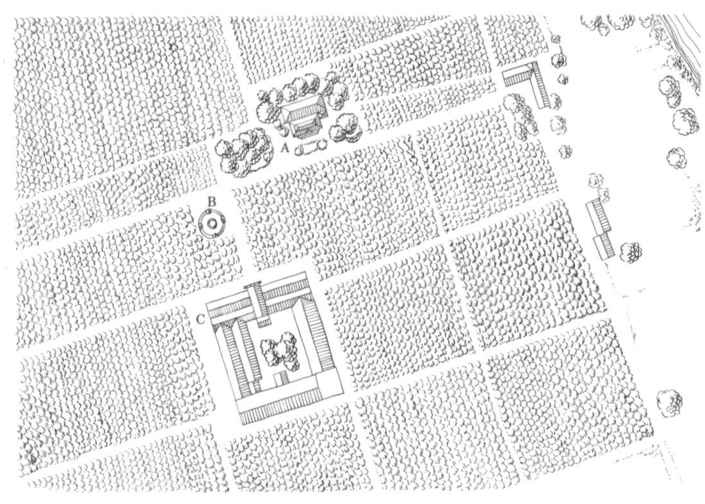


*Right:*
*Plan of Château Latour in the midst of its vineyards; in the upper right hand corner the Gironde.* **A** *The château,* **B** *the famous tower,* **C** *the chais, cuvier and offices.*



permits very thin walls, which facilitates efficient cooling of the fermenting must as and when required: cold water can be automatically poured over the outside of the tanks. A third reason for choosing stainless steel was because it retains its qualities, with minimal maintenance, for a long time; the vats are only used during three weeks each year, and in view of the large investment it is imperative that vats should last for a long while. The primary consideration was of course that the vats should at least produce the same result as the former ones in terms of wine.

The new vats were baptised with the harvest of 1964. Then there were 12 of them, each containing 200 hectolitres; now there are 14 of 200 hl. and 5 smaller ones of 140 hl. Cooling is automatically started by an adjustable thermostat which measures the temperature in the middle of the fermenting must. Thanks to this, wine can be made at Château Latour under optimum conditions for any particular year. Nature is lent a helping hand, that's all.

### A pump like a heartbeat

After the first fermentation, the wine is moved to new oak casks, where it spends the first two years of its life. The staff at Latour believe that in this critical initial period it should be disturbed as little as possible if it is to mature and develop satisfactorily. For this reason, a special pump has been bought to transfer the wine to the *barriques*, a pump based on the principle of the pumps used in heart operations, which creates a permanent, gentle pulse beat, instead of having a more violent grinding action.

For the same reason, Latour is the only first growth where bottling is still done by hand and not at an automatic bottling line. At Latour the wine is directed smoothly into the bottle, whereas elsewhere it is injected by machine. Even the presses for the *vin de presse*, not all that important, are chosen with a view to handling the wine with the utmost care. Again, these are modern machines which have the advantage of working with minimum pressure, so that Latour's *vin de presse* is of superior quality.

### Extension of the vineyard

Despite the high degree of mechanisation in the vineyard, the wine makers of Latour have traditional views about planting. There is a strict rule that, of the 60 hectares, at least 48 must always be covered with old vines, because *'Il faut des vieilles vignes pour faire du grand vin'* (old

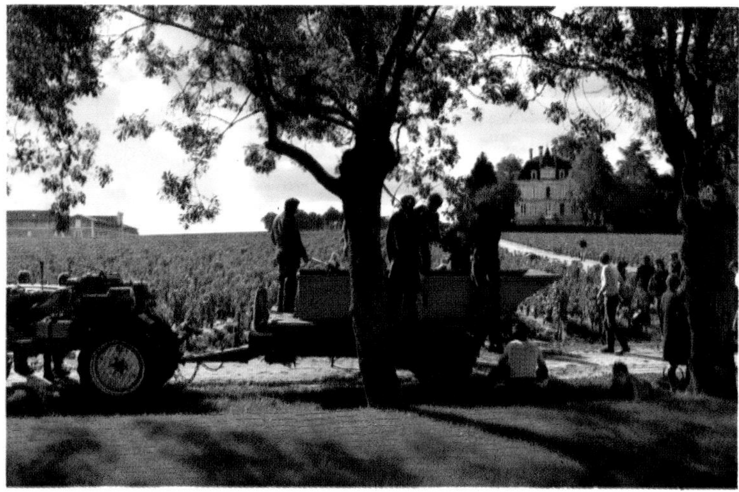

*Left:*
*The grapes are no longer deposited in the old, classic* douils *but in large metal hoppers coated on the inside with plastic. The capacity of each of these is equal to six* douils, *or six casks of wine. The great advantage of the new receptacles is that the grapes no longer need to be pressed down, something formerly inevitable with the wooden* douils *because of their limited capacity. Thanks to this new system the grapes arrive virtually intact at the presshouse, and run no risk of starting to ferment on the way there, which can happen in great heat.*

*Below:*
*Vintageing in full swing, regular workers being augmented by bands of pickers from far and wide.*

From the reception room near the cellars you look out not over Pauillac but over St Julien. A tiny brook, the Ruisseau de Juillac, marks the boundary not only between the vineyards of Latour and Léoville-Las-Cases but also that between the parishes of Pauillac and St Julien.

The Société du Vignoble de Château Latour was one of the first of its kind, and probably the first in France. It was established as early as 1842.



vines are needed to make great wine). Since the British took over, the vineyard has been considerably extended. The new directors – the broker Jean-Paul Gardère mentioned earlier, and Henri Martin, also associated with Château Gloria – discovered that about 3 kilometres from the main vineyard there were two other plots which had previously been planted with vines. One plot was called La Pinada, covering only 2·5 hectares, the other was Petit-Batailley, and covered 10 hectares. So in 1965 both plots were replanted. The existing vineyard was also subjected to careful scrutiny and here the findings caused concern. There was a large number of poor patches, with a maximum diameter of 20 metres, where the vines did very badly. At first nobody could tell why, but it was discovered from old maps that these patches corresponded with the drains which had been sunk at the end of the 19th century, and digging showed that the pipes were blocked. The only solution was to dig up all the pipes in the vineyard, clean and repair them. A start has been made on this costly and lengthy operation, but it will take years to complete. It just goes to show what is involved when an estate changes direction.

In the vineyard, the Cabernet Sauvignon dominates with 75%; the remaining 25% is made up of about 15% Cabernet Franc, 8% Merlot and 2% Petit Verdot, with some Malbec. The production averages 200 *tonneaux.*

### A great gentleman of a wine

The high percentage of Cabernet, and of course the subsoil from which the vines draw their nourishment, largely determine the character of the wine of Latour. But the method of making it is also responsible: the wine is left to rest on its own skins for at least a week, or even more, after fermentation, thus giving more colour and tannin. As a result Latour is the most masculine of the first growths, a wine which in its youth is often very hard, requiring many years to mature fully. If you served the four first growth Médocs at a meal you would probably drink Margaux first, Lafite, Mouton and finally Latour.

In good years Latour is a wine which can be laid up for your children, in great years for your grandchildren. It is a complex, intense wine, full of compact strength. Its bouquet can overwhelm and its style has an immense depth, which discloses more and more gradations the longer you savour it. Latour is like a magnificent Thoroughbred with more staying power than others

*Left:*
*The vathouse of Latour – with the stainless steel fermentation vats in the background. Heads were shaken when they were installed, but they enable the temperature to be minutely controlled.*

*Below:*
*Vintageing is hard work – and back-breaking. But there is a party afterwards.*

It is vital that the vineyard of Latour is well drained, despite its favourable situation close to the Gironde, because the subsoil contains a layer of different kinds of clay. This layer varies between 40 cms and 1 metre. If it is not well drained, the clay layer retains the water, and vine roots do not benefit from this.



because of its constitution: you will hardly ever come across a bottle of Latour which is really over the top.

The Château also has a reputation for producing relatively good wines in off years. I remember the 1954 vintage which, even 20 years later, was still impressive by virtue of its vitality. The colour was only very slightly brown, the bouquet a little reticent, the taste soft, yet sturdy and lingering. You would willingly let your meal get cold just to savour its greatness (luckily I drank it with cheese). The 1963 vintage was also a success. In that difficult year Latour probably made the best wine in the Médoc. I have also tasted the 1965 vintage, which was of lesser quality than the 1963 – the taste seemed to flatten and dry in the middle – but it was still enjoyable. Thanks to strict selection passable wine was produced even in 1968.

Because of this characteristic of producing good wine in off years, the list of interesting Latour vintages is virtually endless, and wine lovers sometimes even prefer the lighter vintages, especially at luncheon. Since 1945, the following can all still be kept: 1945, 1947, 1949, 1950, 1952, 1953, 1955, 1957, 1959, 1960, 1961, 1962, 1964, 1966, 1967, 1970, 1971 (and possibly 1973 and 1974 too).

### Les Forts de Latour

Wine from young vines may be kept separate from the *grand* vin at some estates. Because of the new planting in La Pinada and Petit-Batailley, and replanting in the main vineyard, there are about 12 hectares of young vines at Latour. This wine can either be declassified or a second label can be created; at Latour they do the latter. The idea for the name came from Henri Martin, who discovered on a map several plots called Les Forts de Latour, a few scattered patches of land to the north-west of the vineyard which the property was in the process of buying back.

Thus the Château's second wine came into being, Les Forts de Latour, *A.C.* Pauillac. It is a wine which sells for about half the price of the *grand vin*, but is a worthy younger brother. It is only brought onto the market when it is reasonably mature: in 1972, the 1966 and 1967 vintages were launched. I was in Bordeaux at this time, and both wines made a clean and favourable impression on me. Later I heard that, at a blind tasting session, the 1967 had ended first of 14 fine wines of the same year, and the 1966 fourth! This second wine proves yet again that the skilled management of Latour has made the technical revolution there a resounding success.

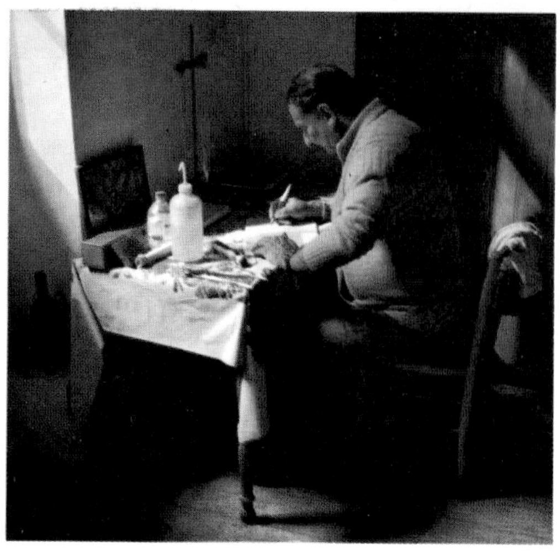

## Château Pichon-Lalande

2nd Grand Cru Classé

When Louis XIV was 20 years old he went down to the Pyrenees to meet his future bride, Marie-Thérèse, the Infanta of Spain. He was to marry not for love but because of various political considerations, and was reluctant to do so. When Jacques de Pichon, Baron de Longueville, invited him to go hunting en route, any diversion was more than welcome. What did the young King think about during his brief stay on the Baron's estate? He enjoyed the gentle landscape of the woods and vineyards, and the delicate bouquet of the wines briefly made him forget his royal duties. That is what it says in the annals of Château Pichon-Lalande in Pauillac.

**Pichon divided**

In the 17th century the woods of the Médoc began increasingly to make way for vineyards. Pierre Mazure de Rauzan was one of the largest proprietors, who in addition to estates in Margaux also owned the large estate of Saint-Lambert-Pauillac. The latter formed the dowry for his daughter Thérèse when she married Jacques Pichon de Longueville, the first president of the Bordeaux *parlement*, in 1700. The property remained in the family until 1850, when it was divided among the heirs, the Baron de Pichon retaining two-fifths and the rest going to his three sisters, the Comtesse de Lalande, Vicomtesse de Lavaur and Comtesse de la Croix. In 1926 the vineyards of the sisters were joined together again in the Société Civile du Château Pichon-Longueville, Comtesse de Lalande. Over half the shares of this company belong to the Miailhe family, the same family having an interest in Dauzac and Palmer. I was told, however, that it is possible the Miailhe holding will be sold in the near future.

**Recent vintages**

Because the various proprietors appear to have been divided among themselves, the recent vintages of Pichon-Lalande have not been outstandingly successful. It would be best to forget the 1972 vintage, in my opinion. The 1973 possesses little refinement and a conspicuous amount of sweetness. The 1974 vintage is no more than (at best) moderate. Moreover, in 1971, 1972, and 1973 a great deal of wine was made at Pichon-Lalande: an average of 220 *tonneaux*. For a classed growth with a vineyard of a good 46 hectares this is almost too much for quality. The fairly new underground *chai* is once again too small. On the roof of this building, completed in 1966, there is a pleasant terrace from which you have a panoramic view of the vines and the buildings of Château Latour; the vineyard of Pichon-Lalande is situated on the other side of the road running from St Julien to Pauillac.

The Château and its adjoining park therefore form a kind of enclave in the Latour estate. This is not necessarily a coincidence. Popular belief has it that a Comtesse de Lalande was the mistress of one of the owners of Château Latour, and that her infatuated lover even sacrificed part of his vineyard in order to build the present château as a comfortable residence for his beloved.

**Older vintages**

To drink a Pichon-Lalande of fine quality one must go back in time. The 1970 vintage is good, but still needs more time to mature,

*Opposite page, far left:*
*The wooden cases in which château-bottlings are packed are handsome in themselves, and the estate brands make them decorative. But increasing costs may eventually result in the use of cheaper packing materials even for great wines.*

*Opposite page, centre:*
*The word 'Comtesse' is now hard to find on the Château label. But serious wine lovers still note a difference between the Comtesse and the Baron estates in the wine as well as the châteaux.*

*Opposite page:*
*Cellar master Hubert Aka in his office.*

*Opposite page, bottom:*
*Latour is literally surrounded by vines, which in the autumn turn red and gold, providing the château with a glowing frame.*

*Right:*
*An old engraving of the château dating from the mid-19th century. Like Pichon-Longueville almost directly opposite, Pichon-Lalande is no longer lived in.*

*Bottom:*
*The grapes are dumped in this large, finely tiled trough, after which they are automatically fed to the égrappoir. The man with the stick is spreading the purple mass evenly over the whole trough.*

When you see the bare rooms of Pichon-Lalande today it is hard to imagine that not so long ago, in 1957, the Comte et Comtesse de Paris, considered by many the heirs to the French crown, were given a glittering reception here. But nearly all the beautiful furniture has been removed from the Château.

The main markets for the wine of Pichon-Lalande are the United States and Great Britain.

The 33 people employed on the estate work under the manager, Jean Jacques Godin, who has occupied this position only since 1970, and who obviously does not have an easy task.

as does the 1966. The 1967 is rather light in colour, but it has a pronounced bouquet with a hint of blackcurrants. The flavour is pleasant but without obvious depth. A wine from Château Pichon-Lalande which I heartily appreciated was the 1964 vintage. I was once given a bottle of it with an excellent *côte à l'os*, which proved to be a perfect combination. The wine had a beautiful colour and a fragrant, fruity style; I found it very appealing. As it happened, no cheese then followed the main dish but rather a strawberry sweet with sabayon sauce. That was just as well, because the decanter had been drained to the last drop, as the wine was so good!

The vineyard of Pichon-Lalande is differently composed from that of Pichon-Longueville, and that is one of the reasons why the two wines are so different. Pichon-Lalande has more Merlot and less Cabernet Sauvignon. The exact proportions are 41·53% Cabernet Sauvignon, 36·25% Merlot, 13·75% Cabernet Franc and 8·46% Petit Verdot.

The lasting attribute of Pichon-Lalande has always been the consistency of its quality under normal conditions. Even in difficult years like 1958 a reasonable result was achieved. But in finer years, as they admit, its neighbour Pichon-Longueville is usually the better wine.

*Below left:*
*Pichon-Longueville vies with Palmer as the most elegantly towered château. It was built in 1851, but is now virtually in ruins inside.*

*Below:*
*Picking starts early – and everyone hopes it will not be interrupted by rain.*

Bertrand Bouteiller told me that the vineyard of Pichon used to be so vast that it cut off several sections of the neighbouring Latour vineyard. This obviously caused friction between the two great estates, with the result that the proprietors of Pichon eventually levied a toll every time the Latour personnel had to cross their land.

The scrupulously high standards of quality at Pichon-Longueville meant that in 1963 and 1965 only a minimal amount of wine was marketed under the Château name, and in 1968 none at all.

# Ch^teau Pichon-Longueville

2nd Grand Cru Classé

As a wine-growing estate, Pichon-Longueville (which is often given the name 'Baron' to distinguish it from Pichon-Lalande) is of modest size. The whole property extends to 50 hectares, of which 30 hectares are under vines. A further 18 hectares used to be cultivated, but because this land was slightly less suitable for fine wine they now lie fallow.

This is typical of Pichon-Longueville: everything testifies to the fact that quality is preferred to quantity, even if it means that production should drop by as much as a quarter. Fully in keeping with this is the low yield per hectare, because the remaining 30 hectares only produce an average of 100 *tonneaux* (compare this with Pichon-Lalande).

Except for a few small plots, the vineyard is in one piece and is virtually encircled by that of Château Latour. Land has been exchanged with the latter, which can never have been to Pichon-Longueville's disadvantage. The vines have a respectably high average age of 30 years, something which greatly benefits the quality of the wine. The division into species is 60% Cabernet Sauvignon, 30% Merlot and the rest a mixture of Cabernet Franc, Petit Verdot and Malbec.

### Supervised fermentation

The soil and the grapes together produce an exquisitely delicate bouquet which often makes you think of violets. It goes without saying that everything at Pichon-Longueville is aimed at ensuring the protection of the subtle charm of the wine. For this reason, the first fermentation is done at a rather low temperature. The normal temperature is 30°C, but at Pichon-

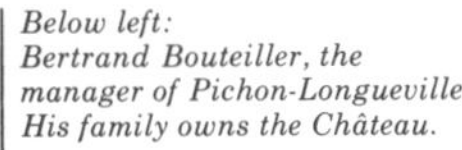

*Below left:*
*Bertrand Bouteiller, the manager of Pichon-Longueville. His family owns the Château.*

*Below centre:*
*Vintageing is not as glamorous as people often suppose. But the bands of pickers – many from Spain – come regularly year after year.*

The wine of Pichon-Longueville is mainly exported to three countries – the United States, Britain and Switzerland.

Every year part of the wine is put into new casks, unless the vintage is exceptionally good, when all the wine is put to ripen in new wood. This was done, for example, in 1961, 1966 and 1970.

Longueville efforts are made to keep the temperature of the fermenting juice below 28°C, and preferably as low as 25°–26°C. The men responsible for this are *maître de chai* Francis Souquet and manager Bertrand Bouteiller (who occupies a similar position at Palmer). The Bouteiller family owns Pichon-Longueville, which they bought in 1935, the proprietor at that time still being a Baron de Pichon-Longueville.

### A Château full of wine

At Pichon-Longueville there is a serious lack of space. Before the period of château-bottling of the whole crop began there was just about enough room, but since château-bottling became the rule the *chais* are too small. It was therefore decided to store the bottles in the cellars under the living quarters, with the result that the wine is now the only living thing in the château (excepting perhaps for the mice). The imposing house, with its slender towers and high-pitched roofs, has been empty for years – a pity, because it is one of the most graceful examples of mid-nineteenth century architecture in the Médoc. With some capital investment it could be turned into a first-class hotel, something which the Médoc lacks, but the sums required have so far proved too formidable.

### Le Baron and La Comtesse

An example of how misleading names can be occurs if you compare the wine of Pichon-Longueville-Baron with that of Pichon, Comtesse de Lalande. Contrary to what you might think, the Baron is the more feminine wine and the Countess the more masculine (although they do sometimes exchange rôles, and in 1966 the Baron seemed to be the sturdier of the two). Generally speaking, the gentleman should be served before the lady – the slightly more refined Baron with the main dish and the Comtesse with the cheese.

I thought a good example of a successful Pichon-Longueville the 1962 vintage. The characteristic bouquet was all-pervading, the colour lovely, velvety and slightly browning, the style fairly light. In complete contrast with this was the 1970 vintage, which had a very delicate nose but whose flavour still contains a considerable amount of hardness. It is, however, certainly neither harsh nor heavy, and through everything you can taste the exquisite flavour. The 1970 also has a deep colour; this too is highly characteristic of Pichon-Longueville, a wine that in spite of its name evokes many terms associated with feminine beauty.

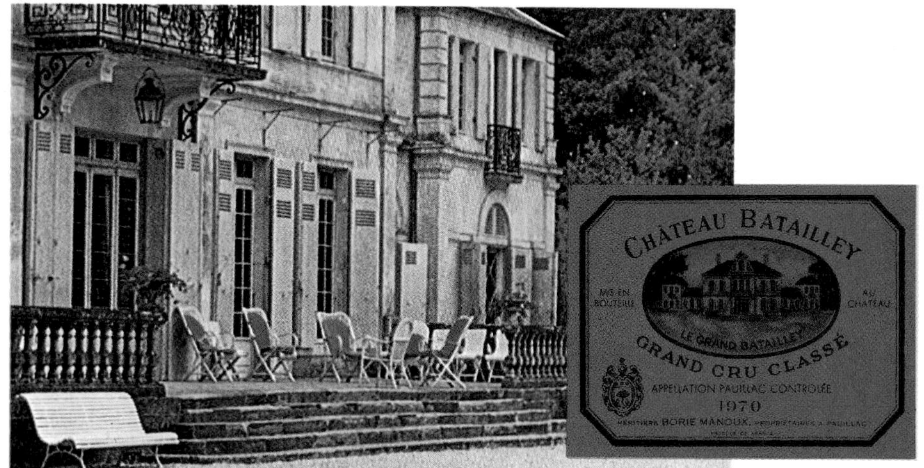


*Left:*
*The terrace of the Château on a fine summer evening. The main building was constructed between 1750 and 1810.*

*Below:*
*Front view of the Château, with a metal signpost in the foreground giving the precise distances to Pauillac and Saint-Laurent. The road past Batailley marks the boundary of two wine growing parishes.*

In one of the long cellars a reception room has been arranged which is well worth a visit. Emile Castéja has had two beautiful sets of antique Delft tiles, depicting life in the 17th century, fixed to the wall.

## Chau Batailley

5th Grand Cru Classé

Thousands of soldiers once fought on the spot where now the vines of Batailley stand in trim ranks. These were the men of the famous Bertand du Guesclin, who defeated a great English military force there; a victory which enabled the French first to lay siege to the fortifications of nearby Château Latour and subsequently to take it. Batailley owes its name to this encounter, and is proud of its association with the admired du Guesclin – so noble a warrior that the French king asked to receive a knighthood at his hand.

### A Bordeaux wine dynasty

The Château, with its 100 hectares (over 50 of which are productive, planted with 75% Cabernet and 25% Merlot) is the property of Mme Denise Castéja, who inherited it from her father, M. Marcel Borie, in 1961. He had bought it in 1929. Madame Denise's husband is Emile Castéja, a descendant of a very old wine family which can be traced back to the 14th century. By a nice coincidence Batailley also came into the Castéja family in the 17th century via a marriage, but then passed into other hands. Ancestors of Emile Castéja – a dominating personality – were mayors of Bordeaux and Pauillac. He himself has his hands full with Batailley and directing the well known shipping house, Borie-Manoux.

Batailley also has an impressive collection of trees. In the garden at the back generations of owners have planted trees from all over the world: from India, Mexico, China and the United States, and the tradition is still kept up. The park is a catalogue of trees. Wild strawberries also grow there and in the autumn the cyclamen, its pink and white flowers looking festive at vintage time as if celebrating the making of yet another fine vintage at Batailley.

*Right:*
*A view of the interior, which has been furnished with antiques and lovingly collected works of art.*

*Centre:*
*The park at Batailley is particularly beautiful.*

*Bottom:*
*One of the long cellar buildings. The 15 families employed at Batailley live in cottages built in typical Médoc country style: long, low, and with claret-red paintwork.*

The Castéjas live at Batailley all the year round, and have transformed the inside of the fine château (built between 1750 and 1810 in the style of the time) virtually into a museum. Nearly every room contains precious antiques which Emile Castéja has collected over the years. Not only the drawing-room furniture is well worth seeing but also the Chinese porcelain, Flemish old masters and the impressive collection of books. In spite of all these treasures, however, the château is still very much a home. You enter through a large hall with a majestic staircase on the right leading upstairs; on the left is the crowded office of the master of the house, where the family usually gathers to enjoy a cup of coffee, perhaps with a digestive, after lunch or dinner.

### Fragrant and constant

In some reference books the wines of Batailley are not thought of very highly. One speaks of a 'limited reputation', 'not one of the leaders' or 'sound, rather unexciting wine'. I tend to disagree; I have come across many good bottles of Batailley, such as the 1955 served by Emile Castéja at luncheon at the château. Already brownish in colour, the wine was wonderful: it had an assertive bouquet and taste, definite finesse and a lot of life. Even better than the 1955, however, is the 1953. In that year Batailley made one of the greatest Pauillacs. I was also impressed by the Batailley 1966, which I have drunk on various occasions, one of them being a two-star meal in the famous Alsatian restaurant, *Aux Armes de France*. This was in the autumn of 1974; with the wine came some delicious *côtelettes d'agneau*. The wine was splendid: it had a full, fruity bouquet with a hint of bay, and on the palate it was fine and long.

The most singular characteristic of Batailley is perhaps its fruity, definite bouquet, frequently followed by an equally definite flavour. It also has a very consistent quality; and even in poor years Batailley succeeds in making respectable wines. It certainly deserves its place among the classed growths, and it is almost always a good buy at a reasonable price.

*Bottom left:*
*The new vathouse of Château La Couronne, where the wine of Haut-Batailley is also made. At many châteaux the second fermentation in the spring is allowed to take place in the cask. At Haut-Batailley, however, the wine stays in the large steel vats. Because the temperature should not drop – and stop the yeasts working – these metal tanks are covered with a kind of tea-cosy made of plastic which conserves the heat during a cold spring.*

*Bottom right:*
*The château is in fact no more than a pleasant farm. The vineyard of Haut-Batailley was split off from Batailley in 1942, and the owner is Madame des Brest-Borie. She leaves the running of the place to Jean-Eugène Borie of Ducru-Beaucaillou. The principal markets for Haut-Batailley are the U.S.A., Britain, France and Switzerland.*

*Right:*
*The emblem and label of Château Haut-Batailley.*

# Chau Haut-Batailley

5th Grand Cru Classé

It was as recently as 1942 that Haut-Batailley was separated from Batailley, so it may be expected that the wines show a marked similarity. This does not mean to say, however, that they do not have individual personalities, because they have. Even a few yards can make a great difference in the world of vineyards. What is distinctive about the wine of Haut-Batailley is that it suggets it is made by people from St Julien, Jean-Eugène Borie (proprietor of Ducru-Beaucaillou) and his cellar master, André Prévôt. You get the impression that here in Pauillac they are trying to produce a wine which is as amiable as the wines of St Julien – and they are succeeding. Even the young wines are amiable. Of course their colour is still purple, the bouquet somewhat reticent, and the tannin still prevalent, but there is no trace of harshness. A pleasant suppleness prevails, together with the what I can best describe as 'ripe fruit'. There are Pauillac wines which in their youth are harsh indeed, but Haut-Batailley tries to charm right from infancy.

Yet it is certainly a wine which is suitable for laying down. For example, I drank a 10 year-old 1964 Haut-Batailley which was particularly good, full, robust and lively. The 1970 vintage is also a wine which requires patience and, like others of this year, will not be at its peak until about the 1980s. As far as lean years are concerned, Haut-Batailley hardly ever seems disappointing: I remember drinking a couple of bottles of 1968 which were nothing exceptionally great but very enjoyable, and certainly bargains at the price.

### A Château to watch

In 1849 the Bordeaux poet Biarnez wrote: 'We must make great wines, not great buildings.' This is particularly applicable to Haut-Batailley, because there is only a vineyard and no château. The wine is made at the adjoining Château of La Couronne (a *cru exceptionnel*), where the *chai* seems to be in a rather shabby state, but appearances are deceptive, and in 1974 Jean-Eugène Borie had new equipment installed.

The production of Haut-Batailley averages between 60 and 90 *tonneaux*. These constitute the harvest of approximately 18 hectares of vineyard, two-thirds of which is planted with Cabernet Sauvignon. The vineyard is divided into two sections: 6 hectares bordering on La Couronne and 12 hectares two kilometres further on. The latter section has a favourable situation on a plateau, where the grapes are ripe for picking about four days earlier than elsewhere – something which in a rainy autumn can make the difference between a good wine and a fine one.

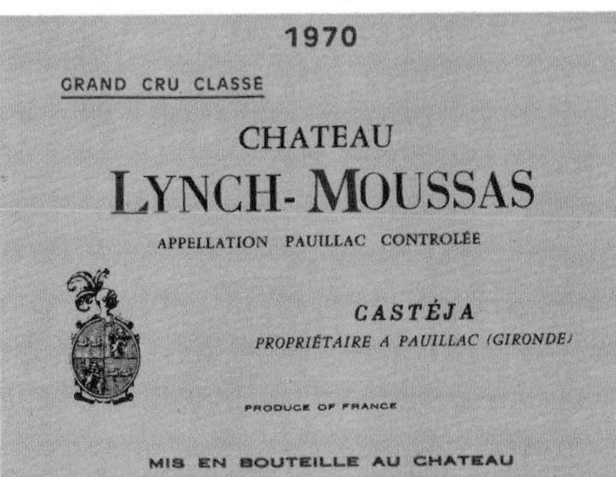
1970
GRAND CRU CLASSE
CHATEAU
LYNCH-MOUSSAS
APPELLATION PAUILLAC CONTROLÉE
CASTÉJA
PROPRIÉTAIRE A PAUILLAC (GIRONDE)
PRODUCE OF FRANCE
MIS EN BOUTEILLE AU CHATEAU

*Left:*
*The name Castéja on the Lynch-Moussas label is one of the oldest in the district, for Castéjas have been one of Pauillac's leading families for generations, and there is also a rue Pierre Castéja in the town.*

*Bottom:*
*Lynch-Moussas stands slightly isolated in the middle of a large, wooded estate. In this picture the château spire (which dates from 1850) is just concealed by the trees. The chais are situated to the right of the main building. Since the 1973 vintage the wine of the château has been bottled here.*

When the father of Emile Castéja bought the estate in 1919, it had belonged for years to a M. Vazquez. Apparently he was either not very interested in the work of growing vines or else he had serious financial problems, because 99% of the vines had been uprooted and had never been replanted. Before his death in 1955, Père Castéja succeeded in bringing 12 hectares under cultivation once again, and this work is now being continued with great assiduity by his son Emile.

In 1973, Lynch-Moussas had a new cellar master in M. Becker, already a veteran in wine.

# Ch^au^ Lynch-Moussas

5th Grand Cru Classé

Château Lynch-Moussas is a typical example of a growth whose name is being completely rehabilitated. When Emile Castéja, the proprietor of neighbouring Batailley, bought the estate from other members of the family in 1969, it was little more than a ruin. The *chai*, the vathouse, the vineyard, everything had to be either completely rebuilt or thoroughly renovated, but little by little this has been done. Red steel fermentation vats and underground blending tanks were installed, an adequate cellar was built and large-scale replanting (70% Cabernet and 30% Merlot) was undertaken. The direct result was a rise in production and quality. At present the production is about 20 *tonneaux*, but it is hoped to step it up to between 60 and 80 *tonneaux* before long. The only thing which has as yet not been improved is the château itself. It is rented to a group of shooting enthusiasts, who have leased Lynch-Moussas' approximately 100 hectares of woodland for pheasant-shooting.

### 'Wait and see' wines

It is, of course, slightly unfair to compare the wines of Lynch-Moussas at the moment with other classed growths, since this estate must be given a chance to prove itself – and that is only possible when the average age of the vines can rise higher than at present. All the vintages from 1969 to 1973 still have the slightly green flavour which always comes from young vines, although the quality of the vineyard does give the wines a good start. What surprised me was the generous amount of fruit in the wines of Lynch-Moussas, which should develop into amiability and charm with time.

The best wines of the ones I tasted were the 1970 and 1971 vintages, of which 1971 might well develop into the better of the two – perhaps because of the slightly more mature vines. This 1971 was fairly light in colour, but the fruit, tannin and firmness indicated that the wine has a lot more in store than might otherwise be supposed.

### A growth to watch

Château Lynch-Moussas will be a name to remember. Because it is as yet little known, the prices will, I hope, remain low, and I am sure the quality, thanks to the effort and skill of Emile Castéja, will improve from year to year.

Whereas the wine of Château Batailley, the other Médoc classed growth owned by the Castéja family, is sold exclusively through the firm of Borie-Manoux, Lynch-Moussas is generally offered to all wine establishments.

On top of a cupboard at the Château I saw a curious painting of a lady squirting wine from her right breast, as Venus is said to have done to create the Milky Way.

In the dining-room there are elongated fronts of four large wooden casks. On these an artist has carved the four elements of earth, air, fire and water into the wood. The casks were originally intended for Russia, but the boat carrying them sank in the harbour of Bordeaux and M. Dupin was quick to gain possession of them.

*Right:*
*The name Saint-Guirons is still found on the label and cases of Grand-Puy-Lacoste, as a M. Saint-Guirons was at one time the proprietor. He was a lawyer at the Bordeaux bar. His youngest daughter – he had three – married M. Lacoste, whose name still survives in that of the Château. M. Lacoste was the grandfather of Madame de Saint-Légier, from whom M. Dupin bought the estate in 1932.*

*Far right:*
*The château possesses a single, slender tower.*

*Bottom:*
*The solid château, which was built in about 1850.*

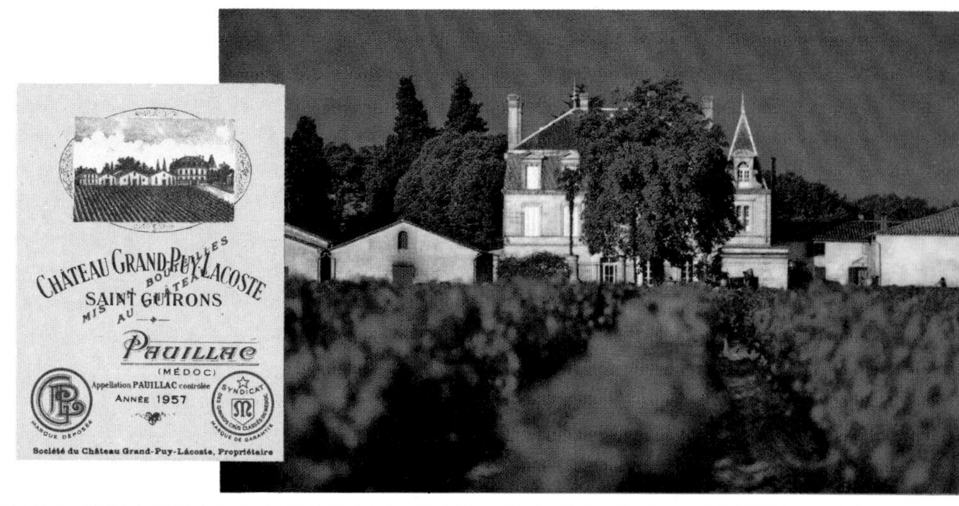


# Chau Grand-Puy-Lacoste

5th Grand Cru Classé

It is always a good thing for a château to have a gourmet owner because anyone who appreciates good food will try to make the best possible wine, if only from personal interest.

The proof of this theory is provided by Château Grand-Puy-Lacoste, where Raymond Dupin, a lover of everything that is good in this life, has his kingdom. Normally a visitor to a château is first asked whether he had a good journey, but when I arrived at Grand-Puy-Lacoste for the first time, M. Dupin asked me where I had lunched that day. I said: 'Somewhere in Pauillac', to which he replied: 'Then it won't have been very good.' I agreed with him and was immediately treated to a brief, pithy speech about where I should go for my lunch in future and what specialities I should order in which places. This is typical of Raymond Dupin. I later learned that he owns Pauillac's only flock of sheep, and anyone who has eaten Pauillac lamb will know how treasured the sheep must be.

## A lucky dip of fine wines

Dupin has definite and cultivated tastes as regards wine. His favourite white wine is the great Graves, Domaine de Chevalier, and he has a reputation for entertaining even the proudest, regaling them with great old vintages. His treasures, are, however, apparently stored haphazardly in a shuttered junk room in the dilapidated château. On the dusty floor I noted piles of cases that make headlines when even single bottles are auctioned – M. Dupin would never put a price on such things: they are for himself and his friends to enjoy.

## A wine like its owners

The vineyard of Grand-Puy-Lacoste is virtually all in one piece, though there is another hectare near Mouton; like that of Croizet-Bages, it is on the plateau of Bages. It is also from its situation that the estate gets its name. *Puy* means peak, and M. Lacoste was once the owner. Overall, the vineyard has 30 productive hectares, planted with 75% Cabernet Sauvignon and Cabernet Franc and 25% Merlot. After the grapes have been picked, destalked and crushed, they are left to ferment in fairly small wooden vats. The wine is subsequently transferred to oak casks, where it remains for one and a half to two years. The production averages 100 *tonneaux*; the U.S.A., Britain, Switzerland and Belgium are the major consumers.

*Left:*
*Proprietor Raymond Dupin is a gourmet renowned throughout the Gironde.*

*Bottom:*
*A typical vintage scene in the vineyard of Grand-Puy-Lacoste. The vineyard is in one piece and is easily viewed from the road as it is situated on a plateau behind the village of Bages.*

Grand-Puy-Lacoste is one of the very few châteaux which uses only standard bottles for bottling its wine. Half-bottles, magnums and other sizes are not used at all.

Over the years Raymond Dupin has managed to build up a fine collection of hand-blown bottles, most of them dating from the nineteenth century; on one of these I saw the date 1854. It is not quite clear what they contain: possibly some may hold Madeira, Cyprus wine or distillates. Typical of the house is the way such valuable things – and many others – are littered haphazardly around.



Characteristic of Grand-Puy-Lacoste is a robust style, with great appeal – like its owner.

### The best wine of four decades

Raymond Dupin bought the estate in 1932 and he can recall exactly the character of each vintage. He told me about the bitter cold of 1938–1939, which was much worse than that of 1956; about 1964, when the last of the grapes were brought in on Wednesday 8 October at noon, and at 2 p.m. the rains began and continued for 3 weeks; and about his 1961 vintage, which he considers to be the best wine Grand-Puy-Lacoste has made in the last forty years.

The production in that year was only 35 *tonneaux*. This need not have been such a problem because nearly all the wines of 1961 were sold for high prices. But what happened? Raymond Dupin had sold a third of his normal crop *sur souche*, well in advance when the grapes were still on the vines and at an agreed fixed price. This often has practical advantages, but in this case it was disastrous, because one-third of the usual harvest was 33 *tonneaux*, which now changed hands for the ridiculously low price of 2,750 francs. M. Dupin only had two remaining *tonneaux* for open sale, and these went for no less than 7,500 francs, a record sum at that period – strange though it now seems.

### A textbook Pauillac

I was lucky enough to be given the 1961 vintage with a good meal. It was a wonderful experience: the wine was still deep in colour and its bouquet abounded in fruit which made me think of an illuminated manuscript: the more I sniffed the more scents were there for discovery, as if you were looking at a miniature with a magnifying glass. The flavour was assertive and already expansive; it was a great wine, demonstrating what a fine Pauillac should be like in a vintage that was everywhere outstanding.

You may not be able to find the 1961 vintage any more, but you can look out for other good vintages of Grand-Puy-Lacoste. In 1945, 1947, 1949, 1952, 1953, 1955, 1959, 1962, 1964, 1966, 1967, 1970 and 1971 first-rate wines were made. The 1960 was fairly light but very pleasing, and it is possible that the 1972 and 1973 vintages will tend to resemble it, though maybe they will not be quite so appealing.

The estate came into the possession of the Lynch family when Thomas Lynch married the daughter of the Domaine de Bages in 1750. Thomas Lynch's son was the famous Jean-Baptiste Lynch, whom we heard about at Château Dauzac, and who was Mayor of Bordeaux. His brother Michel was the last Lynch to be proprietor of Lynch-Bages. In 1824 he sold the Château to Sébastien Jurine, a Swiss wine merchant. It remained in this family until 1935, when it was taken over by Jean-Charles Cazes, father of the present manager. A few years ago the members of the Irish Lynch family paid a visit to the Château, and were warmly received.

Also in the hands of the Cazes family is Château Les Ormes de Pez in St Estèphe, a good *bourgeois supérieur* growth. This wine is bottled at Lynch-Bages.

The Château and *chais* of Lynch-Bages date from the end of the 18th and beginning of the 19th century. During this period the old buildings, which had seen service for centuries, were completely replaced.

*Bottom:*
*The rather plain, angular château is relieved by the ivy on the side wall.*

*Below:*
*In the bottom right-hand corner of the Lynch-Bages label is the Pauillac coat of arms, 'Pauillacus'. M. Cazes is Mayor of this renowned wine town.*

GRAND VIN
CHATEAU
LYNCH BAGES
GRAND CRU CLASSÉ
PAUILLAC
MÉDOC
1972
APPELLATION PAUILLAC CONTROLÉE
J.C.CAZES, PROP
PRODUCE OF FRANCE
73cl


# Ch^au Lynch-Bages

5th Grand Cru Classé

From Lynch-Bages there is a splendid view of the Gironde and the little town of Pauillac, for this Château is situated up on the edge of the Bages plateau, together with a large part of its 58 hectare vineyard.

My first impression of Lynch-Bages was of a big, sprawling, rambling house, and that impression remains with me. The square main building is occupied by the grandmother of the present proprietor, M. André Cazes, Mayor of Pauillac. The *chais* are immediately behind and are more extensive than you might suspect from the exterior. The *chais* are entered through the long vathouse, where wooden fermentation vats are still very much in evidence, though there are a few metal ones as well.

### Traditional methods of vinification

There are no serious plans at Lynch-Bages to change over to metal, steel or cement vats, as may be noted by the fact that not long ago a number of the oak vats were renewed. A visitor gets the impression that winemaking is still very much a craft here. This is confirmed when you see the master-cooper at work in one of the *chais*; he, together with his assisant, makes two to three perfect *barriques* a day. This craftsman prefers to work with oak from the woods of the Allier, in the heart of France, which is considered best for the wine of Lynch-Bages. Another old-fashioned aspect of this property which stresses craftsmanship is the relative lack of such modern equipment as has been in use for years at many other châteaux. Much is still done by hand, including the bottling.

Another thing that catches the eye are the wooden bungs used for the casks containing the first year's wine; elsewhere these are usually made of glass. The wooden bungs give the *barriques* a jaunty appearance, as if they said 'Here I am and I dare you to touch me!' The *chais* are all low, dark and old. In the second-year *chai* I noticed a pleasant, sweetish scent – could

*Left:*
*Vintagers have to be prepared for rain, sun and wind, hence this assortment of headgear on a band about to start.*

*Bottom:*
*In the space above the wooden vats a small press is trundled on rails to its place of work.*

If times improve, the vineyard of Lynch-Bages can be extended by a further 10 hectares, but at present only 58 hectares are under production.

The Château has a Spanish cellar master, M. Jesus Nuñez. Some fifteen years ago he came to Lynch-Bages to make the vintage and stayed on. The estate extends for 127 hectares, and 25 families live on it.



this have been the herald of the bouquet?

### Mouth-filling flavour

Britain, the United States, the Benelux countries, Scandinavia and Switzerland are the main markets for the approximately 200 *tonneaux* which Lynch-Bages produces annually. The fact that the wine is above all appreciated in cool, northern countries is probably something to do with its assertive flavour. It is invariably robust, perhaps lacking subtlety and charm, but appealing to those who like an intense taste and concentration of bouquet.

A Lynch-Bages must always be matured. The individual way in which it is made and the fairly high percentage of Cabernet (60% Sauvignon and 25% Franc) demand patience of the buyer. In its youth the wine may seem hard and inaccessible, and it is only with time that it softens into amiability.

A vintage which I enjoyed immensely was 1962. When young this wine still had a slight astringency, but over the years this gradually disappeared. The last bottle I drank contained a wine with a very deep, still dark red colour, and a bouquet that I noted as intense, soft, and above all deep, together with a lingering, almost delicate taste. To my mind Lynch-Bages produced a 1962 among the best of that vintage.

The 1966 vintage is also a winner, again having a deep colour, much fruit on the nose and a bold flavour. I found the 1967 a pleasant luncheon wine, pleasing, supple and not demanding. In 1970 Lynch-Bages produced a giant, full and tannic, which needs years to develop; already it has an attractive nose. The bottle of 1972 I tasted had a lighter colour, a soft, almost sweet bouquet (it made me think of blackcurrants) and was still firm, even unaccommodating. It is a little lighter in style than usual. As far as the 1973 vintage is concerned, this will probably develop into a fine wine, robust, complete, fruity in every way typical of Lynch-Bages.

# Ch^au^ Croizet-Bages

5th Grand Cru Classé

Like Rauzan-Gassies, Château Croizet-Bages belongs to the heirs of Paul Quié, and here too work is in progress on improvements to the *chais*. In general this work is confined to making them up to date and easy to operate. There are no other major constructions.

Over the years Croizet-Bages has produced sound, healthy wines which needed no apology. The estate has always lived to some extent in the shadow of other

*Opposite page, left:*
*Vintagers awaiting instructions about which grapes they are to pick and where to start.*

*Opposite page, bottom:*
*Although the front of the vathouse might lead one to think otherwise, there is no longer a true Château Croizet-Bages. The chais date from 1810 or thereabouts. To the right, behind the still life of three bottles, can just be seen the house of the* chef de culture, *Claude Ribeaux, who has worked at the estate since the mid-sixties.*

*Right:*
*After the first fermentation the wine is transferred from the cement vats to the oak casks in the* chai.

*Below right:*
*Where the vintage really starts.*

Croizet-Bages gets its double name from the village of Bages and the brothers Croizet. The latter founded the estate in the 17th century. Their family sold it at the beginning of the 19th century to Jean Puytarac, who in his turn sold it to Julien Calvé in 1853. The last-mentioned proprietor felt he had to give his name to the Château as well, and for years the estate was called Calvé-Croizet-Bages. After M. Calvé the estate passed into the hands of M. Monod, an American by birth. Among other things, he brought the firm of Klaxon to France. It was only after the last world war that Croizet-Bages came into the possession of the Quié family, the present owners.

Like many châteaux, Château Croizet-Bages displays on its label some of the medals its wine has won. These are mainly medals from exhibitions and contests of long ago: in this case the Paris World Exhibition of 1878 (silver medal) and 1889 (gold medal).

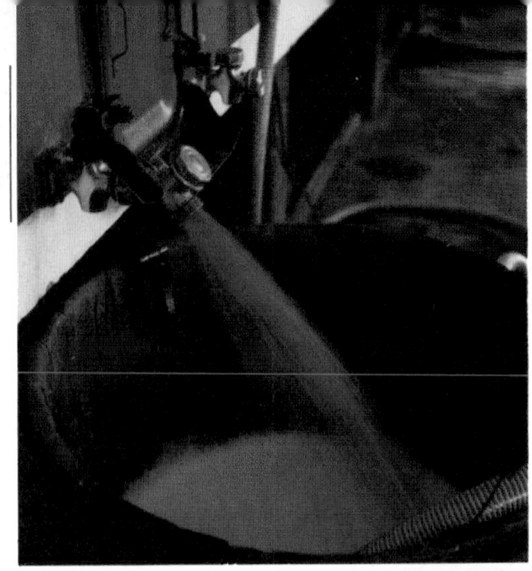



Pauillacs, which is quite understandable, since the production (on average 100 *tonneaux*) is not all that large and the estate has no château of its own, which does not help to promote its reputation. There are just a few cellars and a vathouse in the village of Bages; there is really no suitable place for people to be received. What used to be the château of Croizet-Bages is called Château La Tourrelle; it is situated in Pauillac, and today is a youth centre.

The vineyard is advantageously situated on the plateau of Bages; the first vines begin a few metres from the *chai*. There are 20 productive hectares, which are planted in the classic Pauillac way with 60% Cabernet Sauvignon and Cabernet Franc, approximately 30% Merlot and a small amount of Malbec and Petit Verdot. The wine is mainly shipped to Britain, Switzerland, the U.S.A. and Belgium.

### Some details of wine-making

Paul Quié died on 17 December 1968 and his wife and son now run the estate. Typical of the traditional care of the Quiés is what they did about the *fouloir* which was installed a few years ago. In itself this machine is merely an appliance which removes the stalks and lightly crushes the grapes. To ensure maximum hygiene, such equipment must be regularly cleaned and no lengthy breakdowns must occur during vintageing. So it has to be simple to clean as well as being constructed to enable repairs to be made with a minimum of fuss and loss of time. Both these requirements pose problems of varying degrees at most estates. But not at Croizet-Bages. For a special little passage with descending stairs has been built, so that the workmen can get right into the machine quickly and efficiently and in and out of the hopper without bringing vintageing to a protracted halt. A *fouloir* is already expensive and an extra passage adds to the cost, yet there was never any hesitation at Croizet-Bages. This deserves applause: it is the little details that count!

After the first fermentation has taken place in the cement vats the wine is transferred to oak casks for at least 20 months. In consultation with an oenologist, a strict selection is made every year; anything which is not satisfactory is sold under the second label, Enclos de Moncabon. As regards the label of Château Croizet-Bages, it is worth mentioning that for older vintages two versions were used: one with a red band underneath (the normal label), and one with a blue band (for wine not bottled at the Château). Another tip: good vintages of Croizet-Bages can sometimes be indicated by the size of the bottle, as only the outstanding vintages are bottled in magnums and larger sizes.

### Not reserved, but amiable

The ideal way to drink a wine is at the Château itself, where it somehow always gives of its best. At the château-less Croizet-Bages this is difficult, so when the Quié family invited me to lunch, arrangements were made at Château Bel-Orme-Tronquoy de Lalande, which also belongs to them. This Château lies high up in St Estèphe, but the Croizet-Bages tasted well nevertheless. I drank the 1964 vintage with an excellent *entrecôte*, and the two were happily matched. The 1964 vintage had a splendid colour, a laudable nose and a glowing, velvety taste, soft and generously fruity, clearly a wine which had been harvested before the notorious rainfall of that vintage.

At home I have often enjoyed the 1962 vintage with its rounded, fruity bouquet and flavour to match.

It is often said that Pauillacs are reserved, hard wines, but there is little of this to be found in Croizet-Bages. True, the wine has obvious firmness, but this is packed in an accommodating flavour which comes to meet the drinker. Even young wines are often very supple and – ostensibly – advanced.

Other successful Croizet-Bages years are 1966, 1971, 1973, not forgetting 1970. It was with this last wine that the Château won the gold medal in its category at the 1974 Concours Oenologique International in Milan.

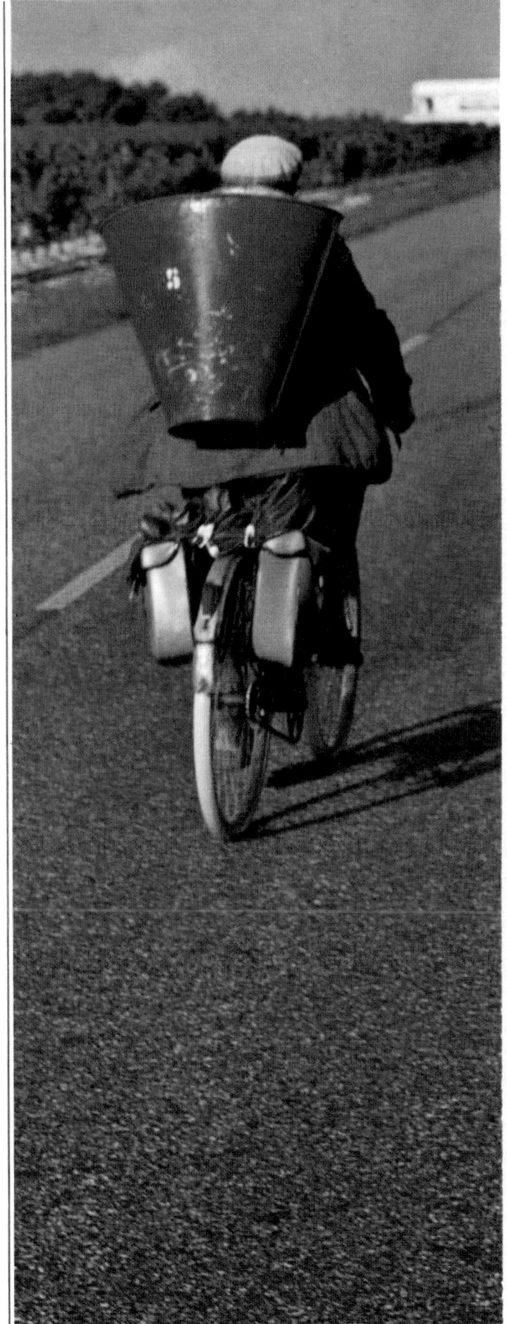

The Maison du Vin of Pauillac is housed at Grand-Puy-Ducasse, as are the headquarters of the *Commanderie du Bontemps de Médoc et des Graves.* The first official ceremony of this wine order was held in 1950 under the magnificent cedars of Lafite-Rothschild. Besides numerous activities in and outside Bordeaux, the Commanderie annually organises three large events. These are the *Fête de Saint-Vincent*, patron of wine-growers, towards the end of January, the *Fête de la Fleur* at the flowering of the vine in June, and the *Ban des Vendanges*, or proclamation of the vintage, just before the harvest. The great wines of the two districts flow freely and abundantly. The brotherhood also has its own blend, which is often served as an appetiser for the lunch or dinner being held.

*Right:*
*A member of the* Commanderie du Bontemps de Médoc et des Graves *during an 'enthroning' ceremony, when new members are admitted. The round hat is* the bontemps, *in the shape of the wooden bowl that holds the egg whites used for fining the wine.*

*Bottom:*
*The back of the small 18th-century château. Part of the garden has been sacrificed for an extension to the cellars.*

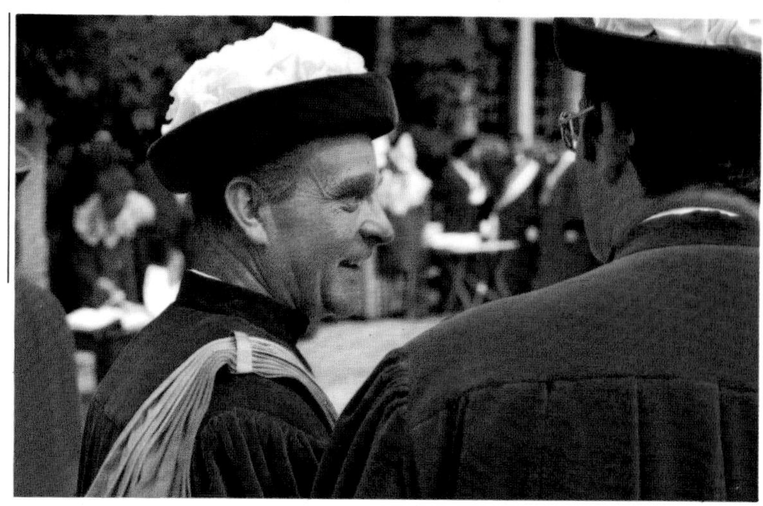

# Château Grand-Puy-Ducasse

5th Grand Cru Classé

In *Bordeaux et Ses Vins* of 1969 it says that Château Grand-Puy-Ducasse only has 10 hectares of vineyard with an average yield of 40 *tonneaux*. Recent developments, however, now mean that these statistics are out of date; in 1971 the estate changed owners, coming into the hands of people

M. Ducasse was a lawyer at the parliament of Bordeaux, and gave his name to the estate when he bought it in 1587. Like Grand-Puy-Lacoste, the property was originally part of the Domaine du Grand Puy, which in the 15th century covered some 90 hectares.

Important markets for the wine are the United States, Britain, Denmark, Switzerland and Belgium.

The Maison du Vin is open on weekdays. There is an interesting museum, and for those who are interested literature is available about the brotherhood, how the wine is made, plus a list of the visiting times of more than 60 châteaux.

*Below:*
*An oblique view of the front of Grand-Puy-Ducasse. Next to the small flight of steps on the right is the main entrance to the museum. The building fronts the river and quays of Pauillac.*

*Bottom:*
*On the right, behind the wrought-iron gate, is the entrance to the recently renovated vathouse. The château is in the middle of Pauillac and its vineyard is outside the town. The wine stands a fair chance of regaining its former popularity.*

who are closely connected with Mestrezat-Preller, a winehouse established in 1815. They appointed an experienced manager, M. Charles Bouilleau (who is also manager of Chasse-Spleen) and immediately started work on ambitious schemes for improvement.

### A vineyard in the making

The vineyard was almost trebled in size to 28 hectares, 13 of which are planted with Cabernet Sauvignon, 13 with Merlot and 2 with Petit Verdot. The vineyard is spread over the parish of Pauillac; the oldest part of it adjoins Mouton-Rothschild and Pontet-Canet, another adjoins Batailley and Grand-Puy-Lacoste, and a third section adjoins Pichon-Lalande and Pichon-Longueville. It is in thoroughly good company on all fronts! Besides the extension of the vineyard, essential improvements were carried out in the *chais*, both to machinery and to method. Four new steel fermentation vats were installed, it was decided that only new casks would be used, the wine was racked according to the latest theories, strict standards of cleanliness were imposed and the wines were subjected to an unprecedentedly rigorous selection – the result being far better wines than had previously been made.

The production rose to no less than 133 *tonneaux* in 1974, although that year produced an exceptional amount of wine anyway. The average production of Grand-Puy-Ducasse is only 30 hectolitres per hectare, which amounts to about 90 *tonneaux*. The increased production forced the estate to extend its *chais* considerably, and part of the garden was sacrificed to create more storage space. So now the bottles no longer need to be transported to Bordeaux for maturation in the warehouses of the shipping establishment, Mestrezat-Preller.

### A wine reborn

It could be said that the wine of Château Grand-Puy-Ducasse was reborn in 1971. This is evident when tasting, once again proving that man's influence should not be underestimated. The attitude of the proprietor is still decisive in the last instance, because it is quite possible to make a disappointing wine even from quality grapes grown on the best soil – as can regrettably be seen in a number of châteaux. In the history of the classed growths you can often read that this wine or that declined sharply in quality over a certain period. This could not be due to any sudden deterioration of the soil or change of climate, but always to the wine maker or owner. Apart from the progress in wine-making techniques and the incidence of vine diseases, the attitude of the owner is the only really variable factor where the quality of a growth is concerned. It can therefore be risky to buy a wine solely by its label. In fact you would do better to buy on the strength of the reputation of an individual or a firm rather than relying on the assumption that the great growths are classified according to quality – of which there are many degrees.

But back to Grand-Puy-Ducasse. The recent vintages I sampled would seem to be worthwhile buys. I personally thought the 1972 vintage successful, and the 1973 vintage is good, too; the latter wine contains a considerable amount of tannin without being harsh; it is even slightly soft. The colour is excellent, the bouquet (and in fact the whole wine) is very promising.

### Headquarters of the wine order

The Château of Grand-Puy-Ducasse is in the middle of Pauillac on the long quayside, separate from the vineyard. The building serves as Pauillac's *Maison du Vin* and is also the seat of the wine order, the *Commanderie du Bontemps du Médoc et des Graves*. This derives its name from the *bontemps*, the wooden bowl in which the egg whites for fining the wine were once beaten. The headgear of its officers, with its white top, is in the shape of this bowl, a cellar utensil of former times, also used for catching any drips from casks. The order's motto is: *'Par le bontemps, pour le bon temps, Graves et Médoc!'*

The Château derives its name from an earlier proprietor, a M. Pédesclaux.

The Jugla family has been making wine in Pauillac for four generations now, and not only on its own estates. Bernard Jugla's grandfather, for example, was for 30 years manager of what is now Duhart-Milon-Rothschild.

*Right:*
*The oil refinery of Pauillac looks horribly close here, though it is in fact over a kilometre away. The existence of 'Château d'Huile' appears to be due mainly to the negligence of the estate owners, who just failed to protest when it was announced that the capacity of the small refinery, which had already long been in existence, was to be increased tenfold. It is a touchy subject among the great growths, who could certainly have brought pressure to bear if they had united to do so. Now nothing can be done. The countryside is spoiled, the odour of the refinery blows over the vineyards of the first growths, although the wine itself so far seems not to have been affected. And French Shell could easily have gone elsewhere.*

# Chau Pédesclaux

5th Grand Cru Classé

If you leave Pauillac in the direction of Lafite-Rothschild, and you go up to the junction of three roads, which is marked by a crucifix, you will see a solid little building standing among the vines with the name *Vignoble Pédesclaux*. The Château is not far away, and you can already see its steeply-pitched roof silhouetted against the silvery expanse of the Gironde. The building dates from the 19th century. I have always been surprised that it looks nothing like the château on the labels, which depict a square, massive building with a few *chais* in the background, and the tower of Pauillac. Or are these perhaps the *chais* in Pauillac itself, which were sold in 1970? But then what are the vines doing in the foreground? Or did the owners want a more impressive house portrayed on their label – and the printer simply designed one for them?

## Reception and tasting

At any rate, Château Pédesclaux exists, and the proprietors have converted the building into flats which are individually leased. Visitors can therefore only visit the *chais*, which have recently been extensively decorated and rearranged. A pleasant reception room has been established behind the vathouse, with its enamelled steel vats, and the bottling hall. This room has been simply but attractively decorated in rough white plasterwork, looking just as though bits of endive have been stuck to the wall and painted over. The tall, moustached, dedicated co-owner and manager, Bernard Jugla, has collected a number of objects connected with wine in this reception room, and in fact he hopes eventually to have enough to form a miniature wine museum. His family is established in many countries, so he can assemble his collection from several continents. Thank goodness he has plenty of spitoons, which I was glad to use during the interesting tasting session which he arranged when I visited Pédesclaux.

## Four recent vintages

We limited ourselves to the 1973, 1972, 1971 and 1970 vintages. The first wine, the 1973, had a surprisingly brownish colour in spite of the wine still being so young. For a cask sample, this was indeed surprising. The bouquet was pleasant and fresh, but without

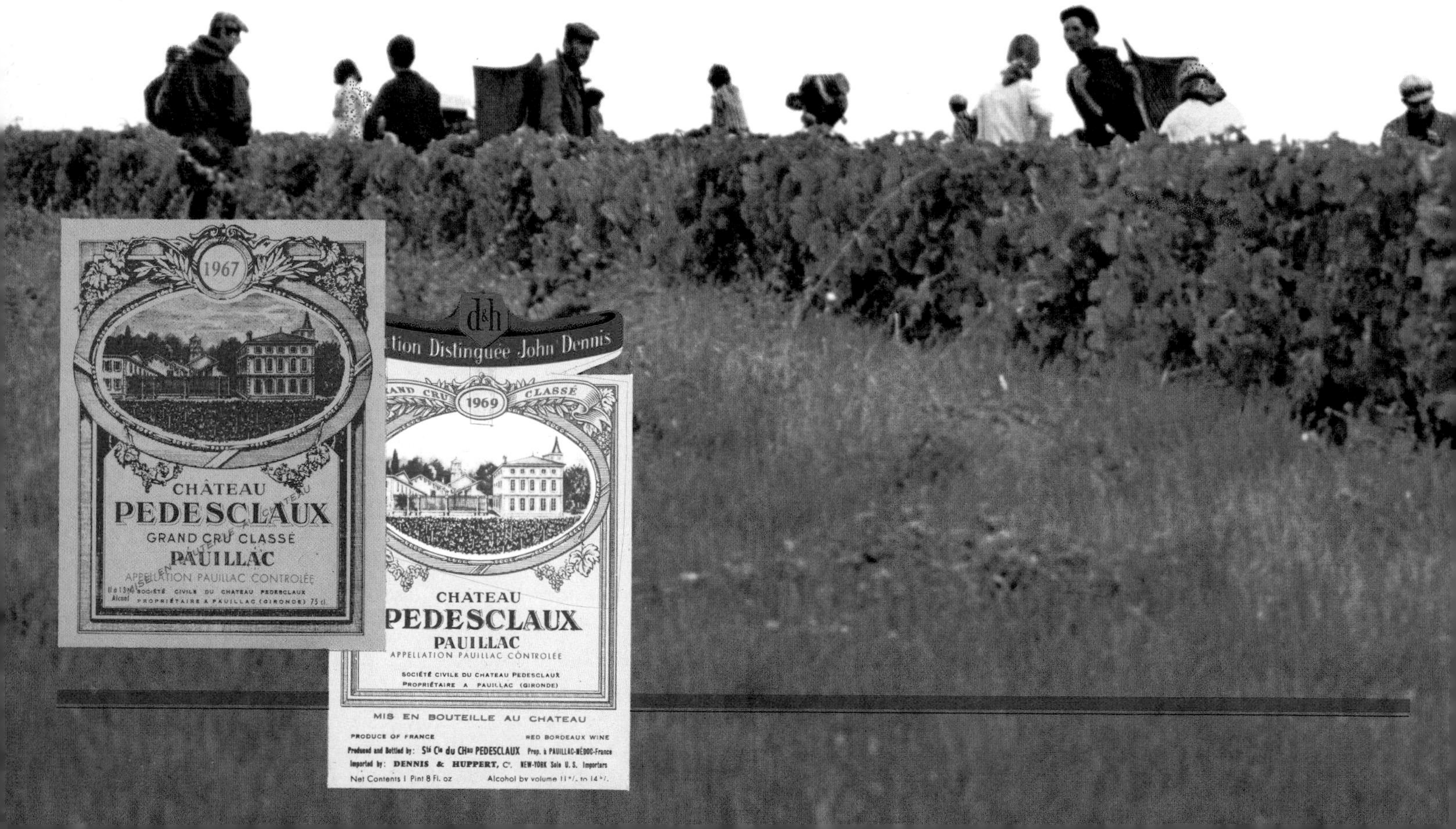

At Pédesclaux new oak casks are used for about a quarter of the wine each year.

The father of Bernard Jugla had already been manager of the Château for seventeen years when he took over from the Counts Xavier d'Erceville and Michel du Lac in 1950. They were grandchildren of de Gastebois, who had bought the Château in 1891.

*Opposite page, bottom left:*
*The wine of Pédesclaux is sold under two different labels: on the left is the original version, which was changed at the request of the American importer. Most of the estates fairly regard their label as sacrosanct, but because the U.S.A. are the chief buyers of Pédesclaux, the alteration was agreed to.*

*Below:*
*A sizeable band of pickers near the château. The vineyard of Pédesclaux is divided into three sections, one section lying near the house and adjoining the vineyard of Mouton-Rothschild, the second section near Pontet Canet and the third closer to Lynch-Bages, some way away.*

*Right:*
*The vathouse of Pédesclaux. The fermentation tanks are of enamelled steel.*

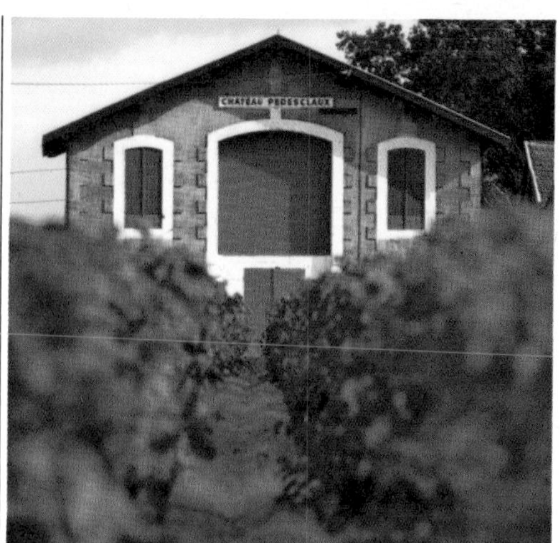



depth, the taste was rather flat with a slight sweetness. 1973 was not a great success for Pédesclaux, as Bernard Jugla agreed. The wine will be ready for drinking in 1976. Can one still respect an owner who has a sufficiently dispassionate love of wine to bring out his less successful vintages? Only the final taste will tell.

The 1972 vintage has an attractive, deep colour, and the characteristic bouquet for a Pédesclaux, which is piquant, perhaps even peppery. The style is fruity, but otherwise tends to be somewhat on the light side – something fairly characteristic of this year. The wine will be ready for drinking quite soon, and will certainly remain good for some 5 to 10 years.

The 1971 vintage was on its own. In that year the Merlot grape at Pédesclaux failed completely, the result being a wine of perhaps 90% to 95% Cabernet (normally it is 80%). This lack of Merlot can immediately be seen from the colour, which is unusually dark. The bouquet and the flavour form a striking contrast with the previous two wines, because the 1971 lacks all softness and appreciable amiability. The wine is solid, masculine and hard – definitely for putting away. I have a few bottles of it at home, but I don't intend to open them before the mid 1980s.

The 1970 vintage was the star. A darkish colour was followed by a concentrated bouquet and a somewhat reserved but fruity flavour, already pronounced, which was echoed in the impressive after-taste.

### A wine family on their new property

Pédesclaux produces an average of 75 *tonneaux* a year from approximately 20 hectares of vines. The wine is exported to the U.S.A. (40%), the Benelux countries (40%) and Switzerland, Britain and Denmark. The Jugla family have been active wine-growers in Pauillac for four generations, but it was not until 1950 that they bought Château Pédesclaux. They are enthusiastic and serious, and the wines they make are worth watching.

# Ch^au Pontet Canet

5th Grand Cru Classé

The history of Pontet Canet goes back to the year 1720, when the vineyard was created by M. Pontet, a rich man with an impressive title: Equerry of the Ancient Order of Keepers of the Seal, attached to the *Cour des Aides de Guyenne*. Such flowery honorary titles disappeared at the Revolution. Besides Pontet Canet, Pontet also owned Pontet St Julien. Both the estates remained in the family for a long time, but were eventually sold, Pontet Canet being bought by Herman Cruse in 1865 after the death of a Madame de Pontet, and Pontet St Julien earlier, in 1821, to Hugh Barton, who renamed it Langoa-Barton.

So from 1865 onwards the Cruse family have reigned over this fifth classed growth, and it says much for this old Bordeaux family of growers and merchants that it succeeded in giving the wine of Pontet Canet such quality that in the past it has frequently been sold at the same price as some of the seconds. In the majority of reference books about the classification, it

*Opposite page, left:*
*The splendid 18th century château, with the entrance to the vathouse on the left.*

*Opposite page, right:*
*A glimpse of the large inner courtyard. The house on the right is the office of M. Ardeloy and the administrative staff.*

*Opposite page, below:*
*The grapes are hoisted up to the égrappoir which, rather unusually, is situated above the vathouse.*

*Right and far right:*
*Two of the comfortable salons in the château.*

*Bottom:*
*The Cruse family no longer lives here except occasionally, but they use the house for entertaining visitors.*

*Below:*
*The vintage of 1972 is the first to be bottled at the Château, as the label states. Previously Pontet Canet was bottled in Bordeaux.*

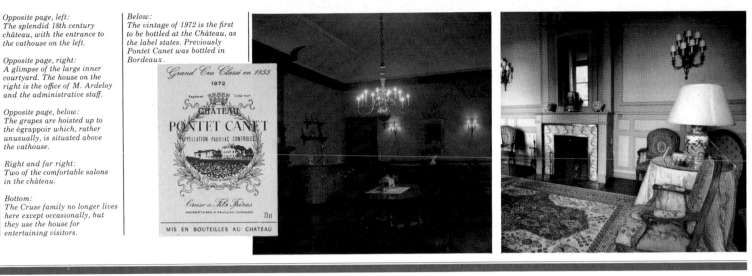

is noted that, as regards quality, Pontet Canet deserves far more than its official status, but, as people do not always understand, the categories of the 1855 classification do not directly imply how good or superior the wine may be. The 1855 classification was undertaken by the Bordeaux brokers at the time of the Paris Exhibition; a number of wines were selected as fine and arranged in the order usual for the prices they fetched on the market. Some were not even tasted by the selectors! All the classed growths are, by implication, fine wines, some more than others. But any revision of this classification in terms of quality is fraught with perils.

### A vinescape around the house

The Château dates from the 18th century but is not now lived in by members of the Cruse family. It has, however, always been beautifully maintained and provides a perfect setting for estate hospitality. From the first glimpse of the house, at the end of curved drive where miniature cyclamen carpet the grass verges, there is a succession of things pleasing to the eye.

The specially privileged are sometimes asked to lunch, when white-gloved staff serve food chosen and prepared as carefully as the wines. Then they usually go up to the adjoining *chai*, on the floor above the presshouse, where they have a panoramic view of part of the vineyard, one of the largest in the Médoc, covering 65 hectares. Two-thirds of the vineyard is situated in the immediate vicinity of the château.

The grapes are brought up to this first floor where the de-stalking takes place, and then they are lightly crushed before being pumped into the fermentation vats, where the must – unfermented grape juice – eventually becomes wine.

### The wine alive in the quiet chai

The vats are mostly of dark oak, except for a few of cement. This is a question of tradition, manager M. Ardeley told me, because in fact the wooden vats make more work, as they are difficult to clean and tend to dry out, which entails extra maintenance; another disadvantage is that the temperature of the fermentation is difficult to regulate. With stainless steel vats you only need to press a button to control this, but the temperature inside the oak vats can be difficult to determine with exactitude from the outside, and cannot be precisely controlled. At Pontet Canet I saw a small, old-fashioned coal stove placed between the vats to raise the temperature of the wine slightly in cold weather so that the secondary fermentation can continue unimpeded.

Immediately behind the presshouse is the *chai* for the first-year wine, one of the tallest I know in Bordeaux. It is not possible to build deep cellars below ground in the Médoc, because the whole region lies so low that they would soon be waterlogged.

*Right:*
*The vineyard is vast, the vintage impressive.*

*Below right:*
*The outside of the big vathouse. The upper floor, where the grapes are hoisted, is sometimes used for receptions, but not at vintage time!*

*Bottom right:*
*A group of guests signing the visitors' book. The major markets for Pontet Canet are the U.S.A., Canada, Great Britain, Japan, Belgium and Holland.*

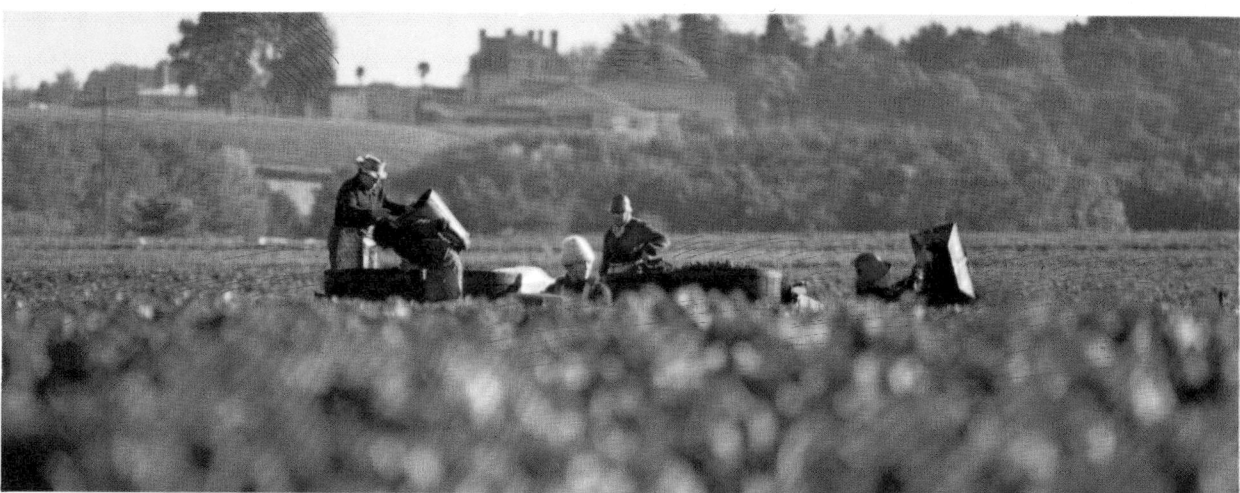



At Pontet Canet there is a personal reserve of the owners kept in deep cellars below ground, but otherwise most new wine, while it is in cask, remains at ground level in two *chais* – first and second year – in wood.

To enter such a *chai*, especially on a hot day in summer, is an impressive experience. You are aware of the wine as a living creature within the long rows of casks. The atmosphere is hushed and redolent of the costly liquid lying in the *barriques*.

### Atmospheric sampling

If you walk through the first-year *chai* you come to the place where the casks are cleaned and the reserves are stored. Everyone working in wine is entitled to a daily allowance to drink and, as both cellar and vineyard work are strenuous occupations, this is generous. However, wine hardly counts as drink – in terms of spirits or fortified wines – in Bordeaux; after all, doctors permit claret consumption in pregnancy and lactation!

The second-year *chai* at Pontet Canet is a genuine cellar, because it is actually under the ground. Here, however, storage conditions are limited. The *barriques* are stacked one on top of the other in fairly narrow, elongated, arched passages running in several parallel lines.

This is, for me, one of the most lasting impressions of tasting Bordeaux – a sample of young wine, before bottling, tasted in the dim light among the casks in the company of those who have helped to create it.

### New times – and new-style wines

Pontet Canet averages 300 *tonneaux*.
I tasted the 1973 vintage in the cellar with the manager, M. Ardeley. The wine had a light colour, not too dark, a slightly sultry, fruity bouquet, and a fairly mature flavour, which surprised me, because to me Pontet Canet has always been such a classic Pauillac (produced from 75% Cabernet Sauvignon, 2% Cabernet Franc, 23% Merlot) that it is usually hard when young. M. Ardeley said this was true, but because the consumer has neither the facilities nor the patience to store wine for years, it was recently decided to modify the vinification process so that the wine is encouraged to become more supple and is therefore easier to drink while fairly young.

M. Ardeley has worked at the estate since 1939 and he seems to regret this decision, but it is dictated by economic pressure.
He expects the 1973 vintage to be pleasantly drinkable in 1978, and by then the 1972 will also be ready for drinking. This is a pleasant wine without much depth, and as yet it seems less complete than its younger brother.

The 1962 was a totally different sort of wine, hefty, clinging to the glass. It had an enticing, sweet, pervasive bouquet and a firm, round taste; it is a genial, forthcoming wine.

The 1966 vintage is one to keep for many years yet. When I saw the slightly velvety colour, with its vague hint of brown, I was prepared for a reasonably developed wine, but the taste proved the opposite. On the palate I noted a great deal of tannin still. The bouquet was typical of Pontet Canet, obviously fruity and slightly luscious – this was a very good year in Pauillac.

The 1967 vintage is less lush and rounded than the 1966, but still has a generous taste and balanced style. This is simply a lighter year, which will be ready for serving and drinking quicker than the 1966.

In my view the 1969 vintage is also pleasant, not overfull of flavour. It is in many respects a lighter version of the 1967 vintage (colour, scent, taste and after-taste), but it still remains very much Pontet Canet, true to its origin.

Finally, the 1970 vintage, like the 1966, must be allowed to mature for some years to come. The wine was still hard and very reticent, though the fine fruity bouquet was an indication of what may develop.
All the wines up to the year 1972 were bottled in the Cruse cellars in Bordeaux, but in 1972 the changeover to château-bottling was made. Mention of this is made on the label of the 1972 vintage for the first time in the history of Pontet Canet.

*Bottom:*
*The modest-looking building of Haut Bages Libéral. It dates from 1850 and is now the home of the* chef de culture *and his family.*

The ceiling of the new cellar resounds so much that, to quote Ardeley, the manager, he feels as if he is working in a church.

The Château takes its name from the location of the vineyard (mainly on the plateau of Bages), and M. Libéral, the proprietor at the time of the classification of 1855.

The wine is bottled using the same mobile bottling unit that is used at other Cruse châteaux, including Pontet Canet and d'Issan.

Each year about a third of the casks used at Haut Bages Libéral are new.

# Chau Haut Bages Libéral

5th Grand Cru Classé

On the label of Château Haut Bages Libéral it says that the estate is the property of the unknown Société Civile Charreules, but in fact it might as well say Cruse Fils et Frères, for the Cruses bought Haut Bages Libéral in 1960 and for administrative reasons turned it into a private company. I mention this because this family, one of the most important of the Bordeaux wine 'dynasties', may well have the same sort of success eventually with Haut Bages as they have long had with Pontet Canet. The emphasis here is on 'eventually', because a transformation like this demands time, as well as money.

It was not until fourteen years after the Cruses had taken over, in 1974, that the *chai* and the vathouse could be completely modernised. Unlike traditional Pontet Canet, everything at Haut Bages Libéral is completely modern. There is the very latest type of *égrappoir*, more than a dozen stainless steel fermentation vats and a neat row of *chais*. The vineyard has been replanned to facilitate efficient working. Replanting has resulted in an increased percentage of Cabernet Sauvignon, now as high as 89% (with 9% Merlot and 2% Petit Verdot). Haut Bages Libéral would therefore seem to be about to enjoy a bright future – and it is indeed time for the resuscitation of this growth.

## Lack of charm

Perhaps slightly spoiled by Pontet Canet, Batailley, Grand-Puy-Lacoste, Mouton Baron Philippe and other Pauillacs I found the wines of Haut Bages Libéral rather a disappointment. My greatest criticism was their lack of charm. Even fairly amiable years, such as 1967, did not quite achieve this, and somehow never succeeded in being wholly pleasing. This may just be my view. The 1967 vintage is slightly more complete and rounded than the 1969 but it lacks the required amplitude. I also detected something too acid, although only in the background. The wines of Haut Bages Libéral which I have drunk otherwise seemed a little thin – the 1969 even meagre; they could do with some more flesh. I prefer to reserve judgement on the 1973 vintage (which was fruity and aromatic), as it is the wines of future years which will and must be the proof of the rehabilitation of the estate.

The Château of Haut Bages Libéral is situated about 800 metres from Château Latour, and the vineyards of the two estates adjoin. In all, the vineyard extends over 21 hectares. The production has fluctuated recently between 71 *tonneaux* (in 1971) and 129 *tonneaux* (in 1970). The main markets up to now have been the United States, Britain, Japan, Canada and Australia.

Shortly after the war, the Baron wanted to reshape the layout of Mouton Baron Philippe and open it to the public so that it would provide a splendid approach to Mouton-Rothschild. The staff and workers, however, were against the idea, because they were afraid that the flowers and trees might be ruined by the crowds. But the Baron pursued his idea and transformed the wilderness into an elegant park with lawns, flowerbeds and new trees. 'In 30 years', Baron Philippe says, 'we have only had one loss: in the mid-fifties a small fir tree was cut down and stolen on Christmas Eve.'

*Right:*
*Some of the 18 big casks, each containing 100 hectolitres. These are used to store the wine in abundant years.*

*Below left:*
*The label of Mouton Baron Philippe shows the same tradition of fine design as the labels of Mouton Rothschild, Clerc Milon and even Mouton Cadet.*

*Below right:*
*The Mouton* chai, *with its beamed roof, is almost luxurious. It has a capacity of 1,100 casks.*

*Opposite page:*
*Baron Philippe de Rothschild photographed by Sir Cecil Beaton, a portrait of which the Baron himself is particularly fond.*

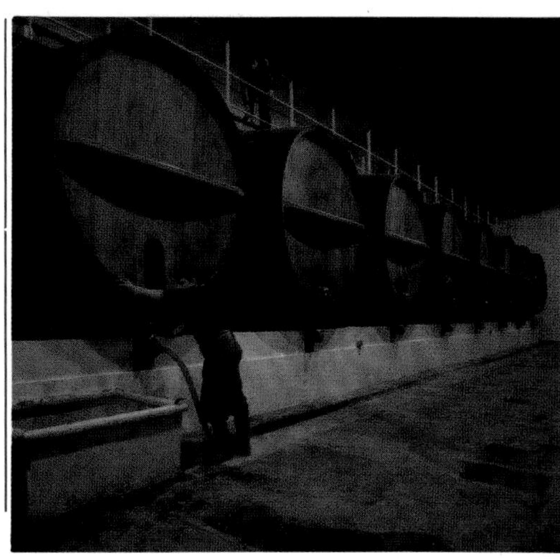

# Ch^au^ Mouton Baron Philippe

5th Grand Cru Classé

Anyone entering the park of Mouton Baron Philippe will be struck by the surrealistic appearance of the Château. It is only half a house, with half a pediment under the roof. Work on the building began between 1820 and 1830, but it was never completed. This is quite typical of the often haphazard methods of the old days; growers were wholly dependent on the weather and were alternately rich and poor as a result of its caprices.

Not only the changeable weather conditions determined the fortunes of the proprietors: the economic situation also played an important rôle. This was most marked in the crisis years of the 1930s, when even the greatest names found themselves in serious difficulties. The fifth

The half-finished Château will remain as it is, but it is being done up inside for three grandchildren of the owner.

The major markets for the wine are the United States, Britain and Japan, while the lesser years do well in France.

The long drive through the park of Mouton Baron Philippe was made by 100 German prisoners of war. The Germans had spent the war at Mouton-Rothschild, then the German air defence centre for south-western France. After the war, the French put the men at the Baron's disposal to clear up the débris left from the war and to put the place in order.

*Right:*
*Cellar work, like that in the vineyard, never stops, though there is great satisfaction in making superb wine.*

*Below right:*
*With a small hand press a quick trial pressing is taken to check the quality of the must during the vintage.*

growth Château Mouton-d'Armailhacq was no exception to this rule. It was bought in 1933 by Baron Philippe de Rothschild, who eleven years earlier had taken over responsibility for the adjoining Mouton-Rothschild. In this way, he brought two wine-growing estates under one proprietor once again – for, during the French Revolution, Mouton d'Armailhacq was split off from the large Mouton vineyard and came into the hands first of the Armailhacq family, and later of the Count de Ferrand.

### A change of name

Legally, Baron Philippe would have been able to incorporate the vineyard of Mouton-d'Armailhacq into that of Mouton-Rothschild, thus considerably enlarging the production of this much more famous and expensive growth. He refrained from doing so because he has always jealously preserved the absolute independence and individuality of his Mouton. So the vineyards remained separate. What Baron Philippe did do was to make every effort to bring the quality of the wine of his new acquisition up to a higher level, according to his own ideas. The size of the vineyard was therefore reduced from 75 to 52 hectares, where necessary it was replanted; new *chais* were built, and modern equipment installed. It was only in 1956 that the Baron considered Mouton-d'Armailhacq good enough to be admitted into the family, and he changed the name to Mouton Baron Philippe. This change was made for two reasons: the important Anglo-Saxon countries could only pronounce the words d'Armailhacq with the greatest difficulty and the Baron was afraid that the name might be confused with Armagnac, the second brandy of France.

Did Baron Philippe buy this fifth growth because it was also a Mouton? Probably not. For years he had been irritated by the fact that Mouton-d'Armailhacq was separated from Mouton-Rothschild by walls, barriers, railings and palings, which greatly obstructed access to his own Château. The purchase of Mouton-d'Armailhacq made it possible to construct the park and the long drive which serves as the entrance to both Moutons. But the Baron had to wait until the death of d'Armailhacq's tenacious owner in 1938, and then the work had to be postponed until after the war.

### Two styles but a single quality

The first wine which was marketed as Mouton Baron Philippe was the 1956, not exactly an auspicious year because of the severe frost. Nevertheless, the estate succeeded in producing 105 *tonneaux* of fairly light wine. The present yield is 180 to 220 *tonneaux*. Minimum production was in the year 1961, when only 120 *tonneaux* could be made. The wine of Mouton Baron Philippe has a style all of its own, completely different from that of Mouton-Rothschild. Sometimes it even tends to resemble Lafite rather than Mouton.

One of the reasons for this is undoubtedly the fairly high percentage of Merlot (25%), which makes Mouton Baron Philippe much softer, friendlier and ready for drinking sooner than Mouton-Rothschild. The wine is made in the estate's own *chais*, and even these are different from those of the parent Château. For example, fermentation vats are of cement instead of wood, and the wine is left to mature mainly in the three-year-old casks from Mouton-Rothschild. If the harvest is large there is not always enough room to store all the wine in *barriques*, so then part of it is stored for a year in large 10,000-litre casks, something which is not done at all at Mouton-Rothschild.

The wines of Mouton Baron Philippe are overall good. The 1967, for example, has a bouquet so agreeably full of depth and nuances that you might forget actually to drink the wine. The same astonishing fragrance is to be noted in the 1966, a year in which the high quality of this Château is masterfully demonstrated. Yet despite its individuality one can taste that the wine has a relationship with Mouton-Rothschild. Appropriately, the motto of Mouton Baron Philippe is *'Bon sang ne peut mentir'*, which roughly means, 'Blood will tell'.

*Left:*
*Since 1945, famous artists such as Jean Cocteau (1947), Salvador Dali (1958), Henry Moore (1964) and Marc Chagall (1970) have designed labels for Mouton. The view is held that the illustrations can indicate the style of the vintage: for example, Chagall's colourful gouache exactly symbolises the exuberance of the 1970 vintage. Every year Baron Philippe's business friends receive a New Year card depicting the most recent of these small works of art.*

*Below:*
*The vineyard of Mouton-Rothschild covers 72 hectares, some 60 of which are under production. The average yield is about 180* tonneaux.

# Chau Mouton-Rothschild

1st Grand Cru Classé

Mouton-Rothschild is one of the most impressive estates in the Médoc. Every year it attracts 30,000 to 40,000 tourists, and has, more than any other château, been the subject of innumerable newspaper and magazine articles. To a very great extent this interest is due to the 118 years' struggle which Mouton has waged against the classification of 1855: to the extreme displeasure of the owners at that time Mouton was not admitted to the *premiers crus classés* but had to be content with being first of the second growths.

The reason for this was probably the time. The Mouton estate was bought by Baron Nathaniel de Rothschild in a somewhat dilapidated condition in 1853 – only two years before the famous classification. In such a short time he was unable to make significant changes to the winery and the vineyard. Mouton was then no more than a farm, and it was not until 1880 that the first steps were taken by Nathaniel's son, James, to turn it into a genuine Château. Alongside the *chais* he built an elegant house, now known as Petit-Mouton. Baron James died in 1881 when he was only 37 years old, but the management of the estate stayed in Rothschild hands through his wife. In 1920 her son Henri found himself encumbered with Mouton and its fortunes, but Henri was more interested in literature and the theatre, and after only two years he transferred command of the Château to his 21 year-old son, Philippe.

The reputation of Mouton-Rothschild by that time was outstanding. Baron Philippe was to be the first of the Rothschilds to try to upgrade Mouton to a first growth.

### Changes and innovations

One of the first things the young proprietor did was to insist that all Mouton should be

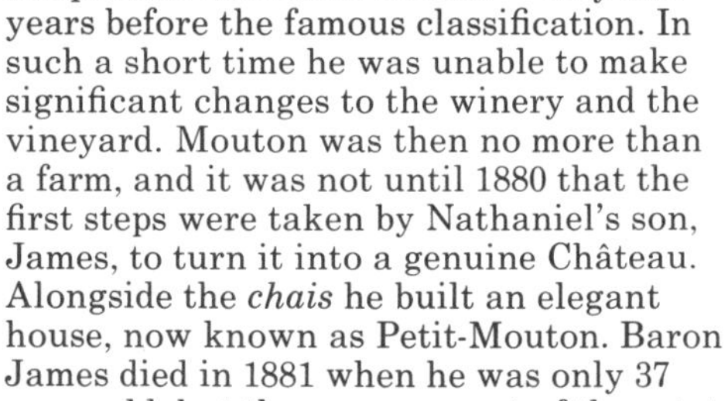

For years, as protest against the classification of 1855, Mouton carried the motto: *'Premier nu puis, second ne daigne, Mouton suis'* ('First I cannot be, second I will not be; I am Mouton'). After Mouton joined first growths the Baron had to change his motto. It is now: *'Premier je suis, second je fus, Mouton ne change'* ('First I am, second I have been, Mouton remains the same').

It is not generally known that the first exhibits in the personal museum were collected by Philippe's father, Baron Henri. He was able to acquire many works of art when the collection of Baron Carl Mayer de Rothschild of Frankfurt came up at auction.

In 1974 Cyril Ray's book on Mouton Rothschild was published by Christie, Manson & Woods. Baron Philippe had hoped for this ever since Mr Ray wrote about Lafite.

In the centre of Pauillac are the offices and cellars of La Bergerie, the marketing organisation of Baron Philippe de Rothschild S.A. A world-wide bestseller is the branded wine Mouton-Cadet, which accounts for about 70% of the turnover of La Bergerie. The wine bears the *appellation* Bordeaux, and is constant in quality, but actually has little now to do with the *grand vin* Mouton-Rothschild, although it was originally made in the Médoc.

From each vintage 24 bottles, 5 magnums and 2 jeroboams are kept at Mouton.

*Far right:*
*A fine 16th century bust of Bacchus by Giovanni della Robbia, another of the treasures of the wonderful private museum at Mouton.*

*Centre:*
*A silver vase, part of it gilded, showing a bearded man's face crowned with vines. It was made in Augsburg, Germany, in the 17th century.*

*Below right:*
*A large wine cup in silver and gold, a Persian antiquity dating from the 5th century A.D.*

*Bottom left:*
*Ground-plan of Mouton-Rothschild.*
**A** *cellars,* **B** *museum,* **C** *the large cellar,* **D** *Petit Mouton,* **E** *visitors' car park,* **F** *private apartments,* **G** *Grand Mouton.*

*Above:*
*Two Persian drinking goblets from the 9th or 8th century B.C., made in gold and delicately decorated.*



château bottled. At this time, even the first growths only bottled a proportion of the wine at the property, the remainder being bottled by the merchants who bought it, not necessarily to the wine's detriment.

It goes without saying that great attention was also paid to establishing the quality of Mouton. Very characteristic is the markedly high percentage of the Cabernet Sauvignon grape – approximately 90%, with 7% Cabernet Franc and the remainder Merlot.

Meanwhile the Baron began to bring the Château into the limelight in other ways. From 1934 each Mouton label mentions the number of bottles vintaged, and each bottle is numbered, and from 1945 (*l'année de la victoire*) the upper part of the label has been designed by a different artist every year, the exception being 1953 when the wine and the label were dedicated to Mouton's first three Rothschild owners to commemorate its centenary.

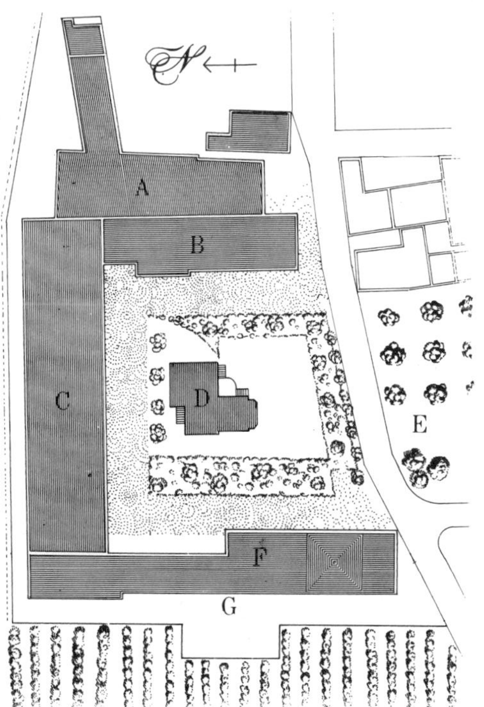


**The wonderful wine museum**

Baron Philippe's most spectacular innovation was the creation of his museum in 1962. With the help of his American second wife, Pauline, he assembled a unique collection of works of art in what was formerly a cellar. Every exhibit is in some way connected with wine. This collection includes a wide range: the finest glass, magnificent old flagons, Persian goblets, antique furniture with grape-patterned upholstery, paintings by Picasso and Dutch masters, tapestries and *objets d'art* from distant lands such as Tibet, Russia and Egypt. The exhibits are cleverly displayed,

*Left:*
*Cellar master Raoul Blondin, amiable and imperturbable.*

Besides their own wines, some 100,000 bottles of other famous châteaux from the Médoc, and from Graves, St Emilion and Pomerol, lie in the Mouton cellars. In many cases Baron Philippe possesses vintages of fellow proprietors which they themselves no longer have. The collection begins with the 1859 vintage, and the bottles are re-corked every 25 years.

The names of Mouton-Rothschild, Lafite-Rothschild and Cos d'Estournel all describe the same thing. Mouton comes from *motte de terre*, which means 'hillock', Lafite from *la hite*, 'hill', and Cos from *coteaux* or *côtes*, 'slopes'.

*Below left:*
*A chart which follows the fermentation process from day to day. The top line records the temperature, the bottom one the decreasing quantity of sugar which is converted into alcohol. The temperature curve levels off because the wine has been cooled during the process to ensure that it does not rise above 30°C, when fermentation might stop.*

*Bottom left:*
*The must ferments in 17 vats such as these.*

*Bottom right:*
*Artist's impression of the* grand chai *where the wine of the latest vintage is laid up.*

*Centre right:*
*Mouton-Rothschild coat of arms*



with imaginative settings and lighting. Everyone who visits Mouton may apply to look around the museum.

### The Baron wins his battle

Baron Philippe's keen sense of publicity and his continued efforts to make Mouton a first growth were eventually crowned with success in 1973. With the assent of the four other first growths Mouton-Rothschild was elevated to a first, but not before many battles had been fought on paper. Philippe Cottin, manager of Baron Philippe de Rothschild S.A., knows all about it: his file on the subject weighs 68 kilos, and it only goes back to 1959!

In fact the success of Mouton was already evident because the wines had been selling at the same prices as the other first growths for about fifty years. Since the second world war people have frequently paid even more for Mouton than for some others. In

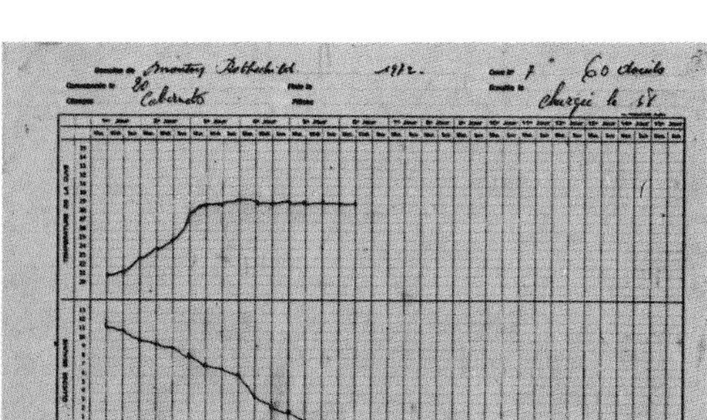

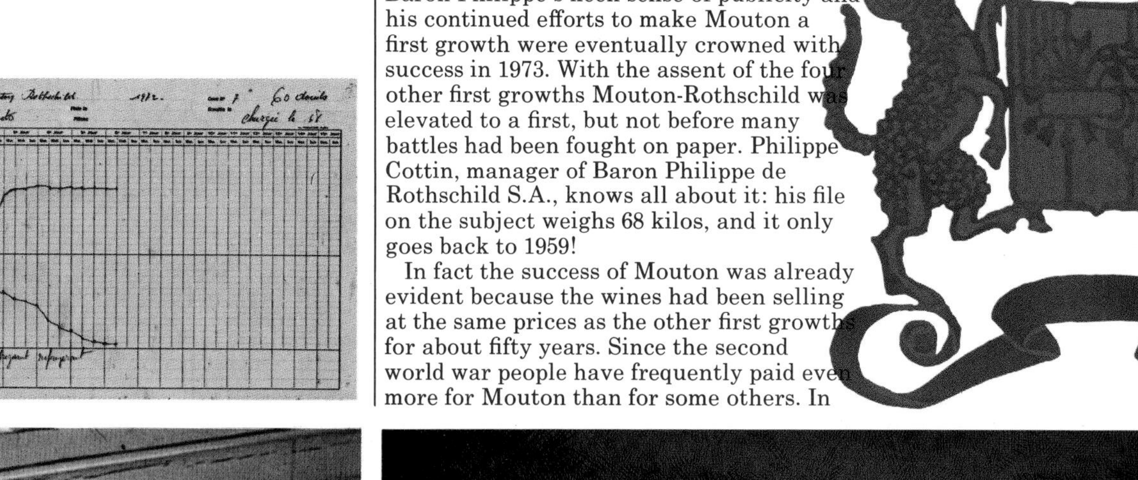

*Right:*
*The cherub who greets all visitors from Bacchus' head.*

*Far right:*
*Part of the Baron's living quarters. He and the Baronne are not often in residence, as they live abroad most of the time. Facing the white stone flight of steps is Petit Mouton veiled in green, and behind is the entrance to the museum and the* chais.

*Bottom: Some of the white doves that flutter in the courtyard of Mouton and perch on the* chai *roof.*



1971, for example, the opening price of Lafite was 110,000 francs per *tonneau* of 900 litres, that of Mouton 120,000 francs. Baron Philippe is passionate about Mouton although his insistence on the altered classification has not, it should be stressed, in any way altered the wine.

### A luxurious chais

In the *chais* at Mouton everything possible has been done to impress the visitor. First, either the *maître de chais*, Raoul Blondin, or his brother Pierre conducts you past the large, oak fermentation vats, after which you are admitted to the vast *chais* where last year's vintage lies maturing in hundreds of brand-new casks. The atmosphere is reverent, even loudly-dressed tourists speak in hushed tones, impressed by the impeccable home of the wine. Specially privileged visitors may sample a little of the purple liquid, still full of tannin, destined to become one of the world's superlative wines.

The wine of Mouton-Rothschild has been praised by many. The description given by a British Master of Wine, Clive Coates, in *Wine Magazine* is typical: 'The concentration of flavour, the sheer opulence, the massive amount of fruit, allied with the unmistakably seductive cedarwood aroma of mature Mouton makes truly exhilarating drinking.'

### Some memorable Moutons

The most impressive Mouton I have ever tasted is the 1961 vintage, a year which has been compared to the great 1870 and the 1945. Raoul Blondin allowed the wine to reach the right temperature and decanted it with care. I remember his exact words when he handed me the first glass: *'Et voilà le grand Mouton'*. Nor was there a grain of exaggeration in this, for it was a very great wine indeed. First, I noticed the amazingly deep colour, then the penned-up, deep, rich bouquet, then the full, woody flavour abounding with fruit. And finally the long, lingering aftertaste – I could still savour the wine half an hour after the tasting. Even Raoul Blondin, who is entirely used to Mouton, refused to spit out this particular wine.

It is sometimes said that the *premiers grands crus* are too expensive, but wines like the 1961 Mouton-Rothschild are truly priceless. The yield per hectare, for example, in 1961 was staggeringly low: only nine hectolitres per hectare.

Another memorable Mouton for me was the 1952 vintage, especially since it is a highly characteristic year with all the best qualities of this great wine. The 1952 vintage at Mouton was classed even higher than the 1953 vintage. The wine of this classic year clearly evoked the *goût de capsule*, which many writers about wine have mentioned. I myself think, however, that it isn't reminiscent of the capsule seal but of iron, for there is iron in the subsoil of Mouton and in dry years like 1952 the roots seek their nourishment deep.

### Recent vintages

The 1970 Mouton is also a majestic wine, proclaimed by some as the best wine of that already exceptional year. After 1970 I expect 1974 to be a year when Mouton may once again score high: the young wine, tasted straight from the cask, had an intense, powerful bouquet full of fruit. Of the 'middling' years – are there any such years with a château of this calibre? – I have fond memories of the 1962 and 1967 vintages. Only in 1964 did Mouton, to my mind, not quite attain its customary greatness, but the property was certainly not alone in this with that rained-out vintage.

# Ch^au^ Clerc Milon

Cru Classé

*Right:*
*The Baron and Baroness used this silver marriage cup from Germany, dated 1609, as a model for the label of Clerc Milon, which they themselves designed. Apparently both the lady's skirt and the cup she is holding were filled with wine, and one had to try to drink the contents of the skirt without spilling a drop from the precariously balanced cup – which would be almost impossible. On the skirt of the original figure is written in German: 'Those who drink beer or wine from me, will always think the best of me'.*

*Bottom:*
*One of the buildings on the estate.*

*Opposite page:*
*The cork and label of Château Clerc Milon.*

In the course of its history the Château has had a number of different names. In *Bordeaux et Ses Vins* of 1850, it is listed as Château Clerc, in the editions of 1868 to 1898 as Clerc Milon, and in those of 1908 to 1969 as Clerc-Milon-Mondon. Baron Philippe has now changed the name back to Clerc Milon, Clerc being the first owner and Milon the village in which the estate lies. It will be interesting to watch the progress of the wines of his new property.

## Château Clerc Milon

'*Notre château Bourguignon*' ('our little Burgundy château') is what the staff of Baron Philippe de Rothschild S.A. sometimes jokingly call the estate of Clerc Milon. By this they mean that everything about this fifth growth is in miniature – Burgundy estates are usually small.

The property is situated in the village of Mousset, and the vineyards are the closest of all the classed growths to the large oil refinery of Pauillac. There is no Château Clerc Milon as such, but rather a collection of small houses and cellars.

### Pocket-size Château

The vathouse is like a high-ceilinged living room, where eleven metal fermentation vats stand side by side. They are numbered on from the vats in the other properties of Baron Philippe, so the eleventh vat at Clerc Milon bears the final number, 54.

The *chais* are very small, but impeccably kept. There is a first-year *chai* where the bright white paint of the interior sets off the creamy brown of the wine casks and the black of the roof beams. In one corner there is a statue of a man. Apparently the sculpture was bought by Baron Philippe years ago in New York, but upon its arrival in Pauillac he decided he did not like it, and therefore banished it to one of the many cellars, where it was recently discovered during a spring-cleaning session.

Clerc Milon was bought in 1970 for a very reasonable sum. The estate was in only moderate trim, but the Baron would not be the Baron if he left things alone, and money was therefore freely invested in the new acquisition.

### Will Clerk Milon get larger?

The improvements were not confined to the *chais*, but extended to the whole estate. Renovations were widespread, and a start was made to regroup the scattered pieces of vineyard. At present Clerc Milon has some 30 productive hectares, which are planted with 85% Cabernet Sauvignon and Cabernet Franc, and 15% Merlot, plus a little Petit Verdot. The production in the first year – 1970 – was 60 *tonneaux*, but the subsequent vintages have risen to an average of 130 *tonneaux*.

Although Philippe de Rothschild is always full of plans, he does not seem to be thinking of extending the vineyard much in the near future. A great deal will depend on the peasant farmers who own pieces of land which could be welcome additions to Clerc Milon. If the price is reasonable there is a possibility of their plots being bought and added to the estate, but if they ask exorbitant amounts (the name of Rothschild is obviously associated with wealth) then Clerc Milon will probably remain its present size – or so a spokesman for Baron Philippe told me.

Extension or not, the first thing to be done is to make good wine at Clerc Milon and to give it a sound reputation. This is the first plan, and twenty years have been allowed for its satisfactory realisation.

### From strength to elegance

It so happens that I have drunk many bottles of Clerc Milon dating from the time that the estate still belonged to its previous owners. I remember 1960, 1962 and even 1963 vintages.

The 1960 was slightly thin in the mouth, slightly browning, pleasantly fragrant and with considerable aftertaste.

I preferred the 1962, whose individual bouquet reminded me for a brief moment of an old Latour. The wine had a rich, penetrating taste, and was clearly more elegant than the Pontet Canet which was also served.

The 1963 vintage was much sturdier than I had expected – and I am speaking about a 10-year-old wine from a year which was virtually a failure! It was even somewhat on the robust side, and showed no signs of premature decline. In nearly all Clerc Milon wines there is a kind of primitive strength which gives the wine a long life; it is only after many years that an elegant style develops, with an aroma which often contains a hint of blackcurrant.

### A fault that time will cure

The 1970 vintage, the first wine which Baron Philippe made with his Mouton staff, was immediately very appealing. I found it to be a perfect Pauillac, complete, balanced, fragrant and with a good colour. The only fault you could find was that it is still too young.

I later heard that this 1970 vintage gained the highest score of 15 wines at a classed growth tasting session in California (no first growths were represented) – which does not surprise me at all. As regards style, Clerc Milon is not all that far removed from Mouton-Rothschild. Could it perhaps be a future *petit Mouton?*

The park of Lafite is separated from the large courtyard by railings and a gate. These look like metal, but when you touch them you find that they are of wood painted with metallic paint.

Manager André Portet has held his present post since 1959. He is in charge of about 75 people who form the permanent staff of Lafite.

The Rothschild emblem is a sheath of five arrows. In the Napoleonic era four Rothschild brothers left Frankfurt, Germany and dispersed to different points of the compass: Salomon to Vienna, Nathan to London, Kalmann to Naples and James to Paris, only Amschel staying behind in the Frankfurt house.

*Right:*
*The Château seen from the front. Little seems to have changed since the time when the engraving was made for the label (opposite page). The pepperpot tower, with the five Rothschild arrows on top, the terrace and the gardens are all still there.*

*Below:*
*The Château seen from the vineyard. This covers 90 hectares and is planted with $\frac{2}{3}$ Cabernet Sauvignon, $\frac{1}{6}$ Cabernet Franc and $\frac{1}{6}$ Merlot.*

1st Grand Cru Classé

To visit the Médoc without seeing Lafite-Rothschild is like going to the Tower of London and not seeing the Crown Jewels. Lafite is the supreme claret – perhaps the finest red wine in the world (unless, of course, you are among those who champion the cause of Burgundy). Lafite represents the superlative in Bordeaux. It is more than a name, it is a concept. Even those who may only get one chance in a lifetime to taste it will cherish the memory of a wine that at least partly justifies all the purple prose written about it.

Lafite is a reserved, dignified place. Visitors are not really encouraged as crowds might interfere with the conduct of the estate and making of wine. No one is allowed to visit the *chais* except the very privileged – such as owners of other estates – and very, very few visitors, even so, are

*Below:*
*A little label for a great wine – only 95 × 70 mm. But Lafite needs no advertising – the name is enough.*

*Bottom left:*
*A panorama of the long second year cellar.*

*Bottom right:*
*Cellar master Robert Revelle, who succeeded his father Georges Revelle in 1966. Revelle senior spent his whole life at Lafite, and as thanks for his services was decorated with the* Chevalier de la Légion d'Honneur *medal in 1959, which he received from the hands of Baron Elie de Rothschild.*

The price which a Dutch syndicate paid for Lafite in 1796 is known down to the last centime: 1,286,606 francs, 25 centimes. The purchase was not very profitable, and in 1803 Lafite was sold again, for 1,200,000 francs, to Ignace-Joseph Vanlerberghe. His family retained possession of it until 1868, when it was bought by Baron James de Rothschild for 4,440,000 francs (exclusive of some 400,000 francs in taxes and other charges).

For some time Lafite made a second wine – Carruades de Château Lafite – made from the younger vines, but it is no longer sold.

The German occupation during the war had one advantage for Lafite: electricity and a modern mains water supply were finally installed in the house.



allowed to taste the wine from the cask. It would make the running of Lafite even more costly, as every tasting sample sends at least one-twentieth of an eventually superb and expensive bottle into the spittoon.

### A privileged visitor

*Pamela Vandyke Price writes:* 'There is good reason for the care with which Lafite guards its privacy, for once when I was being shown the *chais*, it was found that a silver tap from one of the casks had been purloined as a souvenir by an otherwise vouched-for visitor. However, as I was made a member of the wine order at Lafite some years ago, Baron Elie and his staff grant me the privilege of occasionally seeing round.

The entrance is through the vathouse, between the gigantic polished oak vats, with the wider doors at the side for the grapes to come in for pressing from the vineyard that rises above the château and *chais* to the west. (At vintage time no one at all is admitted except those working.) When the wine is made, the vattings are blended, again in these vats, and it eventually goes into the first year *chai*, leading out of the vathouse. It was here that the great vintage dinner was held in 1973, when Mouton Rothschild became a first growth – and for 600 diners the thousand or so casks had to be cleared out.

Lafite makes its own casks, using new ones for each vintage, of wood from the State forest in the Auvergne. The wine is racked four times its first year, and fined – six to seven thousand egg whites being used, and all the workers helping to use up the yolks in endless omelettes. Then it goes into the second year chai, which is actually a cellar, or *cave*, underneath the courtyard; for the part of its third year spent in wood, it is put into another underground cellar. These cellars, manager André Portet thinks, produce some of Lafite's unique quality because of their coolness. Then it is bottled, according to its style, soon or late: bottling the 1972 started in February 1975, and the process can go on until late summer. Also below ground is Lafite's 'Library' or personal reserves – behind prison-like bars. The bottles, thick with mould, go back to 1797, though the entire Lafite crop has been château-bottled only since 1860, the year the Rothschilds first owned it.'

### The priceless vineyard

The vineyard of Lafite is extensive. No less

*Left:*
*The vathouse with its large Bosnian oak vats. Someone once compared it with the wealth-packed cave of Ali Baba! The vats have a capacity from 120 to 240 hectolitres.*

*Below:*
*A bird's eye view of Château Lafite-Rothschild. Part of the cellars lie below the large inner courtyard.*

*Opposite page, left:*
*The Château dining-room, after a watercolour by Cathérine Serebriakoff. The portraits of the ladies on the wall are probably of members of the Italian branch of the Rothschild family.*

*Opposite page, right:*
*This watercolour, also by Serebriakoff, shows the modest library, which includes editions of 19th century Gothic novels in English. Four paintings of Rothschild children of that century are also hung here.*

*Opposite page, bottom:*
*The young wine – possibly the most beautiful and aristocratic drink in the world for all lovers of claret.*

than 90 hectares are in production, 60 of which lie round the château, for the most part on the slope of the hill which can be seen rising above the buildings on the south side. A second section is situated 400 metres further west, and a third – a mere 5 hectares – is strangely enough in St Estèphe, but it has a right to the *appellation* Pauillac, because it has belonged to Lafite-Rothschild for centuries.

The age of the vines is high: manager André Portet put it at an average of 30 years. Cabernet Sauvignon accounts for two-thirds, Cabernet Franc for one-sixth and Merlot for the remaining sixth. The production is generally 250 to 280 *tonneaux*, most of which is exported, to the United States, Britain and elsewhere.

**The Rothschild management**

In the château there are two busts of Baron James de Rothschild, the man who bought Lafite in 1868, but never had the chance to see it. At the time of the sale he was already old and ill. What induced him to add Lafite to the family possessions? Cyril Ray writes that it was not the old Baron but his three sons who wanted Lafite. As members of Europe's new merchant aristocracy. Alphonse, Gustave and Edmond liked the idea of owning the most renowned wine in the world. Nathaniel de Rothschild, of the British branch of the family, was already proprietor of Mouton, then first of the second growths.

After the purchase, the French Rothschilds and their friends undoubtedly had great enjoyment from Lafite's wines, but less pleasure from the revenues. For 80 years not one penny of profit was earned by Lafite – something exceptional, especially for a family of bankers! The first profit was not shown until 1948, two years after Baron Elie, born in 1917, had taken over the running of the estate at the request of his cousins and co-proprietors. He is still the person ultimately responsible for Lafite, but because of his activities in the world of international finance he is unable to stay at the Château on more than four or five occasions a year, and then usually only for a few days. This does not mean that the

Château Lafite-Rothschild

house itself receives less attention than the rest of the estate; for the rooms have been decorated in great taste and with due regard for the Rothschild past. Baron Elie, a fervent polo player and thoroughly up-to-the-minute businessman, has ensured that.

### Discreet style

In the château itself there are only four major rooms downstairs, none of them very large. The hall leads into the *salon rouge* which is in the south-west corner of the château and has three windows. On the walls hang portraits of four of the five Rothschild brothers who fled in the Napoleonic age from the Frankfurt ghetto, to make their fortunes in five different countries. The chairs and sofas in this *salon* are covered with red damask, and in the centre of the carpet is the table at which, in 1870, Bismarck dictated the armistice terms later known as the Treaty of Frankfurt after the Franco-Prussian war.

Adjoining the *salon rouge* is the *salon d'été* with French windows leading out onto the terrace. In the summer, white garden chairs are placed out on the terrace, but the once fine view of the Gironde is now spoilt by the unsightly oil refinery of Pauillac. The interior of this little room is designed for warm, sunny days: the wooden panels are painted with vases, swags and sprigs of flowers on pale buff walls, creating an impression of shadows and coolness.

The library, however, is a less elegant but very personal family room, decorated with green damask and children's portraits. The dining room is a pretty room, with green and white woodwork and the pink and bluish-green Bordeaux china from the factory established in the 1830s by the English potter, D. Johnson. This factory also made the plates showing the Médoc châteaux, now being produced again.

### A wine impossible to describe

To describe the wine of Lafite is a challenge – but one knows in advance that failure is inevitable. So many have tried – yet nobody has ever succeeded entirely. Here are some quotations, from four distinguished wine writers trying to capture the essence of Lafite in words.

Edmund Penning-Rowsell, in *The Wines of Bordeaux*, writes: 'In successful years Lafite is the acme of fine claret, well-balanced, elegant and supple with a delicious aroma.' Alexis Lichine, in *Encyclopaedia of Wines and Spirits*, says: 'In great years, when Lafite is successful, it can be supreme. It has great finesse and a particular softness imparted by the Merlot grape. The wine tends to be firm yet supple, with an eventual lightness developed in age. Lesser vintages are still excellent wines, lighter than those of great years, but always showing breed, fragrance, and depth of flavour.' Frank Schoonmaker in his *Encyclopaedia of Wine* tried to be dispassionate – unsuccessfully: 'The wine of Lafite varies, as all Bordeaux wines vary, from one year to another, although Lafite less than most, but of its best vintages it is hard to speak except in terms of the highest praise. Rarely over 12% alcohol, they have an astonishing authority, impeccable breeding, fruit and fragrance and depth of flavour, all the qualities with which a great claret should be endowed.' Cyril Ray's favourite quote is from P. Morton Shand, who in his *Book of French Wines* wrote: 'Its flavour and bouquet are considered so grand and sublime as to afford a symposium of all other wines.' No one has ever adequately put Lafite into words – and perhaps no one ever will.

### Lafite vintages

What is curious and interesting about Lafite is that it is usually lighter in style than other Pauillacs of the same year. The wine is often so sensitive that to me it is closer to Margaux than to Latour or Mouton. To me Lafite is above all a wine of charm, elegance, refinement – with a constitution of steel, like that of a rapier. Aroma, taste, all its components – colour, bouquet, fruit, body – blend perfectly with each other, as if each had been meticulously and individually selected by a master craftsman. For Lafite is indisputably a work of art: the impression it makes on even the most critical is an indication of this. Perhaps there might be someone who does not like it – but even the most severe competitor could do no other than admit its superb quality.

The best post-war years of Lafite-Rothschild, according to André Portet, are 1945, 1953, 1955, 1959, 1961, 1966 and 1970. These bottles contain liquid gold, yet this does not mean that the other years are of lesser quality. The 1962 vintage is wholly charming and is the wine to drink now and for the next few years. In 1972 the Merlot failed, and as a result this vintage has slightly less of the Lafite bouquet. But it will make enjoyable drinking from 1976 onwards. At Lafite they are much more satisfied with the 1973: this is not a great but a good year, though at Lafite this simply means that it is a wine without fault, albeit of lighter style.

For a long time Duhart-Milon belonged to the well-known Castéja family, owners of other estates such as Batailley and Lynch-Moussas, two other Pauillac classed growths.

Although the vineyard itself is a fair size of 46 hectares (of which 4 hectares are planted with vines less than 3 years old), the total estate is much larger: 80 hectares. Most of this is woodland, and only an additional 10 hectares could be put under vines.

30 people are permanently employed at the Château, including the *maître de chai*, Henri Dargilas, who has held this post since 1959.

The wines of Duhart-Milon-Rothschild are usually bottled $2\frac{1}{2}$ years after they have been harvested, that is, in their third winter. As well as normal bottles, half bottles, magnums and double magnums are also used.

*Below:*
*Duhart-Milon-Rothschild has no château of its own, only a few cellars. This picture shows the brand-new* chai, *which was designed under the supervision of André Portet of Lafite-Rothschild; it was first used in 1974.*

*Below right:*
*The Durhart-Milon label has a marked family resembl nce to that of Lafite. The engraving shows a building symbolising the estate.*

# Chau Duhart-Milon-Rothschild

4 nd Cru Classé

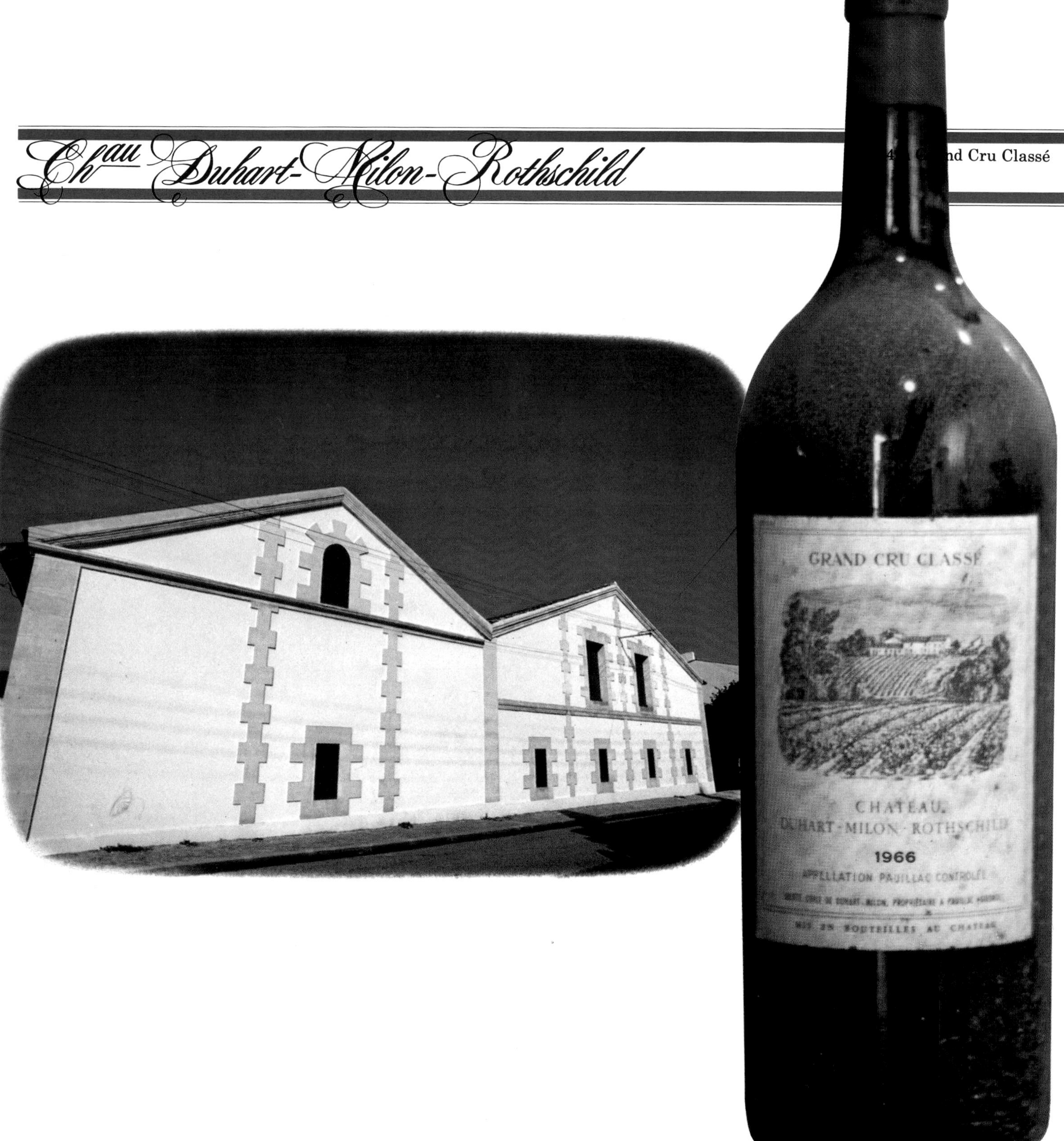

Right:
*Perspective of the new steel vats.*

Below right:
*During the harvest of 1974 some of the wooden vats were still in use, but there is a chance that they may disappear with the passage of time.*

Below centre:
*The second-year cellar of Duhart-Milon-Rothschild, where the casks are stacked up. When the property was bought this chai provided the only storage space.*

Bottom right:
*Young wine, subject to daily changes, is tasted regularly so that its quality is safeguarded.*

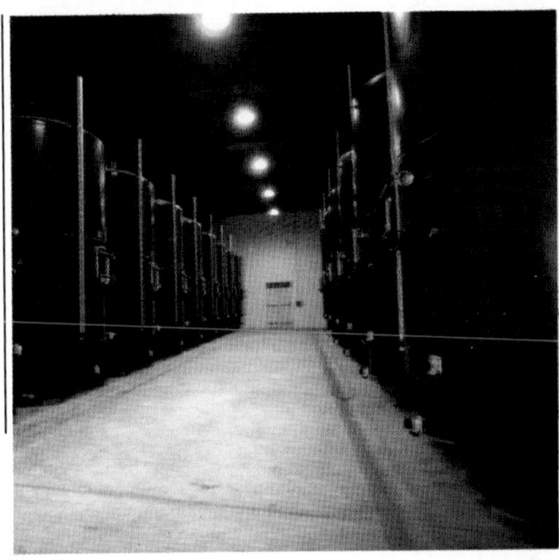

## Château Duhart-Milon-Rothschild

The Lafite branch of the Rothschild family thinks differently from Baron Philippe de Rothschild, who reserves his family name for only the very best wines, which is why Château Clerc Milon will never have 'Rothschild' added to its name, any more than has Château Mouton Baron Philippe. The proprietors of Lafite had no objection to linking their great surname to the fourth growth Château Duhart-Milon, which they acquired in 1962. Naturally enough, the Lafite Rothschilds did not add their name until they were sure that Duhart-Milon was producing wine which completely deserved the association with them.

### Rothschild renovations

Before they could succeed, however, much had to be done, for at the time of purchase the estate was in a deplorable state. The previous family of proprietors had lived partly in Bordeaux and partly in Madagascar having neither the time nor the inclination to make really fine wine. The vineyard extended to only 16 hectares and the *chais* were hopelessly dilapidated.

Duhart is now run by André Portet, the manager of Lafite, who still shudders when he thinks of his first visit to the cellars. Today there is little to remind one of the recent past. The vineyard, situated on the Carruades plateau and bordering that of Lafite proper, now covers 42 productive hectares, and there are plans to extend it another 12 to 13 hectares. The vines are in excellent shape, tended according to the traditional Lafite method. The *chais* have been improved and considerably enlarged, so as to give the wine the space it needs. The brand-new first-year *chai* is spacious, with a high ceiling, which is as it should be, and the vathouse contains a number of new steel fermentation vats. These *chais* are 2½ kilometres from the vineyard, and are right in the centre of Pauillac.

When I asked André Portet whether this location might cause space problems in the event of a possible increase in production, he replied that a further 50 metres of land were available, more than enough for future requirements.

Duhart-Milon has never had a château of its own. The only building which could have claimed to have this function was the home of the proprietor, which stands on the quay in Pauillac, but this was sold after the second world war.

### More colour, more body, more hardness

The wine of the Duhart-Milon-Rothschild comes from a vineyard bordering Lafite, is made by Lafite staff, and matures in used Lafite casks. You might, therefore, expect at least a family resemblance to the great first growth. But Duhart is an entirely different wine, perhaps best described as a gentleman, whereas Lafite is an aristocrat. I once tasted the identical vintage of Lafite-Rothschild and Duhart-Milon-Rothschild in the same morning and the differences were obvious and marked. This is due to a great extent to the soil, for although the vineyards adjoin the subsoils are very different – the vineyard at Duhart-Milon is merely good, whereas that of Lafite is near perfection.

### The rôle of the Merlot

The proportions of grapes at Duhart are more or less the same as those of Lafite (63% Cabernet Sauvignon, 15% Cabernet Franc, 18% Merlot and 4% Petit Verdot), but because the soil of Duhart produces a rather harder wine, it is important that the Merlot gives itself to the full. If this does not happen, the result can be an unattractively hard wine.

This hardness can be seen in the 1972 vintage, when the Merlot crop was scanty, with the result that there was some lack of charm. The 1973 was much better balanced, the bouquet alone of this younger wine indicating its friendlier and more pleasing character. The style was more supple and less austere on the palate when I tasted it.

Duhart's production varies between 160 and 180 *tonneaux*, and it will be fascinating to see how the Lafite influence affects this estate – certainly the direction will not compromise with quality.

*Right:*
*Pigeons are kept at many estates and here, at Cos Labory, there is a dovecote.*

*Below:*
*The pleasant entrance leading to Cos Labory. Nearby is a crossroads on the road that runs from Pauillac to St Estèphe. To the left of this gate there is a cluster of signposts to other châteaux including Montrose, de Marbuzet, Le Crock, Meyney, Canteloup and Tronquoy-Lalande.*

# Ch^{au} Cos Labory

5th Grand Cru Classé

St Estèphe is a parish noted for its assertive wines, which may even appear harsh while still young. They are not always wise choices for the beginner, but they can achieve great quality. The road from Pauillac climbs gradually between vineyards to St Estèphe, and at the top of the steepest incline one sees the Chinese towers of Cos d'Estournel. Cos Labory is right alongside, but completely different – in appearance as well as in the wine it makes.

The château is typically French in appearance, with pointed towers at the corners of the façade. It is undergoing considerable restoration, but priority is rightly given to the work on the *chais* and all the other buildings concerned with the making and maturation of the wine.

**Very distinguished neighbours**

In the 19th century Cos Labory once had the same proprietor as Cos d'Estournel, a Mr Martyn, of London. It passed through several hands until it was bought in 1958 by François Audoy, who runs the estate personally. There is little material available about the history of Cos Labory, but its importance should not be underestimated – the vineyard touches not only that of its neighbour, Cos d'Estournel, but also that of Lafite in Pauillac.

On my only visit to this hard-working estate, the electricians were busy there and M. Audoy preferred me not to see his *chais* and vathouse in an unfinished state.

Not all the storage space is at the Château: a kilometre further on, a cellar has been built for bottling and for storing the bottles. This indicates shortage of space; for now that all the wine is château-bottled, a much larger bottling floor is required than in the old days.

Cos Labory is kept for 3 months in the fermentation vats, and bottled when it is no more than 2 years old – times of maturation vary for classed growths in accordance with variations in the character of the wines.

Château
Cos Labory
GRAND CRU CLASSE
CLASSEMENT DE 1855
COS LABORY
1970
SAINT-ESTÈPHE MÉDOC
Appellation St-Estèphe Contrôlée
AUDOY, Propriétaire à Saint-Estèphe (Gironde)
MIS EN BOUTEILLES AU CHATEAU


*Below:*
*The label of Château Cos Labory, like those of many other estates, bears a coat of arms; this one depicts the Château crowned, flanked by two lions.*

*Left:*
*Château Cos Labory dates from 1830. M. and Mme Audoy have recently started extensive restoration work; when this picture was taken the scaffolding had just been removed from outside the house. The Audoys have owned the estate since 1959. More than half their wine is shipped to the U.S.A. and Great Britain. Belgium, Holland and Switzerland are also regular customers.*

The annual production of Cos Labory averages 60 *tonneaux*. To store this harvest 240 casks are needed, plus enough space for them; four casks of the usual capacity of about 225 litres together make one *tonneau* of 900 litres. This considerable quantity of wine comes from 17 hectares of vineyard, which is divided into three lots within a radius of a kilometre around the château. Forty per cent of this is Cabernet Sauvignon, the most important vine, followed by 35% of Merlot, Cabernet Franc with 15% and Petit Verdot with 10%

M. Audoy finds the vintages 1959 and 1970 the most successful in recent years. Because I had never tasted Cos Labory at all before, I asked if I might possibly taste the 1970 vintage during my visit to the Château. Madame Audoy organised some cheese and other snacks, a magnum was brought up from the cellar, and we settled down in the large drawing-room to the task of sampling the 1970 vintage – the wine which, the owners' consider, will revive the reputation for quality of Cos Labory.

Now I have to admit that I found it disappointing. The smell perplexed me – it was fruity but strange, and the flavour, though attractively robust, seemed curiously unrewarding. Both bouquet and taste had an odd sweetness that I did not expect and that puzzled me.

But I may have had an off day as regards tasting. Also, the wine was in a magnum, and bottles of large size show their quality more slowly than ordinary ones. The St Estèphes, as I wrote earlier, are not beginner's wines, and their intensity and austerity can be off-putting, particularly in those vintages that are powerful and require time to mature to peak drinking. I shall hope to taste Cos Labory again, and I understand that it is the concentration of fruit and the fragrance, extra-sweet at this stage, of the quality of Merlot that can, in time, harmonise in a great wine.

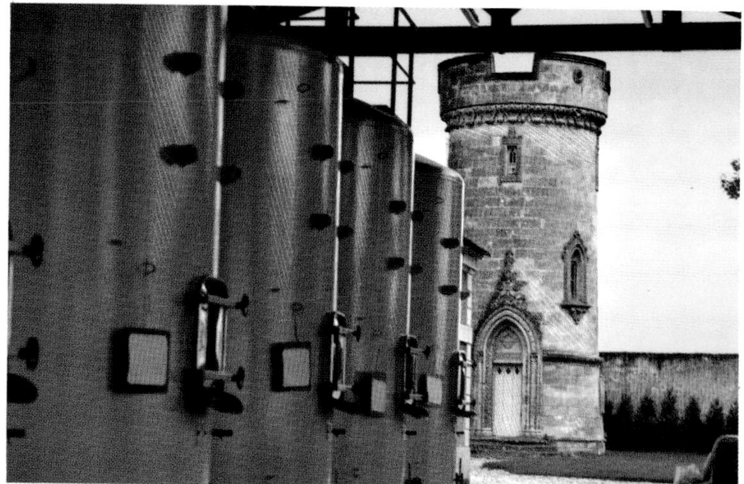

*Left:*
*The cement fermentation vats at Cos d'Estournel are being replaced by steel ones, but because of a shortage of space the new steel containers had to be placed outside, under a lean-to roof.*

*Below:*
'Semper Fidelis' *was the motto of Louis Gaspard d'Estournal who, because he was a horse-dealer, found it natural to introduce a horse into the family coat-of-arms.*

Bruno Prats has a definite opinion about the casks in which he matures his wine. To him the *transport* type is better than the more fragile, traditional *barrique bordelaise.* The *transport* cask is made for moving wine and is therefore sturdier, and the wood is thicker. According to Bruno Prats this can only be good for the wine, for it absorbs less of the outside air.

# Chau Cos d'Estournel

2nd Grand Cru Classé

The story of Cos d'Estournel may begin 'Once upon a time . . .', because it is perhaps the most fairy-tale-like Château in the whole of the Médoc. So, once upon a time there was a certain Louis Gaspard d'Estournel, who in 1810 began to plant the family estate in the hamlet of Cos – just to the north of Pauillac – with noble vines. Soon he was producing good wine, which was partly sold normally, but partly used as barter for M. d'Estournel's other profession, that of horse-dealer. He bought Arab horses in the Middle East and used his own wine as payment in kind.
One day he failed to buy enough horses, and was forced to return to Bordeaux with part of the cargo of wine he had taken out with him. When he got home he opened one of the bottles and discovered that this travelled wine had developed surprisingly well, so well in fact that Monsieur d'Estournel hit on the bright idea of always transporting his wine to Arabia and back before selling it.

But this had to be done in style: everything about his wine had to have an Oriental flavour. So d'Estournel had an exotic park built in the centre of Bordeaux where people could buy his wine, and he also commissioned the building of a completely Oriental château near the vineyard. His wish came true, although not without a long delay. The fantastic project proved so costly that it was twenty years before the Château was finished. During that time it had even been sold once and then bought back again. But the result was worth waiting for. Whoever drives north now from Lafite-Rothschild will suddenly see a white building loom up which makes the

In Bertall's book *La Vigne* there is an anecdote about a famous taster. He was primarily a nose and a mouth – he didn't live, he tasted. One day his carriage turned over, the connoisseur fell out and fractured his skull. His condition was serious, and he was carried into a house where the doctor decided to bathe his wound with old wine. The patient was unconscious, but as some wine trickled down to the corner of his mouth he suddenly blinked and his lips began to move. Everyone bent forward to hear his dying words. And then came his whispered final verdict on wine, weak and choked: 'Cos d'Estournel 1848 . . .'. Having correctly identified both the estate and the vintage, the expert died content.

*Right:*
*Bottles with the distinctive Cos d'Estournel label.*

*Far right:*
*Manager Jean Coudoin, who succeeded his father, M. Emile Coudoin, in 1970.*

*Below:*
*The most unusual silhouette in the Médoc – the fantastic oriental contours of Cos d'Estournel. After the second world war it was completely restored, up to and including the small pagoda bells.*

## Château Cos d'Estournel

unprepared think of a Chinese temple or a set for an Oriental dance company. I believe that no one is really completely convinced that Cos d'Estournel is a wine château until they see the familiar long rows of casks in the *chais*.

### A palace for the wine

In the second world war the German occupiers played great havoc in Cos d'Estournel (one of the things they did was to steal the golden pagoda bells), and this architectural curiosity might have deteriorated and been pulled down after the war to be replaced by a more prosaic building. But on the contrary, Cos d'Estournel was completely restored. The young, talented owner, M. Bruno Prats, told me why. 'To me Cos d'Estournel isn't just an ordinary Château but a palace for the wine – an exceptional home for an exceptional wine. That is why we have done everything to restore it to its former glory.'

The vineyard on which this wine is born extends over some 60 hectares of fairly hilly ground, planted with 60% Cabernet Sauvignon and 40% Merlot, including some Cabernet Franc. The wine is made under the personal supervision of *Ingénieur agronome* Prats, who follows traditional methods, and yet is alert to modern techniques. Hence the fermentation process can be controlled completely naturally and yet in such a way that even in moderate years acceptable results are obtained. Cos d'Estournel 1968, for example, was a successful wine, something which can be attested to in Denmark, for a large part of the vintage was sold there.

In sunny years Cos d'Estournel always has a lot of body – perhaps even a little too much, though that, of course, is a matter of personal taste. I found the 1961 Cos d'Estournel a superb wine, with a wonderfully deep colour and a splendid bouquet, so rich that words fail me. I tasted this wine at the home of the Prats family in

*Right:*
*Cos d'Estournel viewed from the front. The huge wooden doors (far right) are under the centre tower.*

*Far right:*
*A proud Bruno Prats in front of the main entrance to his Château, marked by two fantastic, hand-worked doors. These once formed the entrance to the Palace of the Sultan of Zanzibar. Bruno Prats managed to buy them over the telephone at an auction in Nimes, and now they once again form a fitting entrance to a palace – but this time a palace of wine.*

*Below:*
*A bird's-eye view of this most exotic Château – notice the many unusual features.*

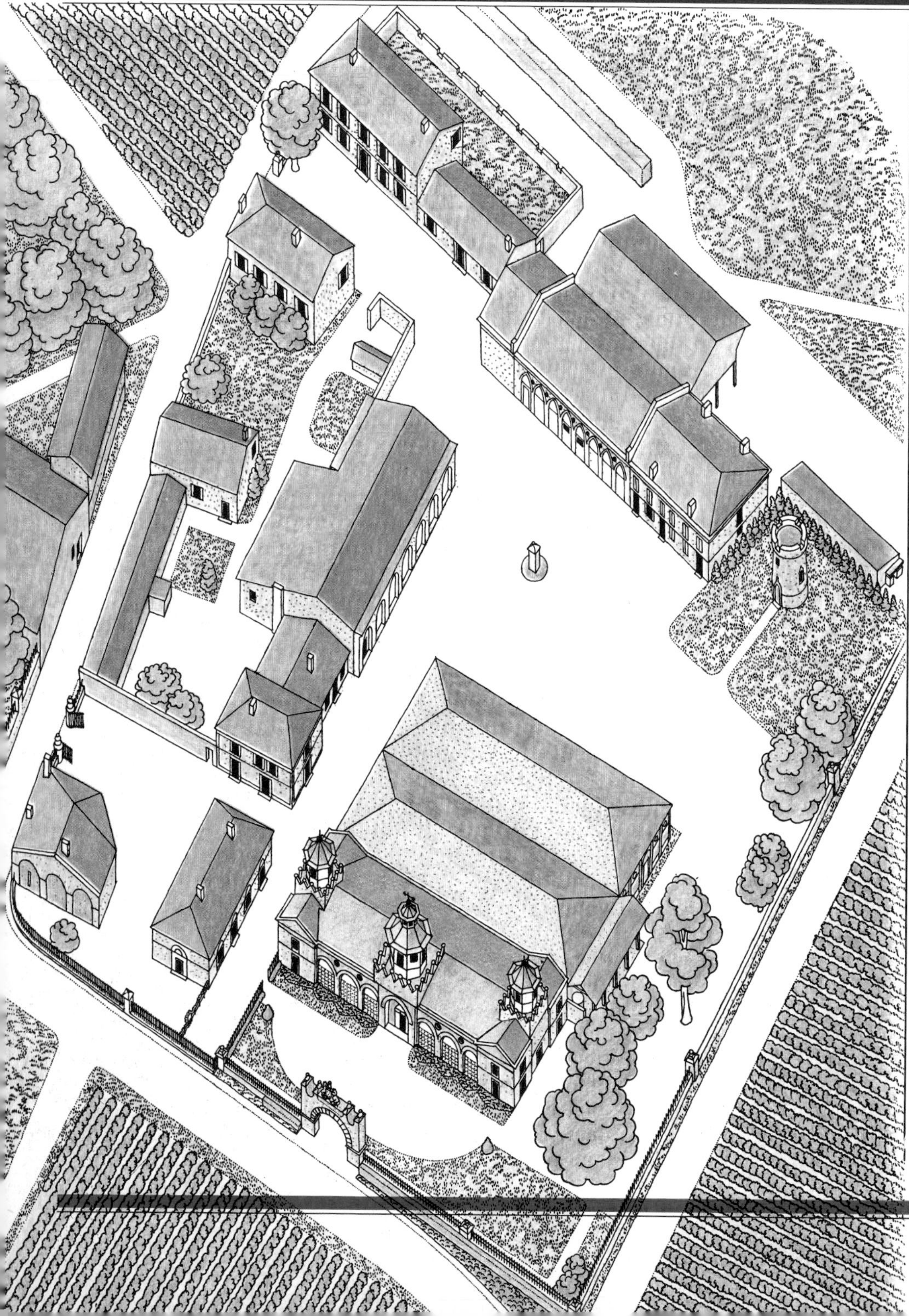

Bordeaux; there are no living quarters for the proprietor at the Château. Just before the 1961 vintage Bruno served the 1966, a vigorous, fruity wine which must wait for years yet. Perhaps the style of this vintage will appeal more if it gains elegance, but this may develop over the years.

The vintage of which Bruno Prats says: 'That's how I'd like to make wine every year', is the 1971. It is a wine with an excellent balance of colour, bouquet, body and tannin – solid yet supple, a wine with a beautiful nose, a lot of flavour and a lot of future; in all respects worthy of a palatial home. But do not drink it before 1984, and even then you needn't hurry, because the wine will remain at the same high level for at least another ten years.

In recent years about 60% of Cos d'Estournel has been sold to the United States, and 20% to Britain. The rest has gone to a large number of other countries including Belgium, Switzerland and Japan. Production averages 200 *tonneaux*.

### The staff of the Chinese Château

It is noticeable that the staff of Cos (the 's' is pronounced) has always felt itself closely linked to the estate. There are about 40 people in permanent employ, under *régisseur* Jean Coudin. Many of them were born at Cos d'Estournel and their families have seen numerous generations of owners. What is also notable is that Cos has special houses for retired employees, who need pay no rent and who at their own request can spend their old age on the ground where they have worked all their lives. There are some who have never even been to Bordeaux.

This strong attachment is partly due to the fact that the vineyard of Cos is traditionally divided up into *sadons* of 800 vines, and that each *vigneron* is responsible for some of these plots of land. And at Cos d'Estournel the system of flexible working hours has been operative for years: those who work the vineyard can fix their own hours of work – providing, of course, that the vines are well tended. And the aristocratic wine provides incontestable proof of this.

*Below right:*
*Cellar master Paul Bussier ready with glasses for a tasting of some of Lafon-Rochet's recent vintages.*

*Bottom:*
*The Château seen from the front. It does not in any way look as new as it really is. Behind and to the right of the château itself are the chais and the presshouse. The entrance to the private cellar of owner Guy Tesseron is on the left.*

Château Lafon-Rochet is entirely surrounded by its vineyard, which extends over 27 hectares. The total area which could be planted with vines is 36 hectares. In addition to this, the estate has a further 16 hectares comprising the park and estate buildings.

Lafon-Rochet is very old, in the 17th century belonging to M. Lafon, adviser to the *parlement* of Bordeaux. The Château remained in his family until 1880, after which it changed hands several times before Guy Tesseron took it over in 1960.

The design for the château was not chosen arbitrarily. The architect studied French provincial houses for an example of a classic style. The plans eventually chosen were based on an old house in the *département* of Vienne.

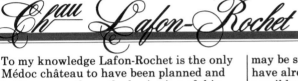

# Ch^au^ Lafon-Rochet

4th Grand Cru Classé

To my knowledge Lafon-Rochet is the only Médoc château to have been planned and built as recently as the beginning of this century. The classic contours certainly do not give the impression that it is new, and the proprietor, Guy Tesseron, made the architect search until he devised a style appropriate to the vineyard itself and to the Médoc. This is typical of the scrupulous care with which M. Tesseron has gone about improving the name and the wine of Lafon-Rochet. If a conscientious owner invests large sums of money in the château, you may be sure that the vineyard and *chais* have already received the same attention – possibly more, if he has maintained his priorities.

At Lafon-Rochet the needs of the wine were attended to first, before those of the possible inhabitants. The vineyard was not only extended by some 25 costly hectares, but also underwent a radical 'grape-lift'. After the purchase it was discovered that the percentage of Merlot was unusually high for its situation, and although the vines were still in their prime, M. Tesseron

*Left:*
*The bottles of Lafon-Rochet are as classic in style as the château.*

*Below:*
*In the back garden is an old chapel which Mme Tesseron hopes to restore. Previous owners seem to have made use of it as a water-tower.*

When you approach Lafon-Rochet you see a flight of steps leading to the entrance; this is much older than the château itself. The Tesserons discovered this flight of steps by chance and found that it could easily be incorporated into the overall style of the château.

Lafon-Rochet used to be a resting place for pilgrims on their way to Santiago de Compostella in northern Spain. They worshipped in the old chapel in the back garden, built on the orders of the first Mme Lafon.



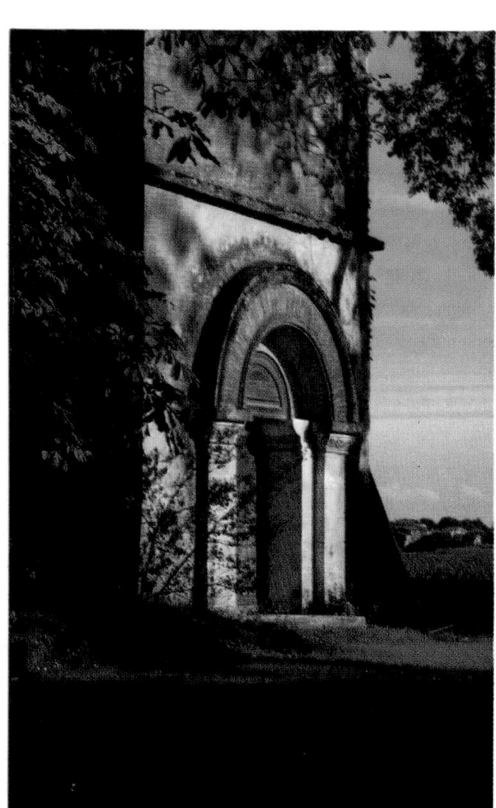

decided to replace them and replant with the more suitable Cabernet. As for the *chais*, a completely new vathouse with immaculate oak fermentation vats, and a new first-year *chai* were built, the second-year *chai* was renovated, and an underground cellar for storing bottled wine was built.

Everything was done with the most detailed care; for example, the cellar floor is made of gravel rather than concrete, so the floor does not sweat and the bottles can breathe! Beneath the château itself, a second cellar has been built for private use. Here again neither expense nor effort has been spared: the wines lie in neat niches at the side of a narrow, white, arched passage which ends at the only imperfect object in the whole of this impeccable property: a headless statue.

### Bordeaux linked with cognac

Guy Tesseron is a dedicated, active man, who divides his time between his property in St Estèphe and his other business, that of dealing in Cognac. The Tesserons therefore lead a busy life and are constantly on the move. They would like to live quietly at Lafon-Rochet, but like everyone engaged in agriculture they are seldom able to enjoy complete tranquillity.

Madame Nicole Tesseron is a member of the famous Cruse family, her father being Emmanuel Cruse, and her mother living at d'Issan. Naturally she is much involved in everything that happens in and around Lafon-Rochet; although the interior of the château was not yet completed when I visited it, she enthusiastically outlined the plans for the gardens and the tiny chapel. With a tradition of fine wines and spirits bred into them, the Tesserons should produce something exceptional.

### The Cabernet in evidence

Because a vine needs four or more years to produce grapes which can be used for a *grand vin*, the effect of the Cabernet planting at Lafon-Rochet is not in evidence until the 1966 vintage. (1964 was too early and in 1965 the harvest failed). The 1966 is a full-bodied tanniny wine, which can be laid up for some years. The colour is dark and the bouquet surprisingly delicate for such a robust wine.

The 1967 vintage is naturally a little lighter, but still big; its bouquet indicates this by the attractive, distinctive appeal to the senses.

In the 1970 vintage I first tasted the Cabernet really asserting itself. Colour, strength and bouquet were well developed and in perfect harmony with each other. It struck me that it was not as hard as might have been expected in a St Estèphe, as Guy Tesseron does not himself like very austere wines. He prefers wines that are noble but which possess charm.

The 1971 vintage will be a very good wine – for those who have the patience to wait – in contrast to the 1972, which possessed a fine bouquet while still young; despite its high Cabernet content, it will already be highly enjoyable in the 1970s.

The 1973 was slightly more balanced and also rather more complete. Tasted from the cask, this proved to be attractive, pleasant and full-bodied; a fine St Estèphe, made to please.

The production of this interesting Château is 100 to 150 *tonneaux* per annum, most of which are shipped to the United States and Britain.

### A privileged situation

Château Lafon-Rochet is one of the five classed growths of the parish of St Estèphe. Three of these – Cos d'Estournel, Cos-Labory and Lafon-Rochet itself – lie close together, on the edge of a small plateau in the extreme south-west corner of the district. The vineyards are drained by a small waterway, the Chenal du Lazaret, which forms the commune boundary. On the other side is Pauillac, with the vineyards of Château Lafite-Rothschild. Perhaps this privileged situation goes some way towards explaining the quality and the reputation of Lafon-Rochet's wines. It is certainly true that their praises have been proclaimed in the past.

After the death of M. Dollfus, Montrose passed into the hands of Jean Hostein, a famous owner of his time. Cos d'Estournel belonged to him as well. His portrait still hangs in the main *salon* at Montrose.

Four carriages – brought back into use during the last war – and a 1920 La Zèbre motorcar are kept at the estate.

*Centre:*
*The trimly kept Montrose estate. The building on the right of the tree-shaded courtyard is the presshouse. This picture was taken from the old frame of the windmill.*

*Below:*
*The front of the château, with some palm trees in the background.*

*Left:*
*The label and the capsule, part of the dressing of the bottle.*

2nd Grand Cru Classé

The word 'slapdash' is totally unknown at Montrose. Everything at this estate is precisely arranged and organised from the moment you arrive: at most other properties motorists enter by whatever drive is convenient – at Montrose there are neat signs directing visitors to the reception area. The paths between the buildings are trim and some of them even have names, for example, Avenue de Mulhouse and Rue d'Alsace. The vathouse and the *chais*, the château, the park and of course the vineyard are immaculate. Montrose has in fact always been an estate with particularly dedicated owners. It has been looked after with loving care since it was first established in 1778, since when it has been considerably enlarged. In 1825 Montrose still had only 5 to 6 hectares, in 1832 it had 32, in 1880, 65, having more than

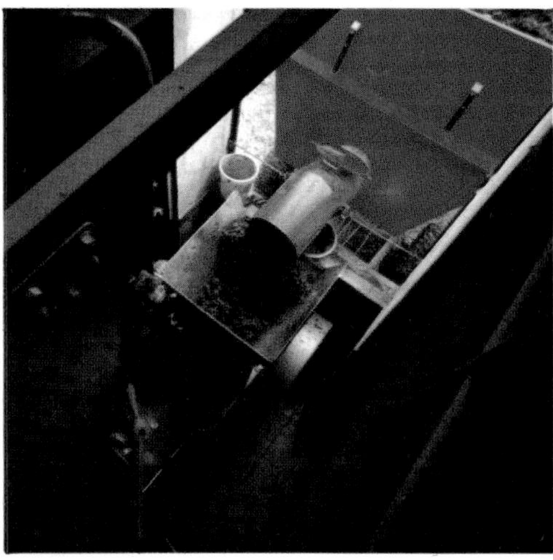

*Left:*
*The de-stalker in full operation.*

*Below:*
*A cellar scene typical of winemaking.*

*Far below:*
*Owner Jean-Louis Charmolüe with one of his staff.*

*Bottom:*
*Paul et Virginie, child hero and heroine of a romantic novel of 1786, with a tragic end: Virginie is drowned because she is too modest to undress and swim to safety; Paul later dies of grief.*

The Alsace street name signs at Montrose were put up by Mathieu Dollfus, who was born in Alsace. Not long ago Jean-Louis Charmolüe had to have them renewed, because generations of the children of the estate had used them as targets and obliterated the names.

In recent years not only the *chais* and outbuildings have had to be modernised but also most of the château. One inner wall was found to be absolutely eaten with dry rot. This is a Médoc hazard. When M. Charmolüe was born, there was no electricity at Montrose – and not even one bathroom.

M. Charmolüe has a fine collection of *tastevins*, the small cups or saucers used for sampling the wine, each district having its own design.

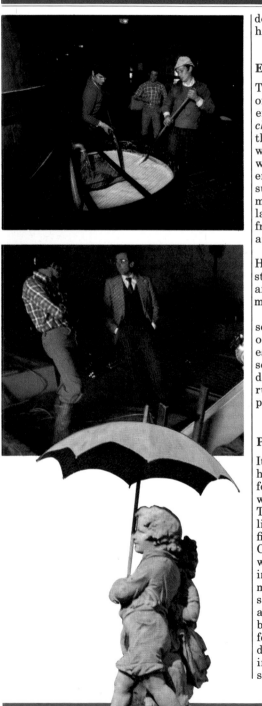

doubled its size. Today it extends over 75 hectares.

### Estate owners of personality

The man who principally has left his stamp on the estate is Mathieu Dollfus. For example, it was he who added the present *chais*, which bear his initials. At the end of the last century they were very modern, which is probably why they still function so well today. Dollfus also built a windmill to ensure sufficient drinking water in the summer. The pump went to a depth of 200 metres and worked until 1960. A few years later the windmill fell down, but the metal frame still stands, and serves as a flagpole and observation tower.

Dollfus was also progressive in business. He divided 10% of his profits among the staff, paid all his employees' sickness costs and had an arrangement to keep expectant mothers.

Dollfus died childless, and his estate was sold to M. Jean Hostein, who then also owned Cos d'Estournel, among other estates. In 1896 Hostein made it over to his son-in-law, Louis Charmolüe, and it is his descendant, Jean-Louis Charmolüe, who now runs Montrose after his mother, a famous palate much respected in the Médoc.

### Perfection down to the last detail

It is often the smaller details that indicate how much a proprietor is involved in the fortunes of his estate, his staff and his wine: such minutiae indicate his character. There are plenty of examples at Montrose, like the tiled floors in the vathouse and first-year *chai*, which Jean-Louis Charmolüe had laid specially because they would be easier to keep clean. There are impeccable wooden fermentation vats. The minibus takes all the young children to school every day; the vintagers' quarters are attractive and a modern kitchen has been installed for them. These are only a few of the details, but they indicate how devotedly the owners continue to re-invest in their estate – sometimes properties are sadly exploited by those in possession.

### The pink hill

Montrose is situated on a hill not far from the Gironde, and it is this hill that gave the Château its name. Where the vines now flourish only heather and broom grew in the 18th century, and when the heather was in bloom over the roughly 80 hectares of the present domain, the ground was carpeted in pink: hence *mont rose* – and why the 't' is still not pronounced.

On the 64 productive hectares, Cabernet Sauvignon takes pride of place with 65%, followed by the Merlot with 25% and the Cabernet Franc with 10%. The production averages 230 *tonneaux*, and the largest markets are Great Britain, the United States, Belgium, Holland and West Germany.

### Château-bottling since 1969

Montrose began to château-bottle the whole of its crop as recently as 1969. As with all estates there could be a considerable difference in the taste of wines bottled at the Château and also of the rate at which, compared with foreign bottlings, they matured. The château-bottlings were not always superior to those handled by merchants in export markets, but it is probably true to say that exact comparisons of the fine Bordeaux, can only be wholly fair when the wines have been bottled at the estate.

A vintage which I find very good was the 1962. This had a deep colour, a beautiful, gracious bouquet and a firm, ripe taste; it was a wine which, like all good Montrose years, can be described as full-bodied, with much charm.

Another vintage which I can wholeheartedly recommend is the 1970. Its profound, generous, lengthy style is heralded by a concentrated, intense bouquet and a dark colour, very deep indeed. The element of great refinement was not yet present, but it possessed a great deal of distinction and firmness. It is probably one of the best St Estèphes of that particular year, a wine to delight you and your guests in 1985 or thereabouts.

Calon-Ségur once used to call itself *Premier Cru de St Estèphe* (see picture) – a reference to the seniority of the estate. But this, other proprietors thought, gave an indication of superiority – so they protested, and Calon is not permitted to give itself this designation nowadays.

Calon keeps its own herd of cows and it is their meat which provides the basic fare for the vintagers. Its reputation encourages friends of the estate to try to wangle a meal at vintage time.

Calon-Ségur has two vathouses, one with wooden and one with metal vats, though the former is now no longer in use.

*Below:*
*An old engraving of the Château. Little has changed over the years, except that most of the trees have been cut down.*

*Right:*
*M. Philippe Capbern-Gasqueton, co-owner and manager of the Château.*

CHATEAU
CALON SEGUR
PREMIER CRU DE
S^T ESTÈPHE
MEDOC

# Chau Calon-Ségur

3rd Grand Cru Classé

Calon-Ségur is a property with very ancient traditions, for in the Gallo-Roman period Calon was the municipal centre around which the parish of St Estèphe later grew up. The name Calon is derived from an old word for wood or forest, and the small boats which used to carry wood for the garrison were called *calones*. Just how closely the history of Calon is interwoven with that of St Estèphe is also evident from the fact that, until the 18th century, the parish was called St Estèphe-de-Calon, or sometimes St Estèphe-de-Calones.

There is little doubt that it was at Calon serious wine-growing in this northern parish of the Haut-Médoc began; documents have been found mentioning levies on vines dating from the 13th century.

Calon-Ségur acquired its present name when it was the property of the Marquis Alexandre de Ségur two centuries ago. He was president of the *parlement* of Bordeaux, and also owned other estates, including Lafite, Latour, Mouton and de Pez. Despite the rising popularity and increasing fame of these properties, he preferred Calon and is reputed to have said: 'I make wine at Lafite and Latour, but my heart is at Calon.' This saying is commemorated today by the heart shown on every label of Calon-Ségur.

### A well loved and famous growth

Just as the Marquis lost his heart to Calon, so did Philippe Capbern-Gasqueton. He is the current owner, and is single-minded about trying to make the best wine possible. He enjoys considerable success, Calon-Ségur usually being one of the best St Estèphes.

The wine of 1973 provides a good example. In that year M. Gasqueton estimates that only 30% of the vintage in the Médoc was wholly successful, 70% less so. Because of this, buyers were naturally cautious, and their hesitation was increased by the general economic situation and by the large stocks of 1971 and 1972 which still remained unsold. Yet the Calon-Ségur 1973 turned out to be so good that it was already all sold before it was bottled.

There is no doubt that this wine seems to be promising, possessing as it does a marked amount of fruit in the nose and taste, complete and well balanced. In my opinion this Calon-Ségur is among the best Médocs of the year. Its classification as a third growth in no way relates directly to the quality of its wines, and the prices usually reached by Calon are satisfactorily high.

*Left:*
*The tall entrance to the old presshouse with the reception hall for the grapes behind it.*

*Below left:*
*The large* chai, *with its strikingly wide arches.*

*Below right:*
*Calon-Ségur is furnished with fine antiques and tapestries, many brought to it by Mme Eliane Gasqueton, widow of the famous Edouard, who did much for the estate.*

Château Calon-Ségur

In the 1969 edition of *Bordeaux et Ses Vins* it says: *'actuellement supérieur à son classement'* – better than its classification.

### Vineyard in one piece

Centuries ago the vineyard of Calon was the largest in St Estèphe, and even today it is still big. The parish consists of 3,757 hectares, with about a third of this, some 1,100 hectares, under vines, 60 hectares belong to Calon-Ségur, and normally 55 hectares are yielding. These 60 hectares are in one piece and are almost surrounded by a wall. The vines are planted mainly to the south and west of the village. The soil contains much gravel and is in general fairly heavy. This can be tasted in the wines, which are both rounded and assertive. Compared with Montrose, for example, the percentage of Cabernet Sauvignon in the Calon-Ségur vineyard is not very high, the ratio of the varieties being one-third Cabernet Sauvignon, one-third Cabernet Franc and one-third Merlot.

As at Château du Tertre, the other classed growth belonging to Philippe Gasqueton, the production of Calon-Ségur is on the low side. This is partly due to a great many old vines, which produce little, and partly due to the slightly less good wines being strictly separated from the rest. In all, the 55 hectares yield on average 155 *tonneaux* of the Château's *grand vin*.

The wine is sold mainly to the U.S.A. and Britain, although Belgium and Holland are also regular importers of Calon-Ségur. There have always been close ties between Holland and St Estèphe, by the way, since the Dutch have drained much marshland there.

Something unusual about Château Calon-Ségur is that better wine is frequently made in normally good years than in outstanding ones. For example, I personally prefer the 1967 to the 1966. The 1967 is a wine with plenty of fruit, an intense bouquet, and considerable body and 'push'. The 1966, however, is rather on the light side for this exceptional year. Similarly, I would prefer to buy the 1973 vintage, mentioned earlier, than the 1971 – although the latter wine is very worthwhile, and particularly well balanced. In 1970 a successful wine was made at Calon-Ségur, as elsewhere; it had a great deal of flavour, much *corps* and bouquet, a lot of strength and a lingering aftertaste. The wine seemed slightly less hard than other wines of that year, but this is probably due to the relatively high percentage of Merlot. All in all M. Gasqueton deserves to be warmly complimented on his wine.

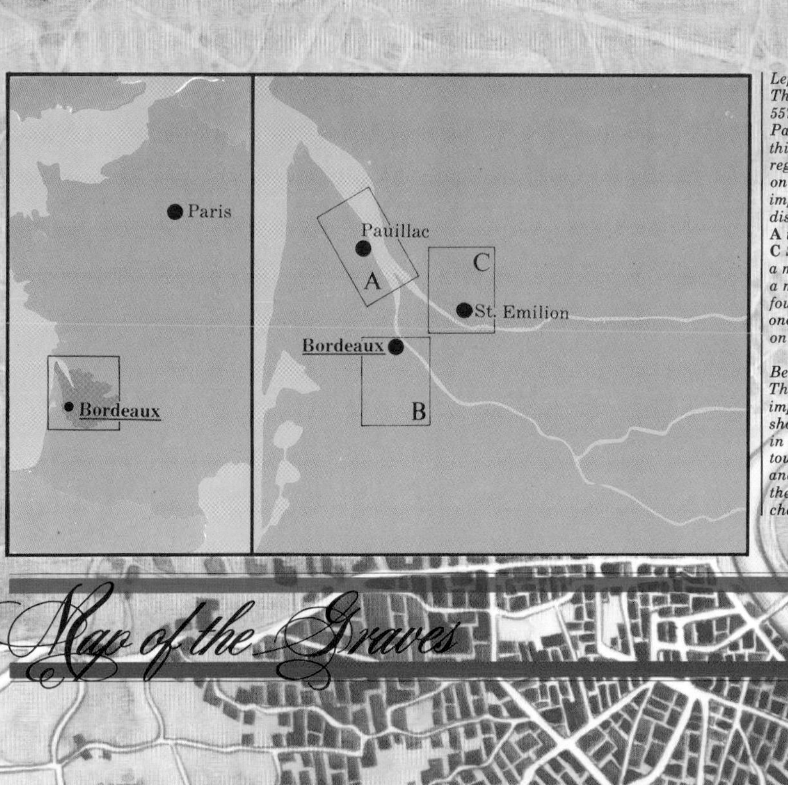


*Left:*
*The city of Bordeaux is situated 557 kilometres south-west of Paris. The city is in the heart of this famous wine-producing region, which is indicated in red on the key map. The three most important districts, each of them discussed in this book, are:* **A** *the Médoc,* **B** *the Graves,* **C** *St Emilion and Pomerol. For a map of the Graves see below; a map of the Médoc will be found on pages 22 and 23, and one of St Emilion and Pomerol on page 167.*

*Below:*
*The map gives a general impression of the Graves. It shows all the châteaux discussed in this section. The names of towns and villages are given, and next to each château symbol, the names of the individual châteaux.*

As a wine district the Graves was a major producer a considerable time before the Médoc. This region is adjacent to Bordeaux, extending 60 kilometres to the south-west of the city. It takes its name from the gravel (*graves*) of the soil, which is often mixed with clay and sand. Different types of wine are produced in the Graves: red, dry, medium dry and sweet white. The great sweet wines are some of the finest in the world. The red Graves have much in common with the Médocs but are often more subtle. Maurice Healy once rather glibly compared the wines of the two areas to two prints of a negative: black and white for the Médocs, sepia for the Graves. Of the total production, about a third is red wine and a sixth dry white. Most of the great wines are produced in the northern part of the district, some in the very suburbs of Bordeaux. The landscape is gently undulating, wooded and picturesque.

# Map of the Graves

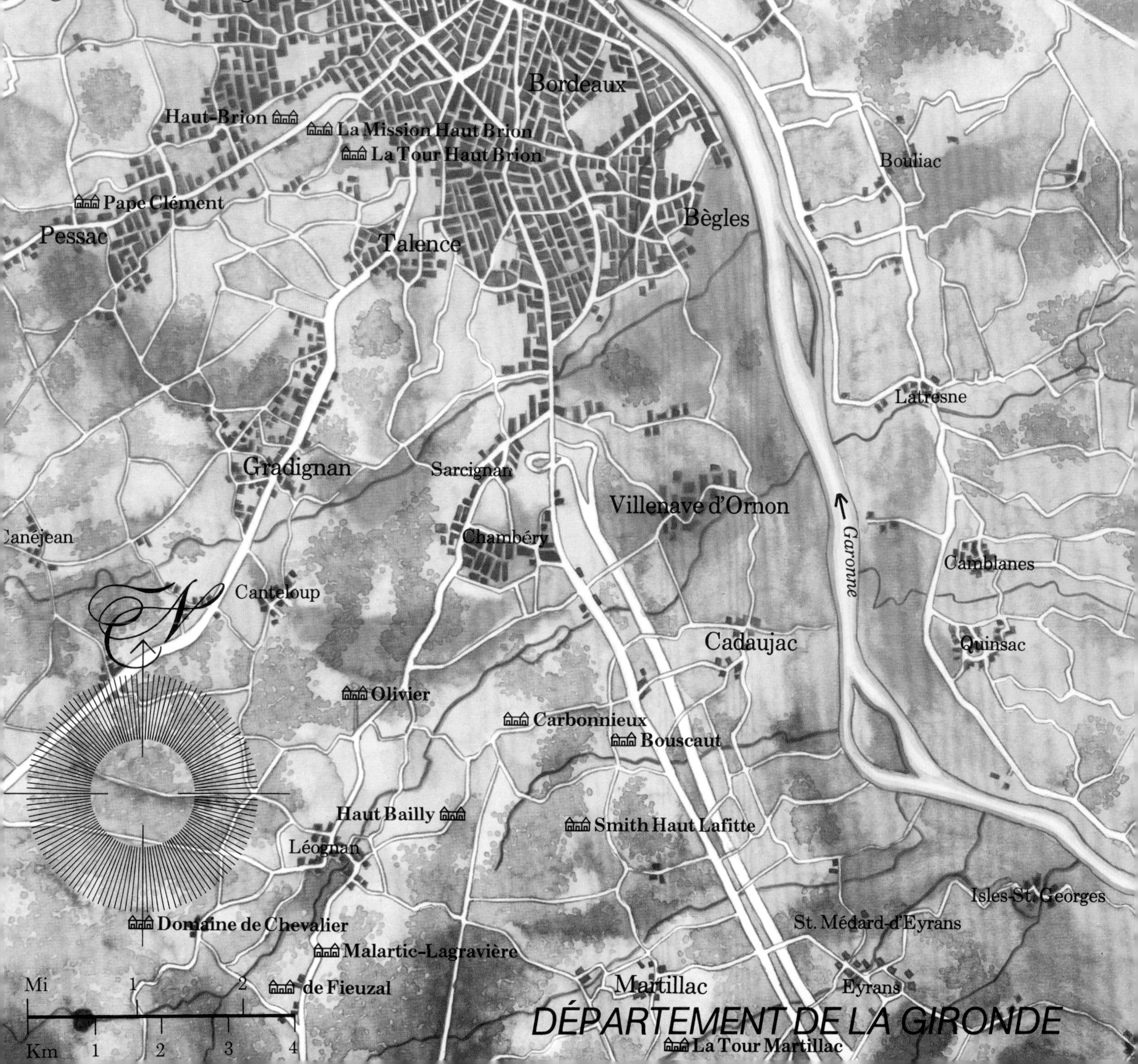

Bordeaux
Haut-Brion
La Mission Haut Brion
La Tour Haut Brion
Bouliac
Pape Clément
Pessac
Talence
Bègles
Latresne
Gradignan
Sarcignan
Villenave d'Ornon
Canéjean
Chambéry
Garonne
Camblanes
Canteloup
N
Cadaujac
Quinsac
Olivier
Carbonnieux
Bouscaut
Haut Bailly
Smith Haut Lafitte
Léognan
Isles-St. Georges
Domaine de Chevalier
St. Médard-d'Eyrans
Malartic-Lagravière
Mi 1 2
de Fieuzal
Martillac
Eyrans
Km 1 2 3 4
DÉPARTEMENT DE LA GIRONDE
La Tour Martillac

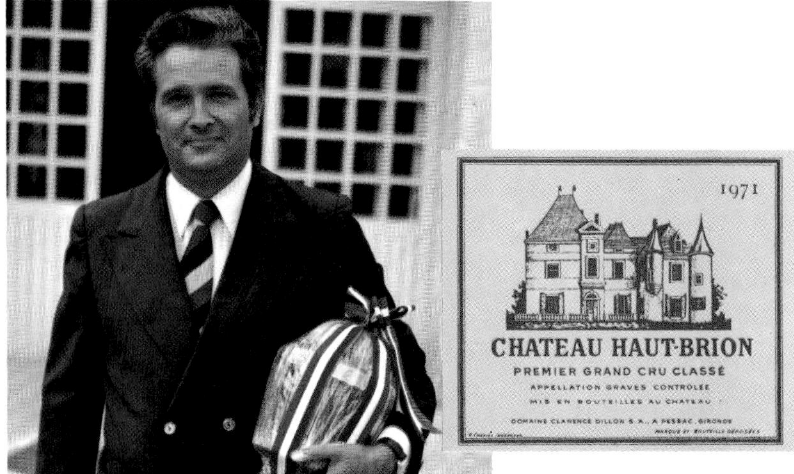


*Left:*
*Haut-Brion's manager, Jean-Bernard Delmas, after being presented with a Dutch cheese, a special gift from a Dutch wine brotherhood, La Confrérie des Vinophiles des Pays-Bas. Dutch cheese is a traditional accompaniment to red Bordeaux. M. Delmas was born at Haut-Brion and took up his present position in 1960. Before that he worked with his father – who was also manager – and studied oenology, among other things. He is now considered one of the greatest experts in Bordeaux. He is also chairman of the Union des Crus Classés des Graves, and in his spare time is an amateur cameraman – having gone as far as Nepal in pursuit of his hobby.*

# Chau Haut-Brion

1st Grand Cru Classé

When the diarist Samuel Pepys drank Haut-Brion in The Royal Oak tavern in London on 10 April 1663, he noted: '. . . and here drank a sort of French wine called Ho Bryan that had a good and most particular taste that I never met with'. This was possibly the first time that an individual growth was referred to by name. Not until the beginning of the 18th century are other names mentioned. Haut-Brion may therefore have the right to claim to be the first Bordeaux estate known on the market.

The property originated from the *Maison Noble d'Aubrion*, the property of the Pontac family during the 16th, 17th and 18th centuries. It was the Pontacs who planted the vineyard and shipped the wine to England. They created the right kind of publicity. In 1666, for example, François Auguste de Pontac opened an exclusive tavern in London called Pontac's Head, which quickly became the meeting place for the nobility – and where Haut-Brion flowed freely.

### Clarence Dillon's takeover

At the end of the 18th century Haut-Brion fell into various hands, and changed proprietors many times before the American financier, Clarence Dillon, took over the estate in 1935. The story of the purchase is amusing, and perhaps at least partly true.

It seems that Mr. Dillon was at first interested not in Château Haut-Brion but in Cheval Blanc; in the depression of the thirties this famous St Emilion estate was on the market for whatever it would fetch, like many other classed growths. Before the sale was concluded Clarence Dillon wanted to inspect the place, and with M. Dubaquié (director of the *Station Oenologique*) and Seymour Weller (the present president of Domaine Clarence Dillon S.A.) he hired a car and set out for St Emilion. It was a very cold day – so cold, in fact, that they had to stop on the way to buy some blankets as the car had no heater. This did not please the impatient Mr. Dillon at all. Not long afterwards, a fog suddenly came down and the party was soon hopelessly lost. This was the last straw: Clarence Dillon had had more than enough of the remote, elusive Cheval Blanc and decided against buying it, although he did retain his interest in acquiring a wine estate; after further deliberation the choice fell on Haut-Brion.

With hindsight it is clear that the wily financier did the right thing, because Haut-Brion, situated actually in the suburbs of Bordeaux, is now worth a great deal more than Cheval Blanc. In 1962 Clarence Dillon transferred Haut-Brion to his son, Douglas, who has been United States Ambassador and was Minister of Finance under J. F. Kennedy. He comes to Pessac once or twice a year; otherwise the Château is run by Jean-Bernard Delmas, a particularly expert winemaker.

### A question of the soil

Why, I asked M. Delmas, was the wine of Haut-Brion the only non-Médoc wine to be included in the classification of 1855, and why is it that it actually resembles Médoc? He replied: 'It is a question of quality and seniority, but also of the soil.' In the geological past, rivers carried stones and pebbles to the Bordeaux estuary and out to the ocean. A complex soil structure resulted, originating partly from that of the central Pyrenees, partly from the Massif Central, partly from the valleys of the Lot and Aveyron. In the Haut-Brion area, however, this soil, excellently suited for wine-growing, was later covered by a thick layer of sand, blown by the wind from the Landes. Only where Haut-Brion itself now stands did the sand not lie, because there are brooks on either side of the estate which over the centuries washed away the sand. Thus the famous gravelly subsoil remained accessible to the roots of the vines. All this provides the explanation for Haut-Brion. As regards the 1855 classification, the Graves was, as Edmund Penning-Rowsell points out, the original centre of Bordeaux wine growing, and other estates seem to have been in a period of recession at that time.

### Separation of unripe grapes

The vineyard of Haut-Brion is planted with Cabernet Sauvignon, which accounts for 55%, Cabernet Franc 25% and Merlot 20%. The estate totals 50 hectares, of which 42 are under production. There is also a patch of land where Sauvignon Blanc and Sémillon grapes are cultivated for the dry, clean-tasting Haut-Brion Blanc. The vineyard lies on two gentle undulations, the one immediately behind the château itself, the other on the other side of the railway line, where La Mission Haut-Brion also has land.

One of the countless points of detail which go to making a great wine is the degree of ripeness of the grapes. Ideally, the grapes must be perfectly ripe, even, according to Jean-Bernard Delmas, a little over-ripe. It is therefore very important that any unripe grapes should be separated out before fermentation. An attempt was made to get the pickers at Haut-Brion to work selectively, but this failed. M. Delmas therefore thought of another method. When the grapes are brought in, and before the de-stalking, they are put onto stainless steel tables, with eight persons standing round each. The group sorts out the unripe grapes, together with any leaves which have accidentally been picked, from the purple mound. It was especially necessary to make a very strict pre-selection for the 1962 and 1972 vintages.

### Estate-designed fermentation vats

The winemakers at Château Haut-Brion were among the pioneers to use stainless steel fermentation tanks: the first one was put into use as early as 1961. The idea originated with M. Delmas. The wooden vats had to be replaced, and he searched for a type which would enable him to regulate the temperature during the first fermentation as and when required, for among other things, the temperature affects the colour and tannin content of the wine. The new vats had to last well and not be all that different in size from the wooden ones in order to avoid extensive alterations also being necessary in the vathouse.
The problem was that the vats which M. Delmas was looking for did not exist in ideal form.

Haut-Brion is now having its history set down in a book by an American writer, Robert Dely. Unlike the serious volumes devoted to Lafite, Latour and Mouton, this is enthusiastic and colourful – almost dramatic – in tone.

Clarence Dillon often visited Jamaica and from there ordered cases of Haut-Brion to be flown out to him. There were many delays and difficulties about arranging these shipments via Paris and sometimes dinner parties had to be postponed.

Every year about 4,000 visitors come to visit Haut-Brion, but they are received by appointment only.

*Right:*
*Picturesque appraisal – though wines are in fact more strictly judged in the north light of a tasting room.*

*Far right:*
*The two red wines the estate produces: Château Haut-Brion and, behind, the non-vintage Château Bahans-Haut-Brion.*

*Bottom:*
*Rear view of the Château, with the door leading to the vathouse on the right.*

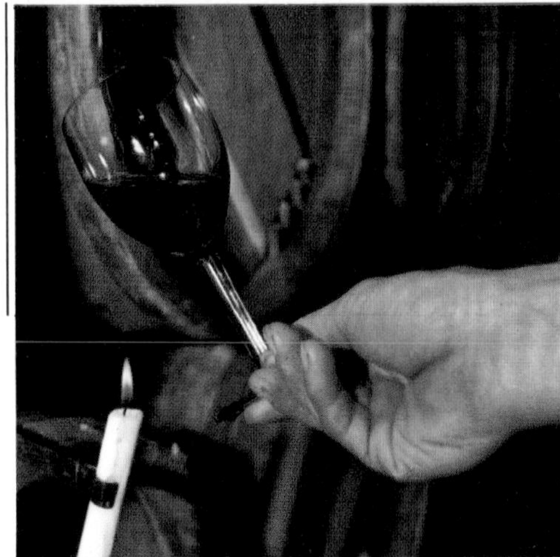

Together with Professor Peynaud and others he started to experiment. Stainless steel seemed to be the ideal material, but it was costly, and the effect of it on the wine and of the wine on it was unknown. Jean-Bernard Delmas remembers many experiments, such as wine to which vast doses of sulphur had been added – more than could ever occur in reality. The aim was to ascertain whether the metal was liable to corrosion. Many more tests and experiments were carried out to study all aspects of the problem. The shape of the first steel *cuve* was designed by M. Delmas himself. He chose a fairly broad structure, with as large a diameter as possible, not only to fit the height of his existing vathouse but to fulfil another aim as well. During fermentation, a thick layer of skins floats on the surface of the wine. It is imperative that the wine remains in contact with this 'hat', because it is from the skins that it acquires its colour. A vat with a large surface area permits more contact than a narrow one.

At Latour this line of argument was not followed, because the temperature control was the factor considered to be of prime importance, and of course cooling takes place faster and more easily if the vats are tall and narrow. It is difficult to say which estate has made the right decision in the

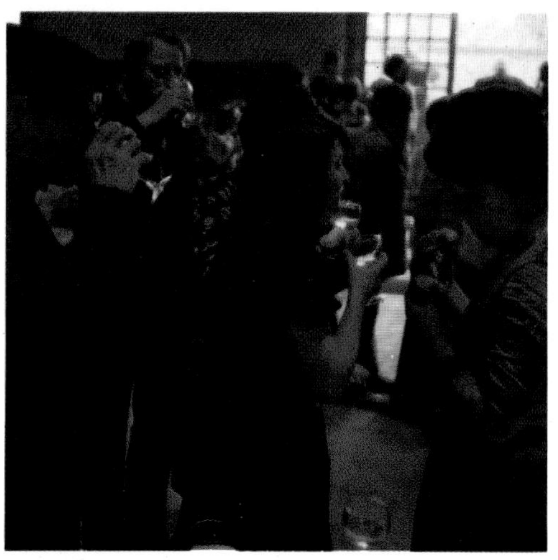

Château Haut-Brion

*Left:*
*At the end of the vintage it is traditional for the workers to be given a party – with plenty of wine to celebrate.*

*Below left:*
*The vintage dinner is held in the cuvier. Jean-Bernard Delmas (standing next to the presses on the right) is thanking the vintagers. The modern stainless steel fermentation tanks provide a contemporary setting for this traditional feast.*

One of Douglas Dillon's daughters is married to Prince Charles of Luxemburg. At her request the château was refurnished in 1973, because she wished to visit it more often. 'But', says Delmas, 'it is still no Versailles!'

The 1974 Haut-Brion was so powerful that it had to be fined with as many as eight egg whites.

The spelling of the Château name has undergone several changes over the centuries. In the records it is given variously as d'Obrion, Daubrion and Hault-Brion.

Because Haut-Brion changed hands several times in the first half of this century, few old vintages remained in the cellar. At Mouton-Rothschild, for example, there are more old bottles of Haut-Brion than at Pessac. Clarence Dillon has done his best to buy back a fair number, so that the Château can now boast a modest collection of bottles from the pre-Dillon years, such as 1906, 1914, 1918, 1921, 1924, 1926, 1928, 1929 and 1934.

long term, but it seems that Haut-Brion has managed to achieve highly satisfactory results.

After fermentation, the various vattings undergo extremely careful selection. First of all, each one is thoroughly analysed, and then Jean-Bernard Delmas samples them a few times – on different days, because the time, the weather, and one's mood can affect decisions of taste. Wine which is found to be too light is marketed as the non-vintage Château Bahans-Haut-Brion, which is exclusive to the house of Johnston. The average 130 *tonneaux* of Haut-Brion are sold to some 20 shippers, who market it mainly to the United States (at least 60%), Britain, Belgium and Japan.

### The character of Haut-Brion

In the first half of last century the Englishman, Cyrus Redding, said about the wine of Haut-Brion: 'The flavour resembles burning sealing-wax: the bouquet savours of the violet and raspberry.' And the authoritative Edmund Penning-Rowsell comments in his book *The Wines of Bordeaux*: 'These parallels are nearly always lost on me, but I pass this one on, in the hope that it will strike a chord with others.' Indeed, if one wishes further to define the qualities which Redding describes in the wine, one must either have hyper-acute senses or a lively imagination.

Easier to understand and accept is what P. Moreton Shand wrote in the present century in his *Book of French Wines*: 'Indeed, many connoisseurs used to consider it out and away as the greatest of the four, and the finest wine on earth, with its stately harmony and massive volume of round, regal flavour.' Haut-Brion is indeed a full wine with a round, noble flavour. Moreover it is a wine with a highly individual personality, which is clearly different from the Médocs. Compared with the Médocs included in the classification of 1855 it is possible to taste the distinctive style of the Graves in Haut-Brion. Normally it is a less reserved wine than the Médocs, although it is the fine red Graves which often bears a close resemblance to certain Pauillacs. A good Haut-Brion always has, in addition to its strength and depth, a velvety quality which gives it disarming charm at a later age. Let me give you a few brief tasting impressions of some recent vintages.

To me the bouquet of the 1964 vintage was very beautiful: rich, creamy, full of character, and the flavour was no less superb. For Haut-Brion, perhaps it is a shade on the light side, but nevertheless fine. The 1966 is definitely a success, and the same goes for the 1967. In 1968 Jean-Bernard Delmas may have succeeded in making the best red Bordeaux of that difficult year, and considering the problems that is no mean achievement. The 1969 vintage is a delicate, light wine, by no means thin or flat, and a pleasure to drink now. The 1970, on the other hand, is a typical wine for laying down, with a great deal of colour, and a nose and flavour of concentrated fruit. The 1971 vintage will also develop into an excellent wine, in colour differing very little from the 1970; the bouquet is soft and powerful, the overall impression is one of a firm, well-balanced, generally great wine. The harvest of 1972 yielded a slightly 'green' wine, that of 1973 a middling one with a pleasing nose, which will develop fairly quickly. Finally, the 1974 vintage promises to be '*très Haut-Brion*', with all the good qualities of this splendid estate well represented. Haut-Brion is a definite aristocrat, invariably of decided style.

CHÂTEAU
LA MISSION HAUT BRION
APPELLATION GRAVES CONTRÔLÉE
Grand Cru classé
1964

SOCIÉTÉ CIVILE DES DOMAINES WOLTNER
PROPRIÉTAIRE
BORDEAUX
FRANCE
MIS EN BOUTEILLES AU CHÂTEAU

*Left:*
*The cross of St Vincent de Paul, founder of the religious order which once owned La Mission Haut Brion, can be seen in many places around the estate, and is on the entrance gates and the label.*

*Below:*
*La Mission Haut Brion has a little ornamental garden. The chapel, which now serves as a museum, can be entered from the main building.*

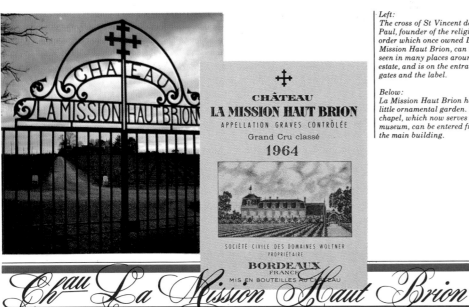

It is related that Napoleon I once craved for the wine of La Mission and sent a messenger to get some. But the owner believed that his wine did not travel and had to be tasted at the estate. So he sent back the answer: 'If the Emperor wishes to drink La Mission, let him come in person.' In fact Napoleon was not the sort of person to appreciate fine wine at all, and the story is probably apocryphal, or La Mission might have suffered.

M. Fernand Woltner has a unique collection of old vintage Cognac, which French law now prevents being made from a specific year.

# Chau La Mission Haut Brion

Grand Cru Classé des Graves

Henri Lagardère is undoubtedly one of the very few managers with a *prie-dieu* in his office – but then La Mission Haut Brion is a Château with a religious history. The vineyard used to be part of the large Haut-Brion estate; in 1682 it was left to a religious order, founded by St Vincent de Paul, which went by the name of Preachers of the Mission (*Prêcheurs de la Mission*). The fathers enlarged and improved the vineyard, and built a tiny chapel, consecrated on 26 August 1698. This is still standing, though it is now used as a small museum, to which successive proprietors have all contributed in various ways. During the French Revolution, the monks were forced to leave La Mission Haut Brion and the estate passed into secular hands. However, the memory of the hard-working fathers still lives on.

### A vineyard divided by road and railway

As one would expect, La Mission Haut Brion lies close to Haut-Brion. The two châteaux face each other at an angle, and the vineyard of Haut-Brion intersects that of its neighbour. La Mission has a total of 18·5 hectares under production, planted with 60% Cabernet Sauvignon, 10% Cabernet Franc and 30% Merlot. The vineyard is divided into four, both by a road and by the 40-metre wide main railway line between France and Spain. Almost half the vineyard surrounds the château.

Further extension, in the Médoc at least conceivable, is out of the question here. 'We have to be extra careful', says Henri Lagardère, 'that urbanisation does not

The wines of La Mission Haut Brion are often preferred by some claret lovers to those of its great neighbour. It is said that Cardinal Richelieu drank La Mission to such an extent that his doctor advised moderation. Richelieu retorted that God would not forbid the drinking of a wine He had made so good.

*Right:*
*Menu of a typical wine dinner at La Mission.*

*Far right:*
*The interior of the old chapel with its fine stained glass windows. Successive proprietors have each contributed to the fine collection of ecclesiastical objects and furniture. In the Château itself are two other collections, one of holy-water stoups and another of Bacchus, which were collected by Henri Woltner. These Bacchus figurines are so rare that they were exhibited at the Brussels Exhibition in 1958.*

*Below:*
*Rear view of the château; the vathouse is in the right wing.*

Monsieur Duijker

CHÂTEAU
LA MISSION HAUT BRION
Grand Crû Classe

Le 17 Janvier 1975
Déjeuner :
Sole du Bassin d'Arcachon
Boeuf grillé sur les sarments
Fromages
Fruits
Desserts
Café
Alcools

Vins
1968 Château Laville Haut Brion
1966 Château La Tour Haut Brion
1949 Château La Mission Haut Brion



encroach on any part of the vineyard that we already have.' Like Haut-Brion, La Mission stands on the outskirts of the ever-expanding city of Bordeaux. Part of the land under cultivation is just in Pessac, but most of it and the château itself are within the parish of Talence.

### The work of a dedicated wine man

After the first world war, La Mission was taken over by Frédéric Woltner, later succeeded as proprietor by his two sons Fernand (the elder of the two) and Henri, and by their sister, Madame Le Gac. It was above all Henri who devoted his life to La Mission. He was one of the most dedicated Bordeaux owners, a man always deeply concerned with the reputation of his wine. Twice a year, for example, he would go round many other great châteaux to find out how his wine compared with the others. M. Woltner was also a gifted taster – according to manager Lagardère, one of the top five of the Gironde. He was also a man who was capable of foreseeing the future of a wine, and predicting its development. M. Lagardère remembers how Henri Woltner was one of the earliest to assert the superiority of the 1966 vintage over the 1967 vintage – a forecast which was by no means a generally held opinion in the early days.

To Henri Woltner, quality was of prime importance. He was prepared to make sacrifices to achieve it. In 1968, for example, he suggested to his manager that all the bad grapes should be snipped off. M. Lagardère pointed out: 'Then you'll have 30% less wine,' whereupon Woltner replied:

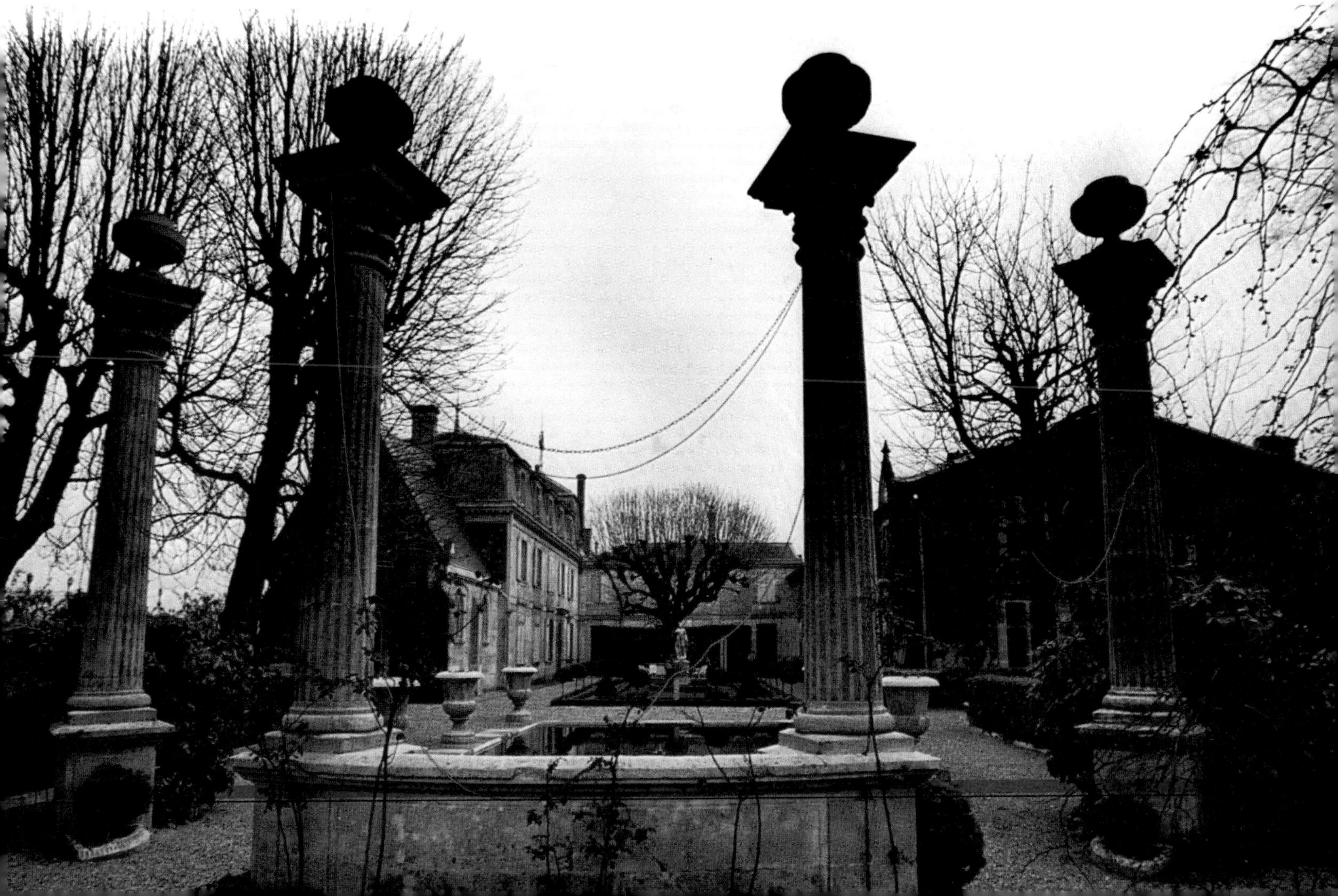

*Left:*
*Oenologist Michel Lagardère samples the young wine.*

*Below left:*
*The steel fermentation tanks with which Henri Woltner experimented for 25 years before he finally installed them. In the foreground a pump of special 'cautious-action' type.*

*Below centre:*
*The chais, typical of a great Graves estate.*

*Bottom:*
*A curious 'watchdog' in the back garden.*

*Right:*
*Plan of the Woltner estates in the outskirts of Bordeaux.* A *Château La Mission Haut Brion,* B *Château La Tour Haut Brion,* C *Château Laville Haut Brion (classed for its white wine),* D *vineyards.*

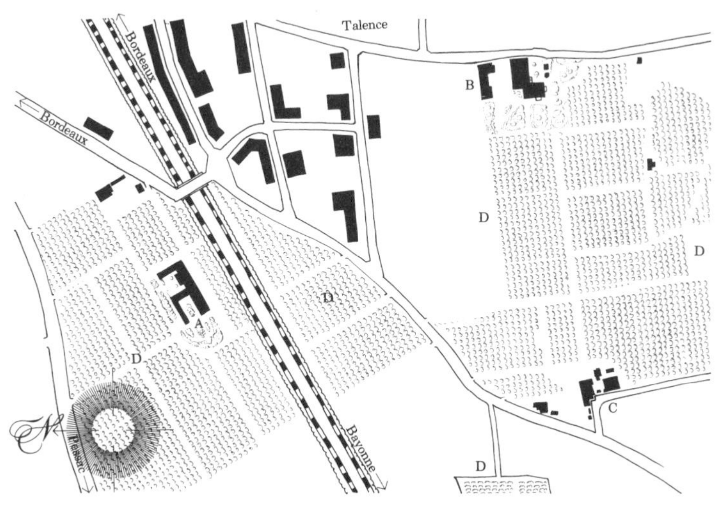

'I want quality.' So the rotten fruit was cut out, and La Mission Haut Brion 1968 was one of the most successful wines of that usually dreary vintage.

### A find in a brewery

Henri Woltner worked and studied at the Station Oenologique and was regarded as an expert on the subject of winemaking. It is therefore not surprising that the vathouse of La Mission is unique in the region of the Gironde. You will not find fermentation tanks like these anywhere else. They are low, angular, metal vats sprayed white on the outside. The wine has no direct contact with the metal, because the interior of each vat is lined with a hard, glass-like substance.

At first sight the vathouse looks quite new. In actual fact the first vat dates from as early as 1926. For 25 years Henri Woltner experimented with his metal vats until he was absolutely certain that the result was not only just as good as fermentation in wood, but even better. The irony of it is that these special vats were first discovered by M. Woltner in a brewery!

This one example illustrates the degree of care taken with everything which might influence the eventual quality of the wine. Another piece of equipment demonstrating this is the cooling machine. To ensure that the temperature during the first fermentation does not rise above 30°C (28°C is regarded as ideal at La Mission) a unit was bought in 1971 which cools the wine carefully and gradually. The precious liquid comes into contact with nothing but stainless steel and is not subjected to violent movement.

Henri Woltner died on 9 October 1974, just as he was preparing for what would have been his fiftieth vintage at La Mission.

### Quality first

The running of La Mission is now directed by Fernand Woltner, who lives in Paris, but comes to Talence about ten times a year. He keeps in touch with developments by intensive correspondence with Henri Lagardère, who is himself assisted by his son Michel, a fully qualified œnologist.

The production of the estate is not large (100 to 120 *tonneaux* in good years) and the *chais* are not as immediately impressive as those of some châteaux. But perhaps this is why they have so much genuine atmosphere. The white plastered first-year *chai* is fairly long, and there is a step leading down to the second- and third-year *chais*. La Mission buys a number of new casks every year, but not for the whole vintage.

It was in the cellars that I tasted the still young 1973. It was a charming, supple wine with a great deal of fruit as regards both nose and flavour: perhaps not sheer perfection, but it will be very pleasant after 5 years or so. The crop of 1973 at La Mission was small, because a heavy storm in September ruined about a third of the almost ripe grapes. In 1974 La Mission was more fortunate; the rain did not come until the last day of the harvest. In that year the production of La Mission was restricted to 42 hectolitres per hectare, very much less than the 80 watery hectolitres of some other châteaux! But then the quality of La Mission is considered more important than quantity. La Mission also has the advantage of being able to call on a large group of pickers from Bordeaux at short notice.

### Recent vintages

Among the wines of La Mission that I have tasted on one occasion or another is the 1949 when it was almost a quarter of a century old: deep-coloured, with a luxuriant bouquet and a full, ripe flavour. The overall impression was that of an elegant, velvety nectar which still showed no signs of fatigue.

Recent successful vintages from La Mission are the 1961, 1964, 1966, 1970 and possibly the 1974. (Perhaps the graceful 1967 should also be included in this list.)

The wines of La Mission definitely show great breeding. They are deep in colour, balanced, elegant, rounded and close-textured. They are the delight of many devotees of claret – who sometimes prefer their refinement and finesse to that of their better known neighbour.

CHÂTEAU
LA TOUR HAUT BRION
APPELLATION GRAVES CONTRÔLÉE
Grand Cru classé
1963
SOCIÉTÉ CIVILE DES DOMAINES WOLTNER
PROPRIÉTAIRE
BORDEAUX
FRANCE
MIS EN BOUTEILLE AU CHÂTEAU


*Left and below:*
*On the label of La Tour Haut Brion the cross has been turned at an angle of 45° to indicate the difference between La Tour and La Mission.*

*Below left:*
*The château, which is now an old people's home.*

La Tour Haut Brion combines two of the greatest names in Bordeaux: Latour and Haut-Brion. Perhaps this is misleading, for La Tour Haut Brion has a distinct individuality.

La Tour Haut Brion wines are not yet very well known, though worth knowing.

It is generally agreed that the 1970 vintage from this estate is particularly good even in this good vintage

The vineyard adjoins that of Laville Haut Brion, an estate which the Woltners bought in 1928.

# Château La Tour Haut Brion

Grand Cru Classé des Graves

Like La Mission Haut Brion, La Tour Haut Brion is the property of the Société Civile des Domaines Woltner. At the beginning of this century it belonged to the same man from whom Frédéric Woltner bought La Mission, M. Cousteau. After the La Mission transaction M. Cousteau continued to live at La Tour Haut Brion for a while, until the Woltner family took it over in 1924.

The two châteaux are situated very close to each other – the railway line is the only thing which really divides them – and since La Mission had a good team of workers and good equipment, the Woltners decided to make the wine of La Tour Haut Brion at La Mission.

The rather uninspired angular château was leased out and is now an old people's home. A pleasant park surrounds the building, which is virtually hidden from view when the trees are in full leaf.

## A plot-like vineyard

The vineyard of La Tour Haut Brion encloses the old people's home on two sides and is diminutive in size, covering only 4·5 hectares. It is a wonder that no project development concern has come along and offered money to build flats or other supposed urban amenities here. The white buildings of the University of Bordeaux are already menacingly close! The production is only 15 *tonneaux*, which are mainly shipped to northern countries such as Germany and Sweden.

Despite the fact that the wine is treated in exactly the same way as that of La Mission, and that the vine species (60% Cabernet Sauvignon, 10% Cabernet Franc and 30% Merlot) are also identical, the wine has a completely different personality.

## Hardness and less finesse

Generally speaking, the prices of La Tour Haut Brion are 25% lower than those of La Mission, understandably so, for the wine is slightly harder and has less finesse. If you were to taste the same vintages of La Mission and La Tour Haut Brion alongside each other, you would find that the latter is almost always less subtle in colour, plainer and harder. Possibly this assertive, robust style may, to a certain extent, explain why people in cooler countries like to drink it. La Tour Haut Brion is nevertheless always a very good wine. I have never been able really to pinpoint the essence of its smell: the bouquet of the 1966 vintage, for example, was both firm and warm, but full of character, typical of the year.

As far back as Roman times there was a ferriferous well on the site of Pape Clément, which gave water that caused stomach ache to disappear. The well is still there today, and is proof that the subsoil contains a good deal of iron.

Pape Clément makes 4 to 5 *barriques* of white wine, kept for the proprietors' use only.

Among the works of Paul Montagne – who wrote under the name of Pol des Causses – are *Les Chants du Cygne* and *Chants d'Exil*. Paul Montagne died aged 94, after having been blind for the last 15 years of his life.

*Right and bottom: The impressive château viewed from two different angles. It was built a short distance from the site of the former palace of the Archbishop.*

*Below: The label shows the insignia of the Papacy: the special tiara and the keys of St Peter.*

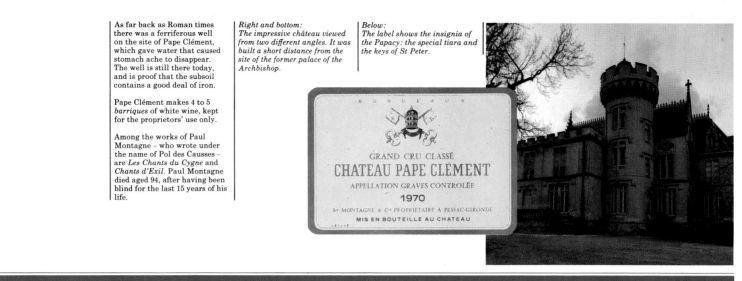

# Chau Pape Clément

Grand Cru Classé des Graves

Archbiship Bertrand de Got may have been a holy man but he was also fond of the good life. In the year 1300 he founded his own vineyard, and tradition has it that a great feast was once held at the Château with Philip the Fair as a guest, a gathering of pretty young women and large quantities of wine. This was possibly considered reasonable behaviour for a priest in those days. In any case, in 1305 the Archbishop was elected Pope; four years later he was obliged by political stresses to move the Holy See from Rome to Avignon, (where he doubtless enjoyed the local wines). His Bordeaux vineyard he made over to Arnaud de Canteloup, his successor in Bordeaux, and the estate soon became known as Pape Clément after the new Pope.

## Complete reconstruction

In the 1930s Pape Clément found itself in an impoverished state. The proprietors went bankrupt, and a firm of bankers specialising in land speculation became the owners. They neglected the vineyard completely, and eventually even those vines which were still productive were ruined by an unusually heavy hailstorm in the spring of 1937.

The estate's salvation came in 1939, for in that year it was taken over by Paul Montagne, a dedicated wine-grower and a poet. He began to replant the whole vineyard and restore the buildings. It took more than ten years before the production was back to something like a reasonable level, but the wine that had been made during those ten odd years was indisputably of good quality. Paul Montagne's heirs now have an excellently kept vineyard of 27 hectares with a production varying between about 60 and 200 *tonneaux*.

## A stylish Graves

The soil of the vineyard contains a great deal of iron and a fair amount of clay. Coupled with the ever-increasing percentage of Cabernet vines (now 60%, but it is hoped to get it up to 80%) and it will come as no surprise that the wines of Pape Clément are usually very definite in style. The 1964 is still extremely dark in colour, with a fine spicy bouquet and an assertive, warm flavour. I find it exceptionally complete and well balanced. It is a red Graves of great subtlety and charm. Even in 1973 – when a record 214 *tonneaux* were harvested – the wine was very dark in colour, markedly fruity, with a fine constitution. Its bouquet is invariably profound and elegant.

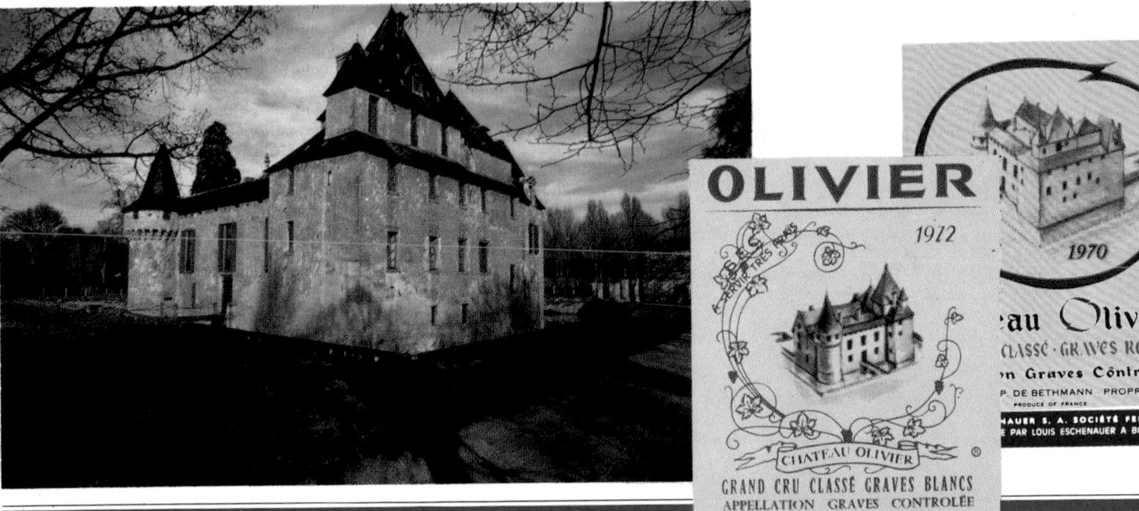


*Far left and below:* *Château Olivier, the oldest part of which dates from the 12th century. In the 16th century a high wall with a tower at each of the four corners was built round the castle; three of these towers were pulled down in the 18th century, but their foundations can still be seen at the bottom of the moat. Inside there are several unexpected features, including a small 15th century chapel and several once secret passages through walls of several metres' thickness.*

*Left:* *The label for the white (left) and red (right) wine of this well known Château.*

# Château Olivier

Grand Cru Classé des Graves

The white wine of Château Olivier is better known than the red for two reasons: far less of the red was formerly produced, and it was sold almost exclusively to the United States. The proportions have now changed, however, the structure of the vineyard having been radically altered in favour of black grapes. The intention is to have only 20 hectares of white grapes with 15 hectares of black grapes, two or three times more than the present area.

The operation is now in progress: all the black grapes have been grouped at the top of the gently undulating vineyard and all the white at the bottom. Since both kinds originally grew side by side, a great deal has had to be replanted, and I saw a large number of plants which were one or two years old. These young vines have caused the workers quite a lot of trouble. The estate totals 160 hectares, including a large area of woodland, the home of rabbits, who are inclined to regard young vines as snacks planted for their especial benefit!

## The white wine

The white Olivier is the product of about 65% Sémillon, 25% Sauvignon and 10% Muscadelle. The yield in 1974 was still 110 *tonneaux* (as against 40 *tonneaux* of red). I have found that the white Olivier does not vary very much from year to year, certainly less than the red. This stability is clearly evident in the recent vintages of 1970, 1971, 1972 and 1974. The 1972 vintage naturally had higher acidity and less fruit than the 1970, but the difference was by no means marked. A good white Olivier has a light colour, delicate bouquet and the distinctive flavour which, besides a certain elegance, usually also possesses a fresh, green quality. It is a good wine to drink as an apéritif, and also as an accompaniment to seafood and such dishes as mushroom omelette.

## Red wines with a future

The red Olivier is clearly a wine in the making. The new plantings, partial change of soil and increase in the percentage of Cabernet (to between 70% and 80%) will certainly influence its character.

The red Oliviers generally need a long time to develop; consequently, the 1967 vintage, which I tasted in 1974, still possessed some tannin, although the colour was already lightening and the developed bouquet was already fully apparent. It will be interesting to follow the progress of this growth in the future.

The extensions to the cellars near the beautiful 12th-century château have created the necessary space for bottling the red and white wines at the Château itself; until now there has not been room for this. The bottling is currently done by Louis Eschenauer S.A., the firm which has leased Olivier since the beginning of this century.

Left:
*The product of this well-known Graves estate.*

Centre:
*The attractive inner courtyard, where receptions are sometimes held during the summer.*

Bottom:
*A fine engraving of Carbonnieux. It was once an awe-inspiring stronghold enclosed by a wall with 12 towers. The estate takes its name from a family called Carbonnieu, which has been traced back to 1234 when Ramon Carbonnieu was baptised in the church at Léognan*

# Château Carbonnieux

Grand Cru Classé des Graves

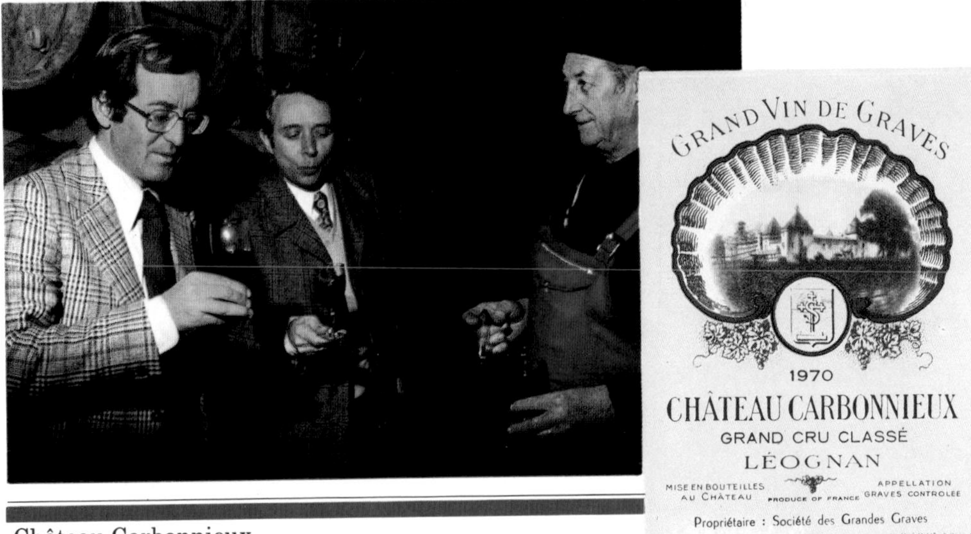


*Far left:*
*Co-proprietor Antony Perrin (left) tastes the wine with some of his staff.*

*Left:*
*The attractive label of Château Carbonnieux. There is also a second label, La Tour Léognan.*

*Below left:*
*The fermentation vats for the red wine are cement. In the foreground a control panel for the highly mechanised equipment which is now used to facilitate work at the Château.*

*Bottom left:*
*After the second fermentation the wine is run off from the lees in the vats. When the red wine has been put in cask, it is left to mature for about two years. The EEC countries and the United States are the main markets for Carbonnieux, although some is also sold in France.*

# Château Carbonnieux

In 1741, when the Benedictine monks from the abbey of Sainte Croix de Bordeaux became the new proprietors of Château Carbonnieux, they set to work in an eminently practical fashion. Not only did they sell the white wine extensively within France itself, they also exported it to the Turkish court. However, as strict Moslems are not permitted to drink alcoholic beverages, the would-be buyers could not openly purchase wine. When the casks arrived in Constantinople, printed on them in large letters were the words: '*Eau Minérale de Carbonnieux en Guienne*', saving the situation. A more romantic version relates that a beautiful Bordelaise, taken in to the Sultan's harem by pirates, persuaded her lord to import this 'mineral water' from her homeland as a preservative of her charms.

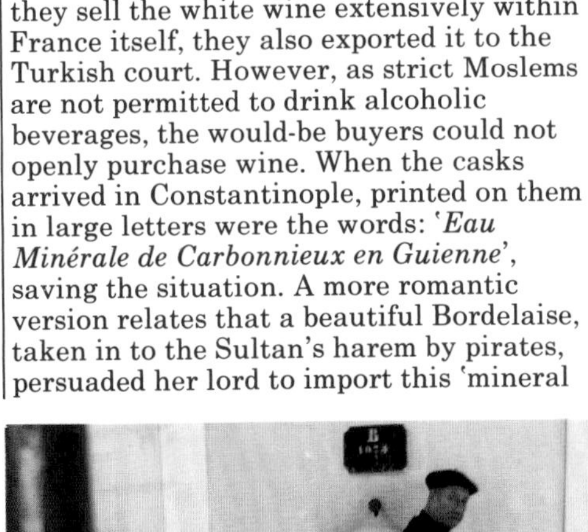

## From Burgundy via Algeria to Bordeaux

As a result of the French Revolution the monks were forced to hand Carbonnieux over to the State, and since that time the property has been in secular hands. The Perrins, the family of the present owner, had been making wine for a couple of centuries in their native Burgundy, but in 1840 they were forced for political reasons to leave France, and went to Algeria – then a French colony – where they started up again in wine making. In 1962 they had to leave, but Marc Perrin had been far-sighted enough to buy Château Carbonnieux in 1956. At the time of purchase the château itself, the vineyard and *chais* were all very dilapidated; the château had been empty since 1910, the *chais* and vathouse had been neglected, and of the 30 hectares of vineyard, as much as 90% had to be completely replanted.

## Fresh white wine

Anyone visiting Carbonnieux today will find no trace of those dreary days. Marc Perrin and his son, Antony, have set to work energetically and have restored everything to its former glory. When you enter the gravel courtyard, one of the most pleasant in the district, the vathouse is immediately on your right. When I visited it in the autumn of 1970 a tractor was unloading, must was being transferred to the underground fermentation tanks, a press for the white grapes was working hard and the air was heavy with the fruity sweetness of the grapes. We drank the wine straight from the hogsheads, and enjoyed its delicious freshness.

The Carbonnieux is never allowed to mature in oak casks but is left for about one year in steel vats. The reason for this is that maturation in wood might well result in three undesirable things – the wine could become darker in colour, it would have a tendency to oxidise, and it might lose some of its freshness.

About two-thirds of the 50-hectare vineyard is planted with white grapes (65% Sauvignon and 35% Sémillon). The white wine production averages 150 *tonneaux*. The Carbonnieux Blanc is certainly a good wine, though to my mind it somehow lacks that special exciting element which makes a great wine. The colour is very light, the nose is often rather reserved, and the flavour is straightforward, dry and light. All recent vintages of white Carbonnieux have been fairly similar.

## Red wine with a prolonged youth

At present a third of the vineyard produces red wine, but Antony Perrin hopes to bring the proportion of red to equal that of the white in the future. World demand is, after all, greater for red quality wine than for white. The black grapes are Cabernet Sauvignon (60%), Merlot (30%), and the remainder Cabernet Franc, plus Malbec. The average production of red wine is 100 *tonneaux*, which is quite high for a vineyard of this size.

The red wines of Carbonnieux have a prolonged youth; that is to say, they retain a slight youthful hardness for a great many years. Take the 1969 vintage: although this wine was the product of a moderately light year, it did not begin to soften until five years later, whereas other red Graves were already making pleasant drinking by that time.

Another wine which I tasted recently is the 1964. This was particularly successful in the red Graves, and the Carbonnieux still has plenty of tannin, although its colour has begun to lighten. The bouquet is still slight – as with the whites, the nose of most Carbonnieux tends to be on the light side.

Before the first world war Daniel Sanders was a linen manufacturer in the north of France. In 1919, however, he became a wine shipper when he married into the family of an existing firm.

At the beginning of this century Haut Bailly belonged to a proprietor who was completely convinced of the wonders of chemistry. He constantly experimented with his wine, at one point even introducing a pasteurised Haut Bailly to the market.

About an eighth of the vintage is sold under its second label, Domaine de la Parde.

*Far right:*
*The simple, angular château as seen from the vineyard.*

*Right and bottom:*
*On the label and on this sign Haut Bailly styles itself both* cru exceptionnel *and a* grand cru classé.

CRU EXCEPTIONNEL
CHATEAU HAUT BAILLY
GRAND CRU CLASSÉ
APPELLATION GRAVES CONTRÔLÉE
1964
Daniel SANDERS - PROPRIÉTAIRE à LÉOGNAN (Gironde)
MIS EN BOUTEILLES AU CHATEAU
DÉPOSÉ


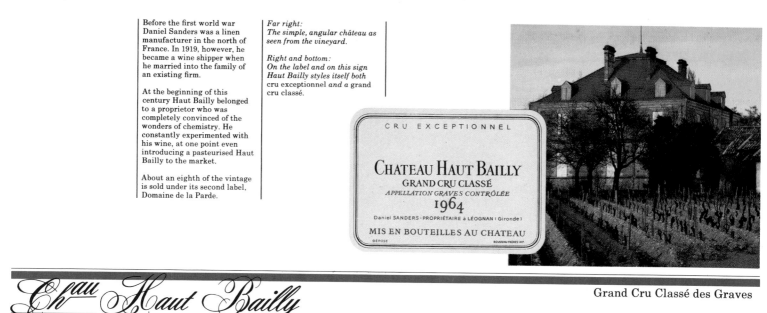

# Chau Haut Bailly

Grand Cru Classé des Graves

My memories of Haut Bailly are chiefly of the sunny day when I drank the fine 1966 vintage in the company of the proprietor, Daniel Sanders, in the almost deserted château. This is a gem of a wine: soft, delicate, elegant, accommodating, very enjoyable, even at 9.30 in the morning.

Haut Bailly is known for its velvety wines full of finesse which, after Haut-Brion and La Mission Haut Brion, rank among the best in the district. This is thanks to Daniel Sanders, who bought the Château in 1955. 'Anyone in Bordeaux', he told me, 'could have bought it, but no one wanted to, for the estate had sadly deteriorated. As a wine merchant, however, I had bought large quantities of the 1945 vintage, a fantastically good wine. I realised Haut Bailly's potential, and it was thanks to this one wine that I bought the estate.'

**Only red wine**

Unlike the other *crus classés* of Léognan Haut Bailly produces only red wine, which can be seen as a healthy kind of specialisation. The vineyard covers 20 hectares and is in one piece.

The Merlot vine accounts for half the production, which explains the distinctive softness of the wine, and a fragrance which is present at an early age, even when the wine is still in wood. The softness of the cask wines does not, however, mean that they are not long-lasting; on the contrary, the wines of Haut Bailly show their charms at a youthful age, but retain them a long time. The secret of his wine, according to M. Sanders, lies not only in the soil and the careful vinification but also in the age of the vines, of which a large number are 50 to 60 years old.

Where the commune of Léognan now lies, many centuries ago there was sea. Evidence of this can be seen in the wall of one of the *chais*, where fossils of shells are still clearly visible.

The annual production of 60 to 90 *tonneaux* of red wine is kept for one or two years in oak casks, about half of which are new. Perhaps Daniel Sanders can manage this rather more easily than other châteaux in the Graves, for his son-in-law owns the leading cooperage of Bordeaux. The countries to which Haut Bailly is exported are Belgium, Britain and the United States.

The fame of this wine, however, stretches much farther afield, for it was this Graves which was served to many monarchs and to the nobility of the world a few years ago at the banquet in Persepolis to commemorate the 2500th anniversary of the Persian Empire.

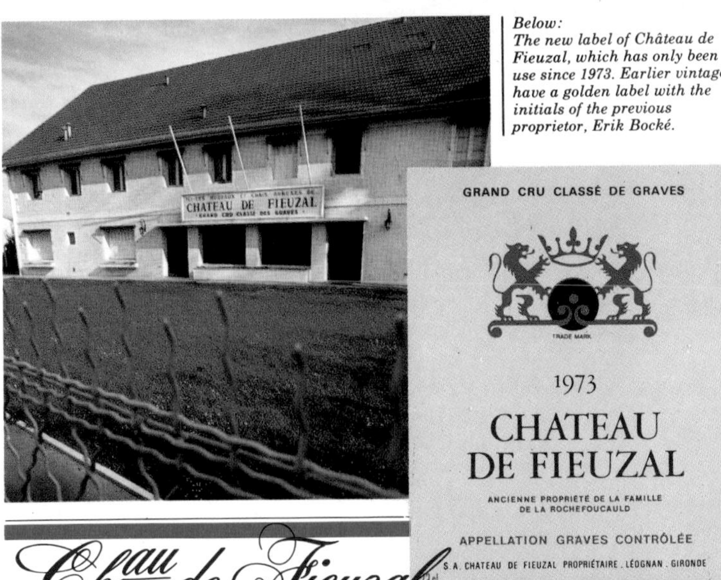

CHATEAU DE FIEUZAL
GRAND CRU CLASSÉ DE GRAVES
TRADE MARK
1973
CHATEAU
DE FIEUZAL
ANCIENNE PROPRIÉTÉ DE LA FAMILLE
DE LA ROCHEFOUCAULD
APPELLATION GRAVES CONTRÔLÉE
S.A. CHATEAU DE FIEUZAL PROPRIÉTAIRE . LÉOGNAN . GIRONDE
MIS EN BOUTEILLES AU CHATEAU


*Below:*
*The new label of Château de Fieuzal, which has only been in use since 1973. Earlier vintages have a golden label with the initials of the previous proprietor, Erik Bocké.*

*Far left:*
*The installation in Léognan where the bottling hall, bottle storage, reception room and offices of de Fieuzal are situated. In 1970 the festivities of the* Ban des Vendages *were celebrated here with a splendid and costly banquet.*

*Bottom:*
*The vineyard of de Fieuzal surrounds the château just outside Léognan. It is planted with the following vines: 60% Cabernet Sauvignon, 30% Merlot, 5% Malbec and 5% Petit Verdot. In addition to the 14 hectares of black grapes there are also 1½ hectares of white grapes: 60% Sauvignon and 40% Sémillon.*

# Chau de Fieuzal

Grand Cru Classé des Graves

Anyone travelling through a wine district will notice that the wine is sometimes better housed than those who tend it. The workers often have to make do with shabby, uncomfortable houses, whereas the wine rests in a spacious, well-kept cellar. I have not seen the living quarters of the employees of de Fieuzal, but the accommodation cannot possibly be as palatial as that of the wine. No one lives at Château de Fieuzal except *Monsieur le Vin*. When you enter the château it looks as if it has just been put in readiness to receive a V.I.P. – everything is so bright, clean and polished. In the first-year *chai* not only the walls and the ceiling have been painted white, but the floor as well, and the gleaming varnished wooden vats are cleaned not with water but with brandy. Everything at de Fieuzal aims at perfection, which is why the wine has built up a strong reputation since the last world war.

## From theatre manager to wine-grower

The person behind this success is Erik Bocké, a tall, lean man with an unforgettable bellowing laugh. He was born in Sweden, but left for America in 1918 and joined the army as a volunteer during the campaigns in France. Two years later he married the daughter of Abel Ricard, the proprietor of Château de Fieuzal. In 1939 war broke out again, and M. Bocké and his wife left France to go and live temporarily in Morocco. When they returned in 1945 M. Ricard had died, the vineyard had been neglected and the cellar ransacked. As ex-manager of the Alhambra Theatre in Bordeaux he knew little about wine-making, but he set to work to repair and restore everything. His efforts were crowned with success, and on 1 January 1974 Bocké, nearly 80 years old, sold the estate, after the death of his wife, for the sum of 10 million francs to Georges Nègrevergne.

## Fruitiness in both red and white

The vineyard covers 17 hectares; 15·5 are devoted to red wine and 1·5 to white. The red wines of de Fieuzal always have a highly individual flavour. In addition they possess a great deal of colour, an interesting bouquet, a sound constitution and usually a fruity taste. They are proud, festive wines. The years 1964, 1966, 1967, 1970, 1971 and 1973 I have all tasted recently; each one is good. While it is young the pleasant, pale white wine of de Fieuzal smells and even tastes of peaches.

Madame Marly keeps pigeons, and this is why the vathouse entrance above the château is protected by a grille, as the birds seem to be very partial to wine.

The youngest son of the house has a fine collection of shell fossils, which he has found in the vineyard.

When she was a little girl, Brigitte Marly had to take round some important visitors on a guided tour and found herself showered with questions she simply could not answer. She remembers that one of the guests asked which was the most common vine species in the vineyard, and all she could do was to reply, with a straight face: 'Mildew'. Her reply was gratefully noted.

*Bottom:*
*The chais, where the wines are maturing and where the bottling is also done. This large building is actually some distance from the château itself, in the centre of Léognan where it forms an entity with the general cellar stock of de Fieuzal.*

*Below centre:*
*This enlarged bottle sticker was used for publicity several generations ago.*

*Opposite page, left:*
*The chais' attractively adorned façade.*

*Opposite page, far right:*
*A view of the château.*

*Opposite page, bottom:*
*A label showing the château, the vineyard, and the vathouse up on the hill.*

*Below and right:*
*Some of the labels which have been used by the property. M. Marly, a mirror manufacturer, wanted one with reverse writing (right), but at the insistence of the trade this was replaced by something more conventional (centre).*

CHATEAU
MALARTIC-LAGRAVIÈRE
*Grand vin de Bordeaux*
1964
CRU CLASSÉ DE GRAVES
APPELLATION GRAVES CONTRÔLÉE
MISE EN BOUTEILLE AU CHATEAU

# Chau Malartic-Lagravière

Grand Cru Classé des Graves

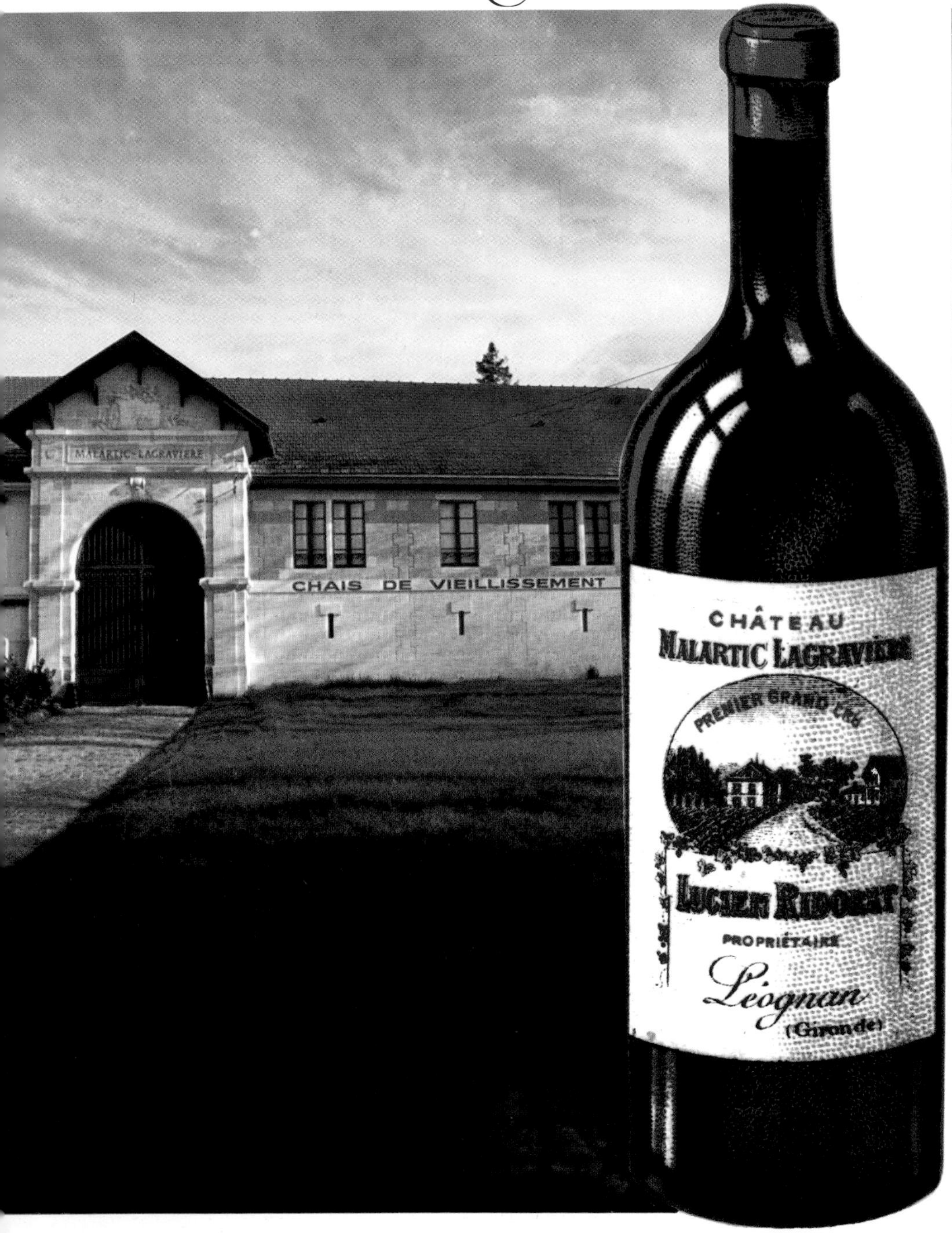

Jacques Marly, proprietor of Château Malartic-Lagravière, says that he and his family are a self-willed bunch of people with fixed ideas. 'We are always the odd ones out, refusing to go with the crowd!'

This non-conformity quickly became apparent when the subject of quality versus quantity was brought up. Unlike nearly all his colleagues, M. Marly holds that the two can go hand in hand – at least on his estate. It hurts him that in some years he has to declassify much Malartic-Lagravière, simply because he has produced more per hectare than the legally permissible amount. Another point which concerns him closely is the character of his wine. Malartic-Lagravière cannot be regarded as immediately appealing, and more than once M. Marly has received requests to make it more supple by adapting his wine-making process. But he has no intention of doing so: 'Soon one wine will be much like another! How absurd that I can't even make my Malartic as I want to any more!'

## Progress in the vathouse

Yet time has not stood still at the estate. In the vathouse there are nine shiny stainless steel fermentation vats, each holding 1,200 hectolitres. These were an enormous investment for this independent, moderately sized Château. Jacques Marly nevertheless feels that the expense was justified. The modern vats will last for a long time, and they also permit control of temperature during fermentation better than any other type. At Malartic-Lagravière all the wine goes into new casks, both the red, of which there are 60 to 70 *tonneaux*, and the 8 to 10 *tonneaux* of white wine.

## Only Sauvignon for the white wine

The vineyard is situated immediately behind the château on a long, wide slope and covers an area of 20 hectares. The black grapes are conventional in proportions: 50% Cabernet Sauvignon, 25% Cabernet Franc and 25% Merlot. The white wine, however, is made only from the Sauvignon. There is no Sémillon at all. According to M. Marly, the Sauvignon on

Château Malartic-Lagravière

its own gives a fruitier, more fragrant wine than a mixture of grape varieties. As proof of his argument he let me taste his white wine, and I admit that it is very good: fresh, light and fragrant – an excellent start to the meal.

### A memorable gamut of wines

I was fortunate enough to be able to taste a number of vintages of the red wine during a lunch at the château. This was on a Saturday, when the owners keep open house for their nine children and their families. They chat, play billiards and during the course of the afternoon sit down to play bridge. The main event, however, is luncheon, an exuberant meal at which outstanding wines are often served. The apéritif on this occasion was a dry Champagne, and the white wine was drunk with the hors d'oeuvre; with the lamb and, later, cheeses, the red 1973 (as 'mouthwash'), the 1964, the 1953 and a magnum of 1929. Not a bad selection for an ordinary Saturday!

Although it required some strength of mind on my part to make notes throughout this family meal I managed to do so. But as I have tasted some of the same wines on other occasions, my impressions are not based only on this visit.

The 1929 vintage was a perfect wine – for a quarter of an hour. Then it was suddenly over: oxidation made it fall apart extremely rapidly. But in those fifteen minutes I appreciated the magnificent colour, the powerful bouquet and excellent flavour. The 1953 still had not completely reached its peak: it was rather austere and will continue to develop for years. I found the 1964 vintage especially enjoyable, indeed, in retrospect, it was perhaps most typical of Malartic-Lagravière, with a suppleness and inner firmness. This too is a stayer. The 1966, like the 1964, had a ripe, fully rounded nose, also with an impression of barely concealed power. The 1970 vintage was still very reticent, although I noted its fruit and a fair amount of tannin, indicating that it too may well last for a long while.

### Winemakers and seamen

This estate was brought into the family by Madame Marly, a charming woman, whose forebears were both wine-growers and seamen: the men sailed round the world while the women tended the vineyard. This explains why you can find engravings from China, rattan souvenirs from Sumatra, and a ship's parrot side by side in this cosy, friendly château. The parrot's teacher, however, could hardly have been a Marly, because the bird enjoys rum and whisky, not wine.

Claude Ricard is a talented pianist and originally wanted to be a professional musician. In 1948, however, his father brought him to Domaine de Chevalier (which became his mother's property in 1942) saying: 'As you have nothing better to do as a pianist, you may as well look after Domaine de Chevalier.' Claude Ricard's son-in-law is an artist, and today many of his paintings are displayed in the house.

The estate's small production was further decimated in 1974 when night frosts came on 25 April and then again on 8 May.

Domaine de Chevalier Blanc is a wine which does not need fining but naturally falls bright by itself after some months.

The white grapes are always ready for vintageing about eight days in advance of the black ones. Claude Ricard therefore has plenty of time to make both the white and the red wine.

As a rule, in a good vintage the red wines from the estate must mature for at least 10 years before they are fully developed.

Thanks to very strict selection Claude Ricard also succeeds in making excellent white wines even in off years: the white 1965 was deliciously fragrant. Even these white wines can improve with as much as ten years' maturation in bottle.

*Bottom:*
*The unpretentious château where such fine wines are made. It was fortunate that Jean Ricard planted a vineyard here in 1856, in the middle of the woods, as a hundred metres further up the soil is quite unsuitable for vines. The building on the far right is the vathouse; behind this are the chais.*

# Domaine de Chevalier

Grand Cru Classé des Graves

Little attention is paid to outward display at Domaine de Chevalier. The house is low, small and modest, the word 'château' is not used and the whole estate has a rustic character. It is situated in a clearing in the middle of the woods behind Léognan, far from the other great properties. You might even suppose that a pleasant rather than a great wine is made here, but this is far from true: Domaine de Chevalier makes excellent red and white wines which are esteemed among the finest Graves. I personally believe that white Domaine de Chevalier is one of the outstanding dry white wines in the world. I once tasted it alongside a Le Montrachet: the white Graves captured my heart with its delicate, aristocratic style.

The vineyard covers 15 hectares, with only 2·8 hectares planted with white vines (60% Sauvignon and 40% Sémillon). Many growers would be tempted to make as much wine as possible from such a limited area, but not proprietor Claude Ricard. Severe pruning of all the vines makes the yield of Domaine de Chevalier probably the lowest of all the wine estates in Bordeaux. In 1970, for example, Claude Ricard was the only proprietor in the whole of the Gironde whose crop was below the statutory permissible maximum per hectare. His highest yield to date was in 1973, 25 hectolitres per hectare. In good years Domaine de Chevalier produces 30 *tonneaux* of red and 10 *tonneaux* of white wine.

### Minute attention to detail

Both red and white wines are made with a fanatical attention to the smallest details, especially the white. Its vineyard is so small that Claude Ricard can control it with minute exactitude.

The wine-making process is as follows: the white grapes are usually picked in three separate operations. First the rows are searched for any rotten grapes. Then all the sound, healthy, ripe grapes are picked, the rest being picked a few days later. The grapes must not be too ripe, or the wine will lose some of its sensitivity. The grapes are then pressed, only the first pressing being used for the *grand vin.* Claude Ricard has conducted many experiments to see whether some of the subsequent pressings could not be used, but even a 2½% addition could be detected, white Domaine de Chevalier being so delicate and fine. After the pressing comes the fermentation. This takes place in wood, because Claude Ricard finds it easier to keep the temperature down. The wine is then left to mature for 1½ years in casks. New ones are never used for the

*Far left:*
*A still life of the great wine of Domaine de Chevalier in various bottle sizes.*

*Left:*
*The label of Domaine de Chevalier, which rather unusually shows a photograph of the estate instead of being an old print.*

*Bottom left:*
*The estate's chais are modest but impeccably kept.*

*Bottom right:*
*Manager R. Tahon has worked at Domaine de Chevalier for 15 years. He, together with Claude Ricard, followed a course in oenology under Professor Peynaud. Different in temperament from his boss, he invariably agrees with him in important decisions.*



white wine, because the young wood affects the flavour. M. Ricard told me that in 1955 he had had too few old casks and had been forced to put part of the white wine into new casks, but 'you could taste the woody flavour for years afterwards.'

This is only a single instance of the many details that are rigorously watched in order to produce this superb wine.

### An individual style of fermentation

The red wine is made from 65% Cabernet Sauvignon, 5% Cabernet Franc and 30% Merlot. The grapes, destalked and slightly crushed, are left to ferment in four 100-hectolitre steel vats. There are still some wooden ones but these are no longer used.

Claude Ricard holds slightly different opinions on the ideal temperature during the first fermentation from those at many châteaux, who do their best not to exceed 28°C; M. Ricard believes that the temperature should be 30°C.

The red wine rests in wood for two years. After careful experimentation M. Ricard has come to the conclusion that in normal years half of the casks must be new; these are placed alternately in the small *chai.* Only in vintages of outstanding quality does the whole crop go into new wood.

### Choice of a great Graves chef

I have already used adjectives like delicate and sensitive for the white wine of Domaine de Chevalier. One that should be added is finesse, because I know of no other dry white wine which possesses more. Among white Bordeaux in several of its attributes Domaine de Chevalier may share the qualities that are associated with Château Margaux. It is therefore not to be wondered at that Ginestet, the merchant side of Château Margaux, have acquired the exclusive right of distribution of Domaine de Chevalier.

The red wines from the estate start fairly hard, but once they mature and soften you are immediately aware of their aristocratic breeding. Because of the great precision and care with which they are made they are never disappointing: varying according to their vintages, they are still constant in quality. No wonder the red 1964 of Domaine de Chevalier was the wine that Raymond Oliver, of the Paris restaurant Le Grand Véfour, chose when he, together with the Champagne house of Krug, gave a banquet for a group of master chefs in 1974, to celebrate Oliver's 50th anniversary as a *grand bonnet.* He too comes from the Graves.

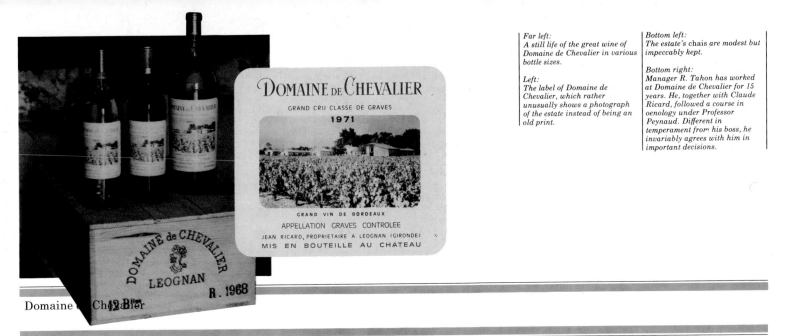

*Left:*
*Close-up of the* chais. *Château Bouscaut is situated in the commune of Cadaujac, a word which roughly means 'I stop here'.*

*Bottom:*
*The magnificent house in all its glory, built in 1710 as a* maison bourgeoise. *The solid round tower was not added until 1847. In front of the Château there is a lake and at the back a private swimming pool.*

*Opposite page, left:*
*One of the magnificent tapestries in the dining room. All the rooms are beautifully furnished, and contain many interesting works of art.*

*Opposite page, far right:*
*Everything has been prepared for a superb meal by the cook. Bouscaut has its own specially designed porcelain and tableware.*

*Opposite page, bottom left:*
*Some of the treasures housed in the château.*

*Opposite page, bottom centre:*
*The cellar staff can regularly be seen topping up the casks, a procedure carried out about three times a week during the first year.*

*Opposite page, bottom right:*
*Rear view of the Château.*

# Château Bouscaut

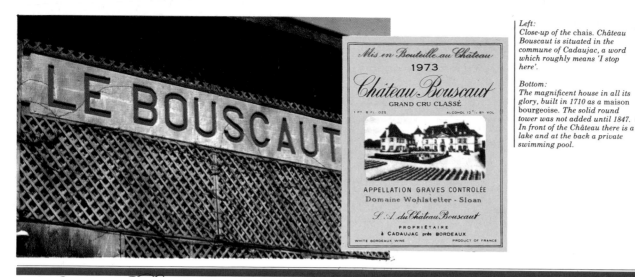

Grand Cru Classé des Graves

Château Bouscaut is to me one of the most fascinating estates in the Graves. What has happened here in the space of a very short time is almost unbelievable. In 1969 Bouscaut was bought for one million dollars by a group of ten people brought together by the American, Charles Wohlstetter. What they received for their money was in fact no more than the certainty that at Bouscaut it must be possible to make a good wine, for apart from that, the property was in a bad way. The cellars had been poorly maintained, the vineyard was uncared for, the château lacked all modern conveniences and the workers' quarters were primitive. All that was to change quickly. The Americans succeeded in securing Jean-Bernard Delmas of Haut-Brion as manager, and gave him and his charming wife, Anne-Marie, *carte blanche* to renovate everything at Bouscaut. Jean-Bernard was to look after the *chais* and everything to do with the wine, and Anne-Marie was to be in charge of the château itself. Together they have performed something little short of a miracle, combining hard work with intelligence and good taste.

### A Château brought back to life

First of all the needs of the workers were seen to: in the space of four years, ten houses were built for the families of the permanent staff. Then came the turn of the château, where guests can now be received in style. Downstairs there is a large reception hall, well-equipped kitchen, a dining room and a library, where an open fire crackles in the large grate during the winter. Upstairs there is a television room with a modern colour set, as well as stocks of light reading matter and games and puzzles for the visitors. On the first floor there is a small breakfast-kitchen with a well-stocked refrigerator at the disposal of thirsty or hungry guests. There are several bedrooms and bathrooms, all luxuriously furnished with every possible convenience. Bouscaut thus provides nowadays the comfort of a first-class hotel, but with the atmosphere of a friendly country house. Most important of all, there is a superb cook with a repertoire of dishes to please even the most exacting of guests – those who visit Bouscaut have a memorable experience.

### $400,000 for vineyard and chais

Much needed to be done to the *chais* as well, as can be seen from the $100,000 invested in them as a start. This is only the beginning; when there are sufficient funds available M. Delmas hopes to replace the wooden vats with stainless steel ones like those at Haut-Brion; an identical de-

Château Bouscaut

stalking machine to the one at Haut-Brion has already been installed.

The vineyard has also been thoroughly renovated. The 40 hectares had to be virtually completely replanted, a project which cost $300,000. In spending these vast sums the new proprietors are demonstrating their belief that Bouscaut can be a great château making a great wine. They are first of all lovers of wine – investors only second, which is how one wishes it could always be.

**Vintages with great futures**

Like several other Graves châteaux, Bouscaut makes both red and white wine. The red is made from the classic Cabernet Sauvignon, Cabernet Franc and Merlot, the white from the Sauvignon and the Sémillon. The yields are 100 *tonneaux* and 20 *tonneaux* respectively. I found the white Bouscaut pleasant and fresh. Its bouquet is considerable and does not belie its origin: most dry white Graves have a light liquorice in their aroma. Drink this wine with Arcachon oysters or with Bayonne ham, as they do at Bouscaut, where they know how to enjoy the good things in life.

Red Bouscaut is a wine which is known for its great keeping properties. While young it is fairly hard, but as the years go by it becomes increasingly amiable. I have happy memories of the 1928 vintage which I once drank, a firm wine with a superb bouquet, though it understandably declined and after about 20 minutes was only a shadow of its former self – the bottle was then over forty years old.

After the difficult period which Château Bouscaut has gone through, there has been a spectacular improvement in the quality of the wine since the 1969 vintage, the year in which M. Delmas took charge. All the wines since then have been finer and deeper than their predecessors, something which is immediately noticeable in their bouquet.

The 1969 vintage yielded a great deal of wine for that year. The nose is a little delicate, but the flavour more assertive. I might describe this full, solid flavour as being like having marbles – or the pebbles of the Graves – in your mouth.

The 1970 vintage is a wine for the year 2000. It will be a giant, with a deep dark colour, it is still reticent and very tannic.

In 1971 Bouscaut also made an assertive wine, very typical and exceptionally good. The 1972 vintage lacks body; it is marketed in its entirety under the estate's second label as Château Valoux.

The 1973 offers a great deal of fruit, is supple and pleasing, and the young 1974 has a good colour, considerable firmness and balance. Claret lovers may hear a lot about Bouscaut in the future.

GRAND VIN DE GRAVES SEC
1972
TRES SEC
CHATEAV
SMITH HAVT LAFITTE
MARTILLAC
APPELLATION GRAVES CONTRÔLEE
LOUIS ESCHENAUER S·A·PROPRIETAIRE
A MARTILLAC (GIRONDE) FRANCE
LOUIS ESCHENAUER S. A. · BORDEAUX
PRODUCE OF FRANCE

*Left:*
*The wines of Smith Haut Lafitte are bottled in the striking bottles of the Eschenauer firm. The Château's red wines mature especially well and are therefore suitable for laying down for a considerable time.*

*Bottom:*
*The large new underground cellar which provides space for 2,000 casks containing both the first and second year wines.*

The 1973 vintage is the first wine to be bottled at the Château and not in the Eschenauer cellars in Bordeaux.

The red wine of Smith Haut Lafitte is the product of 75% Cabernet Sauvignon, 20% Merlot and 5% Cabernet Franc.

The Château acquired its name when a certain Mr Smith acquired a property on the *Haut de Lafitte*, the Lafitte Heights, in the 18th century. The word *fitte* also used to mean 'hill'.

# Château Smith Haut Lafitte

Grand Cru Classé des Graves

It might be said that Smith Haut Lafitte is now in its second youth. A great deal is happening at this important estate, even more than when it was completely renovated for the first time. It was perhaps at its most famous a century ago.

In the second half of the last century, under the energetic leadership of M. Duffour-Duberger, a former Mayor of Bordeaux, the three original sections of the Smith Haut Lafitte estate were reunited. The resulting vineyard was for those days a model: for example, in 1876 Château Smith Haut Lafitte was awarded the prize for the best kept vineyard in the whole of the Gironde.

After the death of M. Duffour-Duberger the estate changed proprietors many times: in the records can be found the names of a German firm and the French treasurer of Indo-China. For years the only constant factor was the house of Louis Eschenauer, which has held the exclusive selling rights for the wine since 1902. In 1957 the firm bought the vineyard (not the château) and now the fortunes of Smith Haut Lafitte show signs of reviving for the second time in its history.

## Wholehearted reconstruction

Under the capable management of Eschenauer's technical manager, René Baffert, much was achieved in a relatively short time. The vineyard was extended from a mere 6 or 10 hectares to 51 hectares (which is still 15 hectares less than the area under cultivation in 1860). A start was also made on the construction of a brand-new cellar complex. René Baffert admits honestly that they were rather carried away by their initial enthusiasm: in 1962 cement fermentation vats were installed, which they would prefer to dispense with now because the steel vats bought subsequently have been found to make better wine.

Near the vathouse Eschenauer has built a vast *chai* on the spot where there used to be living quarters for the workers. This *chai* is 70 metres long and 25 metres wide, and can store at least 400 casks. A second-year *chai*, bottling hall, storage room for the bottles, and a cleaning hall for the 6,000 casks which have to be cleaned every year, were among the other new installations.

'You could call it passionate reconstruction', says manager Baffert, and you have to agree with him. Nor is the reconstruction confined to everything necessary for wine-making; the outward appearance of the estate as a whole has also been considered. There are plans for a park, the reconstruction of the old tower, the equipping of a *salle de réception* and the restoration of an old chapel.

## Love it or leave it

The new château – for that is really what it is – stands in the middle of its vineyard on top of a gentle rise. Of the 51 hectares, 47 are planted with black grapes and 6 hectares with white. The white Sauvignon dominates, in the ratio of 5 to 1; there is therefore only a very small percentage of Sémillon. This was done on purpose when the white wine vineyard was completely replanted in 1967.

I tasted the 1971 vintage, which certainly had a marked Sauvignon smell. The taste was still green, which was all the more surprising, as when I tasted it the wine was already three years old. I believe that with this very individual wine it is a case of love it or leave it: you like it either very much or not at all.

However, it is likely that the wines will

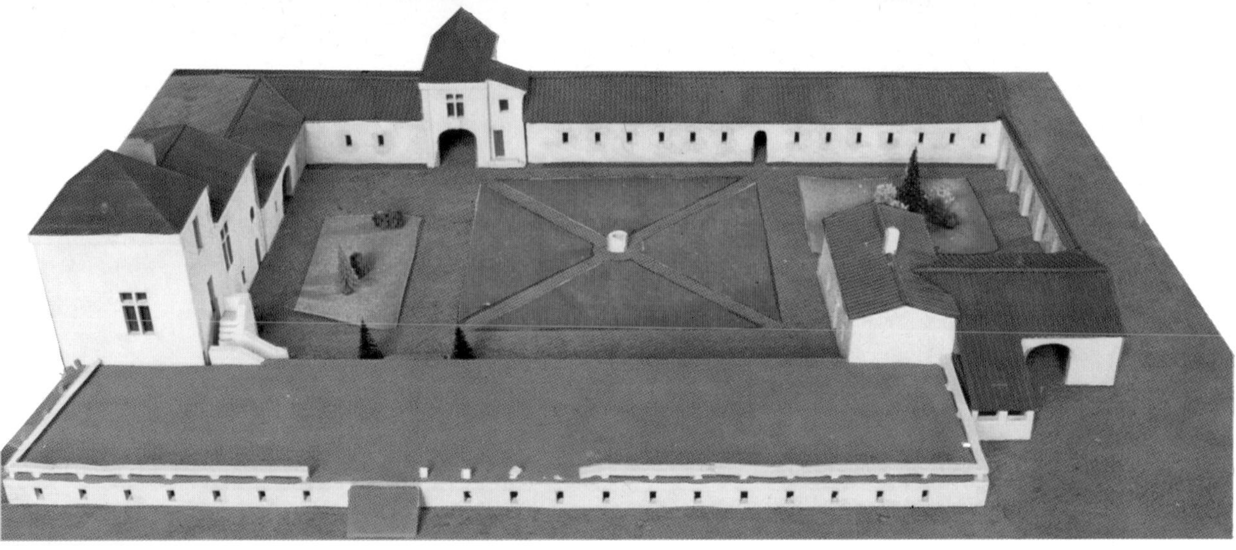

*Left:*
*A model of the new Château. The building at the end of the left wing is the reception hall, the raised section in the front is the roof of the new* chai.

*Bottom centre:*
*The old Château of Smith Haut Lafitte which stands a short distance from the new one and is separate from the vineyard.*

*Bottom right:*
*Manager Claude Guérin, who has worked on the estate since the mid-1960s. He has 11 staff working for him permanently.*



become rounder and more friendly as the vines mature and their roots penetrate deeper into the subsoil. I shall watch with interest the progress of Smith Haut Lafitte Blanc in the coming decade.

The red wine is mainly shipped to the U.S.A., but Britain, Canada and Japan are also important customers. The production averages 250 *tonneaux*, which is about eight times that of the white wine. I think back with pleasure to the 1962 red, which had a lovely colour, a fine, soft bouquet and a flavour to match – it was unquestionably a fine Graves.

A great deal has happened in the red vineyard, however, and I thought I detected this in the more recent wines. Like all other replanted vineyards there is the problem of a great many young vines, which give a considerable yield but lack the delicacy, depth and complexity of the older vines. The 1969 and 1971 vintages which I have tasted were to my mind a bit flat to the nose and on the tongue. But apart from this, the ingredients of a *grand vin* were present: colour, tannin, balance and so on. In my opinion, it is only a matter of time before the red wines of Smith Haut Lafitte will again be exceptional – as they are already described on the top part of the label.

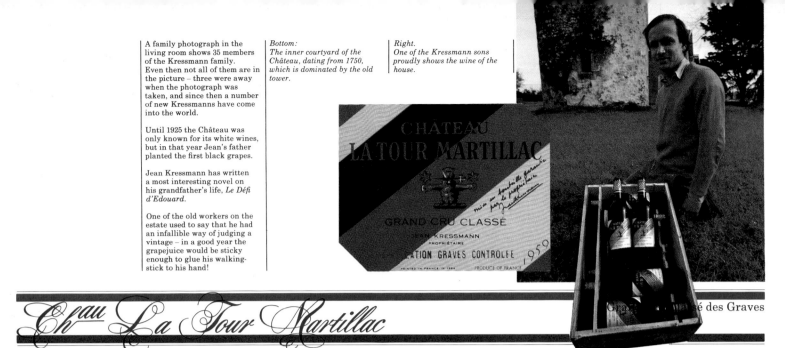

A family photograph in the living room shows 35 members of the Kressmann family. Even then not all of them are in the picture – three were away when the photograph was taken, and since then a number of new Kressmanns have come into the world.

Until 1925 the Château was only known for its white wines, but in that year Jean's father planted the first black grapes.

Jean Kressmann has written a most interesting novel on his grandfather's life, *Le Défi d'Edouard*.

One of the old workers on the estate used to say that he had an infallible way of judging a vintage – in a good year the grapejuice would be sticky enough to glue his walking-stick to his hand!

*Bottom:*
*The inner courtyard of the Château, dating from 1750, which is dominated by the old tower.*

*Right.*
*One of the Kressmann sons proudly shows the wine of the house.*

# Chau La Tour Martillac

…sé des Graves

Château La Tour Martillac is situated in an idyllic part of the Graves region. From the garden at the back you look out over the vineyard, which stretches into the distance to the edge of a wood. On warm summer days the peacefulness is heavenly, and the 'civilised' world seems very far away, especially if you are lucky enough to be able to sit quietly under the trees and enjoy good wine and a huge *entrecôte* grilled over glowing embers of vine prunings. It is not surprising to read that in the 18th century Montesquieu, the political philosopher, would gladly have exchanged his moated Château de la Brède nearby for the rustic simplicity of La Tour Martillac, but was unable to do so. It is therefore understandable that, when Jean Kressmann decided to retire from the shipping house that bears his name in 1965, he settled here as a wine grower.

The first years that Jean Kressmann was at La Tour Martillac were not easy ones. He was not a young man even ten years ago, but he recalls having to drive the tractor himself to cultivate the 16 hectare vineyard. Nowadays things have improved, but the hard work still goes on. The $2\frac{1}{2}$ hectares planted with white grapes require especial time and effort. M. Kressmann says of them: 'My white vines are very old, which means they require twice as much work for half the yield. The quality of the white wine is good, yet I get for it half what I get for my red wine. It's rather foolish to go on making my wine as I do, and I fear my sons will do things differently.' Thanks to the obstinacy of Jean Kressmann, La Tour Martillac Blanc is a fresh, agreeable light wine, a wine which Prince Philip, Duke of Edinburgh, enjoyed when he was installed in the *Commanderie du Bontemps de Médoc et des Graves*, the wine brotherhood of the two regions.

### A red wine of restraint

Whereas the production of white wine is about 6 *tonneaux*, the production of red is 50 *tonneaux*. The striking thing about the red wine is the low percentage of Merlot among the black grapes: only 12%, with 50% Cabernet Sauvignon, 25% Cabernet Franc and 13% Malbec.

The red La Tour Martillac is not usually an exuberant wine: more for intellectual and serious appraisal than for enthusiastic but indiscriminate quaffing. The bouquet does not rush to meet you but it is fine, ripe and soft; if the flavour seems restrained, the quality is definitely there. The 1959 vintage, particularly, gave me a great deal of pleasure, and as regards recent years, 1973 and 1974 are charming wines which will be ready to drink relatively quickly.

*Left:*
*The city of Bordeaux is situated 557 kilometres to the south-west of Paris, in the heart of this famous wine-producing region, indicated in red on the key map. The three most important districts, each of them discussed in this book, are:* **A** *the Médoc,* **B** *the Graves,* **C** *St Emilion and Pomerol. For a map of St Emilion and Pomerol see below; a map of the Médoc will be found on pages 22 and 23 and one of the Graves on page 143.*

*Below:*
*The map gives a general impression of the St Emilion and Pomerol district. It shows all the châteaux discussed in this section. The boundaries of the parishes of St Emilion and Pomerol are shown in dark yellow, the names of towns and villages are given and next to each château symbol, the names of the individual châteaux.*

The fascinating mediaeval town of St Emilion – the whole of it has been declared an ancient monument – is in the midst of 5,000 hectares of vineyards, divided among 1,000 estates. The early ripening Merlot grape is predominant, accompanied by the Cabernet Franc (locally called Bouchet); the white Cabernet Sauvignon plays a supporting rôle. Most of the great wines of St Emilion come from the calcareous slopes near the town itself; only two *premiers grands crus* are situated near Pomerol, where the ground is highly siliceous. Surrounding this district are several other parishes which are allowed to couple the words St Emilion to their own names. They extend over a total of some 3,000 hectares. The soil in the Pomerol district is mostly gravel, but also contains clay, sand and iron. The wines are often more elegant and delicate than those of St Emilion and can be drunk young. Pomerol extends over 675 hectares with 120 estates. Neighbouring Lalande-de-Pomerol covers about 825 hectares.

Cheval Blanc came into the possession of the Fourcaud-Laussac family in 1852 when Mademoiselle Ducasse, whose father owned the estate, married M. Fourcaud-Laussac.

The Château has its own well and windmill.

In the 19th century the building was only a simple farmhouse. It took on its present shape around 1890.

The father of manager Jacques Hebrard was famous. He established the French airline Air Inter, which still flies on domestic routes, and flew the Atlantic at a time when this was still a hazardous adventure. The model of his plane stands in the living room at the château. Jacques Hebrard himself also has a pilot's licence.

The pickers have their meals in the Orangery, which for the rest of the year is full of the orange trees in their pots.

*Bottom:*
*The Château seen from the rear garden. Mass is said in the tiny chapel during vintage time.*

*Opposite page, far right:*
*Topping up the casks, a task that has to be repeated at frequent intervals.*

*Opposite page, bottom:*
*Cellar master Gaston Vaissire in his domain. He has worked at the Château for about 30 years.*

# Ch^au Cheval Blanc

1st Grand Cru classé

It perhaps seems strange that the finest wine of St Emilion is made on the very edge of the parish: Cheval Blanc touches Pomerol, its vineyard being separated by a narrow road from that of Château La Conseillante, *A.C.* Pomerol. The landscape here is different from that round the picturesque town of St Emilion, 4 kilometres away, which stands above fairly hilly, rugged country, whereas around Cheval Blanc there are only gentle, undulating slopes.

Even more marked than this difference in appearance is the difference in the subsoil: the slopes of St Emilion are largely calcareous and those around Cheval Blanc silicated. Separating these two types of soil is a strip of sand, 3 kilometres wide. The soil around Cheval Blanc is not only gravelly; the vineyard extends over patches of clay and also of iron. It is this unusual combination which gives Cheval Blanc its unique style – in conjunction with the right grapes and the right human care.

The vineyard covers 34 hectares, of which 29 are fully productive. It has been a lot smaller: there is a map dating from 1834 which shows less than half the present acreage. The vineyard was increased to its present size by a series of purchases of adjoining land (mostly pasture or wood with a good subsoil) during the 19th century. Highly characteristic of Cheval Blanc is the unorthodox way in which the vineyard is planted: there is no Cabernet Sauvignon at all. The vine species used are two-thirds Cabernet Franc, almost a third Merlot and just one hectare of Malbec. This has been done deliberately, and when many of the vines were destroyed by frost in 1956 there were no changes, although modifications could have been made in replanting. In fact, as few vines as possible were uprooted in the hope that most of them would eventually sprout again; where replanting proved necessary, the existing varieties were kept. In the terrible year of 1956, only one cask of wine was made at Cheval Blanc.

Cheval Blanc probably owes a good deal of its great reputation to the fact that the same family has maintained a consistent

Château Cheval Blanc

policy of quality for many generations. These are the Fourcaud-Laussacs, or more specifically their descendants, for none of the present owners bears that name; they are all nephews, nieces, cousins and relations by marriage.

Co-proprietor Jacques Hebrard has been manager of Cheval Blanc since 1970. He is a giant of a man, taciturn, but both dedicated and painstaking in his work. It was he, I discovered, who was the one to make a number of improvements, such as building a new, cool *chai*, with a spacious reception room above it. He is deeply involved in the fortunes of his vineyard, and is the first of the many proprietors in his family to live at the château all the year round. He is a great wine expert, and a respected authority on wine, and has also gained practical agricultural experience in Central Africa.

### Why the 'white horse'?

The château where Jacques Hebrard and his lovely wife live is perhaps not as grand as those of the Médoc first growths, but it is a comfortable home. It is said that on the spot where the building – painted white, naturally – now stands, there used to be a post-house where horses could be changed. Apparently Henri IV once stopped here when he wanted to change his horses, traditionally always white, on the road from Paris to Pau, his birthplace, and after that the inn was called Cheval Blanc. The authenticity of this story would be difficult to check, but it is a rather charming one, and quite in keeping with the various legends of Henry of Navarre, even if the scrupulously accurate historians of the region say that for various reasons the Béarnais would have changed horses somewhere else.

### Château-bottling since 1974 vintage

You gain access to the cellars of Cheval Blanc from the château. The vathouse dates from 1964 and houses a considerable number of cement fermentation vats, each of which holds the quantity of grapes picked in a day. According to M. Hebrard this makes it possible to control the wine-making exactly. The cool, white first-year *chai* is roomy and has indirect lighting. The casks there are largely new; the wine is usually left to mature in wood for two years.

It is in this new installation that the first vintage to be bottled at the Château, the 1974, will be handled. The bottling of all previous years was done in Libourne. The cellars in this little wine town date back to the time when most of the wines of St Emilion were brought in either for bottling by the Libourne shippers, or alternatively were shipped further down the River Dordogne. In those days the Libourne quays, relatively quiet now, would have been very busy.

For the sale of its wine, Cheval Blanc has an agreement with five houses: those of Calvet, Delor, Cruse, J. P. Moueix and Horeau-Beylot. The chief markets are Britain, Belgium, Scandinavia, Holland and, to a lesser extent, the United States, France and Japan.

The amount of wine available varies considerably from year to year, the production fluctuating between the 40 *tonneaux* of 1957 and 1961 and the 150 *tonneaux* of 1970. The figures for some recent years are: 1966: 79, 1967: 140, 1969: 75, 1970: 150, 1971: 68, 1972: 64, 1973: 128. In 1965 no Cheval Blanc was marketed, and in 1968 only 4,000 to 5,000 bottles. The latter bore the usual label but without the words *Premier Grand Cru Classé.*

*Left:*
*From the new reception hall at Cheval Blanc there is a view over Pomerol. The little tower which can just be seen in the distance is the village church.*

*Below left:*
*Everything is freshly painted white in the new reception building, which has been extended from the cellars.*

*Bottom:*
*Cheval Blanc is largely surrounded by trees, and in the summer it is impossible to see much more than its spire from the road.*

Jacques Hebrard is the first person to live at Cheval Blanc all the year round. His predecessor lived in Libourne, next to the old *chais*.

Some 18 people are employed at Cheval Blanc. *Maître de chai* Gaston Vaissire is responsible for the work in the cellars, *chef de culture* Guy Haurut supervises the work in the vineyard.

## Implications of luxuriance

Every time I drink Cheval Blanc – unfortunately not nearly often enough – I feel for a moment as if I were very rich, for the luxuriance of this wine is fantastic, you taste such a concentration of claret. This was marked in the 1964, which I drank in the château's blue dining-room, with *confit* of turkey. This vintage was dark, with a marvellous bouquet which became progressively richer, and a luxuriant, very fine flavour with elegant undertones.

Even more impressive was the 1961, to me a perfect wine, less solid perhaps than some other red Bordeaux of that fine year, but still a beauty. It was as if the nose of this wine folded you in its embrace, its bouquet was so full and penetrating, and then there was the superb flavour.

Besides 1961 and 1964, the 1966, 1970 and 1971 vintages are also excellent. The 1970 is a tannic, long-lasting wine with a promising bouquet. I found it slightly more sensitive than the 1971, although this is also a marvellous wine: round, complete, powerful and full of fruit. When I tasted it it was still a little hard, but this will undoubtedly soften with maturity. The 1972 vintage will not reach the heights of its two immediate predecessors, but will certainly be enjoyable.

Jacques Hebrard does not drink Cheval Blanc at every meal – this would be too costly, even for him – but the substitute is wholly acceptable. This is the estate's *vin de consommation courante*, or everyday wine, obviously lighter, but very pleasant – indeed, far superior to the sort of carafe red to which most of us are accustomed.

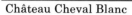

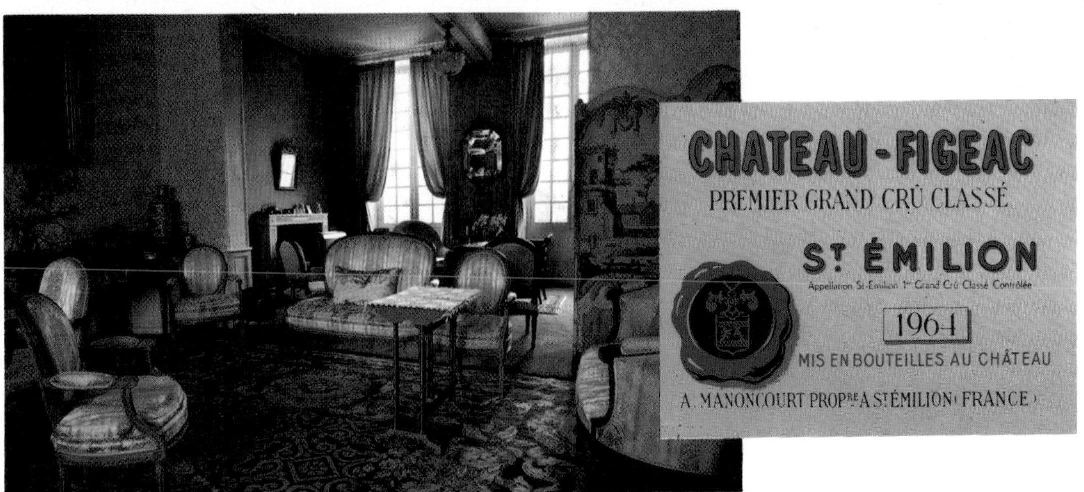


*Left:*
*One of the rooms in the main building, which are only used for guests, as Thierry and Marie-France Manoncourt live in a side wing of the Château.*

*Bottom:*
*Figeac's cellar master, who uses mostly new casks for each year's wine.*

# Château Figeac

1st Grand Cru Classé

Figeac has to some extent been overshadowed by its great neighbour across the way, Cheval Blanc, but unjustifiably so, for its wines are among the most aristocratic St Emilions and deserve to be treated accordingly.

There are probably three reasons why Figeac's fame has tended to be modest. The first is the existence of a large number of châteaux with Figeac in their name – La Tour-Figeac, Petit-Figeac, Yon-Figeac, Grand Barrail Lamarzelle-Figeac, to mention just a few. These estates all make good wine, though it is not of the same quality as that of Figeac. The second reason for the estate's lack of fame is that the grandfather of today's owner, Thierry Manoncourt, regarded it as a holiday house; he was an important civic official in Paris and had little time to come to St Emilion, so the building usually remained closed. This impaired regular contact with the various wine brokers, still influential links between growers and shippers. Finally, the frost of 1956 badly damaged Figeac: a large part of the vineyard subsequently had to be replanted, with the result that production dropped sharply for a time. Not until 1970 was the former yield again attained – 200 *tonneaux*, the same as in 1928.

Thierry Manoncourt relates that in December 1966 he presented sample bottles of his 1953 vintage to the *Académie du Vin de Bordeaux*. All five were Figeac, made and handled identically. But each one had been made from only a single vine, instead of several together, so there was a straight Cabernet Sauvignon, a Merlot, Cabernet Franc, Petit Verdot and Malbec, plus one bottle of the usual blend of these grapes. The majority of the tasters (who had not been told what was in the bottles) in fact preferred one wine above the rest, which was the blend of the vines. But this experiment made M. Manoncourt decide to uproot the Malbec from his vineyard, as this grape proved very disappointing. The noble Cabernet Sauvignon justified its reputation by making excellent wine even by itself.

The first conference of the associated makers of *produits d'origine* – consumer goods of legally defined origin, was held in Bordeaux. Besides wine makers there were representatives of the cheese districts, rearers of the free-range chickens of Bresse, and so on. Château Figeac was one of the three Bordeaux wines served at the gala dinner, with a Mouton-Rothschild and the great dessert white of Château d'Yquem (Sauternes).

Château Figeac has another second wine, Château de Grangeneuf, named after an estate far from Château Figeac.

The 1971 Figeac is expected to be ready for drinking quite early, something unusual for the long-lived wine of this estate.

*Right:*
*Proprietor Thierry Manoncourt, whose family have owned Figeac for nearly a century. Good wine has always been made here, but the fame and reputation of the Château have increased under his direction.*

*Bottom:*
*The Château seen from the park.*

Château Figeac

*Right:*
*The inner courtyard of Château Figeac, with the old vathouse on the left.*



Since Thierry Manoncourt took over the running of Figeac from his grandfather, the estate's fame has rapidly increased. Not only did he improve the structure of the vineyard and construct new *chais*, but he also concentrated on ensuring that many people in the wine business and any other interested individuals should taste his wine. M. Manoncourt is also interested in the fortunes of St Emilion in general, because for over 10 years he has held the office of *Premier Jurat* in the *Jurade de St Emilion*, the oldest wine fraternity in the Gironde and a tradition dating from when the different regions were run by their *Jurades*. M. Manoncourt's interests include history, architecture and geology as well as wine.

### An old-established Château

A visitor to Château Figeac may receive a lengthy lecture on any of the various aspects of the estate. On the history of Figeac, for example, Thierry Manoncourt knows that there were formerly five *maisons nobles* around St Emilion, of which Figeac was the largest. The names of these *seigneuries* often remain in those of the estates. Corbin was also a *seigneurie*, a name which survives in the estates of Corbin, and in Grand Corbin d'Espagne.

The Château de Figeac originally dates from the second half of the 15th century, and one of the old walls, with an opening for a window, dates from this period. Another trace of history is found in a turret and the two columns near the main entrance, which date from around 1590, at the end of the Renaissance.

### Improving new installations

In this historic group there are new *chais* adjoining the existing old ones. The transition from the one to the other is great: when you step from one old, dark *chai* into the spacious, light vathouse with ten shiny stainless steel vats you suddenly bridge a century. Behind you lies the 19th century, in front the 20th century. When the metal vats were installed, the ten old wooden vats were not removed, and they are now used to hold any over-production. This makes working during the vintage much easier, as the cellar workers no longer have to continue through the night if the crop is abundant.

In 1972 the extensions for the storage cellars were completed, once again as the result of inspiration and hard work. A first-year and second-year *chai* was built, plus a truly impressive underground cellar, which is where the bottling is done; there is also enough space to store many tens of thousands of bottles, either binned or already cased. All this gives the impression that the owner has been guided by the principle, 'If a thing is worth doing, it is worth doing well.' Neither expense nor effort have been spared and Figeac can now probably boast the best new cellar installation in the district.

The extensions were in fact a necessity, as at many properties. At the beginning of this century 90% or more of every vintage was generally sold in wood to the merchants in Bordeaux after the first year, and as a result the property would have had to store hardly any wine at all. Nowadays, however, châteaux are expected to mature and bottle their wines themselves. So it is necessary for them to be able to store three vintages in their cellars – two kept in wood and one bottled.

### Siliceous plateau

The wine for the average 125 to 130 *tonneaux* yield comes from a vineyard covering 37·5 hectares. The highest point lies about 35 metres above the Dordogne and gives a magnificent view of the surrounding district. Cheval Blanc is nearby, and the area known as the *graves* of St Emilion can also be seen. In fact these *graves* consist of a plateau with three undulations, on which two of the greatest vineyards – Figeac and Cheval Blanc – are situated. Thierry Manoncourt told me that the thick siliceous layer of this plateau was mainly brought down from the Massif Central by the Isle, a small river which divides Fronsac from St Emilion and Pomerol. He added that with the exception of Ausone all the great Bordeaux wines are born on siliceous soil: Lafite, Latour, Margaux, Mouton, Haut-Brion, d'Yquem, Cheval Blanc, and many more.

With this kind of soil the temptation is naturally very strong to exploit every square metre for wine – something which would be excusable in St Emilion, because except for the vine little else will flourish. At Figeac, however, they uphold the tradition that nature must be cared for – whatever is done must be done with respect for what already exists. Thierry Manoncourt and his charming wife, Marie-France, will not give up even part of their extensive park or any plots of agricultural land to vines. 'We may well be less worldly than other estates', says M. Manoncourt, 'but we do happen to love nature.'

### The velvety strength of Figeac

The Cabernet Sauvignon is strongly represented at Figeac, with 30% of the vineyard; Cabernet Franc accounts for 40% and the Merlot, 30%. For this reason alone Figeac is radically different from Cheval Blanc. Generally, I find the many vintages of Figeac I have drunk slightly more velvety than those of Figeac's neighbour. They have a soft but elegant opulence and unmistakeable distinction.

Here are some tasting notes made about various successful vintages. The wine of 1953 had a lovely, ripe bouquet, still with some reserve. The flavour was soft and generous, but less assertive than the 1955. The latter was complete, exceptionally firm and with an especially distinctive bouquet – a beauty. The 1959 vintage unfolded splendidly in the mouth; I detected slightly more sweetness than in the other wines (this was later confirmed by M. Manoncourt on the basis of his analysis). The 1961 surprised me with its lively bouquet and voluptuous, warm taste. The 1964 had fullness, elegance and assertive roundness – a fine wine to drink on a cold winter's evening at the fireside. Finally, the 1970 had a notably deep colour, was fine and firm, but for some years it will remain fairly reticent.

Markets where Figeac is often drunk are the U.S.A., Belgium, Britain, Switzerland and Denmark.

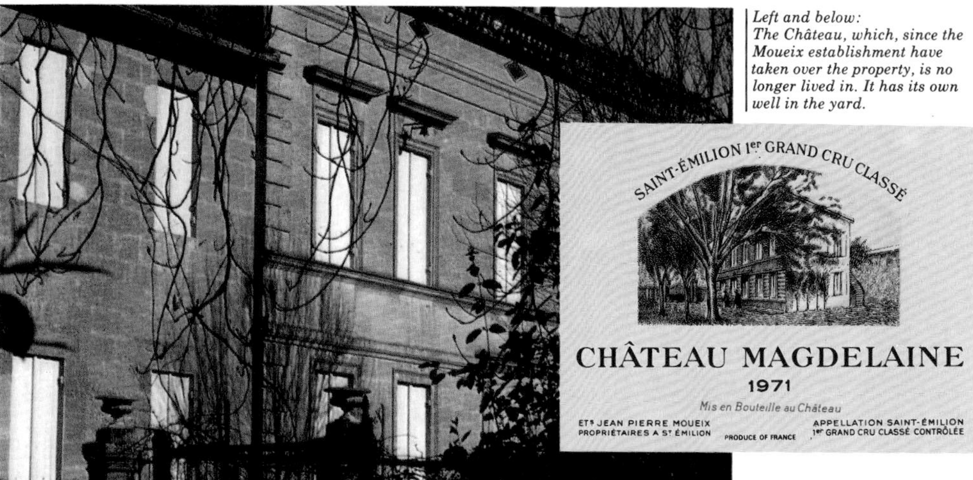

SAINT-ÉMILION 1er GRAND CRU CLASSÉ
CHÂTEAU MAGDELAINE
1971
Mis en Bouteille au Château
ETS JEAN PIERRE MOUEIX
PROPRIÉTAIRES A ST ÉMILION
PRODUCE OF FRANCE
APPELLATION SAINT-ÉMILION
1ER GRAND CRU CLASSÉ CONTRÔLÉE


*Left and below:*
*The Château, which, since the Moueix establishment have taken over the property, is no longer lived in. It has its own well in the yard.*

When Jean-Pierre Moueix bought the estate in 1952 the vineyard was only 9 hectares, but by deforesting some suitable land, 2 hectares have since been added.

By far the most important market for Magdelaine is the American west coast: over half the crop is shipped there. Great Britain and Belgium are also customers.

An exceptionally good, and yet unusual wine is the 1961 Magdelaine. This has much more intensity than usual and has a great future before it. The colour is still dark, the bouquet intense, the flavour firm, and some people detect liquorice and virtually roasted grapes in this and the after-taste.

# Chau Magdelaine

1st Grand Cru Classé

The vineyard of Magdelaine lies in a rough half-crescent, part on the top of a plateau, and part on the slope. It extends to 11 hectares, 9·5 of which are productive. The yield is on the high side, 45 to 50 *tonneaux*, which can be put down to several factors.

First, a high percentage of the productive Merlot has been planted (65%, as against 35% Cabernet Franc). Second, the vineyard's situation is favourable, and third, picking does not begin until the grapes have reached an optimum degree of ripeness. It has been possible to do this since 1952, when Magdelaine was bought by the well-known firm of Jean-Pierre Moueix of Libourne, because this *négociant-viticulteur* has his own group of pickers of more than 100 men and women, who can be put to work at a moment's notice and can get all the grapes in within three days. Consequently, Magdelaine is often one of the last châteaux of St Emilion to start its vintageing.

## Unusual vinification

Throughout Bordeaux it is usual for the black grapes to be de-stalked before they start to ferment, but at Magdelaine only 80% of the fruit is de-stalked, the rest goes into the cement vats with stalks, pips and all. The reason for this is explained by Jean-Claude Berrouet, a fully-qualified oenologist who is responsible for all the wines produced at the Moueix châteaux. He introduced the system to make the wines of Magdelaine a little sturdier; they otherwise tend to be too light. After fermentation – which sometimes takes 20 days – the wines are transferred to casks. Usually three-quarters of these *barriques* are new; they are made by Moueix in their own cooperage. After the wine has been left to mature for 22 months, the casks are transported to Libourne where the bottling is done.

## A bouquet of vanilla

The wines of Magdelaine are generally fairly delicate, but attractively so; a genuine heavyweight is rare. I find the 1973 a charming wine with a friendly, gentle flavour. It still smells of wood. In 1971 the Merlot grape turned out very well, and so, therefore, did Magdelaine. I noted it as a lively, fine wine, with an interesting bouquet, in which a trace of vanilla could be detected. The 1970 has a creamier smell with more finesse; its flavour is complete, full and very fine indeed. In the 1967 Magdelaine a trace of vanilla can be detected once again in the bouquet; the colour is deep, the flavour good, with its characteristic delicacy.

*Left:*
*Trottevieille is a small but striking building. The Château dates from 1870 and has not been inhabited since 1960.*

*Bottom:*
*The Château seen from the vineyard. Long ago white grapes were planted here, and manager Jean Brun can still point out a few vines of the white Alicante. Trottevieille stands on a hill behind St Emilion. If you look out from its small chai you can see the church tower of St Emilion between the rows of casks. The wine matures for about two years in wood before it is bottled.*

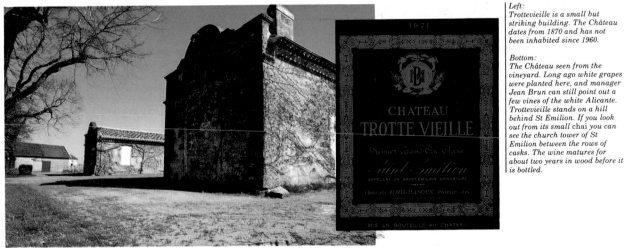

# Chau Trottevieille

1st Grand Cru Classé

As far as its outward appearance goes Château Trottevieille is the most modest first classed growth of St Emilion. The château is a low, rather unsightly little building, with a small garden at the back and a vineyard surrounding it. There used to be an inn here, with an aged but active serving woman who brought tired horsemen, coachmen and travellers their meals at the speed of lightning. It was probably she who gave the estate its name, because 'Trottevieille' literally means 'the old lady who rushes about'.

**One manager – many estates**

Just to the south of the uninhabited château are the *chais* and the small vathouse extension. Everything is simple, even rustic. The vats, however, are cement, though the casks have already been used. Since 1939, Château Trottevieille has had M. Jean Brun as its manager, but the estate is so small that it cannot afford to employ him full time; this is true of estates elsewhere in St Emilion, too. Thus Jean Brun is responsible for seven châteaux besides Trottevieille, including Les Grandes Murailles and Croque-Michotte.

**Twenty-five years of new ownership**

Trottevieille has 10 productive hectares planted with 75% Cabernet Franc and 25% Cabernet Sauvignon with Merlot. Relatively speaking the vineyard is still young, because it was completely replanted when, in 1950, Marcel Borie took over the estate from Jean Guibaud. The production is usually between 40 and 50 *tonneaux*, which are for the most part sold by the house of Borie-Manoux in France, Belgium, Holland, Britain and the United States. There is no room to extend the vineyard and increase its yield, because the estate is bounded by three roads.

**Five good vintages**

The best recent vintages of Trottevieille are held to be 1964, 1966, 1967 and 1970. Of this foursome, my favourite is the 1970; a good, well made, firm wine with a great deal of fruit in its bouquet and depth in its colour. I found the 1971 vintage a charming wine with lots of fruit in its flavour, but still perhaps lower in quality than the 1970. I also noted a great deal of fruit and attractive suppleness in the 1973. This is a pleasant wine, to be drunk soon.

*Left:*
*Bottles of Beauséjour Duffau-Lagarrosse with the traditional type of engraving typical of many labels.*

*Bottom:*
*The modest château; the cellar for bottled wines is in the rock under it.*

*Bottom right:*
*The present proprietor married in 1922 and, to celebrate the occasion, drank the 1870 Beauséjour, a wine which at the time showed no signs of fatigue. He remembers stories told by his grandfather, who went around on horseback to sell the wine. It was not always safe for the solitary traveller, and he thus armed himself 'with a good cudgel rather than a pistol'. Fortunately for him he never had occasion to use it.*

# Château Beauséjour Duffau-Lagarrosse

1st Grand Cru Classé

In 1869 M. Ducarpe divided up the Beauséjour estate between his two children. Both received a more or less equal share, and each was allowed to continue to call his vineyard Beauséjour, which is why there are still two Châteaux Beauséjour in St Emilion. They are situated close to each other and are both first classed growths. Descendants of Ducarpe's sons still live at Beauséjour Duffau-Lagarrosse, but the other Beauséjour has been in other hands for some time.

### All in the family

As a house, Beauséjour Duffau-Lagarrosse has no pretensions. It is a fairly square, simple building, no more. But this is in keeping with those who live there. The Duffau-Lagarrosse heirs are friendly, unassuming people who love their land and look on their home as a family residence rather than just a château. The family is in fact closely connected with the vineyard, for the 5 children and 18 grandchildren all help as much as possible, working the land and vintageing. When possible, the children's friends also lend a helping hand, so there is no shortage of enthusiastic workers at the property.

### Long-lasting vintages

The vineyard is small, covering about 8 hectares. It lies to the south of the château, on a fairly steep slope. The vines are one-third Merlot, one-third Cabernet Franc and one-third Cabernet Sauvignon. As soon as the grapes have been picked, de-stalked and crushed, they ferment in the cement vats which, it is hoped, will soon be replaced by stainless steel ones. After fermentation, the wine is left to mature in oak for an exceptionally long time – 2½ to 3 years. This gives the wines a great deal of tannin, and therefore they develop slowly.

The powerful 1961 vintage, for example, which I tasted in 1974, had still not lost its youthful ruggedness. It is not an exceptionally full wine, but it has a lovely colour and a very fine bouquet (which improves the longer the wine is in contact with the air). The 1970 vintage has a great deal of body and fruit, but it is still very reticent and will remain so for many years, and is a wine to lay down.

To my mind, the wines of Beauséjour Duffau-Lagarrosse can best be described as classic, long-lasting clarets which are made without commercial concessions and are usually very successful. The production is 20 to 25 *tonneaux*, which are mostly sold to the United States.

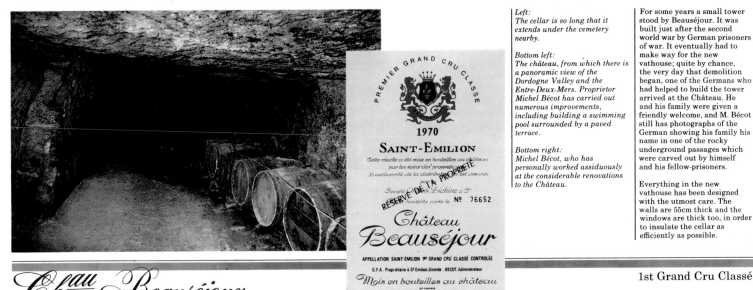

*Left:*
*The cellar is so long that it extends under the cemetery nearby.*

*Bottom left:*
*The château, from which there is a panoramic view of the Dordogne Valley and the Entre-Deux-Mers. Proprietor Michel Bécot has carried out numerous improvements, including building a swimming pool surrounded by a paved terrace.*

*Bottom right:*
*Michel Bécot, who has personally worked assiduously at the considerable renovations to the Château.*

For some years a small tower stood by Beauséjour. It was built just after the second world war by German prisoners of war. It eventually had to make way for the new vathouse; quite by chance, the very day that demolition began, one of the Germans who had helped to build the tower arrived at the Château. He and his family were given a friendly welcome, and M. Bécot still has photographs of the German showing his family his name in one of the rocky underground passages which were carved out by himself and his fellow-prisoners.

Everything in the new vathouse has been designed with the utmost care. The walls are 55cm thick and the windows are thick too, in order to insulate the cellar as efficiently as possible.

# Chteau Beauséjour

1st Grand Cru Classé

Michel Bécot is very proud of his new *chais*, and rightly, for they are impressive – and they are only one of the many improvements he has made at Beauséjour in a short time.

M. Bécot bought the vineyard, which was very dilapidated, in 1969. The wine was so bad that this Beauséjour (not to be confused with Beauséjour Duffau-Lagarrosse and other Beauséjours elsewhere) risked being excluded from the ranks of the first classed growths. Michel Bécot at once set to work to rectify this state of affairs. He devoted all his time – and probably all his money – to restoring or improving the *chais*, the vineyard and the château. Today, Beauséjour can proudly boast a range of ten of the very latest stainless steel fermentation vats in a brand-new vathouse, a new reception room, which can seat 200 persons, and underneath this a magnificent cellar carved out of the rocks. Here is storage space for bottles and casks and even another reception room, complete with bar and dance floor.

## An investment for another estate

From this, you might well think that Beauséjour is a vast estate. On the contrary, the vineyard covers only $7\frac{1}{2}$ hectares. The gigantic investments are, it is to be hoped, nevertheless justified, because the wine of the neighbouring Château La Carte (*grand cru*), another property of M. Bécot, is also made at Beauséjour. The production of Beauséjour is around 20 *tonneaux*, coming from the following vines: 70% Merlot, 30% Cabernet Franc and Cabernet Sauvignon.

The 1969 vintage is the oldest wine which can be tasted at Beauséjour, because Michel Bécot, fairly enough, refuses to let anyone sample wines made by the previous owner. The 1969 is still somewhat reserved, but it has a fine colour and is sound. Its flavour retains something of oak. The 1970 is a treat for the eye with its brilliant deep colour, and the taste is as yet mainly fleshy, with some tannin. I found the 1972 surprisingly solid for that year. Again, the wine has a deep red colour and an attractive taste, with fine undertones. It would seem that this estate is well on the way to producing excellent wines, and its future looks bright, increasingly so since Professor Peynaud, the famous oenologist, has been called in to give advice on methods of vinification.

*Left:*
*Château La Gaffeliere dates from the 11th century, but the wings were rebuilt in the 17th and 18th centuries. In the 19th century the château was thoroughly restored in accordance with the current fashion for the supposedly Gothic style.*

*Bottom:*
*A bird's-eye view of La Gaffelière, where in 1969 the remains of a Gallo-Roman villa were discovered. The Romans enjoyed the region, their villas being pleasantly remote from the city of Bordeaux, and there were many country houses here.*

In the park of La Gaffelière stands what must be the largest cedar in the Gironde, and it is guarded by what are probably the most aggressive swans of the region, too.

It goes without saying that Roquefort is seldom absent from Count Malet de Roquefort's cheese board.

## Ch$^{au}$ La Gaffelière

1st Grand Cru Classé

There are certainly many more felicitous names for an estate than La Gaffelière: the word originally meant 'leper colony', and to *faire une gaffe* in French is 'to put one's foot in it'.

The advantage of such an odd name, of course, is that it is not easily forgotten. The owner, the Comte de Malet Roquefort, told me that he once received a letter from abroad addressed to 'Château La Cafetière, France'. A post office official had written on the envelope 'France or Brazil', and the letter did reach its destination.

The road which bisects La Gaffelière is also an asset. The Château is separated from its *chais* by a busy tarmac road, but this means that most visitors to St Emilion will discover exactly where La Gaffelière is. The road used to be a private pathway which was presented to St Emilion by de Malet's grandfather (then Mayor) in order to connect the town to its railway station.

### A vineyard with a double contribution

The vineyard of La Gaffelière covers 21 hectares which are planted with 60% Merlot, 20% Cabernet Franc and 20% Cabernet Sauvignon. About 10 hectares are situated on the hill near Ausone; the soil gives the wine its substance. The remaining 11 hectares are situated at the foot of the hill; the soil here gives the wine its soundness. The total production averages 110 to 120 *tonneaux*, but this always includes some wine that does not satisfy the requirements and is therefore sold under the second label as Château de Roquefort. The selection imposed by the proprietor is strict: in 1973 more than a third of the wine was not good enough, and in 1974 nearly a third. On average, some 80 to 100 *tonneaux* remain to be marketed as La Gaffelière, which is sold through five shippers in Bordeaux and Libourne, mainly to Belgium, the U.K., Switzerland and the U.S.A.

La Gaffelière is well worth visiting. The château is elegantly furnished with comfortable pieces, tapestries and old paintings. On one of the walls I saw a canvas, dating back to 1486, depicting Louis Malet, *Amiral de France*. Next to the tall château is the modern vathouse, which has been used since the harvest of 1974. Here there are a dozen stainless steel vats, all beautifully polished and shiny, on the well-scrubbed and spotless tiled floor. It is necessary to cross the road to get to the *chais*, where the wine lies maturing in oak casks (a third of which are new each year)

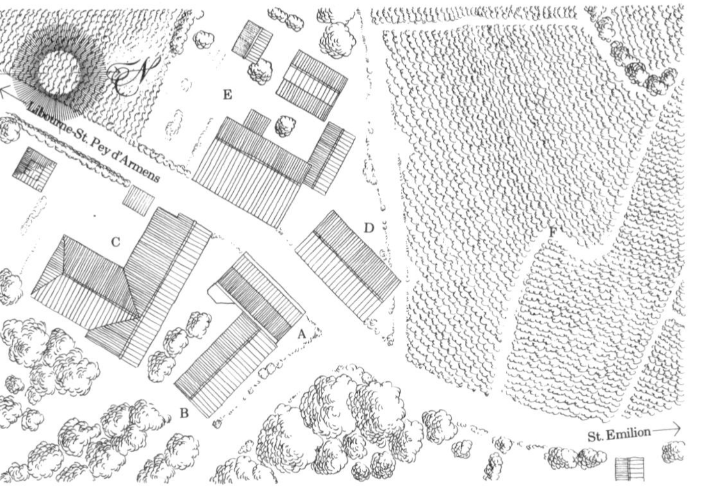


*Far left:*
*The cellar master of La Gaffelière, who lives next to the* chais.

*Left:*
*Plan of La Gaffelière.*
**A** *the château.* **B** *extension to the living quarters.* **C** *the vathouse.* **D** *bottling hall and storage room.* **E** *the* chais.
**F** *vineyards.*

*Bottom:*
*Here all the wine of the château is bottled. On the left in the background note the cardboard cartons which have been designed so that they resemble the wooden cases formerly used. They weigh 5 kilos less than the cases, and are of course also cheaper.*



for about two years. I tasted the 1973 and 1974 vintages here: both are well made, and the 1974 in particular seems to promise well.

### Vintages from the house

For the older wines which we were to drink with lunch, my host guided me to his private cellar. This is in the château itself, very near the main boiler, although the temperature in the cellar is not too high, thanks to an ingenious ventilation system which creates a kind of protective layer of cold air, enabling the temperature in the wine cellar to remain ten degrees cooler than the temperature outside. Count Malet de Roquefort asked me whether I would like to choose for myself, and after some hesitation I picked out the 1961 and the 1947 from among the many good bottles there. Perhaps I was greedy, but given such an opportunity you should take advantage of it as you may otherwise miss the chance of tasting wines which you may never be offered again.

Both bottles were superb. After the oysters with champagne – rather unconventional for the Gironde we first drank the 1961 La Gaffelière. This originally had so much strength that the Count had had to fine it twice, once with four egg whites per cask and then with three. As was to be expected, the wine had a deep colour and a full, round taste. I found the bouquet very fine indeed, with many rich shades of smell in it. The flavour of the wine was very firm, and still even a trifle reticent. After this perfect 1961 the 1947 was served; it too was a revelation with its superb breed and surprising youthfulness.

My host told me this 1947 had been made by his father and the 1961 by himself. His father had been in his time an advocate of a short wine-making process, so as to make the wine ready for drinking quicker. The son, on the other hand, tends more and more towards a long vinification, which endows the wine with greater keeping qualities and distinguishes it from the many St Emilion châteaux where nowadays wines are produced which are quickly ready to drink. His views are clearly demonstrated by the 1967 vintage, which I had drunk on another occasion. This, approximately seven years after its vintage, still had a considerable amount of firmness and tannin backing its distinctively round style. The 1970 is in my view one of the best St Emilions of that vintage – but give it enough time to reach full maturity.

*Right:*
*The façade of the château; nobody lives there now.*

*Bottom:*
*The entrance to the underground cellars. In this part of St Emilion the estates sometimes have their storage and bottling areas in the galleries and caves which have been hewn out of the relatively soft limestone. The region is pitted with such natural cellars, many centuries old, and St Emilion's monolithic church (the visible one is above ground) now stands where the hermit, St Emilian, first built his cell.*

The casks of Clos Fourtet have metal hoops of galvanised iron, because normal iron rusts too quickly in the damp grottoes.

The vine species in the 16-hectare vineyard are Merlot (55%) and the two Cabernets (45%).

The oldest vintage which is still in the cellars of Clos Fourtet is the 1950. All the bottles of previous vintages were stolen, apparently because a potholing enthusiast accidentally discovered a passage which led to the cellars; with a few friends he made good use of this entrance. The theft was discovered when a bottle of Clos Fourtet 1949 was suddenly found in the middle of the vineyard. The thieves' booty has never been recovered.

Clos Fourtet has an exclusive export agreement with the firm of Jean-Pierre Moueix of Libourne. In addition, much of the wine is also sold direct to France.

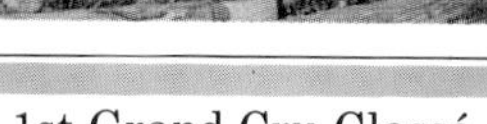

# Clos Fourtet

1st Grand Cru Classé

Every visitor to St Emilion sees Clos Fourtet, because the Chateau is situated opposite the large car park near the church, only a stone's throw away from the famous Hostellerie de Plaisance. There used to be a modest fortification on this spot: the word *fourtet* means a small fort. As a building the château is not awe-inspiring: it is a pleasant house covered with a thick growth of ivy. The most interesting part of it lies underground. This is the region of the slopes, the calcareous, rocky hills around St Emilion, out of which many grottoes, passages and cellars have been hewn. Under Clos Fourtet there are in fact three levels of galleries which have been hewn out of the rock. A small part is used for ripening the second-year wines, the largest part for growing mushrooms. (Did you know that in the Bordeaux region almost as many people cultivate mushrooms as do grapes?)

## Pleasure without patience?

Clos Fourtet is owned by a family company belonging to the Lurtons: three brothers and a sister. All of them have their own châteaux elsewhere, and I wonder whether, as a result, Clos Fourtet is sometimes pushed slightly into the background. The production is small, only 50 to 70 *tonneaux*, so its importance is mainly that of its reputation for quality wines, and it would have been easy to devote attention to more profitable activities.

However, a firm policy has been worked out by André Lurton, who has been directing Clos Fourtet for several years now (it is administered by his daughter, Christine). It was his idea to change the method of wine-making in 1972, and in view of present circumstances this may have been a wise decision, for Clos Fourtet has always made a wine that tended to be hard for many years. Only after long maturation did the wine begin to appeal – as with the 1949 vintage, as much as 23 years after being made. The 1952, 1959 and other good years still presented a reticent, reserved impression in 1972, to say nothing of the 1966, 1970 and 1971.

André Lurton's new motto is 'Pleasure without patience', and I shall be interested to see whether this change of policy will prove successful. The 1973 I tasted was not very dark in colour, had a reticent bouquet, but fairly supple flavour with a considerable amount of fruit – a wine that may quite soon prove to be a surprise.

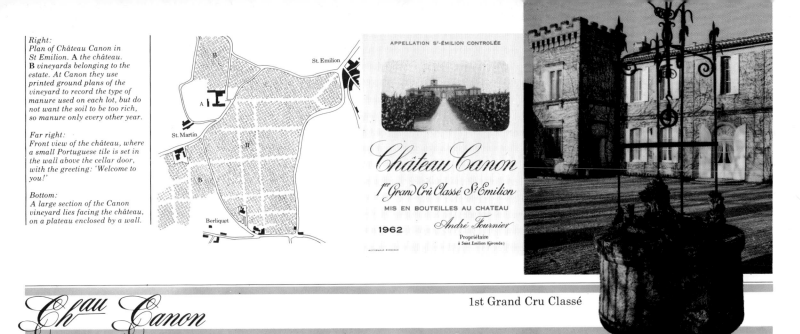

*Right:*
*Plan of Château Canon in St Emilion.* **A** *the château.* **B** *vineyards belonging to the estate. At Canon they use printed ground plans of the vineyard to record the type of manure used on each lot, but do not want the soil to be too rich, so manure only every other year.*

*Far right:*
*Front view of the château, where a small Portuguese tile is set in the wall above the cellar door, with the greeting: 'Welcome to you!'*

*Bottom:*
*A large section of the Canon vineyard lies facing the château, on a plateau enclosed by a wall.*

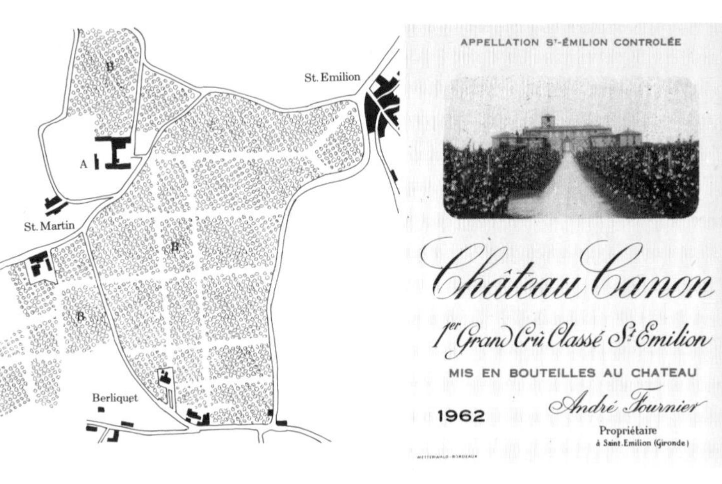

# Chau Canon

1st Grand Cru Classé

An estate that still uses horses to work the vineyard must surely make wine the traditional way – and that is certainly true of Canon. Fermentation vats other than wooden ones are not even considered, 'because other systems are more like a factory'. Similarly, the remainder of the process is carried out by old, well-tried methods. The young director, Eric Fournier, hastens to point out that this is not a question of thriftiness but of loyalty to tradition. New wooden vats today cost almost as much as stainless steel ones, and manual labour is always slower – and therefore more expensive – than mechanised labour.

**Minimal replanting**

The vineyard lies around the château in a shape resembling an open fan. All the lots are clumped together, occasionally separated by paths or walls. In the distant past a large part of the area under cultivation was surrounded by a wall; this *enclos* directly faces the château. The total acreage is 19·4 hectares, planted with 58% Merlot, 30% to 35% Cabernet Franc, and the remainder Cabernet Sauvignon and Malbec.

The vines are often a respectable age: many are more than 40 or 50 years old and the average age is between 25 and 30 years. These old vines are tended with great care and the annual replantings comprise only what is absolutely essential. This usually turns out to be a patch of land as large as a third of a *journal* – a *journal* being the amount of land which one man can work in one day, or 3300 square metres.

The production of Canon averages 80 to 85 *tonneaux*, all of which are bottled by hand straight from the cask. Much of the wine is sold in France, but it is also exported to countries such as Belgium, Britain, the U.S.A. and Japan.

I consider Canon to be one of the best St Emilion wines; it is often a generous, robust wine, with a lovely smell. I still remember the bouquet of the 1961 vintage clearly: it evoked the scent of warm, ripe apples. The colour was deep, the flavour and aftertaste magnificent. This wine is already formidable with game. The 1962 has rather less push and tannin, but is nevertheless sound, complete, with a lovely bouquet – a superb luncheon wine. As for more recent vintages, the 1970 will without a doubt be superb, the 1971 is amiable, perhaps to be drunk fairly soon.

Ausone is still rather irritated by an article in Paris-Match in 1973. The magazine ran a feature about Mouton-Rothschild, and published an aerial view of what was captioned as Mouton – but was actually Ausone and its vineyard.

The general view at Ausone is that its fine wines need a minimum of ten years' maturation.

*Below right:*
*A display of bottles of Ausone near the entrance to the vathouse.*

*Bottom:*
*The famous view of Ausone as visitors to St Emilion see it when they approach the little mediaeval town. Ausone stands on the top of the hill on which its vineyard is planted. From the bottom of the slope all you can see of the château itself is the outline of the roof.*

# Chau Ausone

It was the Roman poet Ausonius who gave his name to Ausone, although no one really knows whether his villa did actually stand where the Château is now. Ausonius is associated with several villa sites and was both a great host and a great guest – but to visit Ausone today is to understand how its owners have loved it. The Château stands high on the edge of a plateau, and the vines are planted in rows running steeply down the hillside. From the little park with its palm trees there is a magnificent panoramic view across the slopes of St Emilion, clad in a cloak of green vineyards. It is a landscape unusual in the Gironde, otherwise an undulating or flat countryside; here the terrain is somewhat more extreme.

**Commanding site**

The château itself is a fairly extensive building, in fact a set of buildings, its most distinctive characteristic being a rectangular tower with a steep, pointed roof. In the course of centuries the main block has been extended by various proprietors so that it is now difficult to distinguish its original plan. At present Château Ausone is occupied by two sisters, Madame J. Dubois-Challon and Madame C. Vauthier, each having her own apartment there.

Madame Dubois-Challon is the widow of Jean Dubois-Challon, who died in 1974. He was born at the Château in 1896, three years

*Right:*
*Here the bottles are 'dressed' once the wine is ready for despatch.*

*Bottom:*
*A characteristic view of the large cellar where the sunshine only briefly penetrates in the morning.*

after the man, later his father-in-law, who inherited the estate from an aunt of his wife's. His widow is now trying to continue his good work, closely assisted by manager Chaudet, who has worked on the estate since the 1950s. M. Chaudet worked for a long time at Château Carbonnieux in the Graves; he is a dignified man, formally dressed even in this remote estate, and with a rather old-fashioned manner quite in keeping with his appearance.

Ausone is more of a small fortification than many estates: in the drawing room there is a view over much of the property. The rooms are high: in the dining room there is a cupboard so high that the top shelves can be reached only with the help of a ladder. Immediately behind the château is the small vathouse, where St Emilion's particular saint, St Valéry, presides over several wooden fermentation vats.

**Treasures underground**

The cellar is as impressive as the vathouse is modest. Behind the château the steep cliff rises, and an enormous gallery has been hewn out of the rock. In this underground vault, with its massive pillars, the wine matures. It is a damp, cool place, where the temperature is constant; on the hottest summer day the temperature never rises by more than two degrees above the minimum level during the winter. The galleries date from about 1580; like most others of this sort in St Emilion they were originally part of a quarry. The wine matures here for about $2\frac{1}{2}$ years, in new casks. Alexis Lichine says that, for a period, no new casks were used – which may have affected the quality of the wine at that time. Bottled wine is also stored here, both Ausone and that of nearby Belair (which belongs to one of Ausone's proprietors). I noticed several vintages from the beginning of the last century – 1831, 1817 and even 1800. Ausone, like other great growths, keeps its 'library'.

**A vineyard of ancient traditions**

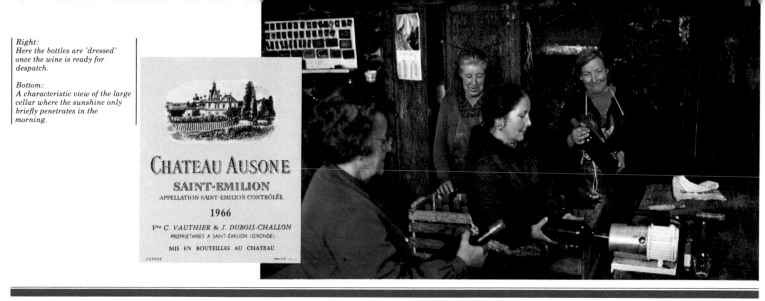

In *Bordeaux et Ses Vins*, 1969, Cocks and Féret state that the average production of Ausone is 25 *tonneaux*. The reason for this low yield is said to be the *vieilles vignes françaises* (old French vines) which have been preserved, thanks – among other things – to the careful use of insecticides. The authors refer to vines which are more than a hundred years old, which means that they must have survived the phylloxera. I have not been able to find confirmation of the existence of these old vines, but certainly the average yield of Ausone is now higher than 25 *tonneaux*; at the Château itself the figure of 40 *tonneaux* was reported. For a vineyard of 8 hectares, this

*Left:*
*Next to the cellar is a small chapel, the* Chapelle de la Madeleine, *hewn out of the rock. Years ago a magnificent mural painting was discovered here, but unfortunately the damp and erosion have since virtually erased it, and now only a few lines can be traced. This illustration is a rare photograph of the mural, taken years ago by an American who travelled specially to Ausone to record it.*

*Bottom:*
*Front view of Ausone. The original shape of the house is difficult to discern, as through the centuries there have been many alterations and additions to it.*

Before the first world war Russia was a very important market for Ausone, but today the principal market is the United States.

In 1963, 1965 and 1968 no Château Ausone (or Château Belair) was offered for sale as such, as the vintage was judged unworthy of the estate labels.

To fine the wine at Ausone six egg whites per cask of 225 litres are generally used. The estate's average production is 160 of these casks.



is a yield of 45 hl. per hectare, much more than very old vines could give, so I am inclined to think that although these old vines might formerly have been cultivated, they have since largely been replaced.

The major vine species at Ausone is Merlot; nearly two-thirds of the vineyard is planted with it. The remaining third is made up of Cabernet Franc and Cabernet Sauvignon. It is interesting that traces have been found at Ausone of wine being produced in Roman times: the growers then dug long trenches in the rocky ground in which they planted the vines. An indication of how well the Romans had mastered certain wine-growing techniques may be given by the fact that in St Emilion the vines are generally planted the same distance apart as they were in classical times.

**A revival of popularity?**

Ausone, together with Cheval Blanc, heads the wines of St Emilion in the classification of 1855. Both are indisputably great wines, praiseworthy even in the company of the great Médocs and Graves. Some claret lovers might even rate them higher. Is Ausone on a level with Cheval Blanc? There are certain wine writers who have their doubts. In *The Wines of Bordeaux*, Edmund Penning-Rowsell, whose opinion I greatly respect, writes: '. . . since the war I have never met an outstanding Ausone', and in other books similar comments are made. The auction prices at Christie's in London give some indication of how Ausone is rated on the market, expressed in terms of the prices the public will pay for it. Generally speaking, Cheval Blanc is the favourite: the price per dozen bottles is usually higher than the price for Ausone of the same vintage. A slight exception is the 1966, when prices between £82 and £140 were paid for cases of Ausone, whereas the sums for Cheval Blanc only reached between £96 and £120.

Prices may, of course, be suddenly and deceptively affected by fashion. Ausone was once very fashionable and then seems to have fallen rather out of favour. In 1945, for example, Ausone fetched £270 at Christie's, Cheval Blanc £370. But it is also true that in the rather small vineyards of St Emilion variations between estates can be very great as far as quality is concerned.

The owners of Château Ausone have obviously been aware of the apparent decline in the wine's international reputation, which is why some improvements in the wine-making have recently been made; the use of new casks is one indication of this. So perhaps a revival is on the way. The 1970 vintage, however, was obviously below standard, and only with the 1971 have I heard better reports. However, from my own tasting notes I can recall only qualified impressions: the wine was deep in colour, still reticent as to bouquet, with an assertive flavour and marked, lengthy finish. It is to be hoped that Ausone will soon be great again.

For a long time the wine of Belair enjoyed greater fame than that of Ausone. In the 19th century, *Bordeaux et Ses Vins* listed Belair as the best property of the *côtes* of St Emilion, before Ausone.

Belair is a wine which is not widely known. A major part of its production is in fact drunk in France.

There are no less than 30 properties in Bordeaux with Belair or Bel-Air in their name, so take care that you have the correct name, label and A.O.C.

*Right:*
*The figure of St Emilion's own patron saint, St Valéry, looking out over the Belair vineyard.*

*Bottom:*
*This distinctive square building is a separate part of the Château and stands on the edge of the plateau. It is usually the only thing the visiting tourist sees of Belair. The actual château is modest. It is lived in by M. Chaudet, manager of both Ausone and Belair.*

1st Grand Cru Classé

Château Ausone only partly belongs to Madame Dubois-Challon, but she is the sole owner of Château Belair. The estates are situated close to one another, with no more than a few hundred metres between them. Like Ausone, Belair offers its visitors a splendid view of the district, but it looks out to the south rather than to the east.

For a long time the Château was in the hands of the English; during this era it belonged to Robert de Knolles, then the Governor of Guyenne. After Charles VII had expelled the English, the descendants of Robert de Knolles continued to live in the district and Belair remained in the family. At the time of the French Revolution, however, the estate fell into other hands. Eventually, in 1916, it was bought by M. Dubois-Challon, father-in-law of the present owner. Only the old fortifications alongside the château now remind one of the English.

### A grotto of wine

The vineyard extends to 13 hectares, 5 hectares more than at Ausone, but still not very impressive an extent. The vines (approximately two-thirds Merlot and the rest Cabernet) give an average annual production of 60 to 65 *tonneaux*. The wine matures in a cool, dark cellar behind the château. As at Ausone, this was originally hewn out of the calcareous rock base of the plateau above. The cellar is slightly smaller than that at Ausone, but this has the advantage of being easier to warm – which is why banquets are sometimes given in the grotto of Belair for visitors to Ausone.

The wine of Belair usually remains underground for about 2 years. Almost without exception, it is ready for drinking sooner than Ausone – often as soon as seven or eight years after its vintage, whereas Ausone usually needs at least ten years. Château Belair makes its impression in this respect as a smaller-scale version of a claret like Ausone.

The château itself is frankly not very attractive, its *chais* are less impressive and the wine does tend to be of lesser quality – but the yield is higher. The 1966 vintage made highly successful wines which can be kept for a long time, but the 1966 Belair is fairly light, and eight years after being made is already browning in colour. The bouquet of this wine is rather disappointing and I find the flavour decidedly thin. Nor was the 1967 vintage truly impressive. Belair, even more than Ausone, in my view, needs rehabilitation.

*Right:*
*View of an odd corner in the cellars.*

*Below:*
*An old engraving of the château, showing how little it has changed. However, the high rock wall rising up behind the buildings has disappeared. Bottom right is the vathouse of Pavie, to the left the working areas, living quarters and offices, and against the slope the château itself.*

*Bottom:*
*The château as seen from the vineyard above it.*

1st Grand Cru Classé

In the large underground cellar there used to be room to store 3,000 *barriques*. Fewer can now be accommodated there, as some parts present hazards of dilapidation.

The man who gave Pavie its great reputation some seventy years ago was Ferdinand Bouffard. He won many prizes, including a medal for his fight against the phylloxera, the insect which nearly destroyed the world's vineyards in the 1870s.

Pavie also markets a second wine, the *grand cru classé* Château La Clusière.

Pavie is owned by the Consorts Valette, a *société civile* with ten shareholders. The firm is run by Pierre and Jean-Paul Valette.

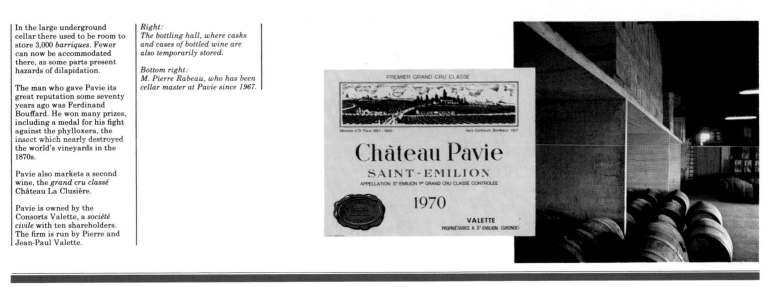

*Right:*
*The bottling hall, where casks and cases of bottled wine are also temporarily stored.*

*Bottom right:*
*M. Pierre Rabeau, who has been cellar master at Pavie since 1967.*

Château Pavie is perhaps the most hilly estate in St Emilion. Vineyard and buildings are situated on a steep slope: at the foot of the hill stands the vathouse, about halfway up is the château and right at the top the *chais*. The difference in height between the vathouse and the *chais* is some dozens of metres; on average about 600 casks (150 *tonneaux*) are produced per year, and the moving of this quantity of wine involves a great deal of hard work.

The place where the wine matures in wood, for about a year and a half, is a very old cave, dating from the 11th century. It is a perilous place, because over the centuries the rocks have gradually been eroded by rainwater, and the present owners have twice seen a section of the cellars collapse, the first time about twenty years ago, the second in December 1974. A damp cellar is ideal for slow maturation, but the advantages here are balanced by the risks involved – the workers may be hurt and much wine lost. In 1974, for example, Pavie lost 43 casks of good wine in the subsidence.

### Almost historic cement vats

The vathouse of Pavie is one of the oldest of its kind in St Emilion. The cement vats date from the beginning of the 1920s, when oak vats were still considered the best. It must have been revolutionary at the time to switch to the new material: the first models were lined on the inside with glass, but this has now been changed, as it turned out that cracks in the glass, however fine, could retain wine – and thus present a danger of infection. This is why Pavie also has many vats now lined with plastic.

The man responsible for the wine-making is *maître de chai* Pierre Rabeau, who has been at the estate since 1967. His counterpart in the vineyard is Lucien Castang, who has been the *chef de culture* since 1970. About twenty people are employed full-time at Pavie, in itself an indication that this is a property of importance.

### Many old vines

The vineyard of Pavie has a good situation, running from south-west to south-east. It covers 36 hectares, of which 33 are under production. As at other quality-conscious châteaux, the percentage of old vines is kept as high as possible by very prudent replanting of only small patches at a time. Thanks to this policy, Pavie still has gnarled rootstocks which are 80 to 100 years old. The yield from the vineyard fluctuates considerably; in 1974, 52 hl. per hectare were harvested, but in 1971 only 27 hl. The vineyard is planted with the following vines: 60% Merlot, 25% Cabernet Franc and 15% Cabernet Sauvignon, classic St Emilion proportions.

### Vintages of breed and charm

What director Jean-Paul Valette and his team try to avoid making is the sort of harsh wine which has to be left for years in the hope that it may eventually soften. On the contrary, the aim at Château Pavie is to make pleasant wines which are both imposing and supple. My personal impression has been that these wines are not especially full-bodied, but they do have a great deal of softness and a generally trim style.

I have never had the opportunity of sampling very old wines of this Château: the oldest I tasted was the 1962. This was exceptionally friendly, with a fine, deep colour, a soft, almost sweet smell with that element of freshness which is typical of Pavie, and a pleasing flavour.

The 1964 vintage was quite different. This was a wine with very definite assertiveness and a fine finish. In addition to a slight hint of spiciness its bouquet possessed real distinction and breed. It is said that the nose of Pavie is sometimes redolent of currants, though I have never been able to detect this.

In the 1966 I thought I tasted something of really baked grapes – from a very hot year. The bouquet was splendid and full, retaining the aroma of new oak casks. Although the wine in itself had many good qualities, the nuances of flavour, the tannin content and the aftertaste were, I thought, slightly inferior to those of the 1964.

Finally, the 1970 vintage is a wine which must definitely be laid up for ten years; dark in colour, fruity as to bouquet, underlying a firm constitution. The wines of Château Pavie are certainly good and worth sampling whenever you see them listed.

*Centre:*
*Rear view of the château. The lowest tower is the oldest. One of the previous owners thought the low towers unworthy of the status of the wine, so he planned to replace them with tall ones. He had only erected one when a lack of funds put a stop to the project.*

*Bottom:*
*An attractive sign indicating where the vineyard of Vieux Château Certan begins.*

*Right:*
*Bottles of Vieux Château Certan in their cases, ready to meet the demands of export markets.*

*Opposite page, right:*
*Léon Thienpont, who with his wife has lived at the Château since 1943. They now have seven children.*

*Opposite page, far right:*
*A view of the château from the vineyard. As early as 1796 the estate had a great reputation, and its wines fetched high prices. At that time 16·2 hectares were under vines, now there are 13 hectares. At the beginning of 1800 the vineyard was divided.*

*Opposite page, bottom:*
*As you enter the house, you come into this long corridor, with the various salons beyond.*

# Vieux Château Certan

Vieux Château Certan is situated close to a crossroads in the heart of the quality vineyards of this area: if you drive some hundred metres northwards, you arrive at Château Pétrus, the greatest of the Pomerols; if you choose to turn south-west, you soon reach Château Cheval Blanc, the outstanding St Emilion. The reputation of Vieux Château Certan is hardly less than that of its illustrious neighbours, and many regard it as Pomerol's second great estate after Pétrus. Whether this is justified what outsider can say? Other properties, such as L'Evangile and La Conseillante, also produce fine wine. Be this as it may, Vieux Château Certan certainly ranks among the great châteaux of Bordeaux.

In 1924 the estate was bought by Georges Thienpont, a Belgian wine merchant. Three years before he had taken over Troplong-Mondot in St Emilion. Thienpont visited both properties three to ten times a year, but he always stayed at Troplong. In 1935 he found himself forced to sell one of the two estates, but which should be choose? Emotionally, he was more attached to Troplong-Mondot, but financially he saw greater potential in Vieux Château Certan, and it was in the end Troplong which was sold.

In 1962 Léon, son of Charles Thienpont, became co-owner of Vieux Château Certan. He lives at the Château with his family the whole year round, and it is he who has increased the reputation of the wine to its present level.

Vieux Château Certan

### No insurance against hail

M. Thienpont boasts that his vineyard has a micro-climate all its own. This has disadvantages – for example, the spring frost strikes quicker here – but it also has advantages: his vineyard has not been hit by hail since 1935. This is why Vieux Château Certan pays no insurance against the possibility of hail damage.

The vineyard encircles the château and covers 13 productive hectares, 2 more than when Georges Thienpont bought the estate in 1924. The average production is around 70 *tonneaux*, which mainly go to the U.K., the U.S.A., Japan, Australia, and of course Belgium.

Léon Thienpont still has close ties with his mother country; other members of the family company which owns the Château live there – and he sold the whole of his 1973 crop to Belgium. It is easy for the Belgians (and for the Dutch) to do business with M. Thienpont, because he speaks fluent Flemish as well as French.

### Wood is beautiful

At the beginning of the 1970s the cellars of Vieux Château Certan underwent drastic changes: a new first-year *chai* with reddish-brown floor tiles, and a whole new vathouse were built. In the latter there are a few stainless steel tanks, but most of the fermentation vats are made of wood. M. Thienpont says it is 'mostly because it is more attractive – a wooden vat has something classic about it. I often get visitors who wax poetical about my oak vats after all the cement and steel they have seen elsewhere.' The vast fermentation vats were not actually made in Bordeaux, but in the cooperage of the Cognac establishment of Rémy Martin.

The steel vats are rarely used for fermentation. Vieux Château Certan only brings them into operation for the *assemblage*, when the wines of the various grapes are blended into one. All in all, the wine matures in casks for 1½ years, and every year about a third of these *barriques* are new. Just how high the percentage of new casks will be is not known until the wine has been made. As at many châteaux, a set number of casks is ordered every year – in this instance 100 of them – and the percentage of new casks thus varies slightly according to the size of the vintage.

### Some recent vintages

In a restaurant the bottles of Vieux Certan can be picked out from a distance, for they have a pink capsule encircled with gold – a personal invention of Georges Thienpont. But this frivolously decorated lead capsule is not the only thing which draws attention to the bottle – the wine itself deserves remark and is usually of special quality, and a delight to the discriminating.

Following the 1961 and 1964 vintages, the 1966 was another great success. The wine had a magnificent, deep, brilliant colour, a good (but still somewhat reticent) bouquet, and a flavour full of promise for the future. The 1970 was the next excellent year, with a great deal of colour, aroma and tannin. It would be highly advisable not to drink this wine before 1980. The 1971 vintage impressed me greatly: this too is a wine to be kept for a long time, because it contains a reasonable amount of fruit plus a great deal of tannin. The noble wines of Vieux Château Certan have as their basis 50% Merlot, 25% Cabernet Franc, 20% Cabernet Sauvignon and 5% Malbec.

1970
PETRUS
POMEROL
Grand Vin
Mme EDMOND LOUBAT
PROPRIÉTAIRE A POMEROL. GIRONDE
MIS EN BOUTEILLES AU CHATEAU
APPELLATION POMEROL CONTRÔLÉE


*Right:*
*The estate's label, showing St Peter (Pétrus), was designed in the 1930s.*

*Far right:*
*Above the main entrance, Bacchus extends a greeting to visitors.*

*Bottom:*
*This is Château Pétrus, the great growth of Pomerol, presided over by St Peter (opposite page, far right bottom). Only 200 to 300 special visitors are received here per year, most of whom are shown round by Christian Moueix himself. The small château is nowadays more of a reception hall with a few small rooms above it, for no one lives here. The château as it is now dates from the end of the last century. The shutters were painted the striking turquoise colour according to an idea of Madame Loubat.*

# Chau Pétrus

Cru Exceptionnel

One might say that everything about Pétrus is diminutive except its wine, for the château where this world-famous claret is born is of modest proportions. The house consists of just a reception room, a small hall, a few upstairs rooms and the cellars. Its only immediately remarkable features are the turquoise paint on the shutters (almost the same colour as those at Prieuré-Lichine in the Médoc), and the tall flagpole with its large, gold initial 'P' which catches the sunlight and can be seen from some way away.

The vathouse contains several small cement vats. These are not lined with glass or plastic, so the wine comes into direct contact with the cement – or rather with the purple deposit which has accumulated on it over the years. The *chais*, where the wine matures in wood for 2 to $2\frac{1}{2}$ years, are tiny, like everything at Pétrus, except for the renown of the wine. Sometimes, casks of different vintages have to be stacked on top of each other because of the lack of space.

**The unique topsoil**

The label on the bottle shows St Peter with his key. This is of course the key to heaven, not to the Château. There is only one of the latter, and Christian Moueix has it. He is the manager of all the Moueix properties and treats Pétrus with special care. The estate is only partly owned by Messrs Moueix, the remaining shares being in the hands of the two heirs of Madame Loubat, a woman who created the great reputation of Pétrus almost single-handed. She died in 1961. A portrait of her at the age of 45 is to be seen in the tiny reception room, where many great personalities of wine were proud to be her guests.

If you ask Christian Moueix why Pétrus is so much more impressive than its neighbours, he simply replies: 'The secret lies in the clay.' It so happens that only the Pétrus vineyard has a clay topsoil; most of the other châteaux in Pomerol are directly on gravel.

**Old vines, rapid harvest**

There are many unique things about Pétrus. There are almost exclusively very old vines in its $11\frac{1}{2}$-hectare vineyard; the average age of the vines is about 35 years. This is due to Madame Loubat, who refused to replant after the frost of 1956 but left the vines to pick up again in their own time. Another factor which undoubtedly contributes to the greatness of Pétrus is the rapid vintageing. This is done by the same group of Moueix pickers that I met at Magdelaine. They arrive at what Christian Moueix considers to be the best possible time, and over 100 men and women set to work with 10 tractors. On principle, picking is only done at Pétrus in the afternoon, preferably on sunny, dry days; this is to prevent morning dew as well as rain affecting the must. Despite these restrictions, the crop is picked in four days. Yet another process which contributes to Pétrus' outstanding personality is the limited *égrappage*, for

The Pétrus vineyards cover 11½ hectares, of which 11 are planted with Merlot and the half with Cabernet Franc.

In the reception hall of the château there is a frivolous statuette of a man and woman who are quite plainly not talking about the weather – or about wine. No one seems to know how it came there.

All the wine is bottled by hand straight from the cask. As each cask of wine will develop slightly differently, it is possible for two bottles of the same vintage to show definite differences. In machine bottling the contents of the casks are usually mixed before the bottles are filled.

*Right:*
*The outbuildings of Pétrus lie on the other side of the road. It is here that the staff of two families lives, and where machinery and equipment for working the vineyard is kept. Messrs. Jean-Pierre Moueix acquired the Pétrus shares in 1962. Since then the reputation of this superb wine has risen so that it now ranks in esteem and price with the best* premier crus *of the Médoc.*

between 30% and 35% of the grapes are not de-stalked, which gives the wine extra solidity of construction. Finally, there is the fermentation, which is unusually lengthy for these days: in 1973, for example, it was allowed to take 25 days.

## Superlative vintages

Thanks to the old vines the wine of Pétrus is normally naturally high in alcohol. In the 1970 vintage it reached more than 14% in the vat completely naturally – and 13% is the rule rather than the exception. But this is not the only striking thing about the wine, and I find Pétrus overwhelming in every respect. It is not a wine you take but a wine which takes you. It possesses such an untameable style that it is difficult to know what to eat with it, as many foods are overwhelmed by it – indeed, Pétrus is food and drink together. This is not only true of good and great years, for even in fairly light vintages like 1962 Pétrus loses very little of its style. The 1962 has an intensely deep colour, a gorgeous bouquet of untold wealth and luxuriance, and an overwhelming flavour which only reluctantly leaves your mouth. The 1966 vintage is of course even richer, creamier and stronger; it can be kept literally for generations without declining. I rate the 1970 very high, and the 1971 even more so, for then Pétrus made a wine of fabulous style, even among the many greats of that vintage.

Of all the red wines throughout the Bordeaux region, Pétrus is probably supreme as to colour and power. It is therefore advisable to decant it well in advance: vintages older than 1949 one hour before, 1949 to 1962 two hours, and from 1962 three hours. Unfortunately the production of this wonderful wine is only 40 *tonneaux*, which means that the price makes it available only to a few – but a very fortunate few.

# List of further important growths

Below is a list of châteaux which for various reasons are not included in the official classifications of the red wine regions, but which are known for the fine quality of the wine they produce; sometimes this is even better than that of classified properties in higher categories. It would obviously be impossible to mention all the remaining good wines, but I have chosen these excellent, reliable châteaux according to my personal experience. The selection remains – as with everything about wine – subjective, and does not claim to be exhaustive.

As far as the wines of the Médoc are concerned, it should be mentioned that ease of understanding has been the key word in specifying the various non-official classifications of the bourgeois growths. In the Médoc there are two different classifications, the first that of 1932, the second of 1966. The first includes 103 châteaux, the second some 125. There is some overlapping between the two groups, but there are also châteaux included in the first group which are not included in the second at all. To make matters more complicated, the two classifications use different terms. The first is divided into *Crus (Bourgeois Supérieurs) Exceptionnels*, *Crus Bourgeois Supérieurs* and *Crus Bourgeois*, the second into *Grands Bourgeois Exceptionnels*, *Grands Bourgeois* and *Crus Bourgeois*. Both terminologies are used indiscriminately by the châteaux, so, to avoid confusion, only the terms *Crus Exceptionnels*, *Crus Bourgeois Supérieurs* and *Crus Bourgeois* have been used in this list, as in Cocks and Féret's standard work, *Bordeaux et Ses Vins*. The *crus bourgeois* account for about one-third of all the wine made in the Médoc.

## MEDOC

**Château d'Agassac,** *Cru Bourgeois Supérieur, Ludon (appellation Haut-Médoc)*

The château is a proud little castle, complete with moat. It has been preserved largely intact down the centuries, so that today it is one of the few remaining monuments from the 13th century. The Capbern-Gasqueton family owns the estate and completely replanted the vineyard in 1960. In all the vineyard covers 35 hectares. The Cabernet Sauvignon is dominant with two-thirds, the rest being Merlot. The production is rarely more than 60 *tonneaux*, because the proprietors enforce very strict quality standards. The main markets for this excellent wine are Holland, Belgium, the U.S.A. and France.

**Château Beau-Rivage,** *Macau (appellation Bordeaux Supérieur)*

At Beau-Rivage the wine is still made according to traditional methods. Wooden fermentation vats are used and the wine is left to mature in new casks for at least 2 years. The vineyard covers only 7·7 hectares, and has an unusually high percentage of Petit Verdot: 40% (with 30% Merlot, 20% Cabernet Sauvignon plus Cabernet Franc, and 10% Malbec). The production fluctuates between 24 and 40 *tonneaux*. André Barateau is the proprietor.

**Château Siran,** *Cru Bourgeois Supérieur, Labarde (appellation Margaux)*

The wines of Siran usually achieve the standard of its neighbour Dauzac, a fifth classed growth. The Miailhe family has 25 hectares planted with the classic species. The production varies between 75 and 100 *tonneaux*.

**Château d'Angludet,** *Cru Exceptionnel, Cantenac (appellation Margaux)*

The château is the home of Peter Sichel and his family. Peter, son of the famous wine connoisseur, Allan Sichel, was the first foreigner to become President of the *Syndicat des Négociants en Vin et Spiritueux de Bordeaux*. Since 1961 the vineyard of d'Angludet has been virtually completely replanted with 60% Cabernet Sauvignon, 10% Cabernet Franc, 10% Petit Verdot and 20% Merlot (which is unusually low for Cantenac). It extends to 29 hectares. Production fluctuates greatly: 1971 yielded 19 *tonneaux*, 1973 as much as 137 *tonneaux*. The usually excellent wine ferments in oak vats.

**Château Martinens,** *Cru Bourgeois Supérieur, Cantenac (appellation Margaux)*

Unlike the majority of the vineyards in Cantenac/Margaux, the vineyard of Martinens is in one piece, covering an area of 28 hectares. The production: 35 to 75 *tonneaux*. Vines: 55% Merlot, 30% Cabernet Sauvignon, 15% Petit Verdot. The 18th-century house is the home of the owner, Madame Simone Dulos.

**Château La Tour de Mons,** *Cru Bourgeois Supérieur, Soussans (appellation Margaux)*

The manager of La Tour de Mons is Bertrand Clauzel of Cantemerle. The production is between 52 and 120 *tonneaux* per annum. Overall, the vineyard covers 25 hectares, planted with 40% Cabernet Sauvignon, 40% Merlot, 15% Cabernet Franc and 5% Petit Verdot. Wooden fermentation vats are used here, as they are at Cantemerle.

**Château Citran,** *Cru Bourgeois Supérieur, Avensan (appellation Haut-Médoc)*

Citran was once an important feudal seat, and this can still be clearly seen from its size, which is about 500 hectares! Naturally only part of this is planted with vines. Production fluctuates between 60 and 100 *tonneaux*, but was at one time considerably higher, and it is said that the estate once made as much as 600 *tonneaux*. The director is Jean Miailhe.

**Château Brillette,** *Cru Bourgeois Supérieur, Moulis*

*Régisseur* Jean-Pierre Brun makes his wine in cement fermentation vats and then leaves it to mature in casks which are renewed every two years. In 1974 Brillette had a record yield of 100 *tonneaux*, exactly double that of 1972. The wine is the product of a 30-hectare vineyard planted with

Left:
Château Larose-Trintaudon in the parish of St Laurent, on the road connecting the village with the town of Pauillac. Its production is probably the largest in the whole of the Médoc.



60% Cabernet Sauvignon, 30% Merlot and 10% Petit Verdot, and is mainly sold in France, and to Britain and the U.S.A.

**Château Chasse-Spleen,** *Cru Exceptionnel, Moulis*

Chasse-Spleen is a property with a deservedly high reputation. Year after year it produces excellent wines, even in bad vintages. The 1969 vintage was exceptionally successful and the 1973 and 1974 are also extremely good. The owner is Frank Lahary, but the estate is run by Charles Bouilleau, together with *maître de chai* André Raspaud. The cellars might be those of a classed growth, and contain crops of 150 to 230 *tonneaux*. In the 50 hectare vineyard, the Cabernet Sauvignon accounts for 50%, the Merlot for 35%, the Petit Verdot for 10% and the Cabernet Franc for 5%. All the wine matures in brand-new casks.

**Château Poujeaux,** *Cru Bourgeois Supérieur, Moulis*

About 60% of the wines of Poujeaux are sold in France from the estate by the proprietor, François Theil. In spite of the fact that not a single shipper is involved, the wine has been popular in government circles in France for years. The vineyard covers 40 hectares; the grapes are 60% Cabernet, 30% Merlot and 10% Petit Verdot; the production is between 110 and 200 *tonneaux*.

**Château Maucaillou,** *Cru Bourgeois Supérieur, Moulis*

The vineyard of the 'bad stones' (and therefore good wine) is the property of the Dourthe family. Pleasing, elegant wines are produced here which can compete with many classed growths. In 1973 the production was 185 *tonneaux*. Additional land has been bought in recent years and replanted, so the yield will now continue to rise. The grapes are 45% Cabernet Sauvignon, 20% Cabernet Franc, 30% Merlot and 5% Petit Verdot.

**Château Fonréaud,** *Cru Bourgeois Supérieur, Listrac*

The United States, Canada, Belgium and Britain are the largest markets for Fonréaud. Between 1950 and 1965 fundamental reforms were carried out in the vineyard, which is now planted with half Cabernet and half Merlot. It extends over 44 hectares, of which 42 hectares are productive. The lowest yield in recent years was in 1969 with 70 *tonneaux*, the highest in 1974, with 240 *tonneaux*.

**Château de Lamarque,** *Cru Bourgeois Supérieur, Lamarque (appellation Haut-Médoc)*

This is one of the most attractive buildings in the Médoc, dating partly from the 12th century and partly from the 14th. It is beautifully maintained by the proprietor, Gromand d'Evry and is certainly worth a visit. The wine is left to ferment in cement vats lined with plastic, and it then matures for nearly two years in casks, a third of which are new. The most important vine is the Cabernet (70%), followed by the Merlot (25%) and Petit Verdot (5%). The production fluctuates between 90 and 225 *tonneaux*.

**Château Lanessan,** *Cru Bourgeois Supérieur, Cussac (appellation Haut-Médoc)*

This estate has a very good name, thanks to the efforts of manager Hubert Bouteiller, whose family has owned Lanessan sine 1793. The production is modest (30 to 90 *tonneaux*), and only two varieties planted, the Cabernet Sauvignon (60%) and the Merlot (40%). The vineyard covers 26 hectares.

**Château Gloria,** *Cru Bourgeois Supérieur, St Julien*

The great personality, Henri Martin, lives at Gloria and makes his particularly good wine, well up to the standard of some of the neighbouring classed growths. The modest but comfortable house was built in 1888. Fermentation takes place in steel vats after which the wine lies for two years in cask. The annual production of this fine estate is between 150 and 240 *tonneaux*. In the 44-hectare vineyard, the Cabernet Sauvignon is dominant, 75% being planted with it.

**Château Caronne-Sainte-Gemme,** *Cru Bourgeois Supérieur, St Laurent (appellation Haut-Médoc)*

The vineyard of Caronne-Sainte-Gemme is situated in the very southernmost tip of the parish of St Laurent, very near to Lanessan. Manager Jean Nony annually produces an average of 175 *tonneaux* of generous, deep-coloured wine. The vineyard is about 35 hectares, the whole estate covering 120 hectares.

**Château Larose-Trintaudon,** *Cru Bourgeois Supérieur, St Laurent (appellation Haut-Médoc)*

This estate probably has the biggest vineyard and consequently the top yield of the Médoc: in 1973 the crop gave 719 *tonneaux,* in 1974 574 *tonneaux*. This is why proprietor Henri Forner is experimenting intensively, and successfully, with mechanical picking machines.
About 60% of the vines are Cabernet Sauvignon, 20% Cabernet Franc and 20% Merlot. The vineyard covers 158 hectares already but there are plans to add another 15. Fermentation takes place in stainless steel tanks. Considering this huge production the wine is surprisingly good.

**Château Fonbadet,** *Cru Bourgeois Supérieur, Pauillac*

The vineyard of Fonbadet is in good company, because Mouton-Rothschild and Pontet Canet are its closest neighbours. It is in one piece and is planted with a high percentage of old vines. The Meffre family owns the estate; the production averages 100 *tonneaux* of high quality.

*Left:*
*The attractive façade of Château Siran in Labarde near Margaux. In the summer the wild cyclamen flower in the château park, as they do at many other Médoc châteaux.*

## List of Further Important Growths

**Château Peyrabon,** *Cru Bourgeois Supérieur, St Sauveur (appellation Haut-Médoc)*

The wines of Peyrabon are allowed to mature in cask for a very long time – nearly three years. The proprietor, René Babeau, uses 50% Cabernet Sauvignon, 25% Cabernet Franc and 25% Merlot, and the crop varies between 90 and 175 *tonneaux*. The vineyard covers 36 hectares, a few of which lie in Pauillac. The château itself dates back to the 15th century.

**Château de Marbuzet,** *Cru Bourgeois Supérieur, St Estèphe*

De Marbuzet serves as the second label of Cos d'Estournel (a classed growth owned by the Prats family). This explains why the production labelled De Marbuzet bears no relation to the 10 hectares of its vineyard: in 1972 60 *tonneaux* were produced, in 1973 96 *tonneaux*. The quality of the wine is usually good.

**Château Meyney,** *Cru Bourgeois Supérieur, St Estèphe*

Meyney used to be a monastery – the records go back to 1662. It now belongs to the Cordier family. The grapes ferment in stainless steel tanks and then mature for a full two years in casks, a third of which are replaced annually. The vineyard covers 52 hectares and is planted with 60% Cabernet Sauvignon, 30% Merlot, 6% Petit Verdot and 4% Cabernet Franc.

**Château de Pez,** *Cru Bourgeois Supérieur, St Estèphe*

M. Dousson, the manager, lives at the estate and is a particularly serious wine man. Cabernet Sauvignon dominates the 25-hectare vineyard with 70%, followed by 15% Cabernet Franc, 10% Merlot and 5% Petit Verdot. The production of 120 to 180 *tonneaux* goes mainly to Britain, the U.S.A. and Northern Europe.

**Château Les Ormes de Pez,** *Cru Bourgeois Supérieur, St Estèphe*

This estate is leased by Château Lynch-Bages in Pauillac and the wine of Les Ormes de Pez is bottled there. After fermenting in cement vats the wine stays for 2 to 2½ years in wood. Production is between 65 and 165 *tonneaux*. The vineyard, of 28 hectares, is planted with 80% Cabernet and 20% Merlot.

**Château Beau-Site,** *Cru Bourgeois Supérieur, St Estèphe*

The vineyard of Beau-Site contains vines with an average age of 20 years and covers 30 hectares. Here again the Cabernets are dominant with 75%; the remainder is Merlot. The production is between 80 and 175 *tonneaux*. Fermentation takes place in wooden vats. The estate is owned by the house of Borie-Manoux.

**Château Phélan-Ségur,** *Cru Bourgeois Supérieur, St Estèphe*

This estate is situated to the south of St Estèphe and is the largest in this parish. The total acreage is about 180 hectares, of which about a third is under vines. M. Phélan created the estate by joining up Clos de Garramey and Ségur at the beginning of the 19th century. The production averages 200 *tonneaux*.

**Château Bel-Orme-Tronquoy-de-Lalande,** *Cru Bourgeois, St Seurin (appellation Haut-Médoc)*

A splendid small château where the Quié family (of Rauzan-Gassies and Croizet-Bages) often stay. Many improvements have been carried out in recent years. The vineyard covers 26 productive hectares, and in 1974 the production was 150 *tonneaux*. Generally speaking, Bel-Orme is a wine which must be given time to mature.

**Château Coufran,** *Cru Bourgeois Supérieur, St Seurin (appellation Haut-Médoc)*

This is the most northern estate of the Haut-Médoc, where the landscape begins to flatten out a little. The vineyard is planted with Cabernets and Merlot and covers some 50 hectares. This firm wine is mostly sold in north-west Europe. The average annual production is 150 *tonneaux*.

**Château Loudenne,** *Cru Bourgeois, St Yzans (appellation Médoc)*

Loudenne was bought over a century ago by the Gilbey brothers, and is now part of the Gilbey group. Since 1965 the vineyard has been extended to 37 hectares, with 47% Cabernet Sauvignon, 42% Merlot, 8% Cabernet Franc and 3% Malbec. In 1973 and 1974 the production was over 130 *tonneaux*. The wine has a growing reputation and is often good even in poor years. Fermentation takes place in cement and stainless steel vats. Martin Bamford, head of Gilbey France, lives in the rose pink château. Loudenne is one of the rare Médoc châteaux where a good white wine is also made, *appellation* Bordeaux.

**Château La Tour de By,** *Cru Bourgeois, Bégadan (appellation Médoc)*

In his old vathouse proprietor Pagès makes between 100 and 350 *tonneaux* of wine a year. This is the yield of a 60-hectare vineyard of 50% Cabernet Sauvignon, 40% Merlot and 10% Cabernet Franc. The first vines were planted in 1710; the château dates from 1876. The U.S.A., Holland, Belgium and Switzerland are the major markets.

**Château La Tour-Saint-Bonnet,** *Cru Bourgeois, St Christoly-de-Médoc (appellation Médoc)*

The label of this wine slightly imitates that of Latour, but the wine itself can stand on its own. The 1969 vintage was very good. André and Pierre Lafon, the proprietors, make about 225 *tonneaux* annually, largely the product of siliceous soil. The 40 hectare vineyard is planted with 50% Cabernet Sauvignon, 30% Merlot, 10% Petit Verdot and 10% Cabernet Franc.

*Left:*
*A château that is a true castle – d'Agassac in Ludon. This region is not well known, but the soil has made it possible for one great growth to make famous wines – La Lagune.*

*Right:*
*Flowers spell out a famous name – Chasse-Spleen, a cru* exceptionnel *from Moulis-en-Médoc.*

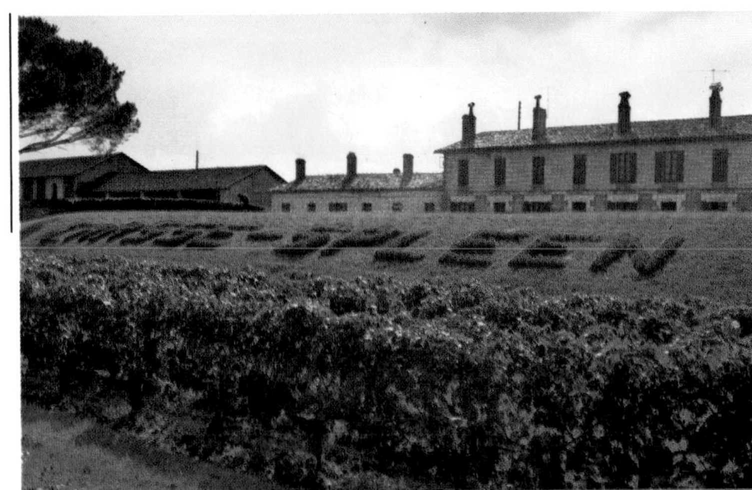

List of Further Important Growths

## GRAVES

**Château Les Carmes-Haut-Brion,** *Pessac*

This small estate, covering only 10 hectares, is situated in the immediate vicinity of Haut-Brion. The Chantecaille family (from the house of the same name) are the owners. Only 15 *tonneaux* of this delicate, fragrant wine are produced each year.

**Château Laville Haut Brion,** *Grand Cru Classé des Graves Blanc, Talence*

Like the red La Tour Haut Brion, the white Laville is made at La Mission Haut Brion. Fermentation takes place in oak vats. As the vineyard only covers 5 hectares, the production is no more than 10 to 20 *tonneaux*. The wine is truly fine and continues to improve in bottle, sometimes for a dozen years. The vines are half Sauvignon, half Sémillon.

**Château Couhins,** *Grand Cru Classé des Graves Blanc, Villenave-d'Ornon*

Co-owner of this estate is the French Ministry of Agriculture, which carries out research here. The very dry white wines are the product of the Sauvignon, Sémillon and a little Muscadelle. A non-classified red wine is also made. In all, the vineyard covers only 10 hectares, from which 30 *tonneaux* are produced in good years.

**Château Larrivet-Haut-Brion,** *Léognan*

This estate's vineyard borders that of Haut Bailly. In all 17 hectares (planted with 45% Cabernet Sauvignon, 45% Merlot and 10% Cabernet Franc plus Malbec) produce between 40 and 70 *tonneaux* of red wine per annum. According to the owner, Jacques Guillemaud – who lives at the château – the U.S.A., Belgium and Holland are the largest customers.

**Château de France,** *Léognan*

The red wine of Château de France is made by proprietor Bernard Thomassin from two-thirds Merlot and one-third Cabernet. After fermenting in stainless steel vats, the wine matures for about 1½ years in casks. The production varies between 77 *tonneaux* (in 1971) and 134 (in 1973).

**Château La Garde,** *Martillac*

Château La Garde belongs to the firm of Eschenauer, which has invested large sums in its estates in the last few years. At La Garde an extension project of 15 hectares for the red wine is in progress. Apart from this the vineyard covers some 31 hectares, of which nearly 29 are for the cultivation of black grapes. These are 51% Cabernet Sauvignon, 26·5% Cabernet Franc and 22·5% Merlot. In the white wines, the Sauvignon dominates with almost 75%. In 1974 the production of red wine was 98 *tonneaux* and of white 11 *tonneaux*. No one now lives in the château.

## ST EMILION

**Château La Dominique,** *Grand Cru Classé, St Emilion*

The vineyard of La Dominique (18·5 hectares) borders that of Cheval Blanc. It has a production of 80 to 100 *tonneaux* which are made in modern style in stainless steel vats. Each year the owner, Clèment Fayat, uses new casks in which the wine matures for nearly two years. This is a fine, fruity St Emilion.

**Château Croque-Michotte,** *Grand Cru Classé, St Emilion*

Manager Jean Brun makes the wine for Madame Geoffrion-Rigal. It enjoys a reputation for quality and finesse. The yield is about 30 to 60 *tonneaux*. The Merlot accounts for two-thirds of the 12-hectare vineyard, the Cabernets for one-third. The wine remains for two years in wood.

**Château Grand-Corbin-Despagne,** *Grand Cru Classé, St Emilion*

The production of this estate of 30 hectares is between 100 and 250 *tonneaux*. The wine is made by Guy Despagne and his staff of ten. Fermentation takes place in cement vats; the maturation is at least 18 months and sometimes as much as 30 months. The vines are two-thirds Merlot and the rest Cabernets.

**Château Corbin,** *Grand Cru Classé, St Emilion*

At Corbin foundations can still be seen of a feudal castle of the 14th century. The present building dates from the 18th century. The vineyard extends over 20 hectares, which are planted with one third Cabernet Franc, one-third Merlot and one-third Cabernet Sauvignon. The average production is 100 *tonneaux* of a wine of quality.

**Château Fonroque,** *Grand Cru Classé, St Emilion*

Fonroque is a property well known for its reliable wines, which retain a pleasing vitality after years in bottle. The vineyard of 20 hectares gives an average of 80 *tonneaux* a year.

**Château Soutard,** *Grand Cru Classé, St Emilion*

The owner, Count de Ligneris, is a dedicated winemaker who leaves nothing to chance where the vinification is concerned. He also enforces strict quality standards and in many years himself declassifies part of his crop. In contrast to the charming old cellar at Soutard the vathouse is equipped with modern stainless steel tanks. The vineyard covers 21 hectares (60% Merlot, 30% Cabernet Franc and 10% Cabernet Sauvignon). The production varies between 85 and 120 *tonneaux*.

**Château Troplong-Mondot,** *Grand Cru, St Emilion*

For St Emilion this estate has a generous yield of 110 to 180 *tonneaux*. The vineyard covers 30 hectares, which Claude Valette has planted with 60% Merlot, 30%

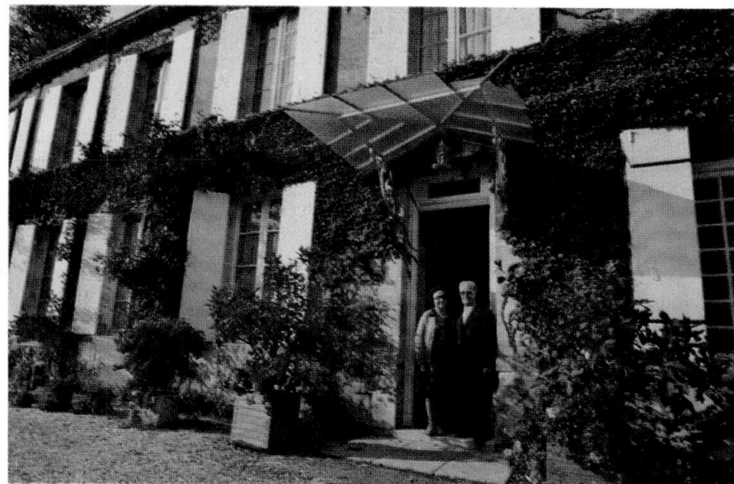

*Left:*
*Poujeaux-Theil, one of the properties of the small village of Grand Poujeaux, formerly a whole great estate.*



Cabernet and 10% Malbec. Fermentation takes place in stainless steel vats and the wine, often of marked finesse, is sold mainly to Belgium, the U.S.A., Holland and Britain.

**Château l'Angélus,** *Grand Cru Classé, St Emilion*

In the modern cellars of l'Angélus a fine, sensitive wine matures, made from half Merlot and half Cabernet Franc. The production is between 66 and 135 *tonneaux*; the vineyard extends over 28 hectares. A major part of the crop goes to the U.S.A. and Belgium. The brothers De Boüard are co-owners.

**Château Bellevue,** *Grand Cru Classé, St Emilion*

Bellevue lives up to its name, for it provides a fine view over the Dordogne Valley. The wine is made here in a traditional way, with the result that it is a typical St Emilion capable of long life. The yield is low, only about 30 *tonneaux*. The wine is drunk a great deal in Holland and Belgium. When you are buying, check that you have the right *appellation*, as there are eleven other Bellevues in the Gironde.

## POMEROL

**Château Nenin,** *Pomerol*

Round attractive Château Nenin are 22 hectares planted with 55% Merlot, 35% Cabernet Franc and 10% Cabernet Sauvignon. These yield 50 to 110 *tonneaux* of wine that is often charming. It matures for about two years in wood after having been fermented in cement vats. Mme Emmanuel Despujol lives at the château, and Pierre Esben is the manager.

**Château Petit-Village,** *Pomerol*

The wine of Petit-Village is pleasant to drink when it is still young, but can continue to develop for a long time. In the vineyard the Merlot grape accounts for 70%, followed by the Cabernet Franc with 20% and the Cabernet Sauvignon with 10%. The production averages 80 *tonneaux*. The vineyard of 11 hectares was completely replanted after the frost of 1956. The owner, Bruno Prats, makes his wine in cement and then leaves it to mature for at least 18 months. No one lives in the château itself.

**Château La Conseillante,** *Pomerol*

La Conseillante can make very fine, long-lasting wine. It is fermented in stainless steel tanks and is the property of the Nicolas family. They have planted the 12 hectares with 45% Merlot, 45% Cabernet Franc and 10% Malbec. The average yield is 50 *tonneaux*.

**Château l'Evangile,** *Pomerol*

Together with Vieux Château Certan and La Conseillante, l'Evangile is often counted among the best Pomerols. M. Louis Ducasse lives here, and makes between 35 and 85 *tonneaux* annually, about a third of which matures in new casks. The vineyard covers 13·25 hectares, planted with two-thirds Merlot and one-third Cabernet Franc.

**Château Gazin,** *Pomerol*

Gazin is an old estate, which used to belong to the Order of the Knights Templar, and is highly esteemed by knowledgeable lovers of claret. The present owner is Etienne de Bailliencourt. He makes between 65 and 115 *tonneaux* from his 23 hectares. About three-fifths of the vines are Merlot and one-fifth each Cabernet Franc and Cabernet Sauvignon. Wooden fermentation vats are used for this distinctive wine.

**Château La Fleur-Pétrus,** *Pomerol*

This estate of 10 hectares, of which 8 are under vines, is close to Château Pétrus and is also run by the firm of Jean-Pierre Moueix. At Pétrus the shutters are turquoise, here they are bright yellow. The grapes are 60% Merlot and 40% Cabernet Franc, grown on a siliceous soil, which causes them to ripen very early. The production is between 14 and 35 *tonneaux*, which mostly goes to Great Britain and the U.S.A. Christian Moueix is the manager of this estate.

**Clos l'Eglise,** *Pomerol*

Clos l'Eglise is situated on the edge of a clayey plateau. The property gets its name from the ancient parish church of Pomerol nearby, built in the 12th century. The owner, M. Moreau, makes 25 *tonneaux* of full-bodied wine every year.

**Château Trotanoy,** *Pomerol*

Trotanoy belongs to the firm of Jean-Pierre Moueix, like La Fleur-Pétrus and a number of other châteaux in Pomerol and St Emilion. Trotanoy has a great name, thanks to the fragrant style of its wine, but the vineyard is small – only 8 hectares. The average annual yield is around 25 *tonneaux*, matured for about two years in new casks.

**Château Clos René,** *Pomerol*

This estate is situated right on the edge of the parish of Pomerol; the wines can have great charm and delicacy. The owner is Pierre Lasserre, *Chevalier du Mérite Agricole*. The vineyard is 12·5 hectares, planted with 60% Merlot, 30% Cabernet Franc and 10% Malbec. Its largest yield in recent years was in 1970 (80 *tonneaux*), its smallest were in 1969 and 1972 (both with 48 *tonneaux*).

# Index

*Right: A fine old castle, Château de Lamarque is in the centre of the Médoc region. With the improved methods of wine making, the wines may become better known.*

## Index

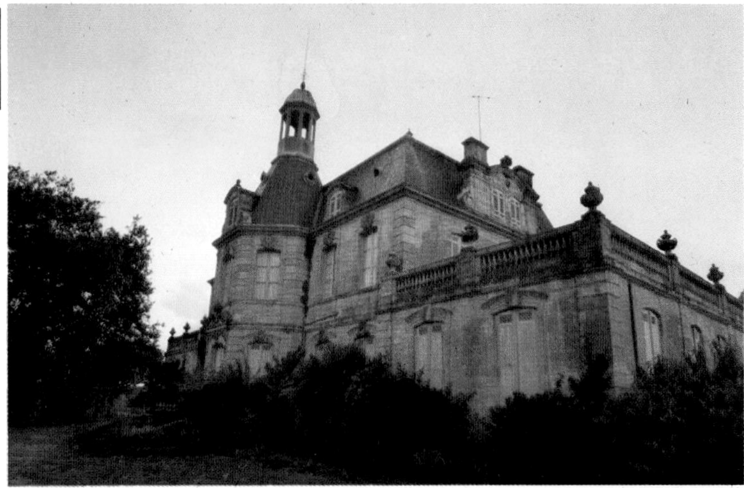

*Right: The monumental contours of Château Fonréaud, a cru* bourgeois supérieur *from Listrac, a parish with its own A.O.C.*

# Index

LYNCH BAGES
PAUILLAC-FRANCE

DULUC DUCRU
ST JULIEN (MÉDOC)

ST JULIEN

PHÉLAN-SÉGUR
SAINT-ESTÈPHE MÉDOC

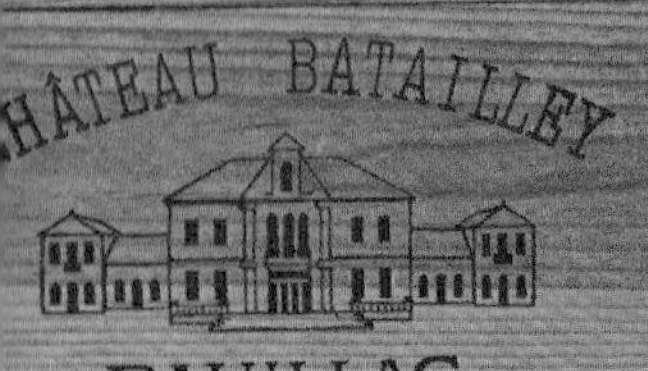
CHÂTEAU BATAILLEY
PAUILLAC
GRAND CRU CLASSÉ

BEAU SITE
SAINT-ESTÈPHE
HÉRITIERS BORIE-MANOUX PROPres

CHau COS D'ESTOURNEL

CHATEAU-LASCOMBES
MARGAUX

CHATEAU MARGAUX
GRAND VIN

CHau LANESSAN
MÉDOC

GRAND VIN DE LATOUR

Château Giscours Margaux

MIS EN BOUTEILLES AU CHATEAU
CHATEAU COUFRAN
ST SEURIN DE CADOURNE
(HAUT-MEDOC)

CHATEAU PALMER MARGAUX

LÉOVILLE
POYFERRÉ

CHATEAU SIRAN
LABARDE-MARGAUX

CHATEAU
BRANE CANTENAC
1er VIN

PONTET-CANET
PAUILLAC

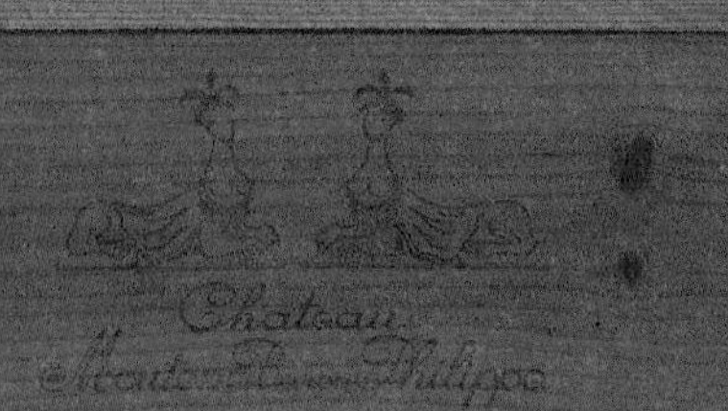
Château

Château Clerc Milon

BEAU SITE
SAINT-ESTÈPHE
HÉRITIERS BORIE-MANOUX PROPres

CHATEAU SIRAN
LABARDE-MARGAUX

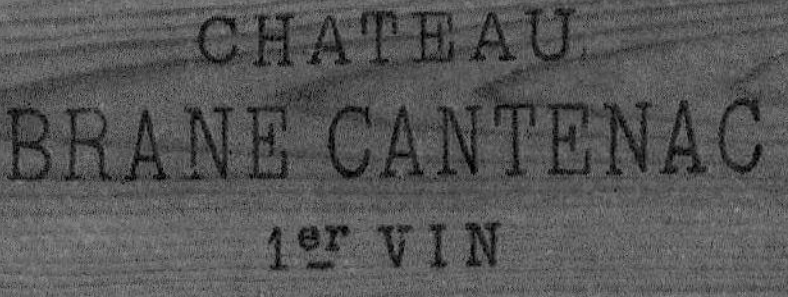
CHATEAU
BRANE CANTENAC
1er VIN

CHau COS D'ESTOURNEL

CHATEAU PALMER MARGAUX

GRAND VIN DE LÉOVILLE
DU MARQUIS
DE LASCASES
ST JULIEN, MÉDOC
12 Blles 1972

CHÂTEAU BATAILLEY
PAUILLAC
GRAND CRU CLASSÉ

LYNCH BAGES
PAUILLAC-FRANCE

CHau MONTROSE

CHau LANESSAN
MÉDOC

Château Giscours Margaux

PAUILLAC
MÉDOC

CHATEAU d'ISSAN

Château Clerc Milon

MIS EN BOUTEILLES AU CHATEAU
CHATEAU COUFRAN
ST SEURIN DE CADOURNE
(HAUT-MEDOC)

GRAND VIN DU CHATEAU
PHÉLAN-SÉGUR
SAINT-ESTÈPHE MÉDOC

PONTET-CANET